CULTURE
and
PROSPERITY

CULTURE
and
PROSPERITY

The Truth About Markets —
Why Some Nations Are Rich
but Most Remain Poor

JOHN KAY

HarperBusiness
An Imprint of HarperCollinsPublishers

HarperCollins books may be purchased for educational, business, or sales promotional use. For information, please write to: Special Markets Department, Harper-Collins Publishers Inc., 10 East 53rd Street, New York, New York 10022.

A European edition was previously published in 2003 in the United Kingdom as *The Truth About Markets* by Allen Lane, an imprint of Penguin Books.

Designed by Nancy Singer Olaguera

Library of Congress Cataloging-In-Publication

Kay, John
    Culture and prosperity : the truth about markets : why some nations are rich but most remain poor / John Kay.
        p.   cm.
    Rev. ed of: The truth about markets. 2003.
    Includes bibliographical references and index.
    ISBN 0-06-058705-9
        1. Free enterprise. 2. Capitalism. 3. Economic policy. 4. Economic development. 5. Culture. I. Title: Truth about markets. II. Kay, J. A. (John Anderson). Truth about markets. III. Title.

HB95.K29   2004
330.12′2—dc22

                                                                    2003056911
04 05 06 07 08 ❖/RRD 10 9 7 6 5 4 3 2 1

{Contents} •

{List of Figures, Tables, and Boxes}

Figures

Tables

Boxes

{Acknowledgments} • • • • • • • • • • • •

The background research took us from the Cro-Magnon cave paintings at Lascaux to the dot.com bubble of 1999–2000, from Auckland to Zanzibar. Many people contributed to this quest: including David Donaldson, Magnus Feldmann, Tim Harford, Alina Jardine, Adrian Lewis, Robert Metz, Scott Reeves, Alex Serbetis, Jorim Schraven, Alex von Tunzelmann, and Kasper Viio. Julian Bene, David Bodanis, Andrew Dilnot, Leslie Hannah, Richard Layard, George Richardson, and Bridget Rosewell helpfully commented on earlier drafts. Stuart Proffitt at Penguin in England helped greatly with the structure of the argument for the European edition. I am grateful to Gabriele Pantucci, Marion Maneker, and Edwin Tan for their help in revising the book for an American audience: this has gone far beyond the conversion of euros to dollars. And Jo Charrington organized both me and the production of both versions of this book with calm efficiency and unvarying good humor. I am grateful to them all.

John Kay

{A Note to Readers} • • • • • • • • • • • • • •

The superscript ^{n} as in Milees^n means the individual referred to has been awarded the Nobel Prize for economics. The superscript ^{w} as in JOKES^w means that relevant Web links can be found by visiting http://www.CultureandProsperity.com and typing JOKES. Other updated material related to this book is also available at www.CultureandProsperity.com. Currency conversions are based on 1 pound (£1) equals $1.67 and 1 euro (€1) equals $1.15, rates prevailing in October 2003, unless otherwise stated.

{part I}

THE ISSUES

● ● ● ● ● ● ● ● ● ● ● ● ● ● ● ●

{1}

A Postcard from France

"C'est l'équipe américaine." The cabdriver smiled gently as the crew descended from the bus ahead. They clustered together on the sidewalk, looking to each other for support. The environment has so many familiar features, but also unbridgeable differences. Insouciant Air France air hostesses wear a uniform with elegance but a clear hint of disrespect for authority.

Delta flies daily between Nice and New York. Most of the traffic originates in the United States. At the front of the plane are celebs dropping in at the Cannes Film Festival or Monaco Grand Prix. Some affluent but louche Americans, following in the footsteps of Frank Jay Gould and Scott Fitzgerald, prefer the south of France to California or the Hamptons. Businesspeople are on their way to the high-tech center of Sophia Antipolis in the hills behind.

There are conventioneers: a desk at the airport will be welcoming dermatologists or real estate brokers. And the plane fills up with tourists. Throughout the summer, crowds of young people, mostly American, squat on the steps outside Nice Station. They wait for trains that will take them on to Italy or Spain, or to Paris. In their backpacks are their European railway passes, tickets to the twenty-first-century grand tour.

I live in Menton, thirty miles east of Nice, on the Italian frontier. The border was determined only in 1860, and in those days a visitor from either Paris or Rome would have experienced great difficulty in understanding the language, or being understood. Each isolated community had its own dialect. The arrival of the railroad a few years later ended this isolation. Poor fishing villages were gradually turned into prosperous communities.

But the border is now eroding. First the customs posts were abandoned, then the immigration controls disappeared. In 2002 the currency-exchange booths closed as the euro became the common currency for a dozen European states.[1] The European Union has become a visible reality.

Within five miles of the sea, a ring of mountains climbs to five thousand feet, establishing one of the most beautiful coastlines and pleasant climates on mainland Europe. A twenty-minute walk leads down to the center of town. On the way you pass the Centre Roger Latournerie, operated by the Caisse Autonome Nationale de la Sécurité Sociale dans les Mines. The Centre is a holiday village for coal miners. The Caisse is neither a public nor a private body. It does not report to an elected official, but is not a charity: it is funded through levies on employers and employees and state subventions. Such organizations play a large role in the life of France and other continental European countries.

There are few coal miners in France today: Europe's accessible coal has long since been used up. French electricity is mainly generated from nuclear power. State-owned Électricité de France built a series of reactors using American Westinghouse technology. The construction program encountered few of the environmental objections or site delays that plagued nuclear power elsewhere.

So visitors to the Centre Roger Latournerie are mostly retired. There are many retired people in Menton. The town has never been famous or fashionable, like Saint-Tropez, Cannes, Nice, or Monaco. But the British have always liked Menton and have given it an elderly tone. There are streets named after Queen Victoria, who wintered here, and Winston Churchill, who painted here. The hotels Balmoral, Westminster, and Hermitage, named after European palaces, date from the late nineteenth century and accommodated English and Russian visitors.

One reason Menton has many retired people is because France has many retired people. Only one Frenchman in six aged sixty to sixty-four works, compared with almost one in two in the United States; one male American in six between seventy and seventy-four has a job,[2] but President Chirac, at seventy-one, is one of the few Frenchmen of his age still in full-time employment. It is said, only half in jest, that Chirac must stay in the job because presidential immunity halts investigation of corruption during his term as mayor of Paris. Retirement ages are closely enforced in France, but most French people would regard it as eccentric that anyone who could retire would not want to, and pensions are generous.

Beyond the Centre Latournerie, you turn left into the center of town and pass Menton's new school, the Collège Guillaume Vento. The Collège Vento is pleasant to look at and study in, impeccably maintained. When the scaffolding came down, I thought "This looks like a private sector building." And then I wondered why I expected a public school to be dowdier than a shopping mall. In Britain and America we believe that austerity is appropriate for the public sector. It has never been a French tradition, and it is not a French habit now.

The Frenchman Jacques Attali was the first head of the European Bank, established to aid the reconstruction of the former Soviet empire. Attali was sacked by British, Canadian, and U.S. delegates for indulgences—the private jet and the marbled reception area—that would have seemed quite normal for the chief executive of a large American bank. The Anglophones saw a difference between appropriate private and public behavior; the French did not.

The Collège Vento has a good reputation, and French schools are generally excellent. The most successful French film of 2003 was not *Matrix Reloaded,* but *Être et Avoir,* a moving documentary of a gifted teacher in a rural school. Rich parents in France do not hesitate to send their children to public schools, although French universities, overpopulated, riven by politics and mired in tradition, are in a poor state. The most internationally mobile couple I know sent their children to lycée in France, to college at Oxbridge, and to graduate school in the United States. These were well-informed choices.

There are shopping malls in France, and they are as dowdy as in the United States. You will find a small supermarket on the outskirts of Menton and several large commercial centers in the suburbs of Nice. The most successful French chain, Carrefour, pioneered Western shopping in Eastern Europe. But multiple retailers are much less visible in France than in the United States. The Marché Municipal is a striking hundred-year-old building in which stall holders present mouthwatering displays of fresh produce. The quality is uniformly high, as are the prices. The market is a tourist attraction, but the crowds that fill it are not of tourists: the daily shopping of local residents takes place here.

Beside the Marché Municipal is a branch of McDonald's. When it opened five years ago, I thought a town principally populated by elderly French people was the least fertile of territories for Big Macs. I was wrong: the tables outside are full all day. But there is no Gap. Most clothes are bought from knowledgeable assistants in small specialist retailers.

Nor a Walgreens. Chain pharmacies are not permitted in France, and supermarkets may not stock even an aspirin. Mom-and-pop pharmacies seem to be on every street. Medical treatment is better than in Britain, less costly than in the United States: a British visitor is surprised that it is available without waiting, and an American that it is available to all at low cost.

Pills and lotions have a central, symbolic rather than therapeutic, role in French medicine. It is rare to leave a consultation with a French doctor, even for hypochondria, without a prescription for three or four items, and filling them at the local pharmacy provides another opportunity for loquacious discussion of ailments. By the end of the morning, the streets are full of shoppers carrying baguettes—long French stick loaves—and paper bags with a green cross, symbol of the pharmacy.

The Marché Municipal closes for the day at 1 P.M. By then all other shops in the center of town will have shut, although they will reopen after lunch. Lunch is a serious affair, and most people will go home for it, although there are many small family restaurants where a plat du jour will cost $10. And holidays are serious too. Five to six weeks is the French norm, and much of that entitlement is taken in August, when it is hard to find a space on Menton's pebbly beach. The last weekend in August is the *rentrée,* when the freeways between Paris and the south are brought to a standstill by traffic.

Time for lunch, then, in Sophia Antipolis, a thirty-minute drive. The autoroute passes to the north of Nice before sweeping down to the coast toward Cannes, and as it does so, it cuts off the suburb of L'Ariane. There is an enormous municipal waste dump, and the housing units beside, all too similar in character, are ridden with drugs and crime. Much of the population is of North African descent. There are similar housing projects in all major French cities.

Local administration has been notoriously corrupt, and organized crime not far below the surface. The novelist Graham Greene, who lived in Antibes, on the coast below Sophia Antipolis, wrote a pamphlet, echoing Zola, titled *J'Accuse: The Darker Side of Nice*. Jacques Médecin, who had succeeded his father as mayor of Nice, fled to Uruguay, was extradited, and ended his life in jail.

French central government is in the hands of perhaps the best educated and most intelligent governing elite in the world. The *grandes écoles*, above all ENA, the École Nationale d'Administration, trains the ablest French students for public service. Both Chirac and Lionel Jospin, his Socialist opponent and prime minister, were Enarchs (graduates of ENA). French national bureaucracy is tainted less by corruption than by the arrogance of power. Daily, it is frustrating and tiresome to deal with but essentially honest.

Fear of immigrants, resentment of the rule of the Enarchs, and contempt for bureaucracy is the basis of the popular appeal of the National Front, whose leader, Jean-Marie Le Pen, caused consternation by defeating the Socialist prime minister Lionel Jospin to qualify for the runoff against Chirac in the last presidential election.

At Sophia Antipolis I am meeting Marie-Louise, a consultant with Accenture, and Gerhard, a divisional manager in Nortel Networks. The town comprises six thousand acres of parkland broken by woods, sculpture, and office complexes. It is the product of a conscious attempt by the local government, the Conseil Général des Alpes-Maritimes, to create a local version of Silicon Valley by attracting footloose but internationally connected industries.

Au Coin Gourmand is set in a row of small shops selling designer clothes and furniture. The tempo is brisker than in Menton. At lunch, single plates of mixed meats, smoked salmon, foie gras, are served, with wine by the glass; the adjoining *traiteur* offers similar products, which busy workers take away for evening meals. Marie-Louise, like every Frenchwoman, professional or housewife, will shop for food every day. Gerhard is German and has spent three years in Sophia. The conversation in Au Coin Gourmand is a mixture of French and English.

A multinational group like ours will probably speak English as we talk about business in France. For a time, the international face of French business was Jean-Marie Messier, another Enarch, who used his position as head of the water company Générale des Eaux to buy Universal Studios and announced the end of "the French exception" as he sought to launch himself as an international media mogul. The end of Jean-Marie Messier came first, however, and a new management team was appointed to dismantle his empire and repay its crushing debts.

A more successful model of international diversification is the oil services company Schlumberger, which probably also provides any smart card you have in your purse or pocket. Other global companies based in France—such as L'Oréal and LVMH distribute the products—fragrances, wines, haute couture—traditionally associated with France. Carrefour is, after Wal-Mart, the world's second-largest retailer; Aventis makes many of the pills in the bags with the green cross; St. Gobain makes glass and other construction materials for a global marketplace: look at the label etched on your car's windshield.

But the French economy depends much more on small and medium-size enterprises than Britain or the United States, and although there are tiresome regulatory obstacles and fiscal burdens to establishing new businesses, there are many of them. Overall, French productivity is slightly higher than that of the United States, but output per head of population is lower: the French retire early, eat lunch, and take extended holidays.

An espresso to finish the meal. So much coffee, so much effort, so much energy, for only a thimbleful of liquid! A taste of old Europe, perhaps. Of a world fated to decline. It does not feel like that from here.

{2}

The Triumph of the Market

The United States won one of the longest and most potentially destructive wars in human history—the Cold War against the Soviet Union—without firing a shot. The battlefield was the economy. Russian productivity was so low that the Soviet Union could not match the military capabilities of the United States, and the attempt to reform its economy led to the collapse of the associated political system. A central lesson of the last chapter of the Soviet Union was that economic institutions cannot be viewed in isolation from the social and political environment in which they function. This lesson was not taken to heart, either by the American victors or by the reformers who subsequently came to power in Russia.

Francis Fukuyama famously captured the triumphalism of America's victory by proclaiming "the end of history."[1] A lightly regulated market economy in a liberal democracy was appropriate, not just for the United States at the end of the twentieth century, but for all countries at all times.

The market economy was victorious not only in the war between the United States and the Soviet Union. In 1959, Russia had shocked the West with its technological prowess by putting *Sputnik* into space. Planning came into increasing vogue in large businesses and advanced Western economies. But this enthusiasm lasted little more than a decade: in the 1980s, all was to change. General Motors, which had for long defined and exemplified the modern corporation, came under acute pressure from the growth of global competition. General Electric, whose strategic planning systems had been the envy of other businesses, prospered through being quick to dismantle them.[2] European states and underdeveloped countries pursued policies of privatization and deregulation.

The United States economy performed well in the 1990s. *Business Week* proclaimed the "new economy": technology had transformed America's long-term growth potential. With the aid of Bloomberg television, this strong economic performance was translated into an extraordinary stock market boom. In 1996, the chairman of the Federal Reserve Board, Alan Greenspan, warned of "irrational exuberance." As he spoke the valuation of stocks was at the highest level ever recorded in American history—surpassing the records of 1929. But far more was to come. The chairman, having once put his head above the parapet, retreated.

Greenspan famously speaks in riddles. His partner, Andrea Mitchell, failed to understand what was being said when he first proposed marriage. But as the paper wealth of Americans continued to grow, Greenspan acquired heroic stature. History will judge whether Greenspan was the man who made millions of Americans rich—or the man who could not bear to tell them that they had only imagined it.

Daniel Yergin and Joseph Stanislaw celebrated this ideological transformation. "What was the conventional, indeed the dominating, wisdom of that time [the 1970s] is now widely criticized, and in some cases discredited and abandoned. . . . All around the globe, socialists are embracing capitalism, governments are selling off companies they had previously nationalized, and countries are seeking to entice back multinational corporations that they had expelled just two decades earlier."[3] But less than a decade later, this ideal was under renewed attack. In 1999, American capitalism was caught up in the largest and most ludicrous speculative bubble in financial history. And as the bubble reached its climax, riots forced the Seattle meeting of the World Trade Organization to break up in chaos.

With the subsequent falls in stock market values, many ordinary Americans lost faith in corporations as their savings were eroded as senior executives were enriched. Antiglobalization protesters gained confidence from their Seattle success, and every subsequent international economic meeting was besieged by demonstrators. Symbols of international capitalism—branches of McDonald's—were stoned and even burned. Environmentalists joined these protesters in denouncing the values of modern business.

So, as the new millennium dawned, the end of history seemed more, not less, distant. International relations took on a new complexity, in which a simple contrast of good and evil became a complex mixture of economics, ideology, religion, and politics. Russian living standards have fallen below the dismal levels achieved under communism, while Russian criminal oligarchs have become billionaires. And the most sinister and threatening opposition to democracy and the market came from fundamentalists who rejected not only the market economy but the values of a society that could give rise to it.

And so the market economy has—at the very least—a public relations problem. As Yergin and Stanislaw went on to observe,[4] few people will die with the words "free markets" on their lips. Despite the demonstrated success of market economies, the term *free markets* evokes disdain rather than enthusiasm in most of the world and in liberal and intellectual circles in the United States. People want the products and the efficiencies that markets bring, but not the markets themselves.

For Yergin and Stanislaw, as for many others, the answer lies in explanation. Business leaders and politicians stress the need for instruction in the merits of free enterprise. After the collapses of Enron and WorldCom and the 2003 settlement between investment banks and New York's Attorney General Spitzer, these calls are perhaps less strident.

The description of market economies they espouse, which I shall call the American business model, believes that greed is the dominant human motivation in economic matters; that regulation of economic activity is mostly undesirable and should be minimized; that the economic role of the state should be limited and largely confined to the enforcement of contract and private property rights; and that taxation should not rise above the levels needed to enable government to achieve these objectives and provide a modest welfare safety net.

These propositions are maintained by many U.S. conservatives and by most people engaged in business and finance around the world. They are, however, hard to sell, particularly outside the United States. In this book, I argue that they bear little relation to a true account of how markets work, and that attempts to redesign market economies in line with such principles have done at least as much harm as good to the effective operation of a market economy.

The Role of Self-Interest

Only saints and fools would deny that self-interest plays an important role in economic behavior. But economic behavior is not governed only by self-interest, and self-interest is itself a complex notion. Bill Gates is the richest man in the world, but as is evident from his dull books,[5] his consuming passion is not money but information technology. For Warren Buffett, "it's not the money, it's the fun of making it and watching it grow."[6] This should not surprise us. In all activities, from tennis to business, the most successful performers are those who are committed to that activity for its own sake, not simply as a means to an end. If Bill Gates had been driven primarily by a search for material pleasure, he would today be on the beach, not in an office at Redmond.

In all societies, there are clever people obsessed by personal gain. They are naturally drawn toward politics: controlling the apparatus of the state is the quickest and surest route to personal enrichment. Rich countries have mostly established mechanisms to exclude such people from government: that is one of the factors that makes some countries rich and others poor. In the United States today and in some other countries, you make money in order to go into politics, you do not go into politics to make money. But experience has shown that greedy people in business encounter the same difficulty as corrupt political leaders such as Indonesia's General Suharto or Joseph Mobutu of the Congo in distinguishing between other people's money and their own. Extreme self-interested materialism is a mark of the sociopath, not a characteristic of the great business leader. In the main, obsessively greedy individuals do not function well for long in complex modern economies where success requires cooperative relationships with other people. The best business leaders care about business rather than about money.

This complexity of motivation is not only true of the people who successfully run large corporations but also for those who work effectively in them. For many people, status, and the respect and friendship of colleagues, are as important as earnings. This variety of rewards enables people to work in teams and so to create and share the organizational knowledge that is the basis of the competitive advantage in many modern businesses. Marx was right to predict that large manufacturing businesses would ultimately fail because mass production facilities would create alienation between workers, managers, and owners. But the mechanism was not the one he described. Workers did not rebel against the bosses. The customers rebelled against the poor quality of products produced in plants organized on such instrumental lines.

The Embedded Market

The triumph of the market was the triumph of an institution that functioned in a social, political, and cultural context. And that context is not an afterthought, an amelioration of the harsh realism of market forces, like a recreational facility that relieves the monotony of the working day. In the absence of a supportive political, social, and cultural context, it is impossible to achieve the cooperative working, the sharing of information, the coordination of economic activity, and the development of trust between individuals and businesses on which the functioning of a complex modern economy necessarily depends. The societies most characterized today by unrestrained individualism and repeated opportunism are not rich free-market economies: they are countries like Nigeria and Haiti, whose economies do not work. Because postcommunist Russia destroyed one set of interrelated social and economic institutions but did not build effective substitutes, its economic performance continues to lag the potential of its people and its natural resources.

This institutional context is often called the rule of law. And the rule of law is an important issue. If there is no means of ensuring that an agreement is enforced, then the ability to establish productive economic relationships is severely curtailed. But it is not the law that coordinates our activities or encourages us to work together. Nor, to any large degree, does the law enforce agreements or establish trust. It is not just in the United States that legal processes are too expensive, and too uncertain, to regulate everyday relationships. We rely on others and fulfill contracts principally because we need to go on doing business with each other.

The phrase *free markets* is almost an oxymoron because markets operate only within a framework of conventions and rules. The San Remo flower market, which I will describe in chapter 12, is the closest approximation I know to the perfectly competitive markets I described to students when I taught economics 101. And yet even that perfectly competitive market functions through an elaborate structure of social relationships. As does the Chicago Mercantile Exchange, the closest approximation I have seen to the competitive display of naked greed. Although electronic trading and high-speed data transmission makes it unnecessary for financial service businesses to have physical marketplaces, the securities industry continues to cluster in a small and expensive area of lower Manhattan. Physical proximity is required to sustain the personal contacts on which the markets depend.

The Regulation of Markets

Personal relationships in which people meet face-to-face allow market regulation to be established by the participants themselves, rather than imposed by a government bureaucracy. Many Americans perceive a sharp distinction between social convention and state regulation. Wearing a suit and tie to work is a voluntary decision, but the speed limit is coercive. This distinction seems less clear to Europeans. In Britain, the mechanism of financial regulation was for decades described as "the raising of the eyebrows of the governor of the Bank of England." This was a metaphor for informal but powerful expressions of regulatory disapproval. The system was made possible by the common social background of market participants. It ceased to be sustainable when the City of London became a more democratic institution, and when globalization brought into the marketplace foreigners who did not understand what these signals meant, or that failure to observe them would have adverse consequences. So Britain acquired a rule book and an analogue of the Securities and Exchange Commission.

The internationalized City of London could no longer sustain the informal regulation symbolized by the eyebrows of the governor. But these structures are pervasive in the world's most successful economies—the small states of Western Europe, such as Denmark,

Norway, and Switzerland. These countries have high incomes per head, low inflation and unemployment, and an environment and physical and social infrastructure unmatched elsewhere. Small, homogeneous communities are particularly well placed to sustain regulatory structures that are both tacit and complex, and modern economies function through such structures: systems that typically work well but are harder to sustain in diverse, multicultural societies.

The young Alan Greenspan wrote that "beneath the paperwork of regulation lies a gun,"[7] but this reveals a profound misunderstanding of the nature of economic regulation in a democratic society: if such regulation requires a gun for its enforcement, it cannot be enforced effectively for long. If you do business in Norway and do not do it the Norwegian way, you will not encounter a gun—there are few guns in Norway—but your venture will not be very successful. Nor will you be faced by a gun in Switzerland, although there are many guns in Switzerland: the Swiss National Army, a universal citizen militia, plays an important role in forming the structure of relationships that underpin Swiss business. Alan Greenspan has distinctive, even distinguished eyebrows, and the raising of them is precisely the mechanism that could, and should, have been used to discourage the speculative excesses of asset markets in the late 1990s.

Globalization, and the development of rights-based models of economic and political behavior, have somewhat undermined the ability to regulate through moral authority. If people are more inclined to question the authority that restrains their actions, it becomes more necessary—but not always useful—to set out its basis. Much of the formal regulation that restricts European economies today is a codification—often necessarily clumsy and inflexible—of the expectations of market participants about the behavior of others.

Many Market Economies

Norway and Denmark do not have a minimal state. Nor, for that matter, does the United States—in fact, it has the most powerful government in the history of the world and is less and less embarrassed to remind people of that. Norway and Denmark also have high tax rates, some of the highest found anywhere. Taxes are lower in Switzerland, but the Swiss have a structure of government like no other: hugely powerful and massively decentralized. Whatever else is true of Denmark, Norway, and Switzerland, they are not societies characterized by unrestrained greed, market fundamentalism, and a minimal state.

Denmark, Norway, and Switzerland are small countries whose total population is less than that of California. But it may not be an accident that many prosperous societies are very small.[8] A small state with open borders can combine social cohesion with a dynamic economy in a manner that larger states find difficult to emulate. And it can sustain its idiosyncratic identity. Norway and Switzerland have chosen not to join the European Union although they participate in its free trade area.

It would be absurd to suggest that the United States should seek to reproduce the economic systems of Denmark, Norway, or Switzerland. But it is equally absurd to suggest the opposite. A market economy in a free society is demonstrably the most effective form of economic organization. But there are many successful variants on that theme. Each is the product of a distinctive process of coevolution of economic institutions and political culture. Not only is it possible for there to be more than one model of a successful economy; it is because different societies have different attributes that globalization, the international division of labor, is so effective in raising living standards.

The world has about twenty economically productive economies, with a total population of around 800 million, of which 300 million live in North America, a slightly larger number in Western Europe, and the remainder in Asia and Australia. It is fashionable to adopt one or other of these rich countries as the current exemplar of success—Japan took that role in the 1980s. As the Japanese sun set after 1989, the performance of the German economy was applauded, and then as that country struggled with the burden of reunification, attention turned to the Asian tigers. After the 1997 Asian financial crisis, the United States assumed the role of the most admired economy for economic commentary and business gurus.

But, as I shall describe in chapter 4, differences in performance among these twenty countries are small relative to the differences between these twenty and the rest of the world. The division between rich and poor states is sharp and has been enduring. China is still extremely poor, but the extraordinary achievements of Chinese people outside China, and increasingly within China, may change this balance of the world economy in the twenty-first century. One of the key issues of economic history has always been why rapid economic growth in the eighteenth century began in northwest Europe rather than southeast China.

No End of History

This diversity of experience demonstrates that there is no single model of a successful modern economy. In an extraordinary reversal, the claims of historical inevitability and economic determinism once made by Marxists are today adopted by devotees of the American business model. Both doctrines appeal to those who seek simple and certain truths to navigate a complex world—the grand narrative of universal explanation.

But the true lesson of Marxism's failure is not that Marxism was the wrong grand narrative. It is that no such theories are valid. The failure of one set of extreme propositions does not demonstrate the truth of their opposite. Greed is not the only economic motivation, but we will not prosper if we rely only on altruism to deliver our groceries and our video recorders. Central direction of industry by the state worked extremely badly, but it does not follow that the state can, or should, have no economic role. Societies do not thrive, socially or economically, without a broad consensus on the legitimacy of the distribution of income and wealth—the absence of such consensus crippled economic development in Latin America for a century and a half—but very high rates of taxation divert effort from creating new wealth to keeping existing wealth in private hands.

And so it goes on. There can be no one-sentence or one-paragraph description of how the market economy works, just as there can be no one-sentence or one-paragraph description of how the human body works, and for the same reasons. The market economy and the human body are both complex, interdependent systems, and they are the product of evolution, not design. A constitution has its framers, a building its architect, but no one designed the market economy. Adam Smith chronicled its development, but he did not invent it.

The Truth About Markets
● ●

An appreciation of how the market economy functions must, like a textbook of medicine, be unfolded topic by topic and chapter by chapter. In this book, I will describe the basic principles of modern economic organization. In Adam Smith's day, most production was still for one's own use, and that remains true in most of the world today. Smith's greatest insight was to identify the emergence of the division of labor. Individuals, businesses, and nations specialize in activities that reflect their distinctive capabilities. (Most people, especially those who have not read Smith's work, regard "the invisible hand" as his fundamental contribution; this is discussed more fully in chapter 17.) As economic development has progressed, that division of labor has become ever more extensive. The products we in rich societies consume every day reflect the efforts of thousands of people and hundreds of businesses. When Smith observed that "the division of labor is limited by the extent of the market," he could never have imagined how far globalization could extend that division of labor and accelerate what he called "the progress of opulence."

But while the increasingly fine division of labor has been a major factor in the evolution of rich societies, the relentless pace of technological and organizational innovation has also been important. If the strengths of the market economy were encapsulated in a single phrase, that phrase would be *disciplined pluralism.* Disciplined pluralism is the process of perpetual experiment in market economies, in which most experiments fail and are terminated, but the few that succeed are quickly imitated. Disciplined pluralism diffuses authority and exploits local knowledge.

In central planning, by contrast, a single voice articulates the right answer, and hierarchical authority is deployed to extract information and execute decisions. The important distinction is not the distinction between state control and private business, but between centralized and decentralized decision making. Often these amount to the same thing, but they need not. The personal computer revolution exemplified the effectiveness of disciplined pluralism, but it happened only because IBM did not—quite—control the industry it dominated. The company unleashed a demon it could not manage.

There are few examples of businesses or businesspeople whose success was based on a sustained record of accurate forecasting. Innovation does not depend on wise men who see the future correctly. If that were true, the rational assessments of committees of planning agencies would often produce better outcomes than the instincts of entrepreneurs. Innovation occurs because, among these confused and conflicting entrepreneurial judgments, a few bear fruit; just as, among the endless mutations of natural selection, a few—and only a few—benefit the species. With hindsight, of course, we will applaud the wisdom of the decision makers whose choices were vindicated by events. Sometimes this applause will be justified, but often these individuals will have displayed only the same prescience as those who picked the winning numbers in a lottery.

Despite the naive faith many people have in the effectiveness of market forces, the superiority of disorganization over organization is deeply counterintuitive. Businesspeople who recognize the weaknesses of centralization and planning when undertaken by a state authority do not understand that centralization and planning will fail in their own organizations, and for the same reasons. The truth about markets is not that businessmen are cleverer than bureaucrats: mostly they are not. The genius of markets is that they are not dependent on the genius of any individual. They do not rely on knowledge that no one can hold or depend on information that it is impossible to collect.

But this is not enough to explain how the spontaneous order of the market achieves the complex job of implementing and coordinating the division of labor much more effectively than deliberate and centralized systems of planning. The two centuries that have elapsed since Smith wrote of the "invisible hand" have not yet provided a definitive answer to this question. But in the section of this book that I found most difficult to write, and you may find most difficult to read, I shall sketch some of the answers that have been proposed.

The Role of Context

We derive gains—huge gains—from production and exchange through the specialization achieved by the division of labor. We benefit from the promotion of innovation through disciplined pluralism. The market economy achieves coordination through the emergence of spontaneous order from decentralized decisions. These are the core components of our understanding of the truth about markets. Yet this account is seriously incomplete.

In modern economies, we routinely trade in markets in which the seller knows far more than the buyer about the nature of the product. Social institutions—branding, advertising, reputation, and regulatory agencies—secure the comfort of our hotels, the predictability of our Big Macs, the competence of our doctors, and the solvency of our banks. Some of these institutions emerge from the voluntary actions of individuals, others are established by government. Often the two interact. Branding by manufacturers is the result of individual action, but would be pointless if regulation did not prevent competitors using the same brand.

We cannot build the complex products that consumers in modern economies require through arm's-length negotiations between unconnected traders. If everyone in the production line has to bargain to receive a product and bargain to pass it on, there will be a lot of bargaining and not much manufacturing. The costs of operating markets are large, and we rely on the efficiency of markets to repay their costs and on social institutions to reduce them.

Only if we build teams, share information, and develop trust relationships both within and between corporations can businesses achieve efficient production, far less develop competitive advantages. If institutions are built on the assumption that individuals are not to be trusted because their motives are purely instrumental, then these expectations will be fulfilled. The quality of output and the flexibility of production will be correspondingly low. This is the lesson that Japanese companies taught U.S. manufacturers in the 1980s.

The competitive markets I described in economics 101 do not produce the new fundamental knowledge on which technological innovation ultimately depends. Self-interested individuals in unregulated markets would only have ideas that they could profitably sell. Understanding that the earth revolves round the sun, the laws of thermodynamics, and the helical structure of DNA do not fall into this category.

Nowhere is the contrast between the reality of the American economy and the caricature of the American business model more evident than in the management of fundamental research. American dominance of advanced science is today almost complete. Yet the rise of American institutions in this sphere is not the result of any application of the principles of the American business model: self-interest, market fundamentalism, and the minimal state. It is the product of institutional and financial pluralism and the powerful motivation of the thrill of discovery.

These examples, drawn from the many that will systematically be presented in this book, have a common theme. Market institutions, characterized by disciplined pluralism, function because of the social context in which they are embedded. And no market economy is more deeply embedded in its society than that of the United States. That is the paradox with which this book concludes. The American business model is not, and could not be, an accurate description of the American economy.

But for ideologically motivated reformers, the failure of the world to correspond to the model requires changes in the world, not to the model. In this way, Marxists imposed untold damage on the economic performance and social structures of the economies they controlled. Today, advocates of the American business model court the same dangers. Their false account of how market economies function has not only undermined the legitimacy of capitalist institutions but has impeded their operations.

The author of a book designed to explain the central content of economic theory has a special problem that the writer of a similar work on quantum mechanics, evolutionary biology, or genomic research does not encounter. Most people know that they know little about quantum mechanics, evolutionary biology, and genomic research. Many people believe they know a great deal about economics from their practical experience—the DIY (do-it-yourself) economics I describe in chapter {15}. The problem with popular and political understanding of economics is, as Josh Billings put it, not what we don't know, but what we do know that ain't so. The object of this book is to dispose of what we do know that ain't so—the power and inevitability of the American business model—and replace it with what we should know: a true account of the complex, elegant, and subtle network of embedded institutions that constitute real market economies. Including the complex, elegant, subtle institutions of the successful market economy of the United States.

{3} •••••••••••••••••••••••••••
People

American Lives
••••••••••••••••••••••••••••••••••

The average American wage is around $23 per hour, so that a typical monthly salary is between $3,000 and $4,000. But there is no average American. Jeff Immelt of General Electric receives over $1 million per month, while a student with a part-time job in a fast-food outlet will do well to gross $100.

Roger and Sandra live with their two children in a four-bedroom house in the Bay Area. They bought the house ten years ago for $320,000; just as well, they sometimes think, because that house is now worth $750,000 and they could not afford to buy it today. Roger earns $8,000 per month as a manager in an insurance company, having graduated in engineering from the University of California at San Diego. There he met Sandra, who was studying history, and who gave up her job as a teacher when their first child was born and now earns pocket money from part-time tutoring.

Roger's drive into his San Francisco office takes about thirty-five minutes in normal traffic in their Toyota Camry; Sandra drives an old minivan. On weekends, they enjoy hiking in the hills around their home, and in the winter may drive up to ski at Lake Tahoe. Last summer, they took a week off to drive up the West Coast to Seattle.

Grant works for Ford in Lorain, Ohio, while his wife, Lanelle, looks after their younger daughter and spends thirty hours per week as a Wal-Mart cashier. Grant drives to the plant in their Escort sedan, while Lanelle takes the bus to the mall on the edge of town. Grant earns $4,000 per month and enjoys a good benefits package; Lanelle receives an average of $1,000 per month. Their two-bedroom house cost only $130,000, but it was in a poor state and Grant spent most of his two-week vacation last year fixing it up.

Harvey and Blythe live together in a two-bedroom apartment in Bainbridge, Georgia, which they rent for $300 per month. Harvey earns $2,200 per month as a janitor in the municipal offices. Blythe is a waitress and much of her income depends on tips, but she can expect $1,500 in a normal month. Harvey and Blythe were both brought up and attended high school in Bainbridge. Blythe dropped out but Harvey finished. Blythe likes shopping and movies, but Harvey enjoys hunting and fishing in the surrounding forests and lakes. Harvey drives to work in an eight-year-old pickup truck, but Blythe's restaurant is within walking distance.

Other Lives

Heidi is playing with her children in the garden of their four-bedroom villa in Küssnacht, an elegant suburb of Zürich. She has just driven home in her Nissan Micra from the primary school where she teaches. A primary-school teacher in Switzerland might expect to earn around $7,000 per month; Heidi, who works part-time, earns about half that. She is married to Hermann, who studied economics and business at the University of St. Gallen and is an executive in a Zürich bank. The Micra is their runabout, but Hermann drives to work in their Mercedes. Heidi and Hermann enjoy eating out in Zürich, where there are many good international restaurants as well as cheerful Swiss taverns. They like opera and play tennis at a club in Küssnacht. In winter they ski most weekends. In summer they visit their small holiday house in Umbria in Italy.

Ravi is cycling to his job at the State Bank of India in Mumbai, where he earns $320 per month. Ravi is a recently qualified accountant, and also recently married. Ravi and his wife, Nandini, live with Ravi's parents in a two-bedroom apartment in the favored district of Worli. The rent of the apartment is $280 per month, paid by Ravi's father. Nandini does not work. It is relatively uncommon in India for the wives of men of Ravi's income and social status to seek employment. A housekeeper visits each morning to clean and cook; she is paid around $25 per month.

Sven is running in the forest near Kivik in Sweden. He is a farmworker and earns the union rate corresponding to his age and experience, which is $2,000 per month. Sven lives with his girlfriend, Ingrid, in a three-bedroom house in the village, and the couple have a four-month-old daughter. Ingrid is employed on the same farm, but is on maternity leave. Swedish parents are entitled to share a year's leave. In a few months Ingrid will return to work and Sven will spend the balance of the leave at home with his daughter. Sven and Ingrid have a mobile phone each and a Volvo 740; they love sports and go skiing in the north of the country. Summer holidays may be spent on Mediterranean beaches or in Sven's parents' summerhouse on an island in the Baltic Sea.

Ivan is taking the metro to work. He is a maintenance engineer for AT&T, the American telephone company. Ivan has a doctorate from MTUSI (Moscow Technical University of Communications and Informatics) and earns $900 per month. He lives with his mother, Lyudmila, his wife, Olga, and two children in Yugo-Zapadnaya, a Moscow suburb. Ivan's father was killed in Afghanistan and his mother receives a pension of $40 per month. Olga teaches English linguistics at MTUSI, where she earns $100 per month, but in a good month, she can earn an additional $300 or more from English translations for businesses. Ivan and Olga have a ten-year-old Ford Sierra, which was imported second-hand from Holland.

Economic Lives

Ravi and Nandini in India, and Ivan and Olga in Russia, have very different economic lives from modern Americans or West Europeans. Those of us who live in rich states have more choices in work and leisure, and a wider range of experiences that leave us better placed to develop our interests and talents. But economic lives are only part of our lives. With choices come mistakes, and material goods do not meet all human needs. Ravi and Ivan do not think of themselves as poor. Like most people, they derive their frame of reference from their local environment. They are well aware that they are much better off than the many destitute people in the streets of Moscow and Mumbai.

Happiness depends far more on personal relationships than the size of house or the capacity to holiday in exotic destinations. But Ravi and Ivan would like to have the resources and opportunities available to those who live in rich states. And the issue of why economic lives differ so much is interesting whatever its consequences for happiness. The economic question is an important question even if it is not the only question, or the whole story.

And the answer to the economic question—why their economic lives are so different—is not at all obvious. Heidi and Ravi, Sven and Ivan, are different people. But they are sufficiently similar that we can see that the differences in their economic lives are mainly the product of differences in the environments within which they operate, not differences in the innate capabilities of the individuals themselves. Heidi and Sven, along with the American couples, have higher material living standards not because they are more talented, or more hardworking, but because they were born and live in Switzerland, Sweden, and the United States. Ravi and Ivan have lower material living standards not because they are less talented or hardworking, but because they were born and live in India and Russia. We often talk of globalization as if the world were becoming homogeneous. But globalization has emphasized, not eliminated, these facts of geography.

And facts of geography have an overriding importance for Raoul and Pedro. The Rio Grande is a wide, sluggish river, of no great natural beauty or interest. But because it forms the border between the United States and Mexico for a thousand miles, it has great political, social, and economic significance.

Raoul is a skilled and experienced machinist in a factory in northern Mexico. He earns $700 per month, a good wage in Mexico. His brother Pedro works illegally as a kitchen porter in a Los Angeles restaurant. Pedro takes home twice as much as Raoul. Raoul has sometimes thought of joining Pedro, but he prefers to stay with his friends and family in Mexico. He thinks that money is only part of life.

Why Do Economic Lives Differ?
• •

What features of the environment into which people are born or migrate make such a difference to their economic lives?[1] For most of economic history, it was believed that the explanation was found in the availability of physical resources. What mattered was access to fertile land. Or valuable minerals—gold and silver, coal and oil. Or the availability of scarce, specialist goods like sugarcane or saffron. The attempt to gain access to these resources has been a principal cause of wars for thousands of years.

The United States is well endowed with natural resources; it is some way ahead of Japan and most European countries, although behind Canada, Venezuela, and (probably) Russia. But every six months, the United States creates output more valuable than its entire stock of productive natural resources. It is a modern cliché that Silicon Valley is not built on reserves of silicon. That is why countries with limited natural resources, such as Japan, have not been greatly disadvantaged in international competition. Rich states have easy access today to natural resources, not because of geographical proximity, but because they have the financial resources to buy them.

If not resources, perhaps technology. While Sven is an employee on a Swedish farm, Sicelo owns his own farm. But Sicelo's farm is in a small village in KwaZulu-Natal. He lives in a hut with his own wife, the two wives of his brother, Patrick, and five of the six children of the marriages. The hut has no electricity or sanitation.

Sicelo earns around $150 per month from the sale of milk and vegetables. The women help on the farm and contribute to household earnings by making baskets. Patrick works in a gold mine in Carletonville, five hundred miles away. He earns $250 per month and sends most of this back to support the family. He usually returns to the village twice a year. Sicelo's eldest son is a domestic worker in Durban and sends $75 per month to his parents.

There is a world of difference between the sophisticated modern agricultural machinery that Sven uses every day and the simple tools available to Sicelo. In principle, the global marketplace makes the same technology available everywhere in the world. For Ivan, this is a reality. AT&T deploys the same equipment in Russia as in the United States. But for Sicelo access to modern technology is a dream. Like

Table 3.1

Resources per Head, U.S. $000
(includes mineral resources, oil and gas, agricultural land, forests)

Top Ten Countries		Other Rich States	
Saudi Arabia	71.9	Austria	7.6
New Zealand	51.1	Belgium	1.8
Canada	36.6	Denmark	11.1
Australia	35.3	France	8.1
Norway	30.2	Germany	4.2
Venezuela	20.8	Italy	3.4
Ireland	17.8	Japan	2.3
USA	16.5	Netherlands	4.1
Finland	15.9	Sweden	14.6
Uruguay	14.8	Switzerland	3.1
		UK	4.9

Hong Kong and Singapore were not included in the study; the figures for both would be extremely small.

SOURCE: *Expanding the Measure of Wealth,* appendix table I: "Country-Level Natural Capital Estimates," World Bank Environment Department, Washington, 1997

most South Africans, Sicelo has neither the education nor the capital to use the equipment to be found on every farm in Sweden.

Is it education that makes the difference? Ravi and Ivan are more skilled than most workers in rich countries. It is hard to imagine that Sven could do either of their jobs, but they could probably do his. But if Sicelo had a better education, that would probably not, of itself, raise his productivity much.

Is it capital that is key? Since common sense tells us that rural South Africa needs capital far more than Sweden, why does Sven have so much and Sicelo so little? In a global capital market, owners of capital can readily shift funds from country to country and business to business. And they do not do so on sentimental or patriotic grounds, but in hope of higher returns. In the 1990s, foreign investors formed exaggerated views of the prospects in Southeast Asian economies such as in Thailand and Indonesia, which, though still poor, were rapidly developing. Far more capital flowed into these economies than they could absorb.[2]

Globalization of capital markets has brought little benefit to South African agriculture because the infrastructure readily available in Sweden is missing. A better social infrastructure would give Sicelo the education to operate competently capital equipment that others might pay for. A better physical infrastructure—proper roads, for example—would give him access to markets on which he could sell his output easily and cheaply. A better institutional infrastructure would enable capital to be passed to Sicelo in an intelligent and discriminating way—and give investors confidence that they would profit from their investment if it succeeded. None of these infrastructures exist for Sicelo.

Raoul and Pedro were born in the same Mexican town and received the same education. Pedro in Los Angeles makes *less* use of his education and capabilities than Raoul. The average American worker has far more capital at his disposal than the average Mexican.[3] Yet Raoul, whose employer manufactures for an American corporation, utilizes more capital equipment than Pedro. Mexico has ready access to American technology, and firms have established plants, like Raoul's, to use American technology in this lower-cost location. We cannot explain all the differences in outcomes by differences in skills, education, capital, or technology: none of these factors, nor all of them together, are sufficient to account for the differences between the economic lives of Pedro and Raoul, between the prosperity of the United States and the poverty of Mexico.

Economic Systems Matter

Productivity is not simply the result of the availability of capital and technology, or differences in the skills of individual workers. In the modern world, skills can be developed everywhere, and capital and technology flow freely among countries. Economic differences persist because output and living standards are the complex product of the economic environment intersecting with social, political, and cultural institutions. The economic lives of individuals are the product of the systems within which they operate.

No modern experience illustrates this as starkly as the difference between the economic lives of Friedrich and Heinz. Brothers, they were born between Hitler's accession to power in 1933 and the outbreak of war in 1939 and brought up in a suburb on the outskirts of Berlin. At school during the war, they experienced acute privations after much of Berlin was razed, and the physical infrastructure of Germany destroyed, by the Allied advances in 1944–45.

After the war Friedrich and Heinz began engineering apprenticeships. Both trained in plants that had been established by Siemens, Germany's largest engineering business. Friedrich moved to Nuremberg, while Heinz started work in a former Siemens plant now controlled by the East German state. Both married in their early twenties and rented apartments in the cities where they had settled. In the early 1950s, the differences in the economic lives of the two brothers were still small. Their families saw each other regularly, although, as the boundaries between the German occupation zones became more marked, visits became less frequent. After the building of the Berlin Wall in 1961, they talked to each other only by telephone, and less and less often.

When the Wall came down in 1989, Heinz, like millions of other Easterners, drove his Trabant into the Western zone to see for himself. He had known that the range and quality of goods in the shops was far superior; now that was a reality. His clothes, his furniture, looked shabby compared with Friedrich's; his cramped apartment in a barracks-style block hardly matched Friedrich's semidetached house with a garden. When Heinz described the equipment he used at work, Friedrich laughed.

Heinz and his colleagues enthusiastically supported reunification, believing that Western living standards would soon be theirs. It didn't happen. Today Heinz lives on a pension from the German government. Friedrich, with a Siemens pension added to his state entitlement, receives twice as much. The Siemens company reacquired the plant in which Heinz worked, scrapped virtually everything inside it, and runs it today with a workforce less than half the number Heinz remembers. Many of his former colleagues, like Heinz himself, never worked again.

In 1945, the roads, railways, and factories of Germany had been destroyed. The country had been the victim of a bombing campaign designed to reduce its productive capabilities. But, within a few years, West Germany was again among the richest and most productive economies in the world,[4] while the East struggled. The division of Germany into two economic zones is the nearest approach ever made in social science to a controlled experiment. And the results were decisive. From 1961 the Berlin Wall divided the two zones. Otherwise the experiment would have ended prematurely with the flight of population from the East. Twenty-eight years later the citizens of the two zones literally tore down the wall that separated them.

The destruction of physical capital does not lead to enduring differences in economic performance; the implementation of different mechanisms of economic management does. The stark differences in economic lives that we see around the world are not the result of differences in the availability of resources or education or capital or skills. They are the product of differences in the structure of economic institutions. These latter differences in turn determine the availability of resources, education, capital, and skills.

This book is about the institutions that define our economic lives. And it will become apparent that not just economic institutions matter. Economic institutions function only as part of a social, political, and cultural context. This is what I describe as the embedded market.

{4}

Figures

There are no average people, only real individuals, like Harvey, Heidi, and Ravi. But only through economic analyses using aggregates and averages can we move from the particular to the general. Economic statistics are simply the averages of the daily economic lives of households and firms.

The comprehensive set of world development indicators compiled by the World Bank is an obvious starting point for systematic comparison of the economic lives enjoyed in different countries. These include estimates for 2001 for gross national income (GNI) per head for 208 countries. Excluding small countries whose population is below 2 million, that leaves Switzerland, with GNI of $37,000 per head, at the top, and the Congo, where the average income is around $100, at the bottom.

Table 4.1 lists the nineteen countries with highest per capita GNI. That range extends from Switzerland down to Italy, whose income level is just over half the Swiss average. These are the rich states of the world. Thirteen of the nineteen are in Western Europe, including eleven of the fifteen members of the European Union.[1] The other EU members are Luxembourg, which is too small, and Greece, Portugal, and Spain, which are too poor. But Norway and Switzerland, which head the list, have chosen to stay out of the EU.

There are six rich countries outside Europe: Australia, Canada, and the United States, and three Asian economies—Japan, Singapore, and China's Special Administrative Region of Hong Kong. The

Table 4.1

• •

The World's Richest Countries

Gross National Income per head, 2001, current U.S. $
at market exchange rates

Switzerland	38,330	Austria	23,940
Norway	35,620	Finland	23,780
Japan	35,610	Belgium	23,850
USA	34,400	Germany	23,560
Denmark	30,600	Ireland	22,850
Hong Kong	25,780	France	22,730
Sweden	25,400	Canada	21,930
UK	25,120	Singapore	21,100
Netherlands	24,330	Australia	19,930
		Italy	19,390

SOURCE: *World Development Report, 2003,* World Bank

total population of the nineteen is around 800 million, of which 300 million live in North America and slightly more in Europe.

Moving on down the income rankings, eight states have levels of GNI per head more than half that of Italy. The richest of these "rich intermediate" countries is Israel, and the poorest Slovenia, a small state—the most economically successful region of the former Yugoslavia—on Italy's eastern border. It has a population of just over 2 million, similar to that of greater Cincinnati. "Poor intermediate" countries—which rank behind Slovenia but have per capita GNI more than half the Slovenian level—form a group that includes such disparate countries as Hungary, Mexico, and Saudi Arabia.

Many of these intermediate countries—Spain, South Korea, Slovenia—are clearly on the way up and will one day join the rich states of Table 4.1. One is on the way down: New Zealand would until the 1980s have been grouped with Australia, the United States, and the prosperous economies of Western Europe.

Table 4.2

Intermediate Economies

Rich intermediate—2001 per capita GNI between one-quarter and one-half of Swiss levels		Poor intermediate—2001 per capita GNI between one-eighth and one-quarter of Swiss levels	
Country	Population (m)	Country	Population (m)
Israel	6.4	Saudi Arabia	21.4
Spain	41.1	Mexico	99.4
New Zealand	3.8	Czech Republic	10.2
Greece	10.6	Hungary	10.2
Portugal	10.0		
Taiwan	22.3		
South Korea	47.6		
Slovenia	2.0		

SOURCE: World Bank; Center for Economic Planning and Development, Taiwan

But rich countries tend to stay rich. Only one other country has suffered the ignominy of New Zealand's fate, and to a much greater degree. At the end of the nineteenth century, Argentina's economy was vibrant, but a century of relative and often absolute decline followed. In the first, European, edition of this book, Argentina was still among the intermediate economies. Following its subsequent economic crises, it is no longer even there. I will return to the experiences of New Zealand and Argentina in chapter 5.

Countries whose economic performance lags that of Hungary have GNI per head less than one-eighth of the Swiss level. In these states, economic life is altogether different. This environment defines the economic lives of most people in the world—Ravi and Nandini, Ivan and Olga, Sicelo and his family. They form five-sixths of the world's population.

But the most remarkable characteristic of the list of intermediate economies is how short it is. It includes only twelve countries. It has a total population of 300 million, one-third of whom live in Mexico, and a further third in South Korea and Spain.

The distribution of GNI is "twin-peaked" whether we measure it by the number of states or by the population of these states.[2] At first sight,

Figure 4.1

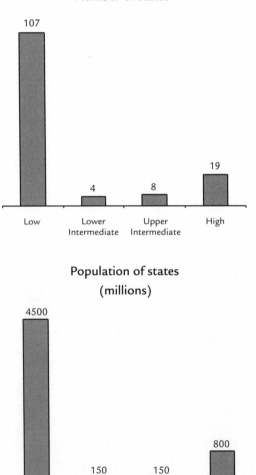

The Distribution of World Income

Number of states

Population of states
(millions)

SOURCE: World Bank

this may not seem surprising. Don't we all know there is a gulf between rich and poor? There is indeed a gulf between rich and poor. Heidi's economic life is very different from Ravi's, and Bill Gates's economic life is very different from mine. But the gulf is not empty. However you define rich and poor households, a lot of households are in between.

Distributions of most variables—height, weight, examination performance, the number of hours individuals spend watching television—are clustered round the average.[3] The further away from the center of the distribution, the fewer observations you find. The distribution of income *within* a country is like that.[4] Most households have incomes close to the local average, and as you move away from that average, there are fewer households. Not only do more households have incomes twice the local average than have incomes that are three times the local average, but more households have incomes that are half the local average than have incomes that are a third of it.

These distributions of income within countries have the statistical shape of a conventional distribution known as the lognormal or Pareto. There is no sharp distinction between rich and poor households, simply a steady gradation from one to the other.[5] The distribution of income among states is quite different. There are numerous poor states, a small number that are neither rich or poor, and a persistent group of about twenty rich countries.

Table 4.1 raises two immediate questions. What do these figures mean—what exactly is GNI? And what is the explanation of the extraordinarily wide range of economic performance that they record? This book is directed toward the second of these questions, but it is necessary to begin by answering the first.

Box 4.1
● ●

INEQUALITY IN WORLD INCOME DISTRIBUTION

Is the world distribution of income becoming more or less equal? The answer to this central economic question is hotly disputed, in academic discussion, among international agencies, and in popular debate.* Yet the main disagreement is not about the facts—most protagonists draw their data from the same sources—but about the way these facts are described.

Some of the confusion arises because there is no single measure of inequality.† In a poor country like India, for example, the majority of the population have similar, low, standards of living, and a small minority is very rich. From one perspective, this is a more egalitarian distribution than we find in productive economies, because almost everyone is in the same boat, and the proportion of national income that accrues to rich people, even in aggregate, is quite small. From another perspective this structure is very unequal. We cannot sensibly say that one of these points of view is right and the other wrong. Each draws attention to different and important aspects of Indian economic life—the gap between rich and poor, and the similarity of the economic lives of most of the Indian population.

In the last two decades, the distribution of income within countries has tended to become more unequal. This is certainly true in Britain and the United States, and probably true in some other rich states. It is probably also true in China and India, where growth has been rapid, but uneven. Across the world as a whole, the very poorest countries—mostly in Africa—have become poorer and the rich have become richer. But the population of these countries is relatively small. Two populous poor countries—China and India—have grown much more rapidly in income than the rich countries of the world. Since these two countries alone account for about one-third of world population, the overall effect of this growth on the world distribution of income is huge.‡

If forced to vote, I would probably conclude that world

income inequality—as measured by the distribution of income per household—has probably gone down. But it is far more important to understand the complex changes that have occurred, and why they have occurred, than to engage in rhetorical debate about rising or falling inequality.

* *See Wade and Wolf in* Prospect, March 2001. *Firebaugh (1999), Melchior et al. (2000), Henderson (2000), Castles (1998).*

† *See Atkinson (1970), Kakwani (1980), and Atkinson (1983) for discussion of the problems of statistical measurement of inequality.*

‡ *Pritchett (1997), Sala-i-Martin (2002).*

Accounting for Our Economic Lives

Economic lives have three different aspects—work, income, consumption. We mostly work in organizations. Grant works in a Ford plant, Heidi teaches in a Swiss school, Ivan works for a Russian subsidiary of AT&T, Pedro washes up in a Los Angeles restaurant. Sicelo works for himself, but in a cooperative South African community. Organizations are teams. Grant works on a production line, where every component contributes to the final product. A meal in Pedro's Los Angeles restaurant requires the services of a chef, a waiter, and a washer-up. The owner of the restaurant, the bank that finances it, and the property company that owns the building also receive a share of what the diner pays. The revenues of the organization become the incomes of individuals—employees, investors, shareholders.[6]

We work in organizations, earn as individuals, and consume as households. Sven and Ingrid work in the same business unit, receive separate paychecks, and make joint consumption decisions. Lyudmila has her own, miserably low, pension, but she survives because she lives with her family. There are cultural differences in the way households pool resources. Harvey and Blythe, unmarried, live together. Ravi, though married, lives with his parents. Sicelo's tribal village is supported by family members working elsewhere; Pedro also sends money back to his family in Mexico. The units in which individuals work and consume are determined by economic necessities and social norms.

These three perspectives on our economic lives—work, income, consumption—are interrelated. What we earn depends on what we produce, what we spend depends on what we earn, what we consume depends on what we make. These links between earnings, production, and expenditure apply to the individual, the household, the business organization, and for the economy as a whole. (Figure 4.2)

Figure 4.2

The Dimensions of Economic Lives

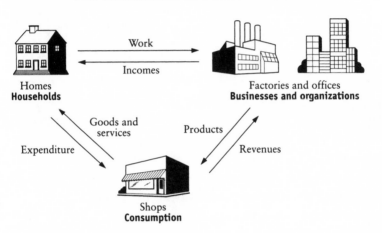

National income accounting systematizes these aggregate relationships, just as household budgeting brings order into domestic lives and financial accounting provides the framework for our business activities. The first national accounts were created by Simon Kuznets[n] just before World War II. The outbreak of war gave rapid impetus to the development of national accounting because it provided a framework for analyzing and managing the resources available to wartime leaders. Two young British economists, James Meade[n] and Richard Stone,[n] under the tutelage of Maynard Keynes, produced the first official and comprehensive set of national accounts.

Modern national accounts are still based essentially on the framework devised by Kuznets, Meade, and Stone, and this framework records and integrates the three elements of economic life—incomes, output, and expenditure. All of them converge on the central concept

Table 4.3

What America Spends, 2001

	$ billion
105 million households spend on average $67,000	6,987
Government spending (equates to $5,325 per head of population)	1,513
Business investment	1,869
Trade deficit (net purchases from abroad)	-349
Gross domestic product	10,020

SOURCE: Annual National Accounts; OECD

Table 4.4

What America Earns, 2001

	$ billion
124 million workers earn on average $47,500	5,881
Profits of businesses	3,596
Taxes (less subsidies) on businesses	660
Statistical discrepancy	-117
Gross domestic product	10,020

SOURCE: Annual National Accounts; OECD

of national income accounting, gross domestic product. When politicians talk about economic growth, they are talking about growth in gross domestic product (GDP). When pundits discuss booms and recessions, they are discussing movements of GDP.

International agencies have encouraged countries to produce their national accounts in a common framework, and this data is the basis for the rankings in Table 4.1. Gross national income is derived by

Table 4.5

Redistribution of Income Among Households, America, 2001 ($ Billion)

Earnings of workers	5,881	
Investment income (net)	2,006	
Total household income from current production		7,887
Benefits and pensions:		1,171
from government	507	
from private sector	664	
Less tax and nontax deductions from income		-1,292
Less personal contributions to social insurance		-372
Left for households to spend		7,394

SOURCE: U.S. National Accounts, Bureau of Economic Analysis

adjusting gross domestic product, a measure of a country's output, for the income its residents derive from the assets they own overseas.

Ravi's income is in rupees. Ivan is paid in roubles, although his wife is often paid dollars for her translations. Comparisons across countries are easiest if figures are translated into a common currency. The simplest way of doing this is to look up the quoted exchange rate between currencies. One obvious problem in making comparisons this way is that exchange rates fluctuate from day to day. Since the euro was established in 1999, its value has ranged from $0.82 to $1.18. Table 4.1 is based on a three-year average to reduce this volatility.

Table 4.6

What America Produces, 2001 ($ Billion)*

Sector	Total output	Sold to other businesses	Sold directly
Agricultural	299	264	35
Mining	163	221	-58
Construction	1,150	244	906
Manufacturing	4,330	2,551	1,779
Transportation, communication, and utilities	1,461	795	666
Trade	1,811	528	1,283
Finance, insurance, and real estate	2,854	1,100	1,754
Services	4,221	1,702	2,519
Other	1,228	92	1,136
Total	17,517	7497	10,020
Gross domestic product			10,020

SOURCE: U.S. National Accounts, Bureau of Economic Analysis

*Latest available figures are 1999. The 2001 estimates shown here are constructed by scaling up 1999 figures by nominal GDP growth between 1999 and 2001.

Box 4.2

● ●

WHAT GDP IS, AND ISN'T

GDP is often criticized because it is not necessarily a measure of sustainable output, or of economic welfare. Two frequent criticisms are that it fails to take account of degradation (or improvement) in the environment, and that it does not measure unpaid work undertaken within the home.*

There is some validity in these claims. But the measurement of GDP and the framework of national income accounts should be seen primarily as a way of organizing the information we have about the national economy, rather than as an attempt to measure welfare. It is difficult to maintain this position because economic data is widely used in political debate.

In the 1990s the Bureau of Economic Analysis, which compiles the U.S. national accounts, was under obvious pressure, particularly from Chairman Greenspan, to support the assertions then made about the "new economy." On the other side of the political fence, those who argue that GDP should account for environmental costs or unpaid work are more concerned to make environmental or feminist arguments than to enhance the integrity of national accounting frameworks.

GDP and other economic measurements are likely to be of greatest use to a wide range of users if as far as is possible the measurement relates to issues of objective fact. Users can then modify these measures to reflect their own requirements. The pursuit of objectivity and comparability is preferable to repeated modification in pursuit of a concept of accuracy that is both subjective and elusive. (The same is true of commercial accounting.)

GDP (in common with other national accounts measures) is a measure of material output, not welfare.

* *For substantive academic discussion of these issues, see Kenrick (1979) and Nordhaus and Kokkelenberg, eds. 1999.*

● ●

Kivik and Palanpur
• •

Switzerland's GDP is not very much smaller than India's. Yet the population of India is more than a hundred times larger. About 5 million people work in Switzerland and 600 million in India. Can these staggering differences in productivity really be true?

Sven's farm at Kivik produces wheat. Since wheat is grown in many countries, we can make approximate comparisons between the productivity of Sven's farm and the productivity of Indian farming. For several decades now, economists have regularly visited the village of Palanpur in Rajasthan, living with the people and studying their economy rather as anthropologists study culture.[7]

Sven's farm produces about twenty times as much wheat per person employed as does Palanpur. In both places, the yield varies from year to year: rather more in Palanpur than in Kivik. Yields have been rising. Since 1960, the green revolution (the adoption of new crop varieties adapted to tropical climates) has almost doubled the Palanpur crop. There have been productivity gains in Sweden too.

The average yield per acre at Kivik is around four times the yield at Palanpur. Sven uses more fertilizer (although new crop varieties have made fertilizer much more productive in India) and modern pesticides. If you were to choose a climate in which to grow wheat, you would probably not select either Kivik or Palanpur. Kivik is too cold and Palanpur is too dry (except in the monsoon, when it is too wet). The Canadian prairies, and the American Great Plains, have the best blend of temperature and moisture for wheat. The land at Kivik is more fertile than at Palanpur, but it is hard to say how much of that is intrinsic and how much the result of poor farming in the Indian village.

Sven has much more machinery. The village employs about five times as many people per acre. The difference in labor input both causes and is caused by the difference in income levels. Because Swedish labor is expensive, Swedish farmers use costly equipment, and Swedish agriculture is consolidated into large commercial plots. Palanpur villagers use bullocks, plows, and scythes as they have done for centuries, and many of them work their own small pieces of land.

Every aspect of economic life is different, so that there is no single explanation of why Swedish productivity is twenty times as great. Wheat cultivation is one of a small number of activities for which

Indian and Swedish output are comparable because wheat is more or less wheat wherever it is grown.[8] Many Swedish goods could simply not be manufactured in India. There are no Indian cars of Volvo quality. Goods like Volvos command high prices in world markets, and that is why the average difference in GDP per worker is well above a ratio of twenty to one.

Material Living Standards

Roger and Sandra ski around Lake Tahoe. Ivan and Olga also ski, in northern Russia. Roger and Sandra have access to a network of modern ski lifts, built to exacting safety standards; the few lifts available to Ivan and Olga are old and poorly maintained. Sven and Ingrid use high-tech skis and bindings, but Ivan and Olga have very basic equipment. Development around Lake Tahoe is controlled to preserve the environment. Ivan and Olga ski in the forests of the Komi republic, which has suffered sustained damage from atmospheric pollution and inappropriate logging.[9]

But a week's skiing at Lake Tahoe would cost ten times what Ivan and Olga pay. Roger and Sandra have a better experience—both couples would prefer to use American facilities and equipment. But is the American experience ten times better? Most of the joy of skiing comes from snow and sun, freedom and companionship, and these are as exhilarating for Ivan and Olga as for Roger and Sandra.

Heidi and Hermann share an income whose dollar value is more than thirty times that of Ravi and Nandini. Heidi and Hermann are certainly much better off, in material terms, than Ravi and Nandini. They have all the material goods that Ravi and Nandini have, and many more: the Indian couple would readily exchange their economic lives for those of Heidi and Hermann, but Heidi and Hermann would not want to live the economic lives of Ravi and Nandini. Heidi and Hermann are better off, but not necessarily happier.

But is Heidi thirty times as well off as Ravi? An objective approach to the measurement of material living standards might ask what it would cost Heidi and Hermann to live the economic life of Ravi and Nandini, or Ravi and Nandini to live the economic life of Heidi and Hermann. But the question is tough. You cannot rent an apartment like that of Ravi and Nandini in Switzerland—the Swiss authorities would not allow it to be built. You can find a house like that of Heidi and Hermann in India, but in an enclosed compound with private security guards.

The food that Nandini buys cheaply every day in the market is available in Zürich only from a delicatessen at high prices. Heidi does not have a housekeeper and does much of the housework herself. Nandini does have a housekeeper and does little domestic work. The cost of an automatic dishwasher in India corresponds to three years of a housekeeper's earnings, but Heidi's salary pays for her machine in less than a week.

The more distant comparisons are in space and time, the more strained they become. Nathan Rothschild, probably the richest man in the world in 1836, died despite the best medical attention money could buy. The infection that killed him could today be cured by antibiotics available even to Sicelo for a few coins.[10] Isn't Sicelo, alive, better off than Nathan Rothschild, dead?

Despite these difficulties, international agencies make estimates of "purchasing power parity" (PPP), the cost of maintaining a given material standard of living in different countries.[11] These comparisons suggest that international disparities in material living standards are less wide than international disparities in productivity. Services and property are generally cheaper in poor countries than in rich countries. Services and property are also cheaper in Australia and North America than in Europe or Japan.

Productivity and Material Living Standards
● ●

These national accounts concepts are the building blocks for the measurement of all aspects of representative economic lives. Table 4.7 provides estimates of material living standards (private consumption per head) and of productivity (output per working hour) for the nineteen rich countries of Table 4.1.

The nineteen countries with the highest GNI are both the nineteen most productive countries in the world and the nineteen countries with the highest material standard of living. This equivalence is not inevitable. But it is likely, given the fundamental connections between the different aspects of our economic lives—output, incomes, and consumption. And it has an important implication that will be developed

John Kay

Table 4.7
· ·
· ·

Living Standards and Productivity, 2001, U.S. $

Country	Consumption per head, PPP exchange rates	Output per hour, PPP exchange rates	Output per hour, market exchange rates
Australia	16,300	32.3	22.6
Austria	15,600	40.0	33.2
Belgium	14,700	46.3	37.0
Canada	16,000	33.6	25.9
Denmark	13,500	39.0	39.8
Finland	13,500	36.4	32.0
France	14,300	45.2	37.1
Germany	15,000	40.1	34.5
Hong Kong	15,600	30.9	30.0
Ireland	13,400	40.2	36.6
Italy	15,600	40.1	28.9
Japan	14,700	35.3	43.4
Netherlands	14,300	42.0	34.5
Norway	15,200	54.0	55.1
Singapore	11,500	29.6	26.9
Sweden	12,200	33.5	31.8
Switzerland	17,400	34.6	39.5
UK	16,900	34.2	31.5
USA	24,500	39.5	39.5

SOURCE: OECD, Hong Kong Census and Statistics Department;
Statistics Singapore

more fully in this book. The main reasons why some countries are rich and others poor, why some states are productive and others not, is because of the internal economic organization of these countries themselves, rather than the product of international economics. Heidi is not rich because Sicelo is poor.

It is probably best to measure productivity at market exchange rates, because market exchange rates measure what, on average, global markets are willing to pay for a country's output. But market exchange rates are subject to large short-term fluctuations, and in 2001 the value of the euro was extremely low, so the rankings by purchasing power parity (PPP) in Table 4.7 are a better overall guide to the underlying levels of productivity in the various countries.

However measured, Norway has much the highest productivity of any country in the world. It combines large and profitable oil extraction with an efficient industrial sector. The range of productivity among the remaining countries at market exchange rates finds Japan at the top ($43 per hour) and Australia at the bottom ($23 per hour), but the less misleading purchasing power parity basis discloses a narrower range, from Belgium's $46 per hour to around $30 per hour in the still emerging Hong Kong and Singapore. Average output of about $40 per hour is what a productive modern economy with current technology can expect to achieve.

Among rich states, variations in productivity are poorly correlated with variations in material living standards. Table 4.8 explores why. There are large differences in private consumption as a share of national income—almost 70% in the United States as against just over 40% in Norway. Norway enjoys a trade surplus, the United States a trade deficit. Norway has much higher personal savings and higher business investment; Norway has much higher levels of public spending.

Variations in the proportion of the population working are less dramatic, but still considerable: 55% of the Swiss population is employed, but in Belgium, where early retirement is common, unemployment high, and it is still unusual for married women with children to work, the figure is only 39%. There are large variations in average annual working hours. Norwegians take a large part of the benefit of their oil reserves in leisure. The United States is a complete outlier, with much longer typical working hours than other countries. It is also the only

Table 4.8
· ·

Why Material Living Standards Differ, 2001

	Household consumption as a share of GDP (%)	Number working per 100 of population	Hours worked (annual average)	Local cost in $ of consumption of $1
Australia	60.1	47.3	1,779	0.70
Austria	55.6	46.2	1,519	0.83
Belgium	53.2	38.8	1,547	0.80
Canada	55.1	48.0	1,789	0.77
Denmark	46.4	50.4	1,482	1.02
Finland	47.8	45.5	1,612	0.88
France	54.0	40.5	1,474	0.82
Germany	57.5	44.5	1,467	0.86
Hong Kong	57.8	49.7	1,760	0.97
Ireland	44.7	44.6	1,674	0.89
Italy	59.6	40.6	1,606	0.72
Japan	55.2	50.4	1,780	1.23
Netherlands	48.9	50.6	1,376	0.82
Norway	41.2	50.2	1,364	1.02
Singapore	42.3	51.1	1,798	0.91
Sweden	47.0	48.6	1,603	0.95
Switzerland	58.4	55.3	1,566	1.14
UK	63.8	45.7	1,656	0.92
USA	69.7	48.4	1,878	1.00

SOURCE: OECD, Hong Kong Census and Statistics Department; Statistics
      Singapore

Shaded boxes mark median figures.

country in which average hours of work have been rising. The normal trend around the world has been for working hours to fall as incomes rise, and if the United States is excluded, there is a strong tendency for longer holidays and shorter working weeks in richer countries.

The final column of Table 4.8 shows the cost of living in different countries: in 2001 it would have cost $1.23 in Japan, $1.14 in Switzerland, but only $0.70 in Australia, to buy the goods that would have cost $1.00 in the United States. This table makes the United States look like an expensive country in which to live, but this is another consequence of the low value of the euro in 2001. If the same calculation were repeated for 2003, the cost of living in Belgium, France, Germany, and the Netherlands would be similar to that of the United States.

Taken together, the factors described in Table 4.8 lead to the striking out come that the United States, with productivity levels around average, attains much higher private consumption levels than any other country in the world. The principal reasons are the high level of consumption, relative to GNP, and the much longer working hours. In the United States, government spending—which is primarily on health, education, and infrastructure—is much lower than average, business investment is lower than average, and high consumption is financed by extensive borrowing from the rest of the world, particularly Asia. And Americans work much more than residents of other rich countries, with later retirement, shorter holidays, and longer hours. As a result of this relentless focus on private consumption, American levels are 40% above those of the next highest countries, Switzerland and the United Kingdom.

Box 4.3 explores this difference further by comparing directly the structures of the French and U.S. economies. This is the statistical analogue of the tour of Menton in chapter 1.

Box 4.3

● ●

WORK AND LIVING STANDARDS, UNITED STATES AND FRANCE, 2001

1. Consumption is much lower relative to national income in France (shares of GDP).

	France	U.S.
Government consumption in France is higher	23%	15%
Investment in France is higher	20%	16%
Personal savings are higher	7%	2%
U.S. borrows more from abroad	-2%	3%

2. The proportion of the population working in France is lower.

	France	U.S.
Fewer French people are of working age	65%	66%
Fewer women work in France (aged 15–64)	62%	70%
French people retire earlier (average retirement age)	60	65

3. Working hours are shorter in France.

	France	U.S.
France has more public holidays (days)	11	10
French people have longer paid holidays (days)	26	16
The average working week is shorter (hours) (includes part-time working)	31	38

4. The cost of living differs between the two countries.

In 2001 it would have cost 82¢ to buy enough euros to purchase $1 of goods in France

In September 2003, that figure is $1.05

Source: Own calculations based on OECD and GRONINGEN[w] data

Other Dimensions

• •

The nineteen countries of Table 4.1 are the rich states, the productive economies of the world. They are distinguished from other countries in many other respects. Here are some other correlations.

Climate—productive economies are cooler. With the exceptions of Hong Kong and Singapore, and a large area of Australia in which few people live, there are no rich states in the tropics.[12]

Democracy—rich states are normally democracies.[13]

Environmental standards—productive economies mostly have higher environmental standards (less atmospheric pollution, better water quality) and more environmental activism.[14]

Freedom of expression is less restricted in productive economies.[15]

Gender equality—rights and freedoms of women are more extensive in rich states than poor ones.[16]

Happiness, self-reported—the people of productive economies mostly give positive answers to the question "Are you generally happy with your life?" The same is true in some poor countries (Cuba, India). In other unproductive economies, surveys show that few people are happy. This is particularly true of Eastern Europe.[17]

Health—life expectancy is higher and infant mortality lower in rich states. (East European countries do better on this score than their GDP would suggest.)[18]

Height—the population of productive economies is taller.[19]

Honesty—rich states are less corrupt and their citizens give positive answers to questions like "Do you find you can mostly trust other people?"[20]

Inequality can be measured in many ways. But if we consider the ratio of total income of the richest 20% of the population to total income of the poorest 20%, then productive economies are more egalitarian than unproductive ones. Most ways of measuring inequality would lead to a similar conclusion.[21]

Inflation is lower in rich states.[22]

Literacy—the population of productive economies is almost entirely literate. This is also true in East Europe, but only occasionally elsewhere.[23]

Materialism—people in poor economies more often give positive answers to questions of the kind "Is money the most important thing?"[24]

Openness—productive countries have fewer restrictions on trade with other countries.[25]

Population growth is lower in productive economies.[26]

Property rights are more secure in rich states.[27]

Religion—from the standpoint of earthly productivity, it is better to live in a society whose traditions are Christian, and among Christians, it is better to live in a predominantly Protestant tradition than in a mainly Catholic one.[28]

Tolerance—more people in rich states answer yes to questions like "Should people be allowed to live as they choose?"[29]

Correlation does not imply causation. Average height is greater in rich states. Are tall people more productive than short people? Or does higher productivity make people taller? I doubt if either of these things is true. The most likely explanation is that higher standards of living, which result from higher productivity, lead to better nutrition. In turn, better nutrition leads to greater adult height and still higher productivity. The relationship works in both directions, and only in association with other factors that are themselves associated with height and productivity.

Most of the relationships described above are like this. Few, if any, of the factors listed are directly caused by higher productivity or higher living standards. They are components in a complex mixture of factors associated with higher productivity. Our economic lives are embedded in our social and political lives.

The present chapter has illustrated aspects of this embeddedness, which will be the continuing theme of this book. Within the community of rich states, different cultures have made different choices about the ways in which the capacities of their economies are reflected in the economic lives of their citizens. These choices are partly the result of individual decisions—how long to spend over lunch—and of collective decisions—how many resources to devote to public schools or transport systems.

There are no economic criteria, and really no criteria at all, that enable us to conclude that some of these choices are right and others wrong. Still less that some convergence on one system or another is inevitable. Diversity is itself an important feature of economic life.

In the decade since the Cold War ended, admiring eyes have switched from Japan, whose own boom ended with its own bubble in the late 1980s, to Germany, whose successful social market economy struggled with the burden of reunification in the 1990s. Attention was diverted to the Asian tigers—Singapore, Korea, Hong Kong—but ended with the financial crisis of 1997. And since then America's New Economy has occupied center stage.

In superficial economic commentary, trends of a few years or even months are projected into an indefinite future with the transience of designer fashions. The really important observation is that differences in economic performance and experience among rich states are small and temporary, while differences between rich and poor states are large and enduring. Any theory of the relative success and failure of economic systems must explain this central fact. A good starting point is to ask how today's rich states became rich.

{5}

How Rich States Became Rich

Beginnings[1]

Modern economic systems are complex, interacting sets of institutions that have evolved over thousands of years. We are all descended from mitochondrial Eve, who lived in Africa 150,000 or so years ago; and when her great-grandchildren arrived in Europe, 40,000 years ago, they displaced Neanderthal man. We don't know exactly how they did it. But we do know that at their Cro-Magnon campsites, we find objects made from materials available hundreds of miles away; Neanderthal tools use only local materials. The Cro-Magnons must have engaged in trade. They also innovated; we can see the evolution of their tools. Language may well have been the key difference.[2] Communication is essential to specialization and exchange.

Agriculture began in what was then the fertile crescent of Mesopotamia, irrigated by the Tigris and the Euphrates, between eight and ten thousand years ago[3]—the area we today call Iraq. People had always "owned" clothes and tools. But agriculture requires property rights over land and animals. Such rights had to be codified and recognized. These new institutions created opportunities for further technological innovation. Selective breeding and domestication of crops and species came with ownership of seeds and animals. New technologies and new institutions gradually spread out from their places of origin.[4]

Technology and institutions sped rapidly across plains and along rivers, slowly over hills. Agricultural practices can be transferred more easily along an east-west axis than a north-south one, because climate changes less. Today's rich states are in temperate climates not too different from that of Mesopotamia ten thousand years ago.

The next steps in the evolution of modern economic life took place in Europe. In ancient Greece, people organized production and trade. Business and management had been invented. They were not well regarded by the philosophers and writers of the time.[5] Intellectual disdain for the market is not new.

Tourists in Athens can still visit ancient marketplaces—physical locations where competitive buyers met sellers. These marketplaces were public facilities, provided by the state to assist commerce. The Greeks invented the notion of politics. With a political realm comes the possibility of a government whose economic activities are distinct from the economic interests of those who control it. Market economies require disinterested government.

Ancient Greece was a pluralist society. Its citizens began to question the nature of the natural world and the structure of social organization. This restless spirit lay quiescent through the Dark Ages, to revive in medieval times.[6] The Renaissance, centered in Italy, was characterized by pluralism and experiment in art, architecture, and literature. But that pluralism and experiment extended to economic organization, economic institutions, and new ventures. Markets for risk and for capital developed, and with them the idea that you can trade paper rights to commodities as well as commodities themselves. These are the beginnings of modern securities markets. Businesses develop that are distinguishable from the individuals who run them, such as trading companies and banks. Their records are maintained through double-entry bookkeeping.[7]

From the Reformation to the Industrial Revolution

The Reformation followed the Renaissance: revolts, centered in England and in Germany, rejected the established authority of the Catholic Church. And the focus of economic development in Europe moved north. The architectural legacies of Italy and Spain are a demonstration, in stone, of the difference between the relative economic positions of countries at the time of the Reformation, and today.

Was there a connection between religious pluralism and economic development? The correlation between the growth of economic institutions and the growth of Protestantism seems inescapable. Catholic Italy and Ireland became modern rich states only in the later part of the twentieth century, and Spain will become one only in the twenty-first. In countries with mixed populations (such as Switzerland, Germany, and the Netherlands), the economic role of Protestants was disproportionate to their numbers.

But the nature of the connection is controversial. Max Weber explained how belief in predestination led to the austere, hardworking morality we still call the Protestant ethic. R. H. Tawney and Robert Merton gave greater weight to the intellectual ferment that followed the breakdown of clerical authoritarianism: the opportunity to challenge established ideas and practices that is essential to the coevolution of technology and institutions.[8] The combination of moral rigor and free inquiry is the basis of disciplined pluralism—the defining characteristic of the successful market economy.

And the shape of that market economy began to emerge. Britain and the Netherlands became major trading nations in the seventeenth and eighteenth centuries. While Spanish colonists were soldiers in search of gold, British and Dutch colonization was managed by businesses such as the East India Company and the VOC (Vereenigde Oostindische Compagnie) and its purpose was commercial exploitation. The beginning of the eighteenth century was a period of rapid financial innovation, which culminated in the boom and bust of the South Sea bubble.

The Market Economy Crosses the Atlantic
● ●

The Pilgrim fathers came to Plymouth from Britain via the Netherlands. Thus the connection with the two countries at the forefront of the development of economic institutions in the seventeenth and eighteenth centuries was established at the inception of modern America. The colonists of the Northeastern states brought with them the technology and the economic institutions of the countries they had left. In less than twenty years, the first ironworks was constructed at Lynn, Massachusetts. The colonists also brought like-minded people. These colonists were not only Protestants but sectarian Protestants—that was what had led them to flee Europe—and they encouraged the immigration of those who held similar views to theirs. Quakers and other dissenting sects were particularly successful in Europe in economic terms, and the hard work and personal integrity they emphasized yielded returns in the colonies also.

The Puritans of New England and the Quakers of the Delaware Valley were two of the principal groups that established the American republic and developed the economic institutions that framed American economic development and gave the new nation an industrial revolution similar to that of Britain and the Netherlands.[9] Besides the English-speaking colonists, the most important group of settlers were the Dutch who occupied the Hudson Valley. More than fifty years after the Revolution, Tocqueville could still write, "In spite of the ocean that intervenes, I cannot consent to separate America from Europe. I consider the people of the United States as that portion of the English people who are commissioned to explore the forests of the new world."

So whatever the political differences established by the American Revolution, Britain, Holland, and the United States were joint leaders in economic development at the start of the nineteenth century. There was one important difference—a difference that itself provided part of the rationale for settlement. Europe increasingly suffered from too much population for its land; in America, the ratio of land to people was quite different. This had implications for the balance of economic and political power. Adam Smith, the revered founder of modern economics, published *The Wealth of Nations* in 1776, coincident with the American Revolution. "England," he observed, "is certainly, in the present times, a much richer country than any part of North America. The wages of labor, however, are much higher in North America than in any part of England."[10]

Virginia was different. The settlers in New England, and the Hudson and Delaware valleys, were predominantly middle-class religious dissenters. Those of the South were displaced aristocrats, who sought to reproduce in America the economic system from which they had derived their status in Europe. The shortage of labor was met, not by higher wages, but by the import of slaves. This enabled these areas to sustain a predominantly agricultural economy, and to reproduce much of the aristocratic style of life and distribution of income and wealth that had been traditional in Europe. These Southern colonies had less interest in either the technological or the institutional innovations taking place in northwest Europe.

Only with the Civil War was the political and economic hegemony of the North decisively established. The consequences can still be seen today. The financial center of the United States is located in the northeast corner of the country, and traditional industries are still predominantly based in Northern states.

Market institutions were first imported into the United States from Western Europe, but the revolution was brought home, in an economic sense, before the end of the nineteenth century, as the United States became a center for new technology and financial innovation. And in the twentieth century, the United States was to become dominant in management theory and product innovation. By its end, Americans would sincerely believe that the market economy was an American invention, and a comparatively recent one.

Thomas Friedman, a chronicler of globalization for the *New York Times,* would explain that "if one hundred years ago you had come to a visionary geo-architect and told him that in the year 2000 the world would be defined by a system called 'globalization,' what sort of country would he have designed to compete and win in that world? The answer is that he would have designed something that looks an awful lot like the United States of America." "The world is ten years old," he announced.[11] But Friedman is wrong. If you think the world is ten years old, you understand very little about the market economy—or about the origins of America's role in it.

Settlements
● ●

The United States was not the only country of settlement. Modern Canada and Australia, Argentina and New Zealand, were also established by European immigrants. These settlers annihilated the cultures of the native populations and largely annihilated the native populations themselves. Their legal systems and political and social institutions are European in origin. They speak northwestern European languages, mostly English, though French in Quebec and Spanish in Argentina.

Colonies such as India or Indonesia in which immigrants were a minority are not rich states—not even those colonies where settlements were large, as in South Africa, Kenya, or the West Indies.

The countries of settlement not only imported technology and institutions from Western Europe: they also imported people familiar with that technology and those institutions. In European colonies the native population was not encouraged—and often, until late stages of colonialism, not permitted—to assimilate and be assimilated by the imported culture. The transfer of technology and institutions was superficial and transitory.

But even if the building blocks of the market economy were imported, these new countries had to solve one problem for themselves. By the nature of settlement, there is no established system of property in land when settlers arrive in an empty territory. (The territories were not empty and there were existing land claims, if not property on a European model. But the settlers ignored these claims or extinguished them.) There are two principal ways of creating new property rights. They can be allocated, or sold, by the state, or government can recognize and enforce the rights of those settlers who actually occupy the land.[12]

The ability to award, or sell, tracts of empty land is a congenial source of patronage and revenue for government. But decisions made in Washington or London did not necessarily relate to what was happening on the ground thousands of miles away.[13] Settlers would develop local norms to define and protect each other's rights. In the gold rushes—the largest were in California and Victoria, Australia—government was ineffective. A degree of spontaneous order, in which the mining communities regulated and enforced each other's claims, emerged rapidly.[14] These models influenced the general development of land rights. In the end, settlers' claims—squatters' rights—were the principal determinant of property rights in English-speaking settlements, but not in English-speaking colonies or Spanish-speaking settlements. This difference had enduring consequences.

Argentina and New Zealand

Argentina and New Zealand are two of these countries of settlement—once rich, rich no longer. They have many similarities.

Both are low-cost agricultural producers. You can take an eleven-hour direct flight from Auckland to Buenos Aires to see the two nations play international rugby. And they have many differences. The most famous Argentines are Eva Perón, movie-star wife of a populist dictator, and the skeptical writer Jorge Luis Borges. The most famous New Zealanders are Ernest Rutherford, who first split the atom (in England), and Edmund Hillary, who climbed Everest (in Nepal). The symbol of Argentina is the gaucho, of New Zealand the kiwi. And New Zealanders seem to have the same affection for Queen Elizabeth of New Zealand that Argentines had for Evita.

But both are geographically peripheral countries. Geographic contiguity had a large influence on the development of rich states in Western Europe. The two countries to have ceased to be rich states are the two most geographically detached.

Transport costs hardly explain why countries that were rich a century ago are less rich today. In chapter 24, I will examine the unconvincing dependency theory of Argentine economist Raoul Prebisch, which claims that all peripheral countries are disadvantaged. But one consequence of peripheral location is that it leaves countries greater freedom to pursue economic policies different from those of other rich states. The geographical contagion that worked so well in Europe is less strong. This freedom has been exploited in both Argentina and New Zealand to dismal effect. The fame of Evita and her husband is not based on skill in economic management. And New Zealand has inflicted unsuccessful economic experiments on itself.

Argentina was never as well off as Australia or New Zealand. But a visitor to Buenos Aires is still impressed by century-old buildings that match the opulence of other late-nineteenth-century capitals. The shabby surroundings measure the decline in Argentina's relative position. Argentine development was strikingly pluralist (a pluralism that is maintained today in the vitality of Argentine cultural life). Immigration from Italy was almost as important as immigration from Spain. Despite the famous Welsh enclave in Patagonia, few settlers were attracted from Northern Europe. But British economic influence was pervasive: Britons not only built tramways and railways but organized markets for Argentine meat.[15]

But economic institutions are only part of the structures relevant to economic development. While the economic growth of English-speaking settlements has matched or outperformed that of England, Spanish-speaking settlements have struggled to match the—itself unexceptional—performance of Spain. And there is a key economic difference between English and Spanish settlements. In English-speaking countries, tension over property distribution was resolved largely in favor of settlers. In Latin America, central control over land allocation was more effective. Even today, land ownership in Latin America is dominated by the descendants of a small number of founding families.

Absentee proprietors are generally poor proprietors. But the indirect economic consequences were more important still. The inegalitarian distribution of income and wealth lacked legitimacy. These economic and political inequalities have shaped the destructive and confrontational nature of Argentina's politics from the overthrow of Rivadavia by landowners in 1827 to the street demonstrations of 2002.[16]

The problems of New Zealand are more recent in origin. Twelve thousand miles distant, New Zealand became a major agricultural producer focused on the British market. Even in 1960, more than half of New Zealand's exports were to the mother country. This relationship fractured as Britain moved closer to continental Europe and, more hesitantly, New Zealand to Australia and Asia.

New Zealand could find alternative markets only at lower prices, and its economic performance deteriorated. In 1975, Robert Muldoon became prime minister. Muldoon's slogan was "think big." He sponsored the construction of aluminum smelters and petrochemical plants and favored detailed economic intervention. Most of the "think big" projects were eventually written off with large losses.

Muldoon was defeated in the 1984 election.[17] The new Labor government appointed Roger Douglas as finance minister. Douglas pursued enthusiastic free market policies, supported by an able and ideologically committed group of Treasury officials led by Graham Scott. If ever a country has been run by economists, it was New Zealand. From 1984 to 1999, New Zealand followed policies of privatization and deregulation and pursued labor market flexibility and reductions in social benefits. During this period, New Zealand experienced the worst economic performance of any rich state. Its decline was bleakly symbolized in January 1998. The supply cables of the unregulated Mercury Energy failed, blacking out the central business district of Auckland. Seven weeks elapsed before regular power supplies were restored.[18]

No country has modeled its policies more deliberately on the American business model—applause for self-interest, market fundamentalism, and the rolling back of the economic and redistributive functions of the state—than New Zealand after 1984.[19] Not even the United States. When one branch of the U.S. government has maintained a strong ideological position—as under the Reagan presidency or the Republican congress of 1994–96—checks and balances operated within the U.S. system of government. The parliamentary structure that Britain gave New Zealand has few restraints on executive authority (New Zealand even has a unicameral legislature). In 1999, the New Zealand electorate tired of economic experiments and returned a government with conventional policies. After three phases of adverse economic experience—one externally created, two self-inflicted—New Zealand GDP per head had fallen from 125% of the average of rich states in 1960 to 60% of the average in 2000.[20]

The Asian Contrast

Why did the industrial revolution happen in Britain and in northwest Europe and not in southeast China?[21] This is one of the great puzzles of economic history. Earlier in the millennium, Chinese technology had fully matched that of the West. In the second half of the eighteenth century, the two regions had many similarities—in industrial structure, agricultural techniques, in capital per head, and the mild but increasing pressure of population on available land.

But the industrial revolution in Europe was not a purely technological phenomenon. China's institutions lagged its productive capability. And the pluralism that was so important to the evolution of Western European science and Western European institutions was largely absent. China was—is—a more or less unitary state, while Europe has always been fragmented. This contrast can be overstated: the imperial writ ran uncertainly over large areas of China, and European fragmentation produced the disadvantages of military conflict as well as the advantages of economic competition. More important is the degree of pluralism within states, and societies.

The China of that period has given the English language the term *mandarin*. Mandarins were the civil servants of the Chinese court, and the values they prized were the values of tradition and ritual. At the start of the eighteenth century, a French missionary visiting China could write that "they are more fond of the most defective piece of antiquity than of the most perfect of the modern, differing much in that from us, who are in love with nothing but what is new." A hundred and fifty years later, another missionary observed that "any man of genius is paralyzed immediately by the thought that his efforts will win him punishment rather than reward."[22]

China's failure to match European economic performance became more and more obvious through the nineteenth and twentieth centuries. The resulting xenophobia exaggerated the initial problems. It reinforced internal authoritarianism and fueled resistance to external influences. The communist takeover reinforced centralization while replacing stasis with deranged and contradictory directions. The extraordinary economic successes of Chinese people outside China itself—in Singapore, Hong Kong, and Taiwan, and also as settlers in Britain, Canada, and the United States—suggest that Chinese institutions were largely to blame for China's sustained economic failure.

From 1639, Japan was closed to external influence.[23] No foreigners could live there; trade was restricted to two ports. Internally, there was more pluralism than in China. Political organization was decentralized, and many features of European financial markets were independently developed. Still, the exclusion of foreign innovations in institutions and technology was a crippling economic handicap. This changed only in 1853 when Commodore Perry arrived to deliver the American business model and returned a year later, with the aid of American guns, to insist.

Japan began to adopt Western technologies, but the import of Western institutions was slower. With the Meiji restoration came political centralization, leading to the obsessive militarism that culminated in Pearl Harbor and ended at Hiroshima and Nagasaki. General Douglas MacArthur landed in Tokyo in 1945 to impose those elements of the American business model that Commodore Perry had overlooked.

MacArthur's objective was to reform Japanese institutions. The secularization of the role of the emperor undermined the authoritarian state. Subsequent political leadership was fragmented and ineffectual, although the civil service remained powerful. The five *zaibatsu*,[24] which had controlled all large-scale economic activity in Japan, were dissolved.

Japanese industry focused on the production of high-quality consumer goods. Toyota transformed itself from a manufacturer of textile machinery into the principal competitor of Ford and General Motors. Matsushita—*zaibatsu* reinvented as conglomerate—became a leading producer of consumer electronics under brand names such as Panasonic and JVC. Sony and Honda were creations of maverick individuals. Akio Morita, the man behind Sony, became Japan's best-known businessman. For forty years from 1950, Japan experienced the fastest growth of GDP ever seen in a major economy.

Japan's success was to be rivaled by the achievements of two former colonies—South Korea and Formosa (Taiwan). Freed from Japanese control by the outcome of World War II, both countries found themselves on the fault line of mutual suspicion between China and the United States. MacArthur moved to Korea, where a civil war widened into a conflict between China and the United States. In 1953, the country was divided at the thirty-eighth parallel. The difference between the economic performance of the two states created since then is extraordinary—far greater even than the differences between East and West Germany or Finland and Estonia. South Korea will shortly become a rich state, barring accident—or reunification. North Korea has both nuclear weapons and endemic famine.[25]

Taiwan was occupied by the Nationalist forces defeated in the communist takeover of mainland China in 1949. Like Korea, it prospered through a mix of policies combining American and Japanese influences: protection against imports, strong export orientation, openness to external capital and technology, and competition among a small number of diversified industrial groups.

The two small island territories of Singapore and Hong Kong, with British institutions and Chinese populations, became rich states. Thailand, Malaysia, and Indonesia, although still poor, have grown rapidly. IndoChina, ravaged by decades of war, is still one of the most economically blighted areas of the world—GDP per head is around $300 and little more than $1,000 at purchasing power parity exchange rates. But relative peace in the 1990s has been accompanied by rapid growth. The prospects for these countries—Laos, Cambodia, and Vietnam—look much better than for the similarly poor states of sub-Saharan Africa.

Does Asia have a distinct model of economic development, or is its success the result of importing a Western model of development?[26] There are many different structures of modern market economies, and although all have common features, each development path is unique. Perhaps we should not be asking "Why did economic development in east Asia progress so rapidly after World War II?" but "Why did economic development in east Asia not progress more rapidly before World War II?"

Many of the key institutions and technologies of Western Europe were already present in Asia. Yet this potential was long frustrated by

Figure 5.1

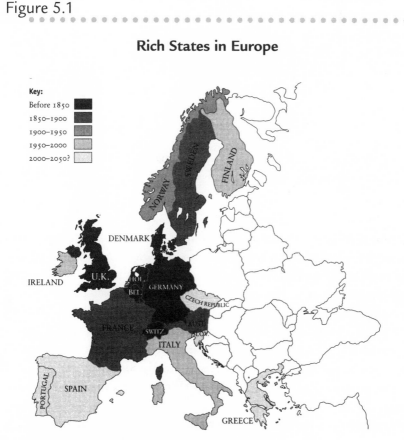

Rich States in Europe

Key:
Before 1850
1850–1900
1900–1950
1950–2000
2000–2050?

SOURCE: Based on Maddison (1993)

Figure 5.2

Rich States in Asia

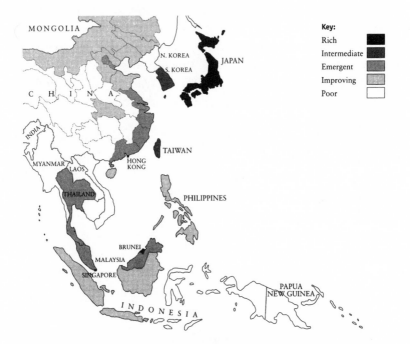

SOURCES: UNDP, World Bank, Statistik Indonesia, Economic Planning
Unit Malaysia (Eighth Malaysia Plan)

Chinese political structures. The Maoist regime inflicted even more economic damage. In other parts of the region, such as Japan and Hong Kong, American and British influence allowed the countries concerned to realize their potential for economic development.

Figure 5.1 shows the geography of the rich states of Western Europe. The group expanded steadily from a central core, gradually encompassing peripheral areas. In Asia, geographic contiguity seems to be equally significant, but in precisely the opposite direction. Richer states (Figure.5.2) are peripheral, and even within China itself, coastal regions have higher incomes. It is as though an economic blight had centered on Beijing—and perhaps this is the right way to see it.

Productive Economies, Rich States
● ●

In the second half of the eighteenth century, there was little difference between living standards in Western Europe and those in the rest
of the world.[27] The nineteen rich states that today account for about
three-quarters of world output, then produced only a quarter of it. But
the modern pattern had been set by 1820. Economic historians have
reconstructed historical series of GDP (even attempting to assess what
national income statisticians would have calculated a million years
ago).[28] We have roughly comparable estimates for twenty-six countries
in 1820.[29] The most productive state then was the UK, but in sixteen of
the twenty-six productivity was more than half the British level. All but
one of these (Spain) are now rich countries. Of the ten others, only two
(Finland and Japan) are now rich. History evidently matters.

Still, the range of productivity in 1820 was small by modern standards. Output per head in the richest countries (the UK, the Netherlands) was then three times the level of the poorest (India, China).
The gap today is thirty to fifty times. This widening has been almost
continuous for two centuries. In the first half of the nineteenth century, a small group began to pull away. In each subsequent period, a
few other states have caught up. Those that have caught up have
mostly been those that were more productive to begin with. And the
productive countries have almost always been on the borders of those
that are already productive.

So if history is important, so then is geography. There were ten
productive economies in 1870—Belgium, Denmark, Germany, Holland, Switzerland, the UK, and the four European settlements of Australia, Canada, New Zealand, and the United States. The European
group form a contiguous block.[30] (See Fig. 5.1)

Before World War I, three more European countries—Austria,
France, and Sweden—became productive. Each of them is on the
periphery of the established group. Norway emerges first as an independent state and then an economic force in the first half of the
twentieth century. The geographical cluster of productive economies
continues to expand after World War II with the accession of Finland, Ireland, and Italy.

If we look at potentially productive economies—those likely to

Table 5.1

Rich and Poor States, 1820*
(income per head in 1990 U.S. $)

Rich countries today†		Others in Maddison's sample	
UK	1,756	Spain	1,063
Netherlands	1,561	Czechoslovakia	849
Australia	1,528	Mexico	760
Austria	1,295	USSR	751
Belgium	1,291	Brazil	670
USA	1,287	Indonesia	614
Denmark	1,225	India‡	531
France	1,218	China	523
Sweden	1,198		
Germany	1,112		
Italy	1,092		
Norway	1,004		
Ireland	954		
Canada	893		
Finland	759		
Japan	704		

SOURCE: Maddison (1993)

* Estimates relate to present boundaries as far as possible.

† Figures for Switzerland not available; the other two rich countries (of nineteen) are Hong Kong and Singapore.

‡ Includes Pakistan and Bangladesh.

qualify before 2050—the geographic theme continues. The Czech Republic, Greece, Hungary, Poland, Portugal, Slovenia, and Spain[31] all border existing rich states. There could hardly be a more striking refutation of the claim that globalization, and improvements in transport and communication, have made economic geography irrelevant. Geography, or something closely related to geography, matters a great deal and continues to matter.

How It Happened
●●●

The history of the world, said Carlyle, is but the biography of great men. Perhaps, but the history of the market economy is not. There was no Paul Revere to summon the industrial revolution, no leaders who defined the structure of economic institutions as George Washington and Thomas Jefferson defined the structure of political institutions. The few heroic figures in my account are inventors of new machinery. Who invented agriculture, insurance, and banking, or corporations? No one did: they evolved. Adam Smith, the revered founder of modern economics, chronicled the market economy, he did not invent or design it.

The establishment of agriculture; the creation of public market-places; the development of banking and insurance; the invention of corporate organization. Each was a step in the coevolution of economic institutions, social developments, and technological innovation. It is a coevolution because there is no linear cause: each strand of development both supports and requires the other.

Market institutions developed within the context of a range of other evolutions—in technology, in culture, in politics, and in the organization of society—and could not have occurred in their absence. But pluralism was common to all these processes. Modern scientific method generated and tested new hypotheses; the principles of science fed into new technologies. Intellectual life emphasized the claims of reason over traditional authority. Political systems made the transition from absolutism to democracy.

This was the common background to the emergence of productive economies and rich states. The lessons that emerge from it—the evolutionary development of market institutions, the need for them to be embedded in a social and political context, and the central role of pluralism in economic advance—will be the repeated themes of this book.

Rich states are rich because of a process of institutional evolution that has taken place over centuries, even millennia. Differences in initial conditions, some of them quite small, explain why these countries, and not others, became rich. In the next chapter, I describe some of these institutions and trace the evolution of some of the most important—the institutions of agriculture, employment, and limited liability.

part II

THE STRUCTURE OF ECONOMIC SYSTEMS

● ● ● ● ● ● ● ● ● ● ● ● ● ● ● ● ● ●

{6}

Transactions and Rules

Going Home

At the end of the day, the Microsoft logo fades. Bill Bridges closes his Internet connection and shuts down his computer. He stops for a beer with colleagues. On the way home, he collects some groceries from the neighborhood store before entering his apartment and watching a movie on television.

Bill's economic life is the result of a series of transactions within a framework of rules. Some of the transactions are contractual, some informal. Some of the rules are legal, others are expectations about behavior. Bill has a contract with his employer. But most contracts of employment say little about the substantive content of the job. They describe procedural matters such as sickness and holiday entitlements, pension and termination arrangements. Bill's Dell computer uses a Microsoft operating system, and a site license for Microsoft Office covers everyone in the building. The Internet service provider uses a Verizon line on terms set out by the FCC.[1] The Internet itself is governed by a nexus of formal agreements and informal understandings.

Bill and his friends understand the conventions of behavior in the bar. But if they were joined by someone from a different culture, they would have to explain the rules. A server will bring you the beer, and you should pay 10% to 20% more than you are asked. You can use the seats, the table, and the other facilities of the bar, but you are expected to refresh yourself, and these rights, by purchasing more drink from time to time. The server will return to remind you of such obligations.

On the subway, Bill's season ticket opens a barrier and allows him access to part of New York's subway network. If a train comes, Bill may or may not find a seat on it. The New York subway is owned and operated by New York City Transit, a division of the Metropolitan Transportation Authority. The MTA is an agency of the government of New York State.

Bill bought a Mars bar, a Granny Smith apple, and a portion of Philadelphia cream cheese. The Mars bar is made by the Mars Corporation. But Granny Smith apples were not grown by Granny Smith. The label describes a variety of apple, and anyone who grows such apples can label them in this way. Philadelphia cream cheese is a trademark of Kraft, and the contents of the packet can be more or less any legal product the company chooses to put in it. It is not cream, it is not made in Philadelphia, and no French person would consider it cheese. But no other company can call its product Philadelphia cream cheese, even if it were identical to the Kraft confection or made in Philadelphia from the cream of that city's cows.

Bill tells people he owns his apartment, but this is misleading. What he has bought is a unit in a condominium—the right to occupy a certain space, and a share in the assets and liabilities associated with the common elements of the building. This complex legal structure is a solution to the tricky problem of how to give people rights of ownership over part of a building. There are different answers to this problem in other countries.[2]

Bill pays to watch television in several ways. Most networks are financed by advertising. A few, such as PBS, are supported primarily by voluntary viewer donations, but also by the taxes he pays. Cable and satellite services are available on subscription or pay-per-view. Tonight, he puts on a prerecorded videotape. The first thing he sees is a description of the terms of his contract with the distributors and the copyright legislation that applies to the transaction.

Contracts Within Rules
● ●

We acquire legal rights in a market economy by statute (a relationship between the individual and the state) or by contract (a relationship between two individuals). This distinction mirrors the distinction between property rights and exchanges, between rules and transactions. But most transactions in a market economy are governed by expectations and conventions, not the law. We are rarely conscious of making contracts. When Bill bought his apartment, he signed a complex legal document, but when he purchased the Mars bar, the law inferred a contract. In many exchanges one party claims to impose a legal contract on the other. Microsoft asserts you have accepted its contract by breaking the seal on its software packs. This unilateral imposition of contractual terms sometimes works, but the courts are not very sympathetic.[3]

In most everyday transactions, agreement is defined and enforced by expectations. Servers in U.S. restaurants expect—and depend on—substantial tips, but tipping is uncommon in Japan or New Zealand. Shops listen to complaints because they value their reputation, not because they fear court action. The costs of writing individual contracts, and using legal mechanisms to enforce them, are prohibitive for most transactions. And the law follows rather than leads the behavior of buyers and sellers. Courts fill in implied contract terms to fulfill the expectations of the parties.

The rules, laws, and conventions that govern our economic lives evolved over thousands of years, and they evolved in different ways in different places. The overpopulated continent of Europe experienced a different coevolution from the isolated and sparsely inhabited island of Australia.

Australian Fish

Twenty or thirty years ago, Australian cuisine was among the dullest to be found. But a recent influx of immigrants from Italy, Greece, and Vietnam has filled Sydney and Melbourne with interesting restaurants. A European visitor will be completely familiar with the meats—beef, lamb, pork, and chicken. But not the fish—advice is needed on the relative merits of trevally, barracuda, orange roughy, and yabbies.[4]

Farmers own animals but fishermen don't own fish. When immigrants arrived in Australia, they brought useful animals—cows and sheep to breed for food, horses for transport, cats and dogs as pets. They shipped these animals because, both legally and practically, they could keep control over them. Cod or sole would have swum off into the Pacific Ocean, so they weren't brought. A few fish were exported from Europe to Australia. Trout are the most (to my mind, only) edible freshwater fish and could be kept in the owner's lake. Carp also made the journey. And once technology made farming possible, Tasmanian salmon appeared on Melbourne menus.

But this is only part of the story. Why was the export of species so heavily in one direction? Most food production in Australia today is of animals and crops of European origin, but Europe cultivates no animals or crops imported from Australia. We enjoy some Australian decorative plants, such as mimosa, but Australia's best-known indigenous foodstuff is processed Vegemite.[5] Yali, a New Guinean, posed the question for his American visitor, Jared Diamond: Why did you offer us so much cargo and we offer you so little? Diamond's remarkable book (1997) is his answer to that question.

Australia was probably not very fortunate in its endowment of grasses and animals. But, in any event, native Australians had little reason to develop agriculture and did not do so. Their sparsely populated environment allowed a nomadic lifestyle. The selective breeding of animals and grasses in Eurasia, which created the docile cow, the affectionate cat, and the nourishing wheat grain, never happened in Australia. These European products followed Captain Cook to Australia. Different continents, different circumstances, different coevolutions.[6]

Labor and Wages

Agriculture developed from population pressures and new technology. The institution of employment developed for the same reasons. Most people in productive economies have jobs. We choose a career, and an employer. We work for agreed hours, we are told roughly what to do, and we receive a wage or a salary. We expect to hold this job for a longish period of time[7]—but not indefinitely. We are so accustomed to jobs that we rarely think about the nature of the institution.

Yet for most of economic history, jobs were unusual. And outside rich states, careers are still unusual. Few people have, or had, any choice about the work they perform. They live in traditional societies and their economic lives were, and are, almost completely determined by where they were born—geographically and socially—and by the traditions and conventions of their society.

Farming for own use is, and has always been, the most common occupation. A farmer would usually share his crop with someone in a more elevated social position or provide his superior with labor. Slavery and serfdom bound peasants to masters who fed them. Other workers were attached to noble households and both lived and worked within them. Apprentices learned from and might live with their masters, until they became independent craftsmen, able in turn to supervise apprentices. Social and economic institutions were linked in all these activities.

The enclosure of land deprived many small farmers of traditional cultivation rights but made wage labor available to landlords.[8] Wage laborers had a lower status than any other social group. Not till the end of the twentieth century were some wage earners—the senior executives of large corporations—the best-paid people in the community with high social status. Today, employment contracts in rich states are standardized, and convention and law make it difficult to deviate far from the norm. Contracts can be neither too precarious or too lengthy: efficiency and public opinion are against both casual labor and serfdom.

In a rich state modern man and—mostly—modern woman goes to work and comes home from work. Working life can be separated from personal life as never before. Marx believed this would change the nature of politics and society, and he was right, though he did not anticipate that economic power at work would be exercised not by the owners of capital but by salaried managers. The separation of work and home makes conceivable the distinction of business and private values.

But, as I shall discuss in chapters 18 and 27, to make that separation conceivable does not make it real. While we can split our time between home and work, it is harder to split our personalities. Although we need not link our working lives and social lives, many people do. And the purely instrumental view of the nature of business—which reached its zenith in labor relations with the growth of mass production in factories like Henry Ford's automobile plant—has receded. The quality of work is influenced by the social context within which it takes place.

Capitalism discovered that Marxian alienation was inefficient, and large manufacturing corporations no longer dominate the economy.

The Limited Liability Corporation
• •

The process by which corporations came to exercise that dominance was lengthy. In Greek and Roman times and in the Middle Ages, business was conducted by individuals, or partnerships of people who knew each other well—who else would take on the risks? When larger partnerships were formed, speculation and fraud followed, and after the South Sea bubble large-scale commercial organization was prohibited. The objective was to restrict investment to ventures the participants might expect to understand. But throughout history, from the tulip mania of 1636 to the dot-com bubble of 1999, greed and gullibility have defeated that purpose.

The precursors of the modern corporation were international trading companies, such as the English East India Company or the Dutch VOC. These companies acted as both businesses and governments in the areas they colonized and controlled territories larger than the native countries from which they came. The development of canals from 1790, and railroads from 1820, required the creation of domestic enterprises operating on a large scale, in Europe and the United States. These organizations would generally be created by legislation that gave them the power they needed to build the canal, or the railroad, and which also defined their capital structure and corporate governance.

The framework of the modern limited liability corporation was created in the first half of the nineteenth century. It is the product of a group of related ideas. One is that an organization exists separately from the individuals who run it, work in it, or invest in it. This concept of legal personality can be dated from a Supreme Court decision in 1819 that effectively acknowledged that status for Dartmouth College. Another idea is that such organizations can be created when individuals get together to define their objects and arrange their governance— they do not need specific legal authority to do so.

The third, crucial, element was that of limited liability—shareholders can restrict their responsibility for the company's debts to the amount they have subscribed. This enabled them to invest in large organizations run by salaried managers. Entrepreneurial individuals without large resources of their own could take charge of businesses, and wealthy individuals could provide private capital to these businesses without becoming involved in their day-to-day operations.

States competed with each other to offer the most attractive environment for new businesses, and this pluralism made the United States the leader in developing this new form of corporate organization. Britain followed suit with laws to permit private limited liability companies, and soon all rich states embraced this new style of business organization. By the twentieth century such businesses dominated all industrial economies.

A French company like Carrefour, with many shareholders, is Carrefour SA, the SA standing for *société anonyme,* "anonymous society." This captures the separation of ownership and control, the distinction between the individuals and the company, which is inherent in the creation of an organization with its own legal—and cultural—personality. Alfred Sloan's General Motors, run by a cadre of trained and skilled executives, became the model for the modern corporation.[9] In the later part of the twentieth century, companies such as General Electric took this professionalization of management to its highest degree. By 2000 most other forms of commercial organization—mutual companies, partnerships, and state-owned enterprises—had been converted into limited liability corporations.

And yet the relevance of this structure is less obvious in the twenty-first century. The distinction between the roles of shareholders and employees was clear when shareholders had bought the plant and employees worked in it. But the principal assets of the modern company are knowledge, brands, and reputation, which are in the heads and hands of employees. What can it mean to say the shareholders "own" these things?

The Internet and the Genome

Every generation must extend the rules of a market economy. In America and Australia, settlement demanded the creation of land rights. Larger-scale production made it necessary to invent corporate organization. Today, new rules are needed for the new technologies of the Internet and the genome.[10]

The architecture of the Internet was established by the Department of Defense and developed by the academic research community. Many businesses hoped to gain control of the Internet by dominating some component. The war between Netscape and Microsoft was bitter because both parties believed that browsers were that key component.[11] Microsoft won the war—by giving away free browsers—but did not gain the influence over the Internet the company sought.

Nor did Excite or Yahoo! or AOL or Cisco. Excite fell by the wayside. Yahoo! became the leading portal. AOL established itself as chatroom host. Cisco was the biggest hardware supplier. But none of these companies achieved a position comparable to Microsoft's dominance of operating systems. Millions of Web sites vied to attract users. The new market for Internet services developed, like so many markets before it, from anarchic relationships between competing providers of complementary services.

Cheap copying and dissemination undermined existing market rules. Napster allowed Web users to exchange collections of recorded music and seemed to threaten the conventional economics of record companies. Music publishers succeeded in closing Napster. But they cannot effectively prevent the electronic distribution of music. The challenge now is to find mechanisms to derive revenue from it.[12]

At Cambridge University in 1953, Francis Crick and James Watson identified the structure of DNA, the molecule that provides the blueprint for human life. DNA is a long string of molecules. Over the following thirty years, further research—and the capacity of computers—made it possible to identify the sequences of the components of the DNA molecule.

In 1989 the U.S. government established the National Center for Human Genome Research, under Watson's direction, with the objective of sequencing the entire human genome by 2005. The identification of DNA was one of the scientific breakthroughs of the century, but the sequencing of genes does not require exceptional intellectual gifts or scientific originality. It is a routine task for a competent researcher with a powerful computer.[13]

The process of academic research was leisurely but private companies sought patents on gene sequences. It seems odd to many people that things that have existed naturally for hundreds of thousands of years should be patentable. Patents were devised to allow the inventors of new manufactured goods to enjoy exclusive rights to the discovery such as the spinning frame. This principle was naturally extended to chemical compounds in the modern pharmaceutical industry, and in recent decades pharmaceutical patents have been among the most valuable of all.

In 1980, the Supreme Court ruled that you could patent a living thing.[14] This proved a wide extension of the scope of the patent system. Companies claimed patents on many advances in genetic knowledge. It is not certain that many of these patents are valid, but the costs of infringing even a dubious patent are large.

Craig Venter, a genome researcher turned entrepreneur, announced in 1999 his intention to decode the entire genome within three years. His company, Celera, subsequently filed tens of thousands of patents. In 2000, with rapid progress in gene sequencing in private and public sectors and on both sides of the Atlantic, President Clinton and Prime Minister Blair held a press conference to announce that the genome had been decoded and that the competing researchers would cooperate in making their knowledge publicly available. Both parts of the announcement were premature, but a complete description of the elements of the genome now exists.

The structures of rules that govern the relationships between the market and the genome, and the market and the Internet, are today unresolved and incoherent. But neither central direction nor absence of direction will produce answers. Markets advance through the coevolution of technology and social institutions.

Framing the Rules

It was important to the development of agriculture to define and enforce new property rights in plants and animals. Once, a plant or animal was yours when you picked it or killed it; today, it is yours when you seed it or brand it. This change was vital if farmers were to invest in crops and husbandry. But this example, along with the variety of property rights encountered on Bill's journey home from work, makes clear that there are many different ways to define property rights, that some are better than others, and that the choice will change with technology and society.

Many economists talk about the rules of a market economy as a distribution of property rights. But the history of the development of market institutions involved far more than the invention of property rights. And many modern market institutions are far too complex and subtle to be easily described in terms of property. The apples in my basket are mine and become yours when they are transferred to your basket. But where is the exchange of property when I turn on the television or use the subway?[15]

When someone smokes in a nonsmoking area, we can say that they violate the property rights of nonsmokers. But it is easier, and shorter, to say they break the rules. And more illuminating, because it reminds us of the variety of ways—legal obligation, private action, social convention—in which the rule can be framed and enforced.

The emphasis on property has a conservative flavor: when we talk of defining and enforcing property rights, the picture in our minds is of a fence, a notice saying KEEP OUT, and a policeman standing guard. This conservatism is apparent in discussion of the Internet and the genome, where music publishers defend what they describe as their property and patentees of gene sequences say they are staking land claims. Market economies must constantly evolve new rules. The analogy with property is unhelpful: the best structures will give encouragement to investment and innovation in new technologies—just as dynamic societies of the past evolved new structures for ownership rights in living plants and animals, developed employment contracts, and invented limited liability companies. These accompanied and allowed the historic development of agriculture, wage labor, and large-scale industrial organization.

This part of the book describes the issues that the rules of the modern market economy evolved to handle. Rich states became productive by facilitating gains from trade and exchange and promoting innovation. The institutional reforms described in the two preceding chapters—agriculture, employment, and corporations—brought about the transformation of economic systems from production for own use to the modern market economy in which we work for others and consume what others grow and make. This division of labor is the most important characteristic of a developed economic system.

{7} •••••••••••••••••••••••••••••

Production and Exchange

Economics began for me on a dark winter morning in Edinburgh, the capital of Scotland, over thirty years ago. An experiment set winter clocks an hour forward. It was still gloomy when Professor Youngson walked from the Adam Ferguson Building to the David Hume Tower to begin the first-year course in political economy.

Several Scottish traditions were being recognized. The names of the buildings acknowledged Adam Ferguson and David Hume, leading contemporaries of Adam Smith in the Scottish Enlightenment. Youngson was fulfilling a convention that the introductory course should be delivered by the senior professor. A tall, gowned figure, he was a gentleman scholar. His finest work was not about economics at all.[1] *The Making of Classical Edinburgh* expressed his love of the city's buildings.[2] Some architectural gems of classical Edinburgh had been demolished to make way for the hideous Adam Ferguson Building and David Hume Tower.

A nervous seventeen-year-old, I was sitting close to the front. Youngson began with a definition of economics—the allocation of scarce resources among competing ends.[3] This was not what I had expected. I had enrolled to learn about inflation, interest rates, and foreign exchange—the economic events that filled newspapers. Youngson talked instead about the nature of economic systems. That seemed to me more interesting, and still does. The allocation of scarce resources between competing ends requires decisions about production, assignment, and exchange. The system must determine what is made—the issue of production. Who gets it—the issue of assignment. And exchange establishes the link between production and assignment.

The shift by Cro-Magnons from production for own use to production for exchange was an institutional innovation to rank with technical innovations such as the manufacture of tools and the invention of the wheel. But only in today's rich states is most production for exchange. For most of history, and in much of the world even today, the main economic activity is the production of food for own use.

And throughout that history, the allocation of scarce resources among competing ends was determined by custom, or by force. In a traditional society, decisions about what to produce, and the division of what was produced, were barely decisions at all. Each year followed the pattern of preceding years. The weather might vary, and with it the crop, but the outcome was distributed according to conventional rules. A customary economic system is an alternative to either a market economy or a planned society. But a static one. Customary economies had little capacity to deal with change and offered little encouragement to initiate change.

In modern society, we make decisions and choices, and the economic system is the framework within which we make them. It contains rules for assignment, production, and exchange. In the late eighteenth and nineteenth centuries, economists established a durable method of analysis for understanding production for exchange. Adam Smith's principal work, *The Wealth of Nations*, described the division of labor. David Ricardo, who became a writer and member of the British Parliament after successful speculation in bonds, laid out the principle of comparative advantage fifty years later. The effectiveness of an economic system is determined by its efficiency in exploiting comparative advantage and the division of labor.

The Colombe d'Or

For two hundred years, European artists have been attracted to the bright light and brilliant scenery of the south of France. The walled village of St. Paul de Vence, which is thirty miles west of Menton, in the hills to the north of Nice, still houses a community of artists.[4] Paul Roux, who bought a small hotel and restaurant at the entrance to the village in 1919, offered food and lodging to artists in return for examples of their work. Today, the Colombe d'Or's collection of modern French art is the envy of many galleries.[5]

Paul Roux was a talented cook and his visitors were talented painters. It therefore made sense for him to cook and Georges Braque, one of the artists he encouraged, to paint. The exchange of food for pictures benefited both parties. It is common to think of exchange as a process in which one party wins at the expense of another. And some exchanges are like that. One party tricks another, or one party makes a mistake.[6] But the exchange between Braque and Roux, like most economic exchanges, was characterized by gains from trade.

The division of labor between Braque and Roux made these gains possible. By getting together, each obtained a mixture of food and art. The two individuals had different capabilities. But these capabilities were, in themselves, insufficient for their needs. Braque needed to eat, and Roux did not wish to live by bread alone. Whenever there are differences in talent and mutual desire for variety, there is the possibility of a division of labor and mutually beneficial exchange.

It seems obvious that if Roux is a good cook and Braque is a good painter, Roux should cook and Braque should paint. But Braque was a much better painter, relative to other painters, than Roux was as a cook relative to other cooks. Braque is one of the towering figures of French twentieth-century art. But even today, when the Colombe d'Or attracts well-heeled visitors from around the world, the Michelin guide will direct those who seek outstanding food to other restaurants in the area.

But even if Braque were a better cook than Roux, as well as a better painter (no evidence survives), it might be best for Roux to cook and Braque to paint. In the time he did not spend whisking mayonnaise by hand, Braque could produce a painting worth many, many meals. This benefit from exchange illustrates the principle of comparative advantage. Comparative advantage dictates that we should focus on what we do best, rather than on what we do better than other people. For exceptionally talented people like Braque, there may be more things they do better than other people than there are hours in the day. And for others, there may be little or nothing that they do better than other people. Comparative advantage requires us to look at our own relative performance in different activities. Both Braque and Roux benefit from following comparative advantage. Braque gets more time for his art, and Roux gets great pictures.

Comparative advantage is a subtle concept. Our instinct is always to ask, "Who is the best person for the job?" and it is a mistaken instinct. We need instead to ask, "Who should be doing this job, bearing in mind his or her productivity in a variety of other jobs, and also the productivity of other people who might be doing this job instead of the variety of other jobs that they currently are or might be doing?" Perfectly competitive markets do that calculation automatically. That claim—a principal cause of economists' fascination with perfectly competitive markets—is the subject of Part III of this book

Specialization and Capabilities in Business

Trade between individuals is possible, and beneficial, because specialization and differences in capabilities offer gains. These reinforce each other. Innate talent brought Braque to painting and Roux to cooking. Training and experience honed these talents.

Trade between firms emerged for the same reasons—gains from specialization, differences in capabilities. Modern firms extended the economic advantages of trade between individuals based on differences in capabilities and on specialization. The moneylender developed into the bank, the blacksmith became the ironworks. Firms not only specialized themselves, but provided the opportunity for specialization in individual tasks by their employees. Adam Smith's famous example of the pin factory[7] described the—still novel—development of the division of labor within commercial organizations. If each focused on one operation, a group could produce many more pins than if each member fabricated a single pin from base metal to finished product.

In the early stages of modern business history, the organization of business was driven mostly by specialization. Large enterprises emerged in activities where economies of scale could be derived from the division of labor—Smith's pin factory—or where the activity required coordination of the specialist functions of many individuals—railroads and oil companies. The invention of steam power provoked a shift from workshop to factory organization in textiles because one engine could power many looms. And factory organization promoted many technical innovations. This is a particularly important example of the coevolution of technology and institutions.

The gains from specialization were believed to be limitless. At the end of the nineteenth century, it seemed that one company would dominate each major industry in each region of the world. That was certainly what business leaders like John D. Rockefeller intended.[8] Standard Oil, US Steel, American Tobacco, were each dominant in the U.S. market for their products.

The concentration of economic power in trusts, and the fear of an associated concentration of political power, provoked a reaction. The Sherman Act, passed in 1890, made it illegal to monopolize any line of business in the United States. When the complacently pro-business William McKinley was assassinated by an anarchist in 1901, Theodore Roosevelt became president and began a populist attack on the power of American trusts and the men who controlled them. Standard Oil and American Tobacco were broken up.

This was a decisive moment in the development of modern market economies. The attack on giant firms was never again to be as fierce. US Steel remained intact, only to experience a slow, sustained decline across the twentieth century. But no similar combinations would be proposed.[9] Firms that became dominant in any line of business would always find their ambitions checked. The U.S. government used the antitrust laws to launch cases against AT&T, the telephone monopoly, against IBM, and in the closing years of the century, against Microsoft. The world's largest economy had chosen pluralism over monopoly in its market structure.

European business was necessarily more pluralist because there was no United States of Europe. But Imperial Tobacco, Imperial Chemical Industries, and I.G. Farben had similar ambitions in their spheres of influence. Both the breadth and the limits of the scope of their aspirations can be seen from the titles that these companies adopted. But large companies like Germany's I.G. Farben and Britain's Imperial Chemical Industries reached informal agreements with Dow Chemical and other firms to share world markets.

After World War II, the occupying powers, concerned at the role companies like I.G. Farben had played in support of Hitler and the contribution of the Japanese *zaibatsu* to that country's militarism, imposed antitrust rules. The founders of the European Union were clear that competition and pluralism, not consolidation, were to be the bases of the economic integration. The Rome Treaty, which established the Common Market in 1964, introduced provisions to this effect. In 2001, it was to be the European Union, not the U.S. government, that checked the expansionist ambitions of General Electric, America's largest business.[10]

But it was not simply government action that prevented indefinite specialization. The division of labor, taken too far, produced organizational disadvantages. The epitome of specialization was the Ford Motor Company. Between 1908 and 1927, 15 million Model T Fords rolled off the company's production lines near Detroit. Adam Smith's pin factory found its apogee in an assembly line on which each individual worker might undertake only a single operation.

But Ford had taken mass production too far. The company was overtaken by General Motors, which offered its customers a choice of color and a variety of models. The tedious nature of assembly-line work meant that the motivation of those who worked on them was wholly instrumental. Labor disputes were common, and no one cared about the quality of the final product. In the 1950s, General Motors, Ford, and Chrysler controlled over half the world automobile market. But that was to be the high point of concentration and specialization. Globalization, far from increasing the power of these market leaders, made it possible for foreign firms with better products to operate on a scale sufficient to compete effectively.

Competitive Advantage

Firms came into existence to take advantage of the division of labor through specialization. But the scale of business today means that gains from specialization are largely exhausted. The structure of industry is today based on differences in the capabilities of companies. The success of the Coca-Cola corporation is derived, in the first instance, from a distinctive capability—the still secret recipe for syrup patented by an Atlanta pharmacist in 1890.[11]

But it is not really the fizzy sugared water. The company has exploited the division of labor through a worldwide network of bottlers and franchisees. And, most importantly, developed an impressive marketing organization in support of the world's best known brand. General Electric (GE) came into existence as the vehicle for the inventive genius of Thomas Edison, who found many more practical uses for electricity than anyone had imagined possible. But the company gained its modern position by developing the most powerful repository of general management skills of any business. These capabilities—Coke's recipe and marketing resources, GE's management—are the commercial analogues of Braque's talent as a painter and Roux's abilities in the kitchen.[12]

The automobile industry today displays the distinctive capabilities of twenty or more car manufacturers. Mercedes and BMW achieve high standards of engineering in production-line sedans. Hyundai benefits from its low cost Korean base. Toyota achieves outstanding component reliability and short model cycles through close relationships with subcontractors.

Firms in other industries build competitive advantages on their distincitve capabilities. Marlboro and McDonald's are brands comparable to Coca-Cola. Hotel chains and law and accountancy practices also rely on distinctive capabilities based on name and reputation. Some companies, such as Toyota, have created competitive advantages from distinctive capabilities in the structure of their relationships with suppliers, the *kiretsu* of producers that manufacture components for final assembly by Toyota itself.

The competitive advantage of innovation is often transitory, because successful innovation is easily copied. But some companies—such as pharmaceutical businesses Merck and Pfizer—are able to protect their innovations legally. Others, like Sony, have an architecture that generates a succession of innovations, and a reputation that wins ready acceptance for everything—from transistor radios to the Walkman to the PlayStation—that they put into the marketplace. The legal protection that Merck and Pfizer obtain for their intellectual property also gives other firms powerful strategic assets—such as Microsoft's copyrights in its operating system, MS-DOS, and graphical user interface, Windows. This variety of capabilities in firms provides the basis for gains from trade between firms, as the difference in capabilities between individuals provided the basis of trade between Braque and Roux.

International Trade

Economies from specialization, differences in capabilities: these are the factors that lead to gains from trade between individuals and trade between businesses. They also lead to gains from trade between countries. Trade between corporations was once mainly based on the benefits of specialization and today relates much more to differences in capabilities. Trade between countries seems to have evolved in the opposite direction.

Ricardo's analysis of international trade in the early nineteenth century emphasized differences in capabilities. Early trade flows were influenced by weather and natural resources. Northwest Europe imported products that could not be grown at realistic cost in its own territory. Ricardo explained how Portugal, where the sun ripened the grapes, exchanged wine for English textiles, which were manufactured in Lancashire, where the damp climate prevented threads from snapping.[13]

Some modern trade is still like this. Countries with natural resources such as oil and minerals sell them to other countries that have none. Differences in soil and climate affect the production of crops and other agricultural products. But many rich countries have been reluctant to rely on such trade. Oil reserves have been developed at great cost in Alaska and the North Sea. The European Union would rather pay Sven to farm than import wheat more cheaply from Canada.

Specialization among countries has become more important than difference in intrinsic capabilities. Most international trade today is in manufactured goods between developed countries, and trade of this kind has grown dramatically since World War II. Trade among the nineteen countries of chapter 4 accounts for almost half of all world trade, and that between these nineteen and poor states accounts for less than one-quarter.[14] Most of this trade is in goods that all other rich states have the capabilities to manufacture.

Like trade between individuals, trade between countries results from mutually reinforcing differences in capabilities and specialization. Differences in national capabilities today have little to do with differences in resources or other natural factors: they have been acquired over time and are embedded in the cultures that gave rise to them. Switzerland relies on exports of precision engineering and speciality chemicals, which account for about 60% of its exports and 25% of its output.[15]

These have nothing to do with Swiss climate or terrain. Nor does Switzerland have favored access to materials from which engineering and chemical products are made. Capabilities and specialization have reinforced each other in another process of coevolution. The choices made—almost by accident—by Swiss businessmen a century ago have had a major influence on the structure of Swiss industry today. The Swiss education system influenced their choices of specialization. Heidi and her predecessors have instilled basic numerical skills of high order even in students who will be employed on production and assembly lines. The system developed further in response to the needs of Swiss business.

Since mutually reinforcing capabilities and specialisms depend on past choices, forgotten or now irrelevant historical events still influence the location of production today. Film producers in the 1920s sought the light of Southern California. Films are rarely made in California anymore, but Hollywood remains the center of the world film industry. Despite technological advances that allow securities dealing on screens that can be located anywhere in the world, the most important trading facilities are in fact located close to each other in a small area of lower Manhattan. Similar accidents of history—the site of Leland Stanford's university and the Xerox corporation's research facility—made Silicon Valley the center of the international software industry.[16]

The competitive advantages of countries and regions—Switzerland, Hollywood, Wall Street, Silicon Valley—are based on the competitive advantages of companies and of individuals. In Switzerland, each firm has a competitive advantage in its own particular line of business, and the common competitive advantages of all these firms are based on the competitive advantages that well educated and trained Swiss workers themselves enjoy. The same is true in Silicon Valley. In both cases, the geographic proximity of businesses to each other reinforces these competitive advantages through the formal and informal sharing of knowledge, experience, and people.

Hollywood and Wall Street are slightly more complex. There is the same phenomenon of competing yet collaborating firms drawing on the same pool of talented individuals. But Hollywood and Wall Street are also themselves marketplaces, and that is itself a source of competitive advantage. Business congregates in the largest marketplace, and that is why historical location remains so important even though its objective basis has disappeared.

Gains from trade are achieved by specialization and by taking advantage of the different capabilities of individuals, organizations, geographical areas, countries. The same principles govern the division of labor between people and companies, regions and states.

With one exception. People, areas of the world, and regions exist and have rights and values independently of their economic function. Businesses exist only for their economic function, and if they have no economic function, they have no reason to exist. So households and countries must do what they are best at, whether or not they do them better than other households and countries. Businesses should only do what they can do better than others. So we speak of comparative advantage for people and for states, competitive advantage for companies. Comparative advantage is relative; competitive advantage is absolute. Production and exchange are governed by a division of labor, based on the advantages of specialization and differences in capabilities. But production and exchange are not ends in themselves. Their purpose is to meet the needs of consumers. The next chapter is concerned with how economic systems find out what their consumers want.

{8} •••••••••••••••••••••••••••

Assignment

The *Portrait of Dr. Gachet*[1]
••••••••••••••••••••••••••••••••••••••

One of the artists attracted by the light and scenery of southern France was a young Dutchman who rented a property at Arles, in Provence. The painter suffered acute bouts of depression and was sent north to a physician in the village of Auvers-sur-Oise, near Paris, for treatment. Dr. Gachet's ministrations were not successful and his patient committed suicide.[2]

The episode brought the doctor unexpected and undeserved immortality. After van Gogh's death, his *Portrait of Dr. Gachet* was sold by his sister-in-law.[3] It was eventually auctioned in 1990 for $82.5 million, still the largest amount ever paid for a work of art.[4] In the last chapter I considered the first part of the allocation of scarce resources among competing ends—issues of production and exchange. This chapter reviews the second part—how the goods and services that are the result of production and exchange are assigned to individuals and households.

Portrait of Dr. Gachet poses the economic problem of assigning a scarce resource in its simplest, starkest form. The painting is incomparable and unique. (Although van Gogh painted two portraits of Gachet: the other, thought to be inferior,[5] is in the Musée d'Orsay in Paris.) There is one scarce resource. But there are many competing ends. Almost every gallery and art collector in the world would like the painting. And many could present strong arguments.

The most extensive collection of the painter's work is in the dedicated Van Gogh Museum in Amsterdam, where the visitor can best understand the development of the painter's talent. The Metropolitan Museum in New York, and the Musée d'Orsay, have stunning collections of the greatest works of van Gogh's time. His achievement can be seen there in its proper historical context. Yet all these collections are already well endowed. Perhaps Dr. Gachet should be hung in a museum in a provincial location or a poor country where there are no masterpieces at all.

How should we evaluate the claims of private collectors against those of national galleries? Art would not thrive without private patronage. There is far more good art than can be displayed in public galleries. These institutions have basements to which they consign currently unfashionable pieces. Still, there is a strong argument that great paintings like Dr. Gachet should be on public display, not in private ownership.

Portrait of Dr. Gachet is now owned by a private collector and has disappeared from public view. A recent exhibition in Boston, Paris, and Amsterdam was specifically devoted to Dr. Gachet's love of painting and painters and his association with van Gogh.[6] The Musée d'Orsay's portrait was at the center of the show, but the world's most valuable picture was not there.

But state ownership does not emerge well from the story either. Van Gogh's talent was not recognized during his lifetime, or for some years after. Decades elapsed before his work would have been accepted even for the basement of a public gallery. His work is preserved only because his sister-in-law had an eye to its commercial value. Private collectors were first to recognize his genius, and most of his pieces are in public collections because of the generosity of these patrons. *Portrait of Dr. Gachet* was donated to the Städel Museum in Frankfurt by a local businessman. It is not on public display now because the German government disposed of it.

Portrait of Dr. Gachet was condemned as decadent art by the Nazis and sold by Reichsmarschall Göring, who pocketed the proceeds. Fortunately Göring, who had a drug habit and was interested in developing his personal collection of tapestries, chose to sell the picture to a private collector—ironically, a Jewish refugee, Siegfried Kramarsky. "Decadent" books were simply burned.

Mechanisms of Allocation
●●

After Kramarsky's death, his family asked Christie's to auction the painting. As the bidding in the New York salesroom reached its climax, eyes were focused on two people. One was Christie's Zürich representative, connected by telephone to her client. The other was a Japanese art dealer. The European bidder—probably a Greek shipping tycoon—offered $74 million, but that proved to be the limit of his willingness to pay. The portrait went to Japan, for $75 million. (The buyer's premium of 10% took the total price to $82.5 million.)

The allocation of the scarce resource—the *Portrait*—among competing ends involved no inquiry into these competing ends. We know what Mr. Saito, the paper magnate represented by the Japanese dealer, did with the painting. But we do not know what use the contenders he outbid would have made of it, nor even, in most cases, who they were.

An alternative means of allocation would have asked these questions in some detail. Public galleries might be asked to disclose their plans, private individuals to explain why they were particularly appropriate owners of the portrait. There would need to be an international art committee to compare and evaluate these claims. We do not assign art or other valuable objects that way. But we do use such a procedure for allocating prized international sporting events.

The 2002 Winter Olympic Games were held in Salt Lake City. The success of the games was tarnished, however, by the enforced resignation of the chair and vice-chair of the organizing committee and the preemptive decision of the mayor who had presided over the city's bid, Deedee Corradini, not to seek office again. The resignations followed allegations that Salt Lake City had offered bribes, including the services of prostitutes, to members of the committee.

The embarrassment felt by Mayor Corradini and the organizing committee that had allegedly given the bribes was not, however, shared by members of the committee that had received them. The president, Juan Antonio Samaranch, explained that the gifts he had received could not constitute bribes since he had no vote in the final decision. The Salt Lake City investigation followed repeated allegations of corruption in the determination of previous Olympic venues.[7]

Where to hold the Winter Olympics was a political decision. Where to hang the *Portrait of Dr. Gachet* was a decision made by the market. Where to hold the Winter Olympics was decided by a process of voice—different people expressed conflicting views. Where to hang the *Portrait of Dr. Gachet* was decided by a process of exit—there was no debate, no discussion, and the auction continued until all but one bidder had left the room.[8]

Where to hold the Winter Olympics was determined by a democratic process—of sorts. Where to hang the *Portrait of Dr. Gachet* was decided by the decentralized decisions of many people and institutions, all but one of whom concluded that they could not, or did not wish to, pay $82.5 million for the painting. Where to hold the Winter Olympics was personalized, decided by named individuals, under the chairmanship of Mr. Samaranch. Where to hang the *Portrait of Dr. Gachet* was an anonymous decision. We know who the auctioneer was—Christopher Burge—but his identity played no significant role in the process. We know who the successful bidder was, although he was not there, and only because he chose to make a public announcement. We do not know who the underbidder was.

These two types of mechanisms define the ways in which goods can be assigned in an economic system. One group is political, hierarchical, and personalized; the mechanism of complaint is voice. The other is market-based, decentralized, anonymous; the mechanism of complaint is exit.

Each of these approaches has merits and disadvantages. Some people regard the anonymity of the market as a virtue; others deplore the impersonality of market forces. Both processes are open to corruption. The squalor of international sporting bodies needs no further elaboration. Auction rings, in which dealers get together to allocate lots outside the salesroom, are frequent. Ten years after the *Gachet* sale, the chairman of Sotheby's was sent to prison for illegal price fixing, and the chairman of Christie's had to remain outside the United States for fear of arrest.

"From each according to his abilities, to each according to his needs."[9] This traditional socialist slogan describes the objectives of any economic system. This requirement identifies the twin issues of information and incentives that any economic system must address. The problem of incentive compatibility is the problem of obtaining the information needed to make decisions about production and assignment. Market mechanisms and political mechanisms deal with incentive compatibility in quite different ways.

Incentive Compatibility in a Planned Economy

To allocate scarce resources among competing ends it is necessary to assess what abilities are—what it is possible to produce—and what needs are—the requirements of firms and the wants and desires of consumers. But almost all this information has to be obtained from the various proponents of the competing ends.

How can they be persuaded to assess it diligently and reveal it accurately? Most people are honest and well-intentioned, and if you ask them for information, they will give it. But they may discover that doing so is not to their advantage. If targets are set and resources allocated on the basis of information revealed, then you will do better if you are conservative about what is possible, pessimistic about what is needed, and optimistic about the benefits that will result. But the people to whom you supply the information will realize you are doing this and calibrate their expectations accordingly. In socialist economies, this process became known as plan bargaining.

The submissions made by the various cities that hope to host the Olympics are unashamedly propagandist. Just as investment appraisals put to the senior managers of large businesses are always optimistic, and the business plans that utilities show their regulators are always gloomy. The hospitality offered to IOC members who wished to inspect the alternative venues was lavish. No doubt some of these members managed to penetrate the haze of smoke and alcohol and find the information they needed to take an objective position. Others found this difficult.

Obtaining the information needed to plan production encounters similar problems. No society in history offered such a wide range of rewards and punishments as the Soviet Union, from the economic and political privileges of the *nomenklatura* to the slave camps of the Gulag. The Soviet economic problem was not an absence of incentives: incentives to conform to the dictates of the center were strong. The Soviet economic problem was that the planners did not have good information on which to base their directions to production units.

Above all, the Soviet economy foundered on these problems of information and incentives. And the information problem is the more fundamental. If a powerful state could accurately calibrate both abilities and needs, it could enforce production according to abilities and assignment according to needs. That is what the Soviet state sought, and failed, to do.

"Plan bargaining" is not confined to the Soviet Union, though it was endemic there. Plan bargaining is found in any planning system: in government regulation of business, in the control of public services, and in the management of large private-sector organizations. When governments set targets for schools and hospitals, they face the same problem: the information needed to determine the targets appropriately is held by people in schools and hospitals, not people in government departments.

Lenin claimed to have found the answer to this problem: "seize the decisive link."[10] Because the information required to control the system completely is extensive and impossible to obtain, the center must focus on a few supposedly key variables. But these are subject to "Goodhart's Law"[11]—any measure adopted as a target changes its meaning. If corporate executives receive bonuses related to earnings per share, then earnings per share will rise, but whether the business is better or more valuable is quite another question.

The inevitable result of these processes is the proliferation of targets. These become confusing and inconsistent and undermine the authority and morale of those who engage in the activities that are being planned. Do markets manage the problems of incentive compatibility better?

Incentive Compatibility in Markets

People will only be honest in expressions of preference when we impose a cost to these expressions. This is how we tackle the problem in families and companies. Some children must have everything they see and dissolve into tears when they do not get it. Some people in organizations make every requirement urgent and essential. We attach less weight to their claims and protests, and value expressions of wants and needs more highly when they are rarely expressed.

Some mechanism of price and cost is always present when we

obtain subjective information about preferences, needs, and abilities. In personal relationships, these prices are always implicit. When we put down our own tasks to help a colleague with an urgent project, we do not expect immediate reward. But both parties understand that a price is being paid. If our stock of goodwill is called on repeatedly without reciprocation, it will be exhausted. When I tell family and friends that I badly need something, and they defer their own needs, I play a card that loses its value if I play it often. These implicit prices, central to both personal and commercial lives, are called opportunity costs: the price of doing A is that it becomes more difficult to do B.

Among small groups of people who deal with each other frequently and know each other well—friends, families, close colleagues, the inhabitants of Sicelo's village—resource allocation occurs through these implicit price mechanisms. Market exchanges are needed when people deal outside these closed circles. Incentive compatibility is immediately more serious. We understand the real needs of our friends and family better than the needs of people we hardly know.

Market exchanges allow longer chains of wants. If I had to find a plumber who needed lessons in economics, my tap might drip for a long time. I might look for a bank needing economic advice that would offer the plumber a loan, but this would be complex to negotiate. With money, or some form of tokens, the coincidence of wants can be as extended as required.

Money and prices have emerged whenever economic life has extended beyond a narrow community of people who interact with each other. Villages like Sicelo's may not need to keep score in a formal way. But larger communities need money. Small businesses like the farm on which Sven and Ingrid work use accountants only to deal with the bank and the tax authorities. Big businesses need accounts for internal control as well as external reporting. Money acts as medium of exchange, store of value, and unit of account.

These functions dictate the characteristics of a good money.[12] Money must be well defined—there should be no room for argument about whether a debt has been paid or not. Money must be storable. And money must have high value relative to its volume and weight, otherwise it will be difficult to carry it around. Many objects met these criteria in traditional societies. Some tribes kept score in cowrie shells.

But scarce and decorative metals—gold and silver—were usually found to meet these requirements best. In concentration camps, where none of these were available, cigarettes became the medium of exchange and the unit of account.[13] Long after money first emerged, it was realized that reliable promises to provide gold or silver—bank notes—were easier to carry than the metals themselves. I will come back to the implications of this discovery in chapter 14.

Strategic Behavior in Politics

George Bush took Florida by 537 votes and was therefore declared the winner in the November 2000 presidential election. Some 2.7% of voters preferred Ralph Nader, the Green Party candidate, to Al Gore, but a majority of those who supported Nader also preferred Gore to Bush. If some Nader supporters had cast their votes for Gore, then Ralph Nader would not have become president—but no one could reasonably have expected that he would. What could have been expected, and would have happened, is that Al Gore would have won Florida, and New Hampshire, and been inaugurated in January 2001 as president of the United States.

It is also likely that many of those who preferred Pat Buchanan to George Bush also preferred George Bush to Al Gore. If these people had found it possible to vote for Bush, they could probably have saved New Hampshire, but not Florida, for the Republicans.[14]

It is not necessarily sensible to express your true preferences. Nader supporters could not get what they wanted, but they might have been able to get what they would have preferred.

But to vote strategically, you must guess not just at the preferences of others, but at their own strategic behavior. Voting mechanisms have their own problems of incentive compatibility. Condorcet demonstrated two hundred years ago that majorities can easily be assembled for inconsistent proposals. Kenneth Arrow—coauthor of the Arrow-Debreu results—generalized this to an "impossibility theorem": no voting mechanism can derive consistent social preferences from conflicting views about how society should be organized.

Arrow, who lives in California, must have recognized the practical force of his impossibility theorem as the lights flickered and faded. The electricity blackouts in California in 2000 and 2001[15] occurred because no voting system could prevent the California electorate from simultaneously demanding low electricity prices and no new generating plants while using ever increasing amounts of electricity.[16]

This doesn't mean that politics is impossible. It does mean that political choices are sometimes incompatible and inconsistent. And it explains why we not only have, but need, the variety of devices through which political decisions are made—political parties, horse-trading, and logrolling, mediation in which concessions on one item are traded for favors on others.[17]

Strategic Behavior in Markets

But market mechanisms encounter similar problems. When the British government auctioned television franchises in 1993, Central Television won the exclusive right to broadcast programs to Birmingham and surrounding areas for £2,000 ($3,340). They did not think the license was only worth £2,000. It was worth much more, and the value of the company rose when the result was announced. Central guessed, correctly, that no one else would bid.

Suppose another potential bidder had understood Central's plan and kept its own intentions secret. It could have won the auction with a bid of £5,000. In bidding at auction, you are not just concerned with your own valuation. You are equally concerned with what others will bid. But their bids will in turn depend on their guesses about your bids. Bidding becomes a game in which the bids bear only a weak relationship to underlying values.

Yet in one variant of this procedure it is best to bid in line with your valuation. A judge reviews all the bids. The judge discards all except the highest two and gives the object to the highest bidder at the price offered by the second-highest bidder.

In that auction, you should bid whatever you think the object is worth. Suppose that amount is $100. If the highest bid from anyone else is $80, then you will get the object for $80. If the highest outside bid is $110, you won't get the object, but you wouldn't have wanted to pay $110 for it anyway. A little time with pencil and paper will show that you can never lose by bidding your true valuation, but you might lose out if you enter a false value. Alone among bidding procedures, this "second-price auction" has the property of incentive compatibility: there is no benefit from strategic behavior.

The mechanism sounds arcane and theoretical. It was proposed by an American economist, William Vickrey,[n] who received the Nobel Prize in 1996 for his analysis of this and similar problems.[18] But the Vickrey scheme is, in essence, the allocation mechanism that was used to decide what should be done with the *Portrait of Dr. Gachet* when the Kramarsky family sold it in 1990. We do not know how much Mr. Saito, the paper magnate represented by the Japanese dealer, would have been willing to pay, nor did Christie's auctioneer. We only know that the maximum the second-highest bidder was ready to put on the table was $74 million. And Mr. Saito won the painting for a "nominal" $1 million more.[19]

It seems at first sight extraordinary that Mr. Christie and Mr. Sotheby should by chance have stumbled on the same device that Vickrey discovered two centuries later with the aid of clever mathematics. But it is not. Christie and Sotheby were inheritors of a long salesroom tradition that had tried different auction rules, abandoned some, and developed others.

Social and economic institutions are adaptive: less appropriate institutions are displaced by more appropriate ones. Choices about the mechanisms of the market economy have been made, not by any conscious decisions, but from historical evolution through trial and error. Mr. Christie and Mr. Sotheby had never heard of incentive compatibility when they defined the rules for their salesrooms—their successors have not heard of it yet. They developed, over time, the procedure that in their experience best satisfied their customers. These processes of adaptation and coevolution recur again and again in our search for the truth about markets.

Do Markets Work?

The auction of *Portrait of Dr. Gachet* produced the right answer, in one sense. The bidders honestly revealed their assessments of the value of the painting: the auction assigned it to the person who valued it most. But this mechanism of assignment did not really solve the fundamental economic problem that Youngson had posed—the allocation of a scarce resource between competing ends.

After Mr. Saito bought the painting, it remained wrapped and stored in a high-security warehouse until Mr. Saito's death. We do not know why Saito bought the painting. Or why he bought Renoir's *Moulin de la Galette* at Sotheby's a few days later for $78.5 million. Saito paid not only the highest dollar sum ever paid for a work of art, but the second-highest sum as well. Perhaps he hoped—wrongly— that *Dr. Gachet* would appreciate in value. Maybe he derived satisfaction from the ownership of a masterpiece, or the world's most valuable painting. Still, this satisfaction was not based on any pleasure he or his friends or anyone else derived from looking at it.

If Mr. Saito had been a great benefactor of mankind—if he had designed the operating system for the world's personal computers or discovered an important new drug—we might feel that indulging his wishes, however eccentric, was a reasonable way to assign one of the world's great paintings. It would represent a just reward, and an encouragement to similar achievement by others. But Saito was an undistinguished Japanese industrialist who nearly bankrupted the firm he inherited from his father and later received a prison sentence for corruption. *Portrait of Dr. Gachet* was bought by a vain, silly, but very rich man.

Both political mechanisms and market mechanisms determined, at different times, the fate of *Dr. Gachet*. Neither worked particularly well. Political voices required the painting to be removed from the wall of the Städel Museum. And they were probably reflective of majority public opinion at the time. The behavior of the Nazis was extreme, but political authority in the arts has always threatened pluralism. Before the Reformation, the Catholic Church exercised control over the style and content of painting; arts administrators today exert power through the allocation of subsidies to the arts and galleries.[20] Joanna van Gogh Bonger's speculation in the works of her brother-in-law brought his genius to the attention of the world, as no central authority did or was likely to have done. But market forces did a poor job of allocating scarce resources between competing ends when they consigned *Portrait of Dr. Gachet* to a sealed warehouse near Tokyo.

Choices between economic systems cannot be made on a priori

grounds. Planners and social democrats think that only political mechanisms can deliver well-balanced solutions and legitimate outcomes. Supporters of the American business model believe that market outcomes are just and efficient simply because they are market outcomes. For both sides, much in the history of *Portrait of Dr. Gachet* needs to be explained away.

Political decisions suffer acute problems of incentive compatibility. These may not only produce bad answers to the assignment problem but undermine the integrity of political decision making itself. The consequences of market allocation depend on the origin and legitimacy of the distribution of property and other resources within which markets operate. *Gachet* should not have gone to Tokyo, nor the Winter Olympics to Salt Lake City. In the next two chapters, I consider other aspects of the choice between political direction and market forces as mechanisms for allocating scarce resources between competing ends.

{9}

Central Planning

Great Leaps Forward

In 1959, Nikita Khrushchev was general secretary of the Communist Party and the most powerful man in the Soviet Union. Khrushchev had begun a liberalization following the death of Stalin. In a gesture of great significance, he paid a visit to the United States. He and his aides were dumbfounded when they visited a supermarket. They went home believing shelves had been specially stocked for their arrival.[1]

But a trip to Iowa made the greatest impression on Khrushchev. Khrushchev had long been enthusiastic about maize. As a young official he had made his reputation by expanding maize production. The American prairies were the world's largest source of maize. There was no faking the luxuriant fields that stretched as far as the eye could see. Khrushchev returned to Moscow convinced this was the future of Soviet agriculture. Large tracts of arable land were converted to maize. The experiment was not a success. Production fell. The economic setback that followed was one of the reasons why Khrushchev was toppled from power five years later.[2]

Russian agriculture did badly in this period, but experience in China, the other communist superpower, was far worse. In 1957, Mao Tse-tung announced the Great Leap Forward. The creation of large people's communes would transform agriculture. The first, which covered fifty-three thousand acres and embraced forty-four thousand people, was created in April 1958. By the autumn over 100 million peasant families lived in communes. They ate in a communal facility and no longer produced food for themselves. Every unit was encouraged to produce steel: backyard furnaces were the key to rapid industrialization. Mao declared war on the "four pests": flies, mosquitoes, rats, and sparrows. Much time and effort was devoted to collecting fuel for furnaces and to scaring sparrows from trees.[3]

The Great Leap Forward moved inexorably from farce to tragedy. Agricultural yields collapsed, and in the early sixties famine spread across the country. Between 30 and 40 million people died of starvation.

Khrushchev and Mao made bad decisions. But they were not absurd decisions. Khrushchev simply made a mistake. Maize was not a more suitable crop than wheat in Ukraine. Businesspeople routinely make that kind of error. Mao was right to have concluded that Chinese agriculture should be rationalized into larger units, that China needed to expand its steel production, and that steel production should take place in small units rather than large facilities. The concentration of agricultural production and the growth of steel output have been features of development in most rich states. The world steel industry has been reorganized into smaller plants.

Yet the context of these mistakes turned them into disasters. Decision making was centralized and personalized, and the outcomes were implemented on a huge scale.[4] Those who reported on the consequences did not wish either to hear or to deliver bad news. They were concerned to protect their own positions and to win approval from their superiors. And these powerful leaders were only slowly, if at all, accountable for their failures.

More Great Leaps Forward

Anyone who has worked for a large organization will have similar experiences. The phenomenon of Khrushchev's maize is familiar. A senior executive returns from a trip enthusiastic about a new idea. Subordinates implement the scheme, perhaps cynically, perhaps with enthusiasm. They congratulate their superiors on the wisdom of the strategy until enthusiasm wanes or the executive is fired or retires.

Henry Ford was probably the most important businessman of the twentieth century. In 1911, he established the world's first mass production assembly line. Ford was a mechanical and business genius, but he was not an intellectual man, and many of his views would have been embarrassing even in a saloon bar conversation. He was rabidly anti-Semitic, was pathologically averse to alcohol and tobacco, disapproved of eyeglasses, and plastered his hair with kerosene, which he believed was the cause of the healthy appearance of oil-field workers. As his commercial success grew, he became ever more convinced of his own rightness and was interested only in opinions that conformed to his prejudices.

Bill Knudsen, who had been Ford's right-hand man in the development of the Model T assembly line, was forced out of the company. "I can't stay and keep my self-respect," he said. Knudsen joined General Motors, which steadily gained market share as it responded to more demanding customer requirements. Ford's customers could have any color they wanted so long as it was black; the proprietor explained, "The only trouble with the Ford car is that we can't make them fast enough." When Ford's son Edsel organized the manufacture of an experimental six-cylinder engine, Henry summoned him to watch the destruction of the prototype.

Ford surrounded himself with an ever tighter and smaller group of sycophants, which ultimately included only his brutal chief of security, Harry Bennett. During World War II, the government considered nationalizing the company to ensure that its erratic founder would not impede the war effort. Ford died in 1947 a lonely, embittered man, having almost destroyed the company he had created, and professional management arrived—just—in time to save the company.

An Wang emigrated in 1945 from China to the United States. In 1951 he borrowed $600 to set up Wang Laboratories. The company made several innovative products as electronics advanced and became a leading manufacturer of desktop calculators, but the development of integrated circuits turned calculators into commodity products.

Wang's great success came with the launch of word processors in 1976. These were desktop computers dedicated to document preparation and spelled the end of the mechanical or electromechanical typewriter. Within a short time, every sophisticated office had a word processing system, and Wang word processors were the market leaders.

In 1979, Sam Gagliano, who was in charge of research and development at Wang Labs, proposed that Wang manufacture a personal computer. The Doctor, as An Wang was known inside the company, rejected the proposal out of hand: "He thought it [a small, general purpose computer] was the stupidest thing he had ever heard of."[5]

Only after IBM launched its personal computer in 1981 did Wang reluctantly agree to allow the manufacture of a personal computer. But it was to run a proprietary Wang operating system. And Wang's heart was not in it. He staked the company's future instead on the Wang Office Assistant, a sophisticated word processor with some of the features of a general purpose computer. It sold only a quarter of its initial production run. By the time of Wang's death in 1990, the company he had founded, which had once threatened IBM's dominance of the computer market, was bankrupt. Peter Brooke, Wang's trusted associate and a member of his board, described the collapse: "In the early eighties they developed a we-know-everything attitude. They insulated themselves from any outside advice. Wang bought its own story. You have closed architecture because you've got a closed mind." "'We' meant An Wang," Gagliano explained. "He stopped listening to what the customers really wanted. I think he lost touch in the early eighties, and there wasn't anybody in the company who was going to stop him from doing that."

People and Decisions

There are many similarities between the worlds of Khrushchev and Mao and those of Ford and Wang. Decision making was centralized. Reporting was limited and sycophantic. Accountability for decisions was slow and indirect.

In all cases, the individuals who made decisions were people of great ability and achievement. Khrushchev had demonstrated great administrative prowess in rising through the Soviet hierarchy during the Stalinist terror. Despite that experience he had retained integrity and humor. These qualities enabled him to begin exposing and dismantling Stalinism. In doing so, he captured the imagination and even the affection of a public outside his own country. If he had been born in the United States, Khrushchev would probably have been chief executive of a large corporation.

Mao—through extraordinary political and military skills—had

successfully united the most populous country in the world under a single government after generations of havoc wreaked by competing warlords. This achievement ranks with those of Napoleon or Alexander the Great. If we do not today think of Mao in those terms, it is because, unlike these two, he survived to exercise civil authority in China for twenty-seven years and made bad judgments with disastrous consequences.

"Had Mao died in 1956, his achievements would have been immortal. Had he died in 1966, he would still have been a great man. But he died in 1976. Alas, what can one say?"[6]

Ford also exerted too much authority for too long. People who have been right in the past cannot be blamed for thinking they are more than averagely likely to be right in the future. The adulation that surrounds successful politicians and businesspeople reinforces their understandable self-confidence. Acton's dictum that "power tends to corrupt and absolute power corrupts absolutely" is not a reference to financial corruption. It relates to the corruption of an individual's values that results from the exercise of unchecked authority over an extended period.

The Reshaping of New York City

If you have ever crossed the Triborough Bridge, used the Grand Central Parkway or the Van Wyck Expressway, visited Lincoln Center or Shea Stadium, you have encountered the work of Robert Moses, who was from 1924 to 1968 the dominant influence on the planning and public infrastructure of New York City. Only Baron Haussmann, who remodeled Paris around grand boulevards in the 1870s, has had comparable effect on the landscape of an established city, and only Moses rehoused so many people to make way for his dreams.

Moses began his career as an idealistic municipal reformer who believed that the corruption of New York politics in the early decades of the twentieth century could be tackled by the rigorously objective grading of city employees. The employees themselves had different ideas, and Moses was crushed by the Tammany Hall machine.

Moses learned the lesson. For the rest of his career, he sustained his power with a mixture of inducements—power, contracts, and financial favors—and threats—no detail of personal behavior or family history was too small to be recorded in Moses's files and used to break opposition to his plans.

Moses was highly intelligent—as An Wang certainly was, Khrushchev and Mao may have been, and Ford was not—and also a visionary, who had seen as an integrated whole the system of Long Island parks and roads that still shapes life in New York City. But like all these leaders, he eliminated from his entourage those who disagreed with him, until only admiring supporters remained.

In the later part of his career, Moses became deaf, but refused to wear a hearing aid. His lieutenants installed amplifying systems in offices, ostensibly to permit large meetings, but to little avail. As Moses biographer Robert Caro explains, the physical ailment was symbolic: Moses had effectively been deaf for many years. "Moses was surrounded by a solid wall of sycophancy—the only opinions voiced were his opinions, the only facts and figures presented those that would confirm those opinions."[7]

History has not judged Moses kindly. Baron Haussmann destroyed homes and communities, but no one disputes the elegance of the buildings and layouts he substituted. No one feels the same affection for the Long Island Expressway. As Moses built, traffic grew until his highways were as congested as were the roads before. The Cross Bronx Expressway turned once thriving communities into areas of dereliction. When Governor Nelson Rockefeller finally maneuvered him from office in 1968—when Moses was almost eighty years old—the city he had shaped so dramatically was in a spiral of decline, stricken by urban decay and financial crisis.

Planning in British Electricity

Absolutism of authority is part of the problem. In Soviet Russia and Communist China, as at Wang Laboratories and the Ford Motor Company, decision making was personalized and undemocratic. In New York, Robert Moses, an unelected official, gathered autocratic power in an environment of ostensible democracy. Would it not be better if wise men came together, in a single institution, to assemble the evidence, consider it dispassionately, and set the direction for the industry? That is what central planning in a democratic society is intended to achieve.

In 1947, the British electricity industry was nationalized. Most

of the business was already owned by local authorities. The importance of the change was that it brought the generation and distribution of electricity under central government control.

In the decades immediately after the World War II, there were
great expectations for the peaceful exploitation of nuclear energy.
Britain had developed a limited nuclear technology for military purposes and had experimented with adaptations designed to produce
commercial supplies of electricity. In the winter of 1964–65, power
blackouts resulted from shortage of generating capacity. The newly
elected Labor government—which had declared "the white heat of
technology" to be central to its plans—decided on a program of five
new nuclear reactors, based on an idiosyncratic British design (the
advanced gas-cooled reactor, or AGR) of which a small prototype
had already been constructed. Fred Lee, a trade unionist who had
reached the pinnacle of his career as minister for energy, announced
the decision with pride: "I am quite sure we have hit the jackpot."[8]

He had not hit the jackpot. The average construction period for
these five (subsequently seven) reactors was over twenty years, and
the total cost (at 2003 prices) exceeded $100 billion.[9] In 1996 owner-
ship of the reactors was transferred to a private company, British
Energy, which collapsed in 2003, effectively writing off any value of
these assets and leaving the British government to pick up the substantial costs of decommissioning.

It is obvious who made decisions in the Soviet Union and Communist China, at Ford and at Wang—or in construction plans in
New York City. Yet it would be difficult to say that the decision to
build AGRs was made by anyone at all.

No one was really responsible for the decision, either when it was
made or subsequently. And the real disaster was not so much the
original decision, but the nondecision to continue long after the disastrous consequences should have been apparent. The central figure
was a civil servant, Edward (subsequently Lord) Plowden, who occupied a variety of Whitehall roles from the 1950s to the 1970s, including the chairmanship of the Atomic Energy Authority. One of the
many influential committees Plowden chaired reviewed the structure of the state-owned electricity businesses. The problem, Plowden
concluded, was that there was not enough centralization. The industry needed to "speak with a single voice."[10]

But the industry did its best to speak with a single voice, and a voice that favored the AGR program. Those who expressed doubts found their career progression blocked or terminated. Others learned the lesson.[11] Anyone who provided negative feedback on the program was similarly treated. In contrast to Moses, who was determined to get his way, Plowden was more interested in the process by which decisions were made—and his central role in that process—than in the outcome. The primary virtue is helpfulness, and the concept is deeply ingrained in a bureaucracy such as the British civil service. Helpfulness describes an individual's contribution to the orderly and consensual conduct of business. It does not relate to the nature and quality of decisions.[12]

The purge of those who were insufficiently helpful was far subtler than with the Gulag, the Cultural Revolution, or the peremptory dismissal by Ford and Wang of those who disagreed with them. And it was even more successful, in its own terms. To this day, there has been no inquiry into the AGR program, no audit of the costs, no learning of the lessons. In contrast to the Great Leap Forward or the random initiatives of Henry Ford, decision making for British electricity had the appearance of high rationality. But the consequences were the same: uniformity of opinion in the short run, economic failure in the long.

The Scale of Decision Making

Centralized economic decision making is characterized by the single voice. The voice of an individual, such as Mao, Ford, or Moses. The synthetic single voice of a process orchestrated and minuted by figures such as Edward Plowden. The single voice makes decisions on a large scale.

Khrushchev's experiment with maize was desirable and even beneficial. What distinguished the Soviet experiment was its size. An individual Russian farmer who had visited the United States might have been equally impressed by the productivity of the prairies. He might have brought back some seed. If yields had been disappointing, as they would have been, that would have been the end of the matter. If he had been successful, his rivals would have imitated him.

The scale of Mao's decisions was breathtaking. That most of Chinese agriculture was converted to communal organization within a year was an extraordinary achievement. The chief executives of large companies aspire to, but rarely achieve, this kind of transformational change. But the scale of the change set the scene for the scale of the catastrophe.

No business leaders have ever enjoyed the wide-ranging political and economic authority of Mao and Khrushchev. But the size of the automobile industry and the scale and importance of New York City enabled Ford and Moses to make momentous decisions. In the 1920s the output of the Ford Motor Company accounted for around 1% of U.S. GDP, while New York is the commercial capital of the world's largest economy.

Fred Lee's plan was to build five power stations, more or less simultaneously, to an unproven design. With a single generating business for the whole of England and Wales, you have to make decisions of that magnitude. But nobody—however talented, however well-informed, however well-intentioned—had the capacity to decide which technologies were appropriate for the British electricity industry for the next twenty years. The probability that *any* such decision would have been badly awry is high. To stand any chance of success, a centralized decision-making process must be exceptionally sensitive to the consequences, responsive to the changing environment.

This was not true in Russia, in China, at Ford, at Wang, or in British electricity. The centralization that established the single voice also stifled dissent. The feedback mechanisms in Ford and Wang were similar to the feedback mechanisms faced by Khrushchev and Mao and equally ineffective. Even modest men rarely tire of the praise of loyal lieutenants. To point out the obvious failure of policy in British electricity was to label oneself a disruptive influence in an organization that, by its own values, was performing more than satisfactorily.

That is not to say there was no feedback or accountability. Ford saw declining market share in competition with General Motors, and Wang eventually went bust. This feedback—a crucial element in how markets work—is described more fully in the next chapter. It operated only slowly for Ford and for Wang because of market dominance created by their previous success. In Russia and China, the feedback came from popular discontent with economic perfor-mance, a mechanism that eventually toppled the Soviet Union and produced radical reform in China

But these mechanisms were slow, and with that slowness went a lack of accountability on the part of the decision makers. Ford and Wang were protected from outside criticism by their reputations and the large shareholdings they owned or controlled. The most account-able of these leaders was Khrushchev, ousted by his fellow politburo members. Ford and Mao continued in office until death, Wang until the death of his company, and their only accountability is to the jaun-diced eyes of history.

Feedback and accountability were almost completely absent in British electricity. The few critics were ignored or disparaged, and Plowden, elevated to the peerage, continued to chair committees to the end of his life. New York City mayor Wagner took office in 1954 deter-mined to curb the power of Robert Moses, but not until 1968 did his reign come to an end. There was less accountability in the democracies within which Moses and Plowden operated than in the openly author-itarian structures that Ford and Wang, Mao and Khrushchev, had in place.

{10}

Pluralism

In the declining years of their founders, Ford and Wang were particularly badly managed companies. It is time to look at a well-run private-sector business.

General Electric was the most successful corporation of the twentieth century. Of the dozen largest companies in the world in 1912, only three—Exxon (the modern name for Standard Oil of New Jersey), GE, and Shell, the leading European oil company—were still in that group at the end. GE is the world's most valuable company, having regained the status it briefly lost in the bubble—first to Microsoft and then, absurdly, to Cisco, a manufacturer of Internet routers.

America's leading electrical company in 1900 was bound to do well in the hundred years that followed. Still, you might have been surprised by the nature of its success. General Electric sold its computer business in 1970, after being consistently outpaced by IBM. GE made little impact in consumer electronics in the face of Japanese competition. Its most important activities today are in aero engines, financial services, and medical equipment. The history of General Electric is one of strong management applied to a diverse and changing range of businesses. In consequence, GE is not only the best-managed company in the world but also the most studied. And its chief executive has almost always been the most respected business leader in the United States.[1] From 1981 to 2001, that position was occupied by Jack Welch.

The facts about General Electric are buried in a welter of management-speak. But Welch's most famous initiative, "workout at GE," represented, above all, an attack on the single voice. The structure that Welch inherited at GE represented centralized planning at its most sophisticated and effective. Reg Jones, Welch's predecessor, had developed systems with the aim of understanding and controlling all areas of the world's largest business. "I could look at six planning books and understand them well enough to ask the right questions," he said. The U.S. Defense Department undertook a survey and concluded that the new man in charge at General Electric "was probably inheriting the world's most effective strategic planning system and that Number Two was pretty far behind."[2]

Welch set out to dismantle this structure. Welch described as "superficial congeniality"[3] what the British civil service calls helpfulness. Welch set out to replace General Electric's "superficial congeniality" with a process of substantive debate and argument. The contradictions raised are apparent in a 1982 interview with General Electric's chief planner, W. G. Rothschild. In the spirit of General Electric's earlier tradition, Rothschild asserts, "I can assure you that a guy who doesn't implement the strategy is in big trouble. . . . We tell the CEO when a manager is not on plan." Yet Rothschild goes on, "I like being challenged, and I like people to argue with me. By the way, that happens to be what our new chairman likes too. The new buzzword here is *contention management.* I'd say that's where we are and where we're going."[4] In that, at least, Rothschild was right. Within a short time, Rothschild himself and much of General Electric's central planning staff had disappeared.[5]

The opposite of superficial congeniality was "facing reality"— performance judged by externally measured achievement, not contribution to internal culture. "Facing reality was not one of the company's strong points. Its superficial congeniality made candor extremely difficult to come by."[6] Welch would illustrate "facing reality" with General Electric's nuclear power plant division. Its managers could not accept that both economics and politics had turned against nuclear power. By attacking helpfulness and abandoning superficial congeniality, General Electric recognized these realities— as Britain's centrally planned electricity industry never did.[7] GE's nuclear power plant business was turned into a profitable sales and support operation.

But the most important part of General Electric's reorganization was the systematic decentralization of authority. "I did away with that [approval and appropriation] process and haven't signed an appropriation approach in at least eighteen years. Each business leader has the same delegation of authority that the board gave me. . . . The people closest to the work know the work best."[8]

To advance, General Electric had to embrace pluralism—to replace superficial congeniality by open debate, to dismember the central planning and decentralize authority. Welch attempted to tackle some of the identified key problems of central planning—in particular, decision making on too large a scale, and the lack of effective feedback and accountability.

Yet centralization, conformity to internally generated values, too much authority seized by leaders whose adjutants derive no advantage from telling the truth, are inescapable in large organizations. Welch was a more intelligent man than Henry Ford, and he did not outstay his effective tenure as long as Ford did. But he did outstay it. In his autobiography, the engaging character who takes charge of General Electric in 1981 becomes less attractive as self-confidence is reinforced by success. The word *I* appears more often. And after his retirement, his reputation began to fade as evidence emerged about his personal behavior and the benefits he continued to enjoy at the expense of the corporation.

Xerox Parc

Photocopying was invented by a lawyer, Chester Carlson, who had tired of the problem of obtaining good copies of documents. Carlson had difficulty finding a backer. It is claimed that IBM, General Electric, and RCA investigated the proposal, and all turned it down. Incredible though it seems to us now, they thought there would not be sufficient demand to justify the costs and risks of development.[9] Eventually a small firm, the Haloid Company, decided to risk everything on Carlson's invention. After fifteen years of development, the company launched the first commercial photocopier. Haloid called the patented process xerography and changed the company name to Xerox Corporation.

Early machines were large, slow, and broke down frequently. Office activities were frequently halted as secretaries waited for the Xerox engineer. Xerox's equipment got better, but not sufficiently better, and when Xerox patents expired, market leadership switched to the Japanese optical company Canon. Conscious that revenues from its initial monopoly would not continue indefinitely, the Xerox Corporation sought to diversify into other high-technology office products. A research center was established at Palo Alto, in the center of what was to become Silicon Valley.

Xerox Parc was a fertile source of innovation.[10] The fax machine was pioneered there, as was the laser printer, the Ethernet, and the graphical user interface (the icons and pointers that make modern computers easy to use). Yet, despite the company's stunning achievement with photocopiers, Xerox never succeeded in turning its innovative capability into corresponding commercial success.[11] It would be left to others to exploit the most revolutionary product of Xerox Parc—the personal computer. Xerography had come into being because no single voice controlled the office equipment industry. A cacophony of voices was to be heard in personal computers.

The Personal Computer

For many years, most experts thought that computing power would be like electric power, and if Lord Plowden or Robert Moses had been in charge, it probably would have been. A few gigantic facilities would maximize economies of scale. Everyone would plug into these supercomputers. In the 1970s, a university, or a business, would typically have one computer. The computer industry might also have developed through an extensive range of application-specific machines—the word processor, the games console, specialist calculators for engineers and accountants. This was the vision that An Wang maintained until it was much too late.

A process of diversity and experiment produced a very different answer. In 1971, Intel developed a general-purpose chip—the microprocessor. The logic of applications was found not on the chip, but in the memory. This paved the way for the general purpose minicomputer. In 1973, scientists at Xerox Parc built the first functioning personal computer, the Alto. It was eight years before they unveiled a commercial version. The new product impressed the trade press with its sophistication. But it was by then too idiosyncratic and expensive for the market.

While Xerox was perfecting the Alto, personal computers were developed by hobbyists. The Altair minicomputer was advertised in *Popular Electronics* magazine in December 1974, a self-assembly kit with a price of $400. Two young Harvard students, Paul Allen and Bill Gates, devised a version of the programming language BASIC for the Altair. Toy computers followed, manufactured by companies such as Commodore, with memory provided by cassette tape recorders.

By now, some large companies recognized the potential of small computers for small businesses. Companies such as AT&T and Sony. The first desktop computer I used, in 1980, was made by Sirius, an Exxon subsidiary. But then IBM launched a range of personal computers—the PC. A machine with an IBM label was not a toy. IBM's reputation and market presence were such that whatever they supported would command wide acceptance. It didn't matter that the PC's performance was inferior to that of other machines on the market. IBM's was the system for which people would write software. Within months, *PC* had become the generic term for a small computer.

For the operating system, IBM had turned to a small company, Microsoft, run by Gates and Allen. Microsoft in turn bought the operating system, which it renamed MS-DOS, for $50,000. But IBM did not take exclusive rights. The computer giant had no real sense of the revolution it had launched. When IBM attempted to regain control with a new and more sophisticated operating system, OS2, it was too late. MS-DOS was everywhere.

The choice of the computer enthusiast was Apple. Apple machines were more fun. Gates and Microsoft had understood that commercial success depended on ease of use rather than technical sophistication. Steve Jobs, founder of Apple, extended this vision further—a computer that you could use without understanding computers. To achieve this, Jobs drew on another invention from Xerox Parc—the graphical user interface. Apple machines had screens that resembled a desktop, and friendly aids such as a mouse and recycle bin.

You could access these capabilities only by buying Apple's integrated software and hardware. Apple's determination to maintain its proprietary system lost out to the widespread adoption of the open standard of the IBM PC, just as Sony's proprietary Betamax standard lost out to JVC's open VHS in the videocassette recorder business (chapter 22). The combination of Apple's graphical user interface with Microsoft's ubiquitous MS-DOS operating system was bound to succeed. Microsoft launched an early version in 1988 and an effective version of Windows two years later. The rest—Microsoft's domination of the personal computer industry and Gates's rise to become the world's richest man—is history.[12]

The Process of Pluralism

Nikita Khrushchev, or Lord Plowden, might have asked "who was in charge of the successful development of the personal computer industry?" There is no doubt that whoever was in charge of the development of computers in the Soviet Union would have had much to learn from that person.

But nobody was "in charge." If Khrushchev's hosts had introduced him to the chairman of IBM, or Bill Gates, they would have ensured that their visitor completely missed the point. Markets work because there is never a single voice.

No one saw for more than a few months ahead how the personal computer industry would evolve. Gates and Jobs believed that the future lay with small machines that were easy to use—a widely held view, though not, for many years, a majority view. But Jobs's strategy for his company did not work, and Gates's success derives directly from one event—his association with IBM. The majority of initiatives failed. Some did not work technically. But even those initiatives that were crucial to the development of the industry were frequently commercially unsuccessful—as was most spectacularly true for An Wang.

This is how new industries develop and new products emerge. Many contended to shape the world car industry. Would cars be steam-powered, like railroad engines, or would internal combustion technology win out? Would they remain as the playthings of rich men or be extended to a mass market? Henry Ford made good calls on these issues.

But we do not know the mixture of luck and judgment behind these decisions—and if Ford made some shrewd decisions, he equally certainly made some bad ones. The key point is that there was a race. Many people had the opportunity to back their own judgments, and some of these judgments were right and some wrong. The names that history remembers—such as Henry Ford—are the names of those who made important judgments correctly.

But the race never ends, and that is why Ford and Wang were penalized for their later errors. Ford's global leadership was overtaken by General Motors. Feedback mechanisms within these organizations failed, but the broader feedback mechanisms of the market economy ultimately succeeded in promoting managerial reorganization at Ford, while Wang's failure ensured that the direction of the computer industry was to be in different hands.

Most decisions are wrong. Most experiments fail. It is tempting to believe that if we entrusted the future of our companies, our industries, our countries, to the right people, they would lead us unerringly to the promised land. Such hopes are always disappointed. Most of Thomas Edison's inventions did not work. Neither Ford nor Mao received, or deserved, much respect at the end of their lives. Bill Gates missed the significance of the Internet, and Napoleon died in exile on St. Helena. Even extraordinarily talented people make big mistakes.

But because most decisions are wrong and most experiments fail, it is also tempting to believe that we could manage businesses and states much better if we only assembled sufficient information, cleverer people, and debated the issues at length. This is how decision making is supposed to be in the public sector and many large organizations.

What would Lord Plowden, chairing a committee in the 1970s to determine the future of the computer industry, have done? He would have deplored the failure of the industry to speak "with a single voice," but would have found the best approximation to that voice in the chief executive of IBM. He would have consulted widely in the industry, certainly discussing with Intel what they thought might happen, and commending them on their cooperation with IBM. He might even have gone so far as to hold discussions with Xerox, even though they were not actually making computers at the time of his report. If he had received submissions from the young Bill Gates and

Steve Jobs, he would have smiled gently and passed them to the secretary of his committee to file. This picture is not fanciful. It is more or less how the computer industry developed, or failed to develop, in the Soviet Union. It is more or less how IBM developed its policies and strategy for the future of its industry.

But nobody has the foresight that these processes require. These structures would fail even if the people who staffed them were infinitely intelligent and farseeing. What would an omniscient planner, blessed with the advantages of hindsight, have said when faced with the numerous business strategies described above? He would have told Xerox that they would not develop commercially successful products from the PC and the graphical user interface. He would have explained to IBM that the company's strategy would destroy its core business. He would have foreseen Wang's bankruptcy and would have told Apple that its policy would take the company to the edge of collapse. And he would have said many of the same things to the people who developed the automobile industry or commercial aviation.

There are always well-founded objections to any new proposed course of action. There is always a proposal that might be better than the one currently being considered. As a result, these apparently rational processes frequently fail to make decisions at all and, when they do, often make worse decisions than those that emerge from more intuitive, and certainly speedier, processes.

Failures of Discipline

Pluralism is the key to the success of a market economy. But pluralism must also be disciplined. A consequence of the extraordinary success of pluralism in promoting innovation in personal computers was the collapse of market discipline in the 1990s.

By the mid-1990s it was apparent that the Internet was an innovation of major significance. The key to giving access to the Internet to a wide public was the development of easy-to-use browser software. The best browser had been created by students at the University of Illinois. Jim Clark, who had become rich by developing and selling an earlier software business, Silicon Graphics, hired the team who had created it, settled the inevitable lawsuit with the University of Illinois, and launched Netscape Navigator. Within a few months, Navigator had achieved market dominance, a result not only of its usefulness but its price: it was usually given away, and when shares in Netscape were sold to investors in 1995, the company's sales revenues to date had been less than $20 million.

The demand for Netscape shares was such that the shares closed on the first day at $58, valuing the company at $2.2 billion. These figures were eclipsed as Internet enthusiasm grew: the shares quickly rose to $170, which made Clark a billionaire. Microsoft developed its own browser, Internet Explorer, with similar capabilities, provided free with Windows, and quickly overtook Navigator. In 1999, Netscape was acquired by AOL at a price that still gave early investors a profit. No doubt it seemed a good idea at the time. Today Navigator's market share is below 10%.

Although Netscape never became a successful business, the company did have a proven chief executive, a good product, and a strong market position. As the decade progressed, an increasing number of companies were launched by individuals with no management or commercial experience, no realistic business plan, and no identifiable product.

Priceline, whose main business was the sale of discounted air tickets, was for a time valued at more than the entire U.S. airline industry. Webvan proclaimed itself the future of retailing, its enthusiasts predicting the demise of "bricks and mortars," and even attracted George Sheehan to relinquish charge of the Accenture consulting business for a seat at the driving wheel of this home delivery service, not long before closing in 2001. Pets.com and etoys will forever be symbols of the implausible expectations for online retailing. As these businesses failed, breathless predictions of the future were transferred from B2C (business to consumer) retailing to B2B (business to business). Eventually reality broke in here also.

The ease with which money could be raised to fund businesses such as these was widely applauded as a demonstration of the vitality of financial markets.[13] In reality, it represented a collapse of market discipline. Investors failed to discriminate between proposals, believing that any stake they held in an Internet-related company could soon be sold to someone else at a higher price. Venture capital managers and investment banks received fees for promoting investments in these businesses, yet it required only common sense, not professional expertise, to see that they had little chance of success.

In early 2000, the valuation of technology stocks in general, and Internet stocks in particular, reached a peak and then crashed. The supply of venture capital to new Internet businesses dried up almost immediately. From the Netscape flotation to the market crash, the collapse of market discipline had lasted five years.[14]

Because the world is complicated and the future uncertain, decision making in organizations and economic systems is best made through a series of small-scale experiments, frequently reviewed, and in a structure in which success is followed up and failure recognized but not blamed. The mechanisms of disciplined pluralism. Welch's reputation as the greatest manager of his generation is not based on the big calls that he got right, on his Napoleonic vision, his Fordist determination, or his Edisonian invention. Welch understood that the principal function of managing director of the world's largest commercial organization was to appoint good people and trust them to do the job. It was to introduce pluralism, and at the same time to impose discipline, through audit and accountability. Both within organizations and outside them, the combination of pluralism and discipline describes how markets work.

{11}

Spontaneous Order

Order Without Design

Who designed the market economy? No one did. It is the result of the simultaneous evolution of social, political, and economic institutions over hundreds, even thousands of years. Who developed the personal computer? The answer, again, is that no one did. The industry has emerged from an unplanned process of trial and error within a framework of disciplined pluralism. There is a deep human need to find ordered, personalized explanations of the complexities and vicissitudes of life. Almost all religions have an account of the creation of the world. Most primitive cultures believe that drought or bad weather are expressions of some human emotion, such as anger or revenge.

Similar instincts lead modern men and women to personalize large corporations (and to seek someone to blame for floods and rail accidents). Jack Welch was lionized because it is hard to believe that an organization like General Electric achieves so much through decentralized decision making and negotiations among thousands of autonomous individuals. It is easier to think it is the expression of the will of one man.

For centuries, theologians argued that the complexity of nature was evidence of the existence of God. William Paley drew a famous analogy: if we found a perfectly engineered watch at our feet, then there must be a watchmaker. But the analogy is misleading.

The thinkers of the Scottish Enlightenment, whose names graced those Edinburgh University buildings, were among the first to grasp one of the most powerful, wide-ranging, and elusive ideas of the last two centuries.[1] Structures and systems can have the characteristics of elaborate design without a designer. David Hume anticipated and refuted Paley's theological argument.[2] Adam Ferguson applied the same thought to social institutions: "Nations stumble upon establishments, which are indeed the results of human action but not the result of human design."[3]

A century later, Darwin was to throw back Paley's example with his own metaphor of the "blind watchmaker."[4] And today, we understand that evolution has produced organisms whose complexity far exceeds the capacity of any human mind—organisms such as human beings, General Electric, and the international division of labor.

The success of Darwin's theory has led to attempts at too literal analogy.[5] Genetic selection is only one type of evolutionary process. Black parents have black children, and French-speaking parents have French-speaking children, but for different reasons.[6] The transmission of acquired skills—impossible in genetic selection—is central to business and economic life. And evolutionary mechanisms themselves are only one example of processes that create order without design—others will be described in this chapter. The importance of Darwin's theory outside biology is that it demonstrates the extraordinary potential of spontaneous order. No one who has fully understood it ever thinks the same way again.

Coordination in Market Economies

Adam Smith was the great economist of the Scottish Enlightenment. And his metaphor of the invisible hand is the most famous expression of order without design. Smith had described how the division of labor had fueled economic growth, "the natural progress of opulence." But how was that division of labor organized and coordinated? The answer was the invisible hand. As I shall discuss in chapter 17, I am not sure this interpretation of Smith is right.

But whether or not it was Smith's answer, it is a good question. We can imagine Khrushchev in the supermarket posing his own version: "Who is in charge of the supply of groceries to California?" To anyone unfamiliar with the institutions of the market economy, it seems bizarre that this question has no answer. In the striking phrase of Ken Arrow[n] and Frank Hahn, two of the economists who have framed these issues, "The immediate 'common sense' answer to the question 'What will an economy motivated by individual greed and controlled by a very large number of different agents look like?' is probably: 'There will be chaos.'"[7]

And yet there is not chaos. In rich states, we are so accustomed to the absence of surpluses and shortages that we feel angry when we encounter them—when a shop does not have the size or color we want, when we cannot find a taxi or a bus late at night, and certainly when California cannot maintain consistent supplies of electricity. Indeed the world in which no one is in charge of the supply of electricity in California does not seem to have worked particularly well.

Market economies solved the coordination problem more successfully than centrally planned ones. This discovery astonished Khrushchev, and it should astonish us. Many of the failures of centrally planned economies were failures of innovation. The pluralist program of experiment, failure, and fresh experiment did not occur in the Soviet Union, and so that country did not produce new drugs, modern automobiles, or personal computers.

But the greatest failures of centrally planned economies were in coordination.[8] Queues formed in pursuit of erratic supplies of consumer goods. Factories failed to meet targets because they could not obtain necessary input. Other industrial goods were in excess supply. The Soviet Union had more steel-making capacity than the United States,[9] and it is hard to understand where all the steel went. Some of it was simply left to rust. For the casual visitor, failures of coordination are one of the most obvious differences between rich and poor countries. The electricity supply is often unreliable; some essential goods are not available. This is sometimes the result of poverty, but also a cause.

So how do rich states do it? If Khrushchev had been introduced to Sam Walton,[10] Walton would have told him that he was only one of several people in charge of the supply of groceries in California. "And who liaises between them?" Lord Plowden would have asked. "Which committee orchestrates the single voice?" Not only is there no such committee, to form it would violate U.S. law.

And who coordinates relationships of firms in the supply chain? Who ensures that goods are produced to fill the shelves? Khrushchev might have speculated on the answer. In market economies prices rise or fall when there is a physical shortage or surplus, so there are no empty shelves or unsold produce. This is indeed the mechanism that emerged in Russia when centralized supply chains broke down after the collapse of the Soviet Union.[11]

But raising prices to deal with temporary shortages is so unpopular with consumers that retailers are reluctant to do it. Shoppers accept price fluctuations of seasonal products, but not price fluctuations from coordination failures.[12] When the failure of California electricity supplies did lead to price spikes, the same political outcry occurred that would have been expected in the Soviet Union.[13] The answer Sam Walton would have given to the question "How do supermarkets deal with shortages and surpluses?" is that the problem rarely arises.

Rich states are not free of coordination failures. Coordination in electricity supply is a powerful example, which is why it will recur often: the consequences of even a small and short-lived coordination failure are so obvious—the lights go out. As they did in Auckland in 1998, in California in 2000, and routinely in poor states. Perhaps the most serious coordination failure in productive economies is unemployment, a coordination failure that planned economies largely avoided, although at the price of coordination failures elsewhere. How market systems achieve coordination is the subject of Part III of this book.

At the Supermarket

Khrushchev did not have to worry about which queue to join at the supermarket checkout, but you do. You can look at the characteristics of the queues: how many people, how full are their carts? Will those ahead unload their baskets quickly? Or engage in extended discussion with the cashier?

Or you can simply join the nearest queue. So long as some people—it need not be very many—are scanning the store to find the shortest queue, you can expect that the time you spend in each queue will be much the same. If any queue looks short, these activists will join it. The activists probably wait slightly less time than you, but not much—enough, however, to give them some return on their socially beneficial activity.

This is a simple and banal example of a system of spontaneous order. It is organized, and in some respects efficient, but it is not directed. It is probably more effective at keeping down waiting times than direction by a bossy store manager. The manager would not be able to keep pace sufficiently well with the constantly changing progress at the checkouts, nor would he always find people ready to follow his instructions—the twin problems of information and incentives that confront planners everywhere.

The outcome of this self-organizing system emerges from the individual decisions of shoppers. They are not pursuing a collective goal of short and uniform waiting times, although their actions have this effect. Their actions are self-regarding, but not purely self-interested: if the supermarket were full of people whose only objective was to get through the checkout as quickly as possible, it would not be possible to operate any queuing system at all. The orderly process is the product of limited self-interest and social convention.

Although nobody designed this system, design might improve it. Many customers are willing to allow other shoppers with few purchases to jump the queue. To facilitate this, some supermarkets have responded with separate queues for such people. A system that works well in one environment may fail in another. In a supermarket, you can see how much is in everyone else's cart. But in an airline ticket queue, the person in front may be booking a round-the-world itinerary or simply asking the way to the gate. A single queue feeds several agents.

Our everyday supermarket experience demonstrates two different kinds of process. Individual shoppers are led "as if by an invisible hand" to keep down overall waiting times. No one consciously intended to bring this about, and it might be more difficult to bring it about by conscious intention. The process is dynamic but not evolutionary. But an evolutionary mechanism is at work. In competition with each other, supermarkets adopt mechanisms that efficiently serve the needs of their customers. This combination of processes illustrates, in microcosm, how market economies evolved—and evolve.

Chaos and Path Dependency
● ●

We could develop a mathematical model of supermarket queues. Such a model would be dynamic—the length of queues constantly changes. It would display feedback—the number of people who join a queue will depend on the number of people already in it. I suspect most readers will be skeptical of the value of doing this. But there really is a branch of mathematics called queue theory,[14] and it has practical implications. Much of it was developed to assist engineers in the design of telephone exchanges. Related models are widely used in business today, to plan stockholding and even to manage checkouts.

For two centuries now, social sciences—indeed most sciences—have been overshadowed by the successes of physics. The great physicist Max Planck reportedly said that he had been tempted to take up economics but had concluded it was too hard.[15]

What could Planck have meant? The most remarkable achievements of physics have been with simple systems, such as planetary motion, which can be comprehensively described by two or three variables. Natural sciences have also made great progress in understanding systems where the number of variables—such as molecules or electrons—is large, but where they behave independently or with interactions that can be described by simple rules. The motion of gases and liquids has this character—and so do queues in large supermarkets. But models based on statistical mechanics don't help with the village post office, where the particular behavior of individual customers matters, or with the development of the personal computer industry, where the interactions between firms are complex.

The life of the village post office and the development of the personal computer industry are not simple systems that can be solved analytically. Nor are they characterized by the random complexity that is tractable by statistics. Firms and households interact with each other frequently, and in different and complicated ways. Firms and households are not so large that a model can describe and incorporate their individual idiosyncrasies, nor so small that these idiosyncrasies can be treated as random. The study of economics and business shares these characteristics with other sciences that seem "too hard"—weather systems, movements of the earth's crust, much of biology and medicine. Our knowledge of all these areas of study is still piecemeal and inadequate. Organized complexity[16] is that intermediate area between simple systems and the statistics of random individual behavior.

Meteorologists, biologists, seismologists, and economists have all developed mathematical models of their processes. All have shared the hope that they could use their models to see the future. But meteorological, geological, biological, and economic systems develop in ways that are sensitive to initial conditions.[17] This property has today entered popular discourse under the label *chaos theory*. The idea has been familiar for a long time: "for want of a nail the shoe was lost." In *Sliding Doors,* Gwyneth Paltrow experiences two quite different lives depending on whether she succeeds in entering a subway train before the doors close. Tom Stoppard has the cast of *Arcadia* debate and experience alternative futures. In the most famous metaphor of chaos theory, a butterfly flapping its wings provokes a tornado thousands of miles away and days later.[18]

Systems in which initial conditions affect subsequent behavior indefinitely are path dependent.[19] Path dependency is why the film industry is still based in Hollywood. The design of our computer keyboards is path dependent: the QWERTY layout was devised in the earliest days of typewriting, and although it is ergonomically inefficient, users are familiar with it and the number of QWERTY keyboards and typists is too large to make any change possible.[20] The coevolution of technology and institutions—the development of the social and economic infrastructure of rich states—has been path dependent.

But path dependency in which outcomes are sensitive to small details—the problem of the butterfly and the tornado—is fatal to forecasting. The hopes that were placed in the development of computers and mathematical modeling have been disappointed. Scientists have not been successful in developing models that predict the weather, or volcanic eruptions, more than a few days in advance; that predict earthquakes at all; that anticipate the development of the economy, or the performance of business, for more than a short time ahead; or that tell us how soon we will shake off a cold.

Successful long-range weather forecasting is almost certainly impossible—we will *never* be able to answer questions like "What will the weather be on June 4 next year?"—and the same is true of economic and business forecasting. That is why many fewer resources are now devoted to this kind of meteorology, or to economic forecasting models.

Some scientists have attempted to establish general principles that might be relevant to all problems of organized complexity. The world center for this research is a spin-off from the U.S. nuclear research establishment at Los Alamos, located at Santa Fe in the mountains of New Mexico, and analysis undertaken there goes under the heading of complexity theory.[21] The hope is not to predict the future, but to gain a better understanding of the general properties of complex systems.

We cannot know what the weather will be like next June 4. But meteorologists can give an indication of the average temperature to be expected and the likely range. They can assess the probability of rain and make contingent predictions—it is more likely to be sunny on June 4 if it was sunny on June 3. All this is useful if you are planning a wedding reception on June 4. And that knowledge is considerably more useful than the confident assertion—it will be sunny and the temperature will be sixty-five degrees—that people expect, even demand, from an economic forecaster.

Businesspeople, politicians, and consumers can have the same kind of knowledge—averages, probabilities, contingent predictions—about how the economy will evolve. And this is the only kind of knowledge they can have about how the economy will evolve. People who forecast the level of the stock market next year, or the demand for air transport in 2015, are charlatans.

The Search for Spontaneous Order

Darwin described the behavior of social insects as "by far the most serious special difficulty" for his thesis.[22] Ant colonies cooperate to build nests. They send expeditions to collect and retrieve food with an efficiency that is closer to Sam Walton's Wal-Mart than Khrushchev's Soviet Union. The chemical signals by which ants communicate with each other, and the evolutionary biology that explains their cooperative instincts, are today largely understood.[23]

It is probably not an accident that during the bubble, films were made—such as *Antz* and *A Bug's Life*—that anthropomorphized social insects. The Disney corporation imposed on nature its perception of how the Disney corporation is run. But insect colonies are not like these films. There are no boss ants and no supervisory ants. The queens of colonies do not sit above them directing their activities. They sit below them waiting to be generously fed.[24]

But perhaps the reality of the Disney corporation has some resemblance to the ant colony. The philosopher Alasdair MacIntyre, whom we shall meet again, likens the presidents of large corporations to clergymen praying for rain. The reverse question may really be the more interesting. What can we learn about human organization—such as the coordination of the division of labor in an unplanned economy—from the emergence of spontaneous order in nature?

Imagine a population trying to find higher points on a large, uneven, and unexplored landscape. There are several possible approaches.

One is for everyone to congregate at the highest point yet discovered and to move in a group when plausible evidence of a yet higher point is obtained. This procedure has much in common with central planning. And as with central planning, a good result might possibly be chosen relatively quickly. But the possibility is not large. A more probable outcome is long periods of stasis followed by occasional violent disruptions. And because there is only analysis, not experiment, the process does not naturally generate much information about the scope and scale of the unknown landscape.

Another possible approach is purely individualistic. Everyone searches for higher points in his own immediate locality. This is close to the mechanism of evolution. Steps are chosen at random; if they lead upward, they are maintained, if they lead downward, retraced. No common knowledge is generated, only individual experiences.

And yet another way of dealing with the problem is neither intentionally cooperative or strictly individualistic. The general aim is to find patches of higher ground. Groups that do, encourage others to join them. This is in the interests of both the group and the individuals it attracts: the former gains from more intensive searching, the latter benefit from the experience of the successful group.

This mechanism has a good chance of achieving better results than either of the others. It does so because it strikes a balance between decentralization and coordination. And yet it requires no direction: it is a mechanism that would likely develop spontaneously.

This account follows a model developed by Herbert Simon[n], who studied theories of decision making. Simon's career was devoted to an attack on the picture of rational action in which households and firms define objectives and compute the best means of achieving them. Even if we had such clear objectives, the world is too complex to allow us to achieve them. An instruction to "find the best allocation of scarce resources between competing ends" is, like an instruction to "find the highest point in California," simply not capable of being implemented.[25] The information required to find the highest point on a static landscape is immense; we can do it only because generations of surveyors mapped it. If topography is constantly changing, like the business and economic landscape, the informational task is impossible. Simon asserts that we do not maximize, we satisfy—we follow rules and procedures, like the organization of supermarket queues, that produce results that are good enough.

Simon's example parallels complexity theorist Stuart Kauffman's description of what he calls fitness landscapes.[26] Kauffman is interested in the general mathematical structure of complex systems. Height above sea level in Simon's example might equally be a measure of how well a species is adapted to its environment, or how effectively scarce resources are allocated between competing ends. Kauffman's conjecture is that common models and principles of self-organization describe phenomena as diverse as the emergence of life and the construction of social order.

Complexity theory today occupies a strange, perhaps unique, position within the scientific canon. It has attracted the attention of scientists of exceptional distinction and creativity, yet stands somewhat outside the mainstream of professional knowledge. Economists are particularly skeptical.[27] As I shall describe in chapter 28, the analogy with physics is central to their thinking. The most widely used model of spontaneous order in economics follows the structure of "simple system" physical models. But like the simple system models of modern physicists, it includes many variables and its mathematics is far from simple. This is the model of competitive equilibrium associated with Arrow and Debreu. Part III of this book is devoted to the development of this theory. In Part IV, I will come back to a wider range of ideas about the nature of spontaneous order.

{*part III*}

PERFECTLY COMPETITIVE MARKETS

• • • • • • • • • • • • • • • • • • • •

{12}

Competitive Markets

A perfectly competitive market has sufficiently many buyers and sellers of each commodity that none has much influence over the price. Supply and demand is constructed from the independent decisions of many consumers and many producers. The coordination of these decisions is the extraordinary achievement of market economies.

Perfectly competitive markets require homogeneous commodities. There cannot be a competitive market for *Portrait of Dr. Gachet* because only one original exists (or arguably two). So there can only be one buyer, and one seller. There is not even a competitive market for van Goghs, or master paintings, because there can never be many sellers.

The Colombe d'Or has a unique location. What it offers reflects the particularities, culinary and organizational, of Paul Roux. Coca-Cola has a unique recipe and an unsurpassed brand. Swiss engineering and chemical businesses command high prices for their products because few companies can match their technical skills. These products all face competition, but they are not sold in perfectly competitive markets.

As economies evolve, more and more of the goods and services that are exchanged are idiosyncratic. A little bit of differentiation will not much affect the issue. The Colombe d'Or is unique, but sufficiently many restaurants are like it that the prices on its menu cannot differ much from others in the neighborhood. How much substitution makes a market competitive is a matter of fine judgment. And costly judgment: argument over market definition in antitrust cases has become a lucrative source of employment for economists.[1]

But, even now, many exchanges are of commodity products—goods whose annual production is millions of units that differ little from each other. Such as oil, milk, electricity, and videocassette recorders.

Supply

(a) Oil

Oil was first exploited on a commercial scale in the nineteenth century. Deposits that were easy to find and close to major population centers, such as the oil fields of Ohio, were small and quickly depleted. But much larger quantities of oil were found farther underground. Texas became rich on the productive fields of Spindletop and Corsicana.

The largest accessible deposits of oil today are in the Middle East, particularly in Saudi Arabia. There are also major supplies in Venezuela, Iran, and Russia. The fields there are generally smaller and development more costly, but the methods of exploration and production are mostly routine. The politics may be harder to manage.

The limits of exploration technologies have been extended in Alaska and in deep water. Alaskan temperatures are so low that the ground is permanently frozen and oil cannot easily be piped. The costs of finding and extracting this oil are much higher.

Other oil deposits are even more difficult to tap. There is oil beneath the major oceans, beyond the reach of existing drilling capabilities; at great cost, these capabilities could be extended to make exploitation possible. In the tar sands in Venezuela and at Athabasca in Canada, there is enough oil to satisfy the demands of motorists, airlines, and power stations for decades, even centuries; but the cost of extraction is well above current oil prices.[2] The availability of oil is a commercial rather than a technological question. The reserves of oil that are available at $100 a barrel are many times the reserves available at $10 a barrel. And the more oil is needed, the more of these different sources of supply are required. If the demand for oil were lower, it would be met entirely from the Middle East. As things are, we draw on Alaska and the North Sea, but not the ocean beds or the Athabascan tar sands.[3]

(b) Milk

New Zealand has a wet, temperate climate and more than enough land for 4 million people. New Zealand had no cows until European settlers arrived just over 150 years ago. But today there are more cows than people. New Zealand is ideal dairying country.

The lush grass on which cows thrive is also found in Argentina and Ireland. But costs in these locations are not as low as in New Zealand. Argentina has good dairy land, but it is even better for beef cattle. Ireland's butter is expensive because the European Union's protectionist Common Agricultural Policy means that Irish production is intensive and in small units.[4]

For both oil and milk, we can illustrate how much oil or milk can be produced at what price. If prices are low, only the most accessible oil will be drilled and the best dairy land farmed—Arabian oil, New Zealand dairying. The higher the price, the more extensive the range of producers that will be required.

(c) Electricity

Nuclear power stations are extremely costly to construct and to shut down. But once they have "gone critical"—the nuclear reaction in the core of the plant has begun—they can generate heat and hence electricity more or less continuously with only small additions of uranium. Their operating costs are low. Gas and oil stations are much cheaper to build, but since they must constantly be supplied with fuel, their running costs are higher than those of a nuclear plant. In general, newer stations are more efficient, and older plants are used sparingly. Plants can be labeled according to a merit order—the plant with the lowest running costs at the top, the plant with the highest running costs at the bottom. The more electricity is required, the higher the costs of the plant from which it is generated.[5]

(d) Videocassette Recorders

For oil, milk, and electricity, higher production entails higher cost. The supply curve for a manufactured good like a VCR is different. The first domestic video recorders were manufactured and distributed by Ampex in 1963. They cost $30,000 in Neiman Marcus, and after five years around five hundred had been sold. In the 1970s,

Japanese manufacturers pioneered a consumer market for videocassette recorders.[6]

The more oil or milk is required, the more it costs per liter, because higher-cost production must be employed. But the cost of making video recorders falls as the rate of output increases. It falls because there are economies of scale in their assembly and in the production of components. The cost of making video recorders has also fallen because so many video recorders have been made. Most of the things that could go wrong with video recorders, or in the making of video recorders, have by now gone wrong and been fixed. The accumulated experience of video recorder manufacturers has lowered the cost of production. And steady technological advance has reduced the cost of both components and assembly. These three sources of falling costs—greater annual output, greater cumulative output, and technological advance—can all operate independently of each other, but in practice they have been closely linked.[7]

Demand

(a) Oil

There is a hierarchy of uses and substitution options in the oil business. Airplanes require high-quality kerosene. Automobiles run on gasoline, though we can choose between gas guzzlers and superminis. Cars could run on gas, and less easily on electricity. Electricity generation is a major use of oil, but electricity can also be produced from gas, coal, or nuclear fission. The lower the cost of oil, the further down the list of uses and substitution options consumers go.

(b) Milk

Like oil, milk has a hierarchy of uses. You can do a lot with milk. You can drink it fresh. You can subject it to heat treatment that will keep liquid milk pure, though not nice to drink, for several months. You can make it into butter or cheese. You can turn it into powder, which is cheap and easy to transport. You can turn it into caseinate, which is a form of plastic—your shirt buttons may be made of milk.

And the more milk you have, the more of these things you will do. There is really no substitute for fresh milk, but milk products, such as butter and cheese, do have replacements. The many decreasingly valuable uses for milk—such as in powder for animal feedstuffs or in industrial uses—only occurs when there is oversupply. When there is major oversupply, there are even industrial uses—such as button manufacture—for milk products.

(c) Electricity

It takes a power cut to remind us of the myriad ways we use electricity. It costs two to three cents per hour to power a personal computer. Not many people would prefer a clockwork PC or to switch off their computer to economize on electricity. Computers, televisions, vacuum cleaners are high-value uses for electricity—the cost of the electricity is small relative to the value of the output. But there are plenty of dispensable uses for electricity, such as in electrical space heating, and you really ought to turn off that light.

(d) Videocassette Recorders

The first domestic videocassette recorders were sold in Neiman Marcus to the kind of people who shop at Neiman Marcus. Later, producers developed a consumer market. The evolution of demand followed a common pattern for consumer goods. Prices gradually fell, and the market for the product grew steadily. Demand increased for a bit, but eventually most of those who might ever want to buy a machine had one. Growth fell, and then sales actually declined, sustained only by replacement demand and second purchases.

Matching Supply and Demand for Electricity
• •

Until 1990, the control room of the National Grid received full details of the availability and running costs of all the power stations in England and Wales, which were linked in a single network. Operators were constantly provided with information about actual and expected demand for electricity. As demand varied, they would instruct stations to produce power or to stop. The U.S. electricity grid is much more fragmented, although companies cooperate to reduce costs by trading power and to support each other's networks in the event of systems failures or surges in demand. It was this structure that broke down in the New York blackout of August 2003. The centralized organization of British electricity made a much more extensively integrated system possible.

Demand for electricity is low during the night. Only nuclear stations operate then. As morning approaches, other plants are put on standby. Demand for electricity is usually at its highest in the early morning, when households prepare to go to work at the same time as offices and factories prepare to receive them. As this process builds, more stations are called to produce. In the UK, peak demand for electricity each year usually falls on a cold winter's morning, when users rise reluctantly from bed and additionally turn on a fan heater. There are also freak spikes in demand, as when a commercial break in a popular television program prompts 5 million households to switch on kettles.

Demand for commodities often has a time dimension. Fresh milk needs to be drunk within a few days, and demand for it is stable through the year. But the lactation of cows is not stable. The plentiful milk supplies that are available in spring and summer are used to make butter and cheese. And, if need be, powder and caseinate.

Storing milk is problematic, but storing electricity is almost impossible. A century's technological advance has not come up with a cost-effective battery, and the best way of storing electricity today is to pump water up a hill and let it run down again when you want the power.

The National Grid represented successful central planning. The system that failed so badly in determining the overall direction of the industry worked well at a detailed operational level. This planning system worked because the engineers who controlled it were competent and honest and were supplied with accurate information about operating conditions in all the fifty or so power stations. It helped that the whole network was under the single ownership of the British government.[8] Problems of incentive compatibility had largely been solved.

In 1987, that government decided that it would sell the power stations and end unified ownership and control. This decision seemed perverse to many people in the electricity industry and risked the loss of efficiencies that came from the operation of the merit order. Could another scheme be devised that would do the same job? The government's objective was to find a market mechanism that would preserve the efficiency of the merit order.

The answer was to establish an electricity pool. The owners of each power station would make bids into the pool. Their bid would state the generating capacity they offered, and the price at which they would sell. The engineers of the central control room were replaced by traders, who reviewed the bids. As demand fluctuated, the traders bought supplies just sufficient to meet demand. The highest bid they accepted was called the pool price, and all successful bidders received the pool price.[9]

At first sight, it might seem more appropriate—and cheaper—to pay bidders only the price they had quoted. But the designers of the pool had carefully thought about the issue of incentive compatibility. If the pool paid each bidder its asking price, then the owner of each station would try to guess the maximum the pool would be prepared to pay and would pitch its bid at around that level. Sometimes their guesses would be right, sometimes wrong. On average, the bids would be higher than those made under the pool system. The problem of pool design is similar to the problem of auction design at Christie's and Sotheby's. Under the pool arrangements, it made sense for each station to bid its actual costs. A moment with pencil and paper confirms this property. It is also true, but harder to show, that the pool mechanism is the only system that is incentive compatible.

The Market for Oil
• •

There is a merit order for oil, just as there is a merit order for electricity. Electricity is a special commodity, because even a transitory imbalance between supply and demand is intolerable. But small differences in the supply and the demand for oil can be accommodated for a time without great inconvenience. There is always oil in transit at sea, and it can be stored in tanks and refineries.

So there does not need to be a mechanism in the oil market like the central control room of the National Grid,[10] and there is none. There are large markets for oil in Rotterdam, in Europe, and on NYMEX, in New York. But most oil trading does not take place on any of these exchanges. Oil companies make contracts with each other, and their own subsidiaries, and long-term agreements with producers and customers. But the price in active markets such as Rotterdam or NYMEX is the principal influence on the terms of these trades. The price of oil varies according to quality and its location. Texas crude commands a higher price than oil at Dubai. The market equivalent of leaving a long queue to join a shorter one is called arbitrage: the speculative activity of buying in one market while selling the same commodity in another at a slightly higher price. Where there is more than one market in the same commodity, as for petroleum, arbitrage ensures that prices in all markets are similar, just as activism in the supermarket equalizes waiting times.

In 1973, the Organization of Petroleum Exporting Countries (OPEC) decided to refuse to supply oil except at a much higher price than previously. This disrupted the oil industry's merit order. It stimulated supplies from areas—such as Alaska—outside OPEC's control. In the end, it probably brought little benefit to the OPEC countries.[11] In the meantime it reduced the efficiency of world oil supply.

The pool price in electricity is the price needed to bring forward enough supply to meet demand; the world oil price is also the price needed to bring forward enough supply to meet demand. If the world oil price is $25 per barrel, that is because it needs to be high enough to make exploration in Alaska worthwhile—we need that oil—but not so high that it makes production in Athabasca profitable—we don't need oil that costs that much. At $25 per barrel, however, low-cost supplies—such as those of the Middle East—are very profitable.

The competitive oil market has, without any intervention, the property of incentive compatibility that the government was anxious to create in the electricity pool. The market price—$25 per barrel—is a single price, paid by all buyers and received by all sellers. That common price is less than some buyers would be willing to pay. Most sellers would still be willing to sell their oil at a lower price. The difference between the maximum price a buyer might pay and the market price is called consumer surplus—the buyer's gain from trade. The difference between the minimum price a seller would accept and the market price is called economic rent. It is consumer surplus that makes us happy, and economic rent that makes us rich. I will return to consumer surplus in chapter 19 and economic rent in chapter 25.

The trading arrangements in the electricity market were invented by a government that set out to create a market structure where none had existed before. It is rare for markets to evolve in this way. The oil

Box 12.1

ECONOMIC RENT

A country like Saudi Arabia derives substantial economic rent from its oil supplies because the market price is so far above the cost of Saudi production.

Economic rent is a central economic concept. But the phrase is unfortunate. In everyday language, rent is what we pay for land and buildings. To use the term *economic rent* when we talk of oil is puzzling, and the usage becomes even stranger when applied to Coca-Cola, Madonna, and the Harvard Business School. The explanation is historical. When David Ricardo (the nineteenth-century economist behind the principle of comparative advantage) introduced the concept, the economy was mainly agricultural.

Ricardo's model explained how the rent of land was determined. The land of England could be ordered from best to worst, from the fertile fenlands of Lincolnshire to the acid moors of Dartmoor. The price of corn would determine the margin of cultivation—a graphic term to describe land at the frontier, which was barely worth bringing into production. However low were grain prices, it would be worth planting in Lincolnshire; however high, it would not be sensible to sow corn on Dartmoor. But the margin of cultivation would move back and forward between these extremes. The swings in grain prices experienced during the Napoleonic wars made the issue very real in 1817. Land outside the margin of cultivation earns no rent. It is not worth cultivating and, like Dartmoor, usually not cultivated. The rent of productive land is equal to and determined by its competitive advantage over land at the margin of cultivation.

Ricardo's framework is powerful and general and can be applied to the rewards earned by any scarce factor—not just Saudi oil or Lincolnshire land, but the competitive advantages of businesses and the talents of individuals. The receipt and allocation of economic rent is a central determinant of the distribution of income in modern economies. But perfectly competitive markets have few economic rents, because the assumption of many buyers and sellers of every commodity ensures that few factors are scarce.

market was not invented: it emerged as the world oil business evolved. Most markets emerged spontaneously to match scarce resources to competing ends. Some emerged centuries ago.

The Market for Flowers

If you drive across the border into Italy from the French Riviera, you reach the Autostrada dei Fiori—the motorway of flowers. The hillsides along the Ligurian coast are covered with plastic and glass. The flowers are transported each morning to the market at San Remo.

The market is a stunning spectacle. Full of color and the babble of excited Italian traders. Tens of thousands of blooms change hands every day. The price of each kind of flower can change in the course of the morning if supply and demand are not in balance. Prices vary as particular flowers move in and out of season. At periods of exceptional demand, such as Christmas and Easter, prices rise across the board.

If no one has much influence over the price in a competitive market, how is the price determined? In one sense, prices are not fixed at all. No coordinating mechanism, like the control room of the National Grid, balances supply and demand in the San Remo flower market. Nor does any agency determine the price of different blooms. The municipal market rents space to traders and regulates their behavior, but that is all. Just as in the public marketplaces of ancient Greece.

Within the apparent chaos, the noise and bustle of the San Remo market, a spontaneous order is formed every day. At the beginning of the morning, flowers arrive from a thousand locations along the coast. At its end, they are on their way to an even larger number of destinations across Europe. The assortment in arriving trucks matches the production of individual growers. The assortment in leaving trucks matches the requirements of individual florists.

There are only prices for individual transactions, and yet there is a typical price, a market price that equates supply and demand. In the oil market, the reports of the Petroleum Argus are regarded as definitive of oil prices. San Remo does not have even that degree of formality. Traders in similar products are generally grouped together. This enables them to keep an eye on each other's prices and each other's stocks. They know that they will not sell much if their prices are above their competitors', and they also know that they must dispose of their stock by the end of the morning.

Most traders attend the market every day and use their experience to judge the level of stocks and the strength of demand. They judge each other too: some traders will be particularly influential. A market price for each bloom emerges from the balance of supply and demand, but an experienced trader will leave with a slightly higher average price for his flowers, and a skilled buyer will pay slightly less. Knowledge of other flower markets will be helpful, but not very helpful. It is local experience that is really valuable.

Yet you will not do badly as a first-time trader in San Remo if you simply keep an eye on what other people are doing and buy or sell at the going price. Others will nudge the price up, or down, in response to supply and demand. These more experienced traders will do better than you. But not much. The spontaneous order of the San Remo market is similar to the spontaneous order of the supermarket queue.

In the supermarket, a few activists who watch the length of neighboring queues determine waiting times. At San Remo, similar activism by skilled traders determines the price. Their skill and experience is specific to the San Remo flower market. None of them have any extensive knowledge of the factors that determine supply and demand in European horticulture, or even of other flower markets, such as those in Holland.[12]

Many other markets function like this. In some—such as markets for airplanes or ships—there are brokers. Brokers are professional watchers of the market. They advise a buyer or a seller about the price to expect. They will put buyers and sellers in touch with each other. Brokers normally live by charging commissions on deals they facilitate. Sometimes brokers become market makers, who risk their own capital by buying in the expectation of selling later on at a profit, as in the used-car market.[13]

Trading at San Remo is about as close to a perfectly competitive market as we find. No individual buyer or seller has much influence over the price. And trading at San Remo is also close to being incentive compatible. There is rarely much to be gained by strategic behavior. If you want to buy a lot of flowers, you would be unwise to walk into the market and announce it. But subtle ways of beating the market are hard to devise and likely to backfire. And concern for reputation with fellow traders also encourages incentive compatibility. If one wants to visit the market again, or simply live happily on the Riviera dei Fiori, one will probably want to bear that in mind.

Virtual Markets

Once, almost all competitive markets had physical locations, like the San Remo flower market. There are still markets like this. The largest physical market in the world is at Rungis, on the outskirts of Paris, where millions of dollars' worth of fresh produce are transported in and out every morning, and which replaced Les Halles in the center of the city. The last of Manhattan's traditional produce markets—the Fulton Fish Market in lower Manhattan—is, like other markets in other cities, moving to a less central location. Used cars are bought and sold in auctions around the country. Local cattle and grain markets have existed for centuries.

These markets were social as well as economic events. The social context of the market supported its economic function by establishing personal relationships and facilitating the exchange of information. Less than fifty years ago, dockworkers would be hired daily by employers who matched the supply of labor to the number of ships in port. But with decasualization of dock labor, the last markets in which workers were bought and sold like physical commodities were closed. Spot markets in labor are now more or less dead, although, as at Thomas Hardy's Casterbridge, the annual meetings of the American Economic Association incorporate a hiring fair at which young Ph.D.'s parade before their prospective Bathshebas.

Many markets are securities markets: traders buy and sell paper that confers the right to physical commodities, rather than the commodities themselves. So it is possible to trade even if you do not actually own the oil you sell or want the oil you buy. Trade on these exchanges is in standard contracts, such as "a barrel of Texas crude."

The market for pigs became a market for pork bellies, and you would not be welcomed to the Chicago Mercantile Exchange if you brought along the commodities you proposed to sell. But there was still a place where buyers and sellers met.

The assumption that markets would have a physical location

changed with the invention of the telephone, which made it easy for people who were not in the same place to negotiate deals. But communication by telephone was one to one. Only with the development of modern electronic systems was it possible to secure access to information about other trades and other traders—the access that San Remo traders enjoy by watching each other—without an actual physical meeting place.

If you turn to the inside pages of the *Wall Street Journal,* you find lists of prices in literally hundreds of markets. The price of electricity, milk, and oil. The price of coffee, copper, and pork bellies. Prices in securities markets. Bonds and foreign currencies. You can even trade the risk of a cold winter or a Japanese earthquake.[14]

Today, electronic trading has taken over most of these markets. What were once busy, jostling trading floors are now eerie, empty museum pieces. A "trading floor" is no longer an exchange in which buyers and sellers clamor for each other's attention. It is home to rows of screens on which traders tap their orders. The habit of dealing in big rooms remains—because the marketplace still requires the exchange of information as well as the exchange of commodities. But today these big rooms are the private property of organizations such as Goldman Sachs and Morgan Stanley, not the collective property of the New York Stock Exchange or NYMEX. These traders deal with their counterparts in other, similar rooms.

At the height of Internet mania, it was widely asserted that most trading would soon be electronic. Electronic trading works well for standardized commodities in perfectly competitive markets. One dollar is much the same as any other dollar. But to trade remotely, you need to know exactly what it is you are buying and must rely on the reputation of the other party, or to know that some exchange or intermediary will guarantee performance.

So it is hard to imagine that San Remo will go electronic. Wholesale buyers of flowers or meat or fish will want to see what they are buying, because making these assessments is a key business skill. It was possible, if demeaning, to buy and sell dock labor in a marketplace because what was bought and sold was—literally—a pair of hands. But even there employers knew that some workers were stronger or more reliable and branded others as troublemakers. Almost every technological and institutional development in a modern economy is toward greater differentiation of products. In chapter 19, I will discuss how this changes things.

Rigging Competitive Markets
● ●

No trader has significant influence on price in a perfectly competitive market. All traders wish they could have significant influence on price. In 1979, a fabulously rich Texas family, the Hunts, tried to take control of the world market for silver. For a time, they succeeded in raising the price substantially, and people queued to melt down their family heirlooms. But in the end their billions of dollars were not enough to establish a monopoly, and the price of silver (and the Hunt family fortune) collapsed.[15]

Governments frequently intervene in securities markets to try to influence the price of their own bonds or their own currency's exchange rate. Since central banks can print money, it might seem that their influence on markets would always be decisive. If politicians were willing to make absolute and unlimited commitments, this might be true. But they rarely are. The International Tin Council was established by governments of tin producing and consuming countries with the good intention of aiding poor tin producers and stabilizing their receipts.[16] The council ran out of money with which to buy tin and entered into forward commitments[17] to buy still more tin. Seeing a growing black hole, the member governments refused to provide money to enable the council to honor its contracts, and the council and the tin price collapsed. The diamond market, managed for decades by De Beers, is almost the only commodity market in which a trader has successfully influenced the price over an extended period.[18]

On "Black Wednesday" in 1992, the financier George Soros gambled that he could borrow more sterling to exchange for foreign currencies than the British government would be willing to buy to support its own exchange rate. Soros won his bet, and Britain was forced to leave the European Monetary System.

But not all government interventions fail. The Asian crisis hit all securities markets in 1997. The Hong Kong Monetary Authority knew that its financial system was stronger than those of its neighbors and bought shares on the Hong Kong stock exchange. The authority sold these shares subsequently at a substantial profit (much of it derived from Soros and another speculator, Julian Robertson).

After this debacle, Soros and Robertson announced their retirements from fund management and returned money to their investors.[19] But even the Chinese government blinked. It decided it had risked enough, withdrew market support, and allowed prices (temporarily) to fall.[20]

The complex structure of the British electricity pool was intended to reproduce the efficiencies of the planning system—the merit order—by an incentive compatible mechanism in a competitive market. The scheme would probably have worked if each of the fifty or so power stations had been under separate ownership. But the government's restructuring of the industry did not go so far. Most of the key stations were owned by two firms, which quickly discovered that they could keep prices high by putting in bids above the cost of production. The outcomes were not incentive compatible or efficient, and electricity prices were higher than they need have been. In 2001 the pool was scrapped and replaced by arrangements much more similar to those of the world oil market.[21]

Incentive compatibility is a key objective of a market economy and a specific objective of the electricity pool. But only perfectly competitive markets achieve full incentive compatibility. Once sellers or buyers are sufficiently large for their behavior to influence the price, they begin to behave strategically.

Yield Management
● ●

In perfectly competitive markets, the price that equates supply and demand emerges through spontaneous order as at San Remo. In markets that are less than perfectly competitive, a seller decides what price to charge. Balancing supply and demand becomes a business objective, rather than the outcome of a decentralized process. One of the most sophisticated such markets is the market for airline seats.

Airlines have more or less the same number of planes and seats available every day. Once they have decided the size of their fleet, their capacity is fixed. But demand varies widely. Empty seats on planes are as useless and as unprofitable as flowers left wilting when the San Remo market is closed. But San Remo is a competitive market, in which no one fixes the price. Airlines face only a few competitors. They have sophisticated computer packages—yield management systems—designed to enable them to monitor the balance between supply and demand. These systems are fed basic information—when Easter falls, the date of the Super Bowl, what happened last year. The objective is not to fill the plane, but to maximize revenue from the flight. An airline would rather have some empty seats than a planeful of passengers all on discounted tickets. It hopes to sell seats at high prices to business passengers in a hurry and at lower prices to price-sensitive tourists. Many cheap fares require you to stay a Saturday night. The airline does not care where you spend your Saturday, but business travelers would usually prefer to spend it at home and tourists at their holiday destination. As I write this, I know that the Super Bowl will be held in Houston on February 1, 2004. I know, and airlines know, that demand for tickets for that weekend will be heavy. Even today, a flight to Houston will cost more around that weekend than on a normal day.

But some cities are more relevant than others. Last year's contestants, Oakland and Tampa Bay, are hot contenders this year, so flights from the Bay Area and Florida will be especially expensive. Airlines monitor odds in the betting market to set their fares.

Spontaneous order—the disciplined and effective matching of buyers and sellers that emerges from the apparent chaos of the San Remo flower market—is often found in competitive markets, in which products are homogeneous and market trading is fragmented. Once products become differentiated, and sellers have sufficient market share to influence price, the problem of setting price and managing demand is very different, and more complex. And coordination may actually be more difficult to achieve, as anyone who has experienced an overbooked flight knows.

Oil and milk, electricity and VCRs, flowers and airlines seats, are typical commodities bought and sold in competitive markets. But these are not what Bloomberg television means by "the markets." The traders whom they serve deal in risk and in money. The very particular markets for these commodities are the subject of the next two chapters.

{13}

Markets in Risk

From the Rialto to the North Sea

The Merchant of Venice stood on the Rialto, waiting nervously for his ships to return to Venice. In the city, Shylock sharpened his knife in anticipation of a pound of Antonio's flesh. Only later in the Venetian Republic was marine insurance invented. This enabled the risks faced by merchants to be spread over many individuals. All could sleep easily in their beds, knowing that no single event could expose them to perils as grave as Antonio's. The market was developed further in Edward Lloyd's coffeehouse in the City of London. Lloyd's of London is still a center of the marine insurance market today.

Several hundred years afterward, Hurricane Hugo hit the South Carolina coast in September 1989. The fishing village of McClellanville, halfway between Charleston and Georgetown, was flattened by eighteen-foot waves and 140 mile per hour winds, and the devastation extended to the neighboring cities and some way inland. It was the most costly natural disaster in U.S. history, although that record was to last only three years, until Hurricane Andrew struck Florida in 1992.

About 20% of the $9 billion of insurance claims that followed Hurricane Hugo fell directly or indirectly on the Lloyd's insurance market, the leading provider against catastrophes of this kind. But the greater catastrophe fell on Lloyd's itself. In the traditional structure of the insurance market, an individual or group of individuals agreed to take a share of the risk. They signified their agreement by signing their names to the proposal (underwriting). But the market had grown more complex and sophisticated since Venetian times. Insurers commonly reinsured their risks.

Reinsurance means that another insurer agrees to meet a share of a claim when it exceeds an agreed sum. The reinsurer acts as insurer of an insurer. A different form of reinsurance was known as an excess of loss policy. If the total losses from all claims, whatever their origins, became too great, another insurer would pay the balance.

The size of the claims from Hurricane Hugo meant that they cascaded round the market. The first claims were directly related to reimbursing those who had lost their houses or their boats. But then, through reinsurance, and excess of loss policies, many more insurance claims at Lloyd's were triggered by the losses of the primary insurers. The total value of claims at Lloyd's arising from Hurricane Hugo was many times the original claims of $1.5 billion, and the vast majority of these were claims by one insurer against another. Insurers who had written excess of loss policies for other insurers had, without knowing it, insured against Hurricane Hugo over and over again. Far from spreading risks over many people, the insurance market had concentrated them on a few.

The curious shareholding structure of Lloyd's made the consequences particularly dramatic. Participants (names at Lloyd's) did not actually subscribe capital but agreed to meet their share of losses or receive their share of profits, as required. This scheme had particular attractions for the decaying English aristocracy, and the social cachet that resulted persuaded other individuals, such as sporting celebrities, who had more money than knowledge of weather conditions in South Carolina, to take part. Many of these individuals were bankrupted by Hurricane Hugo and a series of other disasters that occurred coincidentally in the late 1980s.

Something about this story is very odd. Early markets in risk—marine insurance—enabled vulnerable individuals to spread and share their risks.[1] Centuries later, when markets had become more developed, more sophisticated, and more costly, they operated in just the opposite way. Much of the risk associated with Hurricane Hugo was transferred from organizations well able to bear it—U.S. primary insurers and utilities such as Duke Power and Florida Light—to vulnerable individuals who were quite incapable of knowing what the risks were or dealing with them when they hit. In chapter 20, I will try to resolve the puzzle.

Markets in Risk

The economic approach to uncertainty sees risk as a commodity like any other. There are natural calamities whose consequences we cannot easily avoid. Events like adverse weather, or the onset of disease. But our economic and social organization manufactures risks, as it manufactures other commodities. Business necessarily involves the risk of accident at work, the risk of unemployment, the risk that a venture will fail. Risks can be bought and sold, so that every risk has its market and its market price. Trading risks may yield gains from exchange, for the same reasons as other trades yield gains from exchange—differences in preferences associated with differences in capabilities and benefits from specialization.

Some people like taking risks and others don't, just as some people like apples and others don't. The risks in your life may not be risks you want to hold, as the apples that fall in your orchard may not be the fruit you want to eat. Capacity to bear risk varies. The richer you are, the better placed you are to face the risk of a given loss. These differences in appetite for risk are differences in capabilities. Some people have professional skills in the measurement and evaluation of risk—benefits from specialization.

There are also benefits from trading risks if you can offset a risk to which you are already exposed. If Nike decides to have its shoes manufactured in Indonesia, the contractor and its employees will expect to be paid in rupiah. In recent years the value of the rupiah has experienced violent fluctuations against the dollar. But other traders in Indonesia will plan to import goods whose price is fixed in dollars. Hedging enables both parties to reduce the risks to which they are exposed. Enron played a large role in establishing markets in weather derivatives, which enabled traders, especially energy companies, to hedge against unexpected fluctuations in weather. People who would benefit from high temperatures—ice cream manufacturers—could trade with people who suffered from them—sellers of heating products.

Trading on Differences in Risk Assessment
● ●

But most of the trades in risk markets are not the result of different tolerances for risk, the need to spread a risk, or the opportunity to hedge. Most people who trade risks do so because they think they have made a better assessment of the risk than others.

The University of Iowa maintains an electronic marketplace,[2] designed to illustrate the ways in which risk markets respond to the different assessments made, and information held, by different individuals. The market focuses on political events, such as the presidential election of 2000.

There was a market in shares of the popular vote, and a market in the result. Suppose you wanted to back Bush, and the market price of Bush was 47. If you bought Bush in the "share of the popular vote" market, and Bush secured 49% of the popular vote, then you would gain two dollars for every share of Bush you held, just as you would gain two dollars for every share of Microsoft you bought at 47 and sold at 49. Conversely, if Bush won only 44%, you would lose three dollars per share. If you expect Bush to win, Bush is a good buy at 47.

In the market on the result, you would gain 100 if Bush won, but if he lost, you would, like him, lose everything. If you can buy Bush in this market at 47, then the odds are slightly better than even: if your runner wins, you get back just over twice what you put down.

Iowa taxpayers will be relieved to learn that the university does not fix the prices or itself take views on the likely outcome: it simply maintains the market. If there are more buyers of Bush at 47 than there are sellers, then the price will rise until supply and demand are equalized.

Prices in the electronic marketplace reflect the information and assessments of the different participants. In November 2000, the average of these assessments judged—correctly—that the race was extremely close but that Bush had the advantage. On the day before the poll, Bush closed at 52 in the share-of-the-vote market and Gore at 48. In the market for the result, however, Bush stood at 72 and Gore at 27. Recall that in the results market, you get 100 if Bush wins and you have backed Bush, but zero otherwise. A bookmaker would describe this as odds of 5–2 on Bush, 3–1 against Gore. But these judgments represented the average of the opinions of all traders, weighted by the amount of money they had; different participants each had their own, individual opinions about the result, and this disagreement made trade possible.

The difference between the prices in the share-of-the-vote market and the result market is the product of the all-or-nothing character of democratic politics: a small margin translates into a large difference in outcome. No election has ever demonstrated this as dramatically as the contest between Bush and Gore. I will return to the wider implications of this nonlinear character of many social systems in chapter 28.

Prices in the electronic marketplace had fluctuated in the run up to the vote as the fortunes of the candidates waxed and waned. In the share-of-the-vote market, the variations were comparatively small, but in the result market, they had been much larger. In the Iowa market, as in a securities market, you can always close out your position: if you think that the odds on Bush have risen by more than the change in outlook justifies, you can sell your Bush position. The market price reflects the fluctuating balance of average opinion.

The idea that risk markets reveal the information held by knowledgeable participants reached a fanciful extreme three years later, when some policy analysts at the Defense Department proposed a market in terrorist incidents. Al Qaeda and its accomplices, so the theory went, were unlikely to resist the temptation to turn knowledge of their impending activities to profit, rather as corporate executives might (unless threatened by legislation) trade their insider knowledge for cash. In this way, the market could do a better job of surveillance than the CIA. This idea appears to have been taken seriously for some time before being squashed by Deputy Secretary Wolfowitz in the face of political opposition.[3]

In tune with the topsy-turvy election in 2000, the players in the Iowa electronic marketplace got the result both right and wrong. The result market paid out—to those who had backed Gore. The rules declare as winner the candidate with a plurality of the popular vote and take no account of the activities of the electoral college or the Supreme Court.

Bookmakers, like the University of Iowa, try to avoid taking positions on the races they cover because they know, even if their punters do not, that backing horses is usually a mug's game. In financial markets, it is much more common for the banks, securities houses, and others who make markets to form their own views on the likely movements in the assets in which they deal. Most financial institutions believe this activity is profitable for them, even after estimating the costs of the exposures they run, and perhaps this is true.

Enron began as market maker but became an increasingly important energy trader. These trading activities seem not to have been as profitable as Enron executives hoped, or shareholders wanted to believe. Failing to make profits in its business, the company adopted complex accounting devices to manufacture them. The collapse of the company in November 2001 was the largest corporate bankruptcy in history.

When people trade because one has a greater ability to bear the risk than the other, the exchange is mutually beneficial. As it was for Braque and Roux. As it is for San Remo flower traders or those who buy and sell in the electricity pool. But transactions in markets based on differences in the perception of the same situation by different people are not like that. One party's gain is the other's loss. We never know in advance who will lose and who will gain. The answer will be clearer, though not always certain, with hindsight.[4]

Efficient Markets
● ●

The efficiency of perfectly competitive markets is the subject of chapter 16. In risk markets the term *market efficiency* has a specific, and narrow, technical meaning. Efficiency describes how the market assimilates information about the risks that are being traded. Horses have "form," which is reported in detail in the sporting press. Punters often believe they have special knowledge about particular horses; sometimes this is true, mostly it is not.

Companies file accounting records. Their share-price histories are available from services like Bloomberg and Reuters. Analysts describe reports on the outlook for individual shares. Economic prospects for different countries are described in many public documents. Some traders believe they are particularly well-informed about the activities of other traders. Some analysts believe they have insights into businesses or economies that are denied to others. Sometimes this is true, mostly it is not.

The efficient market hypothesis is that all this information forms the background to the risk assessment of market traders, and all these assessments are weighted and incorporated in the market price of an uncertain event. All available information about a risk is already reflected in the price of the associated security.

In an efficient market, it is pointless to act on the basis of information such as "Seabiscuit put in a strong finish in his last race," "GE has excellent management," "demand for mobile phones will continue to grow," or "Dr. Greenspan is an outstanding chairman of the Federal Reserve Board." These observations are well-known, have influenced other people's assessments, and are "in the price." They are the reasons why the odds on Seabiscuit are short, the price of General Electric shares is high, mobile phone companies trade at large multiples of their current earnings, and the dollar is strong.

There is powerful evidence to support the efficient market hypothesis. The theory predicts that the prices of risks will follow a "random walk." A random walk is a process in which the next step is equally likely to be in any direction. Many physical processes have these characteristics, such as the movement of particles in liquids. This is an area where models derived from statistical mechanics seem to work, and the Black-Scholes model described below is grounded in the analysis of physical systems. And numerous statistical analyses of prices in markets for securities and commodities have confirmed that they display the characteristics of a random walk. In an early test of the theory, the statistician Maurice Kendall discovered that all but one of the series he studied fitted the random walk prediction.[5] It emerged that the one that did not was not in fact a series of actual market transactions but had been prepared as an average of estimated market prices. This is the kind of satisfying confirmation of a theory that physicists often experience but is rarely available in the social sciences.

The efficient market hypothesis invites a skeptical view of claims of the ability of experts to make money themselves—and even more, perhaps, of their ability to make money for other people—by trading risks. This skepticism is more readily applied to racing tipsters than to professional investment managers. Still, there are grounds for applying it to both. On average, investment managers do not outperform a random choice of stocks, and the past outperformance of such managers is a poor guide to their future success.[6]

Derivatives

●●●

In insurance markets, securities exchanges, betting shops, one person sells a risk to another. Derivative markets enable risks to be divided, packaged, and repackaged. If Antonio's ship was loaded with a cargo of cloves, Antonio incurred at least three risks—loss of the ship, delay to the ship, and fluctuations in the price of cloves. Different people might be better placed to assess and assume these different components of Antonio's overall risk. A marine engineer might assess the stability of the hull, a meteorologist could calculate the state of the tides, and a spice merchant would be well-informed about supply and demand for cloves.

Or there might be a market in participations in Antonio's venture. This would give the holder a share in the overall profit or loss. The value of this share would be determined by external events as well as Antonio's shrewdness as a businessman. But this primary market could also give rise to many derivative markets. There might be separate markets for insurance against loss and insurance against delay. Antonio might agree to sell his cloves, when they arrive in three months' time, at a price agreed today. This is a forward contract, of the type that the International Tin Council failed to honor. Or Antonio might make a contract under which he will receive a minimum price for his cloves even if the market price has fallen (a put option). If only he had bought such insurance, and a forward contract or a put, he could have slept comfortably at night knowing that he had secured the certain ability to repay Shylock's bond.

Excess of loss insurers of Hurricane Hugo had given a put option to the primary syndicates, which would cap their losses at a fixed sum. A call option gives the right, but not the obligation, to buy something in future at a price fixed in the contract today. If you buy a call, you benefit from price rises but are not exposed to price falls. Of course, you pay a price for either a put or a call option.

Modern portfolio theory—the mathematical analysis of risk markets—was developed at the University of Chicago from the 1950s to the 1970s. In 1973, Fischer Black and Myron Scholes[n] developed a model that allowed derivatives to be precisely valued.[7] The theory was quickly adopted on Wall Street, and the range of derivative securities grew in range and complexity. Derivative markets allow risks to be packaged and repackaged. They enable people to assemble portfolios of risks that meet their own specializations, differences in preferences, and differences in capabilities. They also allow people to gamble on the belief that their own assessments of risks, different from the market average, are correct.

Financial market theory—the theory of risk markets—is the jewel in the crown of business economics. "There is no other proposition in economics which has more solid empirical evidence supporting it than the Efficient Market Hypothesis."[8] The theory combines technical sophistication with immediate practical application. In the 1990s, its practitioners—often described as rocket scientists—were sought after for highly paid jobs in securities houses. Yet all is not entirely well with this theory, and the self-confidence of its practitioners is diminishing. I return to this in chapter 20.

{14} •••••••••••••••••••••••••••

Markets in Money

Market economies trade flowers. They trade electricity. They trade risks. They also trade money itself. Money is different from these other commodities because it has no intrinsic worth. Money is the unit of account in which we keep score and the medium of exchange by which we measure the price of everything else.

But there are many different units of account and mediums of exchange: dollars and euros, Australian dollars and Singapore dollars, pesos and zlotys. So we trade one money against another—dollars for euros. Money is also a store of value: we need money tomorrow as well as money today. We buy and sell different currencies in foreign exchange markets; we exchange money at different dates in money markets.

In chapter 4, I described how comparisons between countries could be made using either market exchange rates or purchasing power parities, which compare the cost of buying the same bundle of goods in different countries. If it costs less than a dollar in another country to buy goods that cost a dollar in the United States, then people will tend to do exactly that. Market exchange rates cannot therefore vary by too much, or for too long, from purchasing power parity.

And they do not. The numbers in Table 4.8 show the cost of buying in dollars, in other countries, the goods that would have cost you one dollar in the United States. Most of them are not very different from one dollar. And if, in 2001, you had looked at the data in Table 4.8 and bought the currencies with figures below one and sold those above it, most of your trades would have made money.

However, before you act on this discovery, you should bear in mind several complicating factors. A foreign exchange rate, like a price on the Iowa Electronic Market, is an average of the opinions of market participators. These opinions change continuously and may be driven by sentiment rather than by any economic reality. Although the signal given by Table 4.8—that most European currencies were undervalued in 2001—was indeed correct, the undervaluation was to become even more marked before it was reversed.

Since currencies are held as an asset, as well as to buy goods and services in foreign countries, this portfolio demand and supply will also influence their price. Individuals—and countries, particularly in Asia— hold large dollar balances; because the United States imports much more than it exports, many dollar assets are held outside the United States, particularly by Asian countries. And the Federal Reserve and other agencies can influence the supply and demand for currencies.

And, as explained in chapter 4, trade across borders will not necessarily equalize prices: while most manufactured goods can be traded without physical or legal restriction, many services are much more difficult to trade. You can't shift property across borders, and it wouldn't be the same commodity if you did. So countries like Canada and Australia have exchange rates that are persistently below their purchasing power parity, while the Swiss franc and Norwegian krone trade persistently above it.

Money Markets

● ●

Antonio was waiting nervously because he had guaranteed Shylock's loan to Bassanio. The purpose of the most famous of all loans was to finance Bassanio's profligacy rather than Antonio's business. In Shakespeare's time the normal purpose of lending was to allow such overspending. Antonio draws a sharp distinction between participating in a venture and lending at interest.[1] That distinction lay behind the Christian prohibition of interest, which survives in other religions, and restricted money lending to excluded groups, such as Jews. In time, governments became the main profligates.

The substantive loan was from Tubal, a rich coreligionist of Shylock's, to Bassanio, a friend of Antonio's. Bassanio could not borrow directly because his credit was poor. Tubal did not lend directly because

he was not in the business of identifying and assessing credits. Interme-
diation was essential. Transactions between Antonio and Bassanio, and
between Shylock and Tubal, were relatively straightforward because of
their social relationships. The transaction between Antonio and Shylock required notarization and security, and that was what caused all
the trouble.

In a money market, traders buy and sell money tomorrow, money
in five years' time, money in twenty-five years' time. The price of
future money is generally expressed as an annual rate of return. On
the day I am writing this, the price of $1 tomorrow is 99.99 cents
today. This is an annual rate of interest of just over 1%. The price
today of $1 in twenty-five years time is around 35 cents.

As in any other market, price is determined by supply and demand.
The overnight rate is volatile. Who borrows money tonight for repayment tomorrow? Mostly banks and businesses, which daily undertake
large numbers of financial transactions and need to balance their
books. But long-term interest rates are much more stable. Borrowers
for five or twenty-five years are households buying long-lived assets,
like cars or houses, and companies that need to finance working capital or new investment.

The supply of capital comes from people who have more money
than they need, or who want to save for their retirement, their descendants, or a rainy day. The activities of intermediaries obscure this. We
see Shylock trade with Antonio, but the underlying transaction is
between Tubal and Bassanio. And as with Tubal, the supply comes
from individual savings; as with Bassanio, demand comes from overspending and investment by households, businesses, and governments.

The supply of capital is not very sensitive to its price. Interest rates
do not have a large effect on how much we want or need to save; they
may have more effect on how much we are *able* to save, or spend,
because the cost of long-term borrowings such as mortgages varies.

Demand is very different. Much investment is insensitive to interest rates. But many households, most businesses, and all governments have a supply of long-term projects that they could undertake
if capital were sufficiently plentiful. Keynes once looked forward to
an era in which more or less everything that could be built had been
built.[2] But this seems fantasy. New technology creates new invest-

ment opportunities. We pull down the old and build anew. Many offices built in the 1960s have already been demolished.

As a result, the price of capital—its long-term rate of return—never goes much below 2%, or much above 4% or so. I explain below what these figures mean and how they are calculated.

Banks

• •

Capital markets match people who have money, like Tubal, with people who need it, like Bassanio. This matching is like dating, but riskier. If you want to lend, you must find a borrower; if you want to borrow, you must find a lender. You must judge the quality of your partner—more important for lenders than borrowers. And you have to explore whether you are each willing to commit for the same period of time.

Banks solve all these problems. You don't have to seek a rich lender, or an indigent borrower: you go to the bank. The bank judges the creditworthiness of its borrowers. As Tubal, you lend to Shylock rather than Bassanio and rely on Shylock's credit rather than Bassanio's. Since the bank has many borrowers and many lenders, it can allow you to withdraw your money without having to call in a loan ahead of time.

The first banks were established by rich individuals, and the banks' reputations reflected their personal wealth and standing. In time, the credit of the bank reflected the reputation of the institution rather than its partners. Even today banks bear names that preserve the memory of their founders—Chase, Morgan—or the grandeur of their pretensions—the Bank of America, Nationsbank—and have extravagant banking halls. They want to convince you that they will be there when you want your money back.

Banks discovered that if their credit was sufficiently strong, they could issue promises in excess of their readily available resources (or even their total resources). Antonio did not lend Bassanio the money himself because he did not have it. His ships were at sea or, as he subsequently discovered, at the bottom of it. Antonio instead gave Shylock a guarantee. Banks could issue guarantees without expecting more than a proportion of them to be called.

The banknote originated as a bank's promise to pay. And since people were confident of the bank's promise, its notes, as valuable as gold or silver but more convenient, circulated widely. Every aspect of economic life came to depend on these promises being honored. From the earliest days of market economies, governments monitored the solvency and integrity of banks and limited their power to issue notes. The right to issue notes was profitable, and the risks of unregulated issue were large. Eventually note issue became a state monopoly.

But even government cannot be trusted with the power to print money. In 1863, the Union armies won a curious victory when they captured the Confederacy's printing press. Much more recently, the Zimbabwe "government" suffered from a shortage of foreign exchange to buy paper and ink to print banknotes.[3] The gravest currency depreciation in history was engineered by the German government in 1923–24 as part of a dispute over the settlement of World War I reparations. The resulting inflation wiped out the savings of many middle-class Germans and helped pave the road for Hitler.

The Federal Reserve Board, which was established in its present form after the Great Depression, is an independent agency that maintains the state monopoly of monetary instruments and policies but is insulated from day-to-day political control. Political independence was enshrined in the constitution of the Deutsche Bundesbank, which succeeded the currency board established in the western zones of Germany in 1948, and this is increasingly widely seen as the best solution. This model was followed in 1999 when its powers were subsumed by the European Central Bank, which administers the currency for the twelve European countries that use the euro.

Central banks control the supply of money and the level of short-term interest rates. But long-term rates of return are still determined by the balance between the supply and demand for capital. Someone needs to own all the houses, offices, and other buildings in the world, and all the assets of global businesses. And these assets are ultimately the total wealth of private individuals—the property companies, insurance companies, and other institutions that appear on the ownership registers are all really you and me (and Bill Gates and a few others). Long-term interest rates equate the supply and demand for all these assets. In this context, even the U.S. government is small. When the Federal Reserve Board cut short-term interest rates from 6% to 1.75% in 2001, one of the most dramatic cuts in history, long-term interest rates moved hardly at all.

Bonds

Short-term interest rates are largely determined by the world's governments. Long-term interest rates are determined by the under-lying supply and demand for capital. The link between short and long rates is called the term structure of interest rates (Figure 14.1). It is compiled by looking at rates of interest in the bond market.

Banks match borrowers and lenders and allow lenders to get their money back before the borrowers repay. Bonds are another means of handling the same problem. The bond market is a second-ary market, in which the right to receive repayment of a loan can be sold to someone else.

Figure 14.1

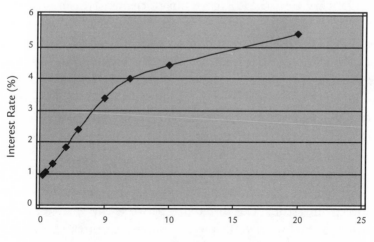

U.S. Treasury Yield Curve (September 30, 2003)

SOURCE: U.S. Treasury (Web site)

The price of a bond in this secondary market will not necessarily be the same as the original amount of the loan. The credit risk may have changed. You can today buy the debt of many telecom companies for less than half its repayment value: these companies borrowed extravagantly and many people are now skeptical of their ability to repay.

A bond gets younger every day. A twenty-year bond, sold after fifteen years, is effectively a five-year bond. Its price will be similar to the price of new five-year bonds. If it is not, then arbitrage between the two types of bond will bring prices into line. If interest rates fall, existing bonds become more valuable; if interest rates rise, they fall in price.

People buy bonds, or make deposits, because they want money tomorrow rather than today. But what they really want tomorrow is not money, but the things that money can buy. If the value of money may change, that will influence the terms on which they buy bonds. The nominal return on a bond or deposit is the extra money you receive when it is repaid. The real return is the extra value that you can obtain with that money. In August 1974, interest rates were around 10%. This return may seem high, but in the next twelve months prices rose by 12%. The $110 you would have received for each $100 invested would only have bought goods worth less than $100. If you had invested in Britain—where inflation soared to 27 percent—the £100 you had invested would have fallen in value to £82 a year later.

In January 1997 the U.S. government created Treasury Index Protected Securities (TIPS), which offered a guarantee of the value of the bond by linking both interest and repayment to the Consumer Price Index. Initially, investors seemed to attach a premium to the security this guarantee provided, and conversely the funds seemed cheap to the government. Unless inflation over the life of the bond averaged between 3% and 4%—higher than recent experience, although still well below the rates experienced in the 1970s—the Treasury would pay out less than it would have on conventional bonds.

Although around $130 billion of such bonds are in issue, interest in them seems to have waned. Perhaps their very security is unattractive to investors. The difference between the yield on indexed bonds, and the higher return in securities that offer no protection against inflation, has narrowed. In 2002, a review by the Federal Reserve Board concluded that the experiment had not been a success. Still, these securities—and the similar inflation-linked bonds of other rich countries, such as Australia, Britain, Canada, France, and Sweden—are the safest of all available investments. Over the twenty years since the first such bonds were issued, the expected rate of return on them has been in the range 2% to 4%. This figure is typical of the difference between inflation and nominal bond rates over a much longer period.[4]

Selling Risk, Buying Capital
• •

If you want a higher return, with more risk, go to the stock market. Over time, the distinction between lending at interest and sharing business risks became blurred. Businesses needed to trade in both risk and capital. They sold risk to spread out and diversify the results of business ventures. They bought capital to finance plant, buildings, and stocks of commodities.

Buying risk and selling capital are different functions, but there is logic in asking the same people to do both. Anyone who assumes the risks of a business will be expected to pay up if things go wrong. The Lloyd's insurance market, which covered Hurricane Hugo, separated the acceptance of risk from the provision of capital. The "names" did not have to put up much money, simply to show that, as wealthy people, they had resources to do so if required. After Hurricane Hugo and other disasters at Lloyd's, the money proved difficult to collect. Some names did not have it, and others were slow to pay or hired lawyers to explain why they should not pay. Today Lloyd's, like other businesses, covers its risks from money subscribed in advance: capital must be sold when risk is bought.

Still, different people have different appetites for buying risk and selling capital. Some may have little capital, but be willing to take high risks. Others want to sell capital, but do not want to buy risks. Financial intermediaries repackage securities to establish different combinations of risk and return. Some repackaging meets consumer demand. Some is smoke and mirrors, designed to encourage people to buy things they would not buy if they understood them, as with the Lloyd's spiral.[5]

Originally a shareholder would provide a proportion of the outlays of a venture and receive a share of the returns. Shareholders bought the risk and supplied the capital in equal proportions. Profit was both a reward for risk and a return on capital. As business became more complex, investors knew less about businesses in which they had placed money. Business speculation without ruin became attainable with the invention of limited liability. The scene was set for the development of modern stock markets.

The Changing Role of Stock Markets

The modern shareholder is very different from a participant in a venture like Antonio's, who put up a share of the outlays and received a share of the revenues. The stock market today, like the bond market, is principally a secondary market. This enables investors to withdraw their money without obliging the company to repay it. An initial public offering—the introduction of a new company to the stock exchange—usually raises some fresh capital from new shares, but its main function is to establish a market in these secondary participations. And because there is a secondary market, businesses can expand and grow: they do not have to return funds to investors whenever their ship comes in.

Modern companies can expect to have an indefinite life. Their shareholders receive dividends, regular distributions of the company's profits. The value of a share rests on the dividends shareholders can expect to receive, just as the value of a bond is in the flow of interest payments. But at the turn of the century, 70% of companies listed in the United States, including such highly rated companies as Microsoft, had never paid a dividend.[6] Why then would anyone buy Microsoft shares? Even if the company makes no distributions, it has earnings and assets, and this gives value to the shares even if none of that value is in practice passed to shareholders.

You may not find that argument entirely persuasive, nor do I; but so long as enough people believe it, you and I can expect to be able to sell our Microsoft shares to them. After the bursting of the stock market bubble in 2000, however, fewer people believed it than before. In 2003, Microsoft announced that it would pay its first dividend.

Valuing Securities

People who claim to predict share-price movements may be fundamental or technical analysts. Fundamental analysis looks at expectations of future earnings and dividends. Technical analysis identifies trends in share prices that will help to predict future movements. Technical analysts talk of support levels and resistance levels. They scrutinize charts in the hope of identifying patterns, such as "head and shoulders" or "double bottoms."

The efficient market hypothesis suggests that both fundamental analysis and technical analysis will fail, because any public information about shares and companies is already reflected in the price. Technical analysis cannot work—everyone can scrutinize the charts—and fundamental analysis only if it draws on private information, such as knowledge of a planned takeover, that would usually be illegal.[7] Chartists (as technical analysts are often called) are the astrologers of the business world: they use arcane language, comprehensible only to themselves, and couch predictions in ambiguous terms that can rarely be falsified.

The case for fundamental analysis is rather stronger. Extreme versions of the efficient market hypothesis have a problem. If it is not worth acting on publicly available information because it is already in the price, no one will act on it, and therefore it will not be in the price. A small amount of market imperfection overcomes this objection. The people who skip from queue to queue at the supermarket wait very slightly less long. Since the stock market is large, picking up a little bit of advantage sufficiently often can yield large profits.

And there do seem to be some—though not many—cases of investors who have outperformed the stock market through fundamental analysis by sufficiently much and for sufficiently long that their success cannot be explained by chance. In chapter 20, I will review evidence against the efficient market hypothesis, while Warren Buffett, the man who seems to be its living refutation, appears in chapter 25.

Intangible Capital
● ●

Investment is present sacrifice for future gain, and anything that may yield a prospective return is an asset. Our assets constitute our wealth or our capital. Our capacity to earn wages and salaries is sometimes called our human capital. We are born with human capital. We can increase our human capital through education and training and depreciate it through idleness, drinking too much, or old age. It is possible to estimate returns on human capital—the value of additional earnings that people can expect from an investment in schooling or an MBA.[8]

Successful businesses—businesses with competitive advantages from distinctive capabilities—are worth more than the value of their buildings, their plant, and their stocks. Accountants used to call this the goodwill of the business. For the shop, the pub, or the small manufacturer, that was an appropriate term. The intangible asset was the loyalty of satisfied customers.

The modern economy has many different kinds of distinctive capabilities and so many different kinds of intangible assets: competitive advantages based on brands or reputations with groups of customers; strategic assets such as patents and copyrights or local monopolies; structures of relationships with suppliers or employees. "Our people are our greatest asset" is a cliché of company reports, and there is a lot in it. All of these factors explain why the value of companies is greater than the value of their tangible assets.[9]

Most recently, the sociologist Robert Putnam has written of social capital.[10] Putnam's thesis—encapsulated in the striking title of his book, *Bowling Alone*—is that group social activity in the United States has declined. Almost two centuries ago, Tocqueville wrote of the desire for association as a feature of American life.[11] Perhaps that association, which was not only the basis for its civil society but an element in its economic success, has been eroded in recent decades.

Market economies, and market societies, are embedded in social institutions. Chapters 18 through 23 will describe many of these, and Putnam is right to worry that the institutions that are the basis not just of civil society but of economic life are being eroded. But there is desperation in the term *social capital*. Putnam fears he can attract the attention of his audience only by expressing himself in economic terms.

There is much to be said for reserving the term *capital* for what can be bought and sold in the market for capital. Some, but not many, intangible assets meet this test; human capital does not, and social capital certainly not. Education and skills are an asset and so is the glue that holds society together, but they are not in this sense capital.

{15}

General Equilibrium

The Coordination Problem Revisited

It is now time to go back to the problem posed in chapter 11. How is it that market economies solved the coordination problems of production, exchange, and assignment so much more effectively than planned ones? The concept of spontaneous order—the idea that complex systems may have properties of self-organization—is powerful; but the knowledge that self-organization is possible falls a long way short of demonstrating either that coordination happens spontaneously or explaining how it might happen spontaneously.

Competitive markets—whether for electricity or for flowers, for oil or for milk, for risk or for money—produce their own local equilibrium that equates supply and demand. The lights stay on, the flowers that arrive at San Remo at the beginning of the morning leave it at the end. This solves part of the coordination problem, but only part. The remarkable feature of the market economy is that it seems to solve a large variety of coordination problems simultaneously. The flower market clears, and at the same time electricity demand balances supply. There are enough trucks at the market, but not too many; enough gas for power stations, but not too much.

Central planners always found it easy to deal with any particular coordination failure. By switching resources you can always relieve a shortage or a surplus: this is what we do when we plan our households or our businesses, and it is what the people who ran the Soviet economy did all the time. The trouble is that there are always knock-on consequences. When you solve one problem, you almost always create another elsewhere. We face this same issue in coordinating our muscles or assembling flat-pack furniture. It is easy to make one piece fit. The tricky thing is to make them all fit at the same time. General equilibrium is the problem of making everything fit at once.

With the furniture, we can be reasonably confident that it is possible to make everything fit at once. Someone at the factory has already tried. Producers in traditional, premarket societies were also confident the coordination problem could be solved, because they too had done it before. The general equilibrium of the system was assured by experience over many generations in which each year was very much like another.

But neither of these answers apply in a complex modern economy. There can be no designer: the problem of incentive compatibility demonstrates that no central planner could ever assemble the combination of information and incentives needed to dictate general equilibrium from the center. And the economic lives of the citizens of rich states are constantly changing. We can't simply rely, as traditional societies could, on the order of the past producing order today.

Still, history is important. What happens today at San Remo, or at the Chicago Mercantile Exchange, is different from what happened yesterday or will happen tomorrow. But it is not completely different. The mechanisms by which the flower market or the grain market function change only slowly, even though the results of the mechanisms change every day. Complex institutions like these did not leap into being: like other complex social or biological organisms, they evolved from simpler versions. That is part of the reason it is so difficult to create sophisticated market institutions where none existed before.

So how do the different bits of a market economy fit together? This question cries out for a mathematical approach. The first mathematical economists were found in nineteenth-century France. Jean-Baptiste Say formulated the idea of general equilibrium in "Say's law"—supply creates its own demand. Say was one of the best economists before Larry Summers—the Clinton administration's last treasury secretary, now Harvard president—to become Minister of Finance. But the most important contribution came from a young colleague,

Leon Walras, with whom Say had established an unsuccessful cooperative bank. After the failure of the bank, Walras retreated to a chair at the University of Lausanne, where he set out, in his *Principles of Political Economy*, the mathematics of a general equilibrium system.

Adding Up

When you assemble flat-pack furniture, you should find that, if you have successfully put together all the bits except one, the last component automatically fits into place. If you are like me, this often doesn't happen. Usually this means you have assembled it incorrectly. In a coordinated system, the position of the last piece is predetermined by the position of all the others.[1] The economic analogue is Walras's law.

Walras's law is an economic application of bookkeeping principles. Double-entry bookkeeping is not as exciting an invention as railroads or the Internet. But double-entry bookkeeping was as important as these innovations to the development of modern market economies. Every expenditure must be matched by a receipt. By keeping track of all entries in a ledger, the activities of a household or business can be regulated and controlled. Double-entry bookkeeping put the discipline in disciplined pluralism.

Double-entry bookkeeping is to economic and commercial life what the second law of thermodynamics is to the physical world, and it has the same role in deflating pretensions of dreamers and fantasists. The claims made by Enron and for the Internet boom were impossible for the same reasons that alchemy and perpetual-motion machines were impossible. Woolly-minded people, and fraudsters who prey on them, assert economic equivalents of alchemy and perpetual motion. But sadly, for an individual or household:

- spending must (more or less) match earnings for firms or institutions (including the government)

- assets must match liabilities

The economy as a whole has similar "adding up" constraints. The most important are:

- production must (more or less) equal consumption

- exports must (more or less) equal imports

- the total value of production must (more or less) be equal to the total value of consumption

- all net assets and liabilities of corporations and of governments are ultimately net assets and liabilities of individuals or households

Because of these bookkeeping constraints, we can't measure the overall consequence of a change to an economic system by simply adding up immediate individual effects. If you alter one component, every other one will have to change, a little, to ensure that the requirements of a double-entry system still hold.

DIY Economics

David Henderson was head of economics and statistics at the Organization for Economic Cooperation and Development (OECD), located near the Bois de Boulogne in the leafy sixteenth arrondissement of Paris. OECD is often described as the club of rich states—its membership more or less coincides with the rich states identified in chapter 4. In 1985, Henderson delivered a series of lectures, born of frustration with economic pronouncements of politicians, on the weaknesses of what he called DIY (do-it-yourself) economics, false propositions that people who have not studied economics know instinctively are true.[2] Anyone who claimed expertise in "practical physics" derived from their experience of driving an automobile or boarding an airplane would immediately reveal himself a fool. It is a measure of the failure of economists to persuade the public of the value of what they do that those who claim practical knowledge of economics suffer no such reactions.[3] There is almost no DIY dentistry, little DIY history or law, rather more DIY medicine. There is much DIY economics.

The most common weakness in DIY economics is the failure to understand general equilibrium issues, often a result of a lack of appreciation of the role of bookkeeping constraints. These constraints mean that what is true at the level of the individual house-hold or firm may not be true at the level of the economy as a whole. This is a subtle source of misunderstanding because economic lives are conducted in households and firms: we do not see the abstrac-tions of general equilibrium. The advocates of DIY economics "know" the truth of what they say from their own experience.

If a firm increases its sales without any reduction in price or rise in costs, the outcome is good for its shareholders and for those who work for it. Conversely, if the firm loses market share to a competi-tor, everyone associated with it is worse off. Applying this simple wisdom to the economy as a whole, we should try to increase national sales—our exports—and diminish national purchases—our inputs—and the more successful we are in this endeavor the better off we shall be. This theory—mercantilism—was believed by most economists before Smith and his contemporaries.[4] It is a widely held thesis in DIY economics today, although it enjoys broadly the same scientific status as the phlogiston theory of heat or the Ptolemaic explanation of how the sun orbits the earth.

The weakness of the argument is the failure to recognize the bookkeeping constraint. The balance of payments must, in the long run, balance. This applies to the national economy, but there is no corresponding constraint at the level of the individual firm. An increase in exports by one firm will be matched either by an increase in imports or by a reduction in exports by some other firm. What is true for an individual company is not true for USA Inc.

The John Kay who invented the flying shuttle was forced to flee to France by Luddites who feared his ingenuity would destroy their jobs.[5] The Luddites had good cause to be afraid for their jobs, many of which disappeared. There are many fewer jobs for bank clerks now that mechanical record keeping is undertaken by computers. But there are not fewer jobs overall. In both these industries employment ultimately increased, because the new technology that displaced the Luddites and the bank clerks led to increased demand for textiles and for financial services. The effect of this increase in demand more than offset the immediate job losses. (This was not necessarily con-soling for the individuals concerned.)

And the adding-up constraints of general equilibrium require this. Lower costs from new technology must lead to lower prices or increased profits, or both. Even if there is no increase in spending on the products of industries directly affected—and there will often be— expenditures on the products of some other industries will increase and generate additional opportunities there. Over the two centuries since the Luddites first wrecked flying shuttles, productivity has increased more than fiftyfold. But instead of having 98% unemployment, we produce fifty times as much.

Current technological changes are no different. In some instances, increasing exports may yield benefits to the national economy (and not just to those who actually export), and new technology will reduce overall employment (and not just the employment of those who are displaced by new technology). But these results are not generally true and cannot be deduced for the economy as a whole from the hardearned experience of individual businesses and the people who run them.

Economic Theory Advancing
● ●

Smith and Ricardo demonstrated the fallacies in the arguments of mercantilists and Luddites. Walras elaborated the implications of these bookkeeping constraints for the economic system as a whole and set out the framework of the general equilibrium issue. But this is far short of demonstrating a solution to the coordination problem. And after Walras, the theory of general equilibrium stalled under the towering influence of the Cambridge economist Alfred Marshall. Although himself a capable mathematician, Marshall derided the use of mathematics in economics. His discourse *Principles of Economics,* published in 1890, follows his injunction to "burn the mathematics."[6]

Marshall's injunction was broadly followed by the man who was to succeed him as the leading Cambridge economist, John Maynard Keynes. Keynes was an extraordinary polymath. He was a leading figure in the literary set known as the Bloomsbury group; he was also active in business and a successful trader in speculative markets on his own account. He played a large political role, most famously in the treaty negotiations after World War I and in financing World War II. And his writing, not confined to economic matters, sparkles with literary brilliance.

Keynes's best-known economic contribution is his 1936 book, *The*

General Theory of Employment, Interest and Money,[7] written in the aftermath of the Great Depression. Keynes claimed to provide an explanation of why the forces of supply and demand in competitive markets had not eliminated unemployment. And although controversy over exactly what Keynes's explanation was continues even today, his analysis and influence provided comfort for those around the world who demanded interventionist policies.

If Keynes was the most influential economist of the first half of the twentieth century, Paul Samuelson[n] was the most influential economist of the second half. While others, such as Milton Friedman, may be better known to a wide public, Samuelson is the economists' economist, whose influence is evident in everything that has followed. Every student knows of Samuelson's best-selling textbook, but it was *Foundations of Economic Analysis,* published in 1947 and based on his doctoral dissertation, that established his reputation, redefined the subject, and announced a shift in hegemony in economic theory from Cambridge, England, to Cambridge, Massachusetts, and from Europe to the United States.

Keynes's *General Theory* contains no mathematics, and that is a principal reason why there are multiple interpretations of his thesis. Samuelson insisted on a rigorous mathematical representation of his argument, and that has been the subsequent style of economic theory. The methods that Samuelson described allowed Kenneth Arrow[n] and Gerard Debreu[n] to set out the theory of general equilibrium, and the Arrow-Debreu model has been central to modern economics ever since.[8] One reason why Smith and his contemporaries could not give formal content to their descriptions of spontaneous order was that the relevant mathematics had not been invented. It had not been invented even in the time of Say and Walras. The discovery of algebraic topology in the twentieth century gave Arrow and Debreu the tools they needed. Fixed-point theorems[9] describe properties of convex sets. A detour is required to explain the economic implications of the mathematical property of convexity.

Convexity

A convex set has the property that a collection that contains two items also contains an average of these two items.[10] If the collection is "things I like," then convexity implies that I also like a combination of "things I like." The averaging process tends to make things better rather than worse.

Addiction violates convexity. Not many people want just a little heroin. And convexity has a problem when goods are indivisible. No one wants half a car. But we see addiction as pathological behavior, and our instincts and our social attitudes commend convexity. We applaud moderation in all things, say that a little of what you fancy does you good, and admire well-balanced, well-rounded individuals.

The desire for convexity seems to run deep in human attitudes. Herrick wrote that "beauty is a golden mean, 'twixt the middle and extreme." This is a good definition of convexity, and modern psychologists have confirmed that Herrick was right. The collection "faces I find attractive" is convex. If you take the faces of two beautiful women and use computer technology to merge them, most people like the result.[11]

It probably isn't an exaggeration to say that the behavior of market economies depends on how convex the world is. To get a sense of why this is so, imagine dropping a ball into a bowl: it circles round, slows down, and eventually arrives at some sort of equilibrium. This happens because the collection of "points inside the bowl" is convex. Now turn the bowl upside down. The set of positions the ball can take is no longer convex: the ball gathers speed and runs away in an unpredictable direction. The shape of the space governs the dynamics of the process.[12]

In a convex environment, minor adjustments, trial and error, piecemeal improvements, tend to make things better. There are many objectives, which partly conflict, and variety is prized. It is in this world that the processes of disciplined pluralism perform well. Market economies don't seem to cope well with urban transport systems, where it probably really is better to focus than to have a little of everything, which is what the market tends to generate.

If specialization pays, the set of "things that I can make" is not convex. Suppose Paul Roux could cook a hundred meals if he cooked all day, and copy four of Georges Braque's sketches in the same time. Convexity would require that if he cooked for half the day and sketched for the remainder, he could cook fifty meals and produce two drawings. But he probably can't. Convexity implies that there are no benefits from specialization, and no economies of scale. If "things that I can make" formed a convex set, then it would be possible, and even desirable, for everyone to be self-sufficient.

The division of labor is rewarding because the world is not completely convex. But it needs to be somewhat convex. If the collection of "things the world economy can make" weren't convex, then the likely outcome would be extreme specialization and extreme instability. The market economy would fail to produce the variety of goods and services that people want, and a planned economy would find it difficult to find a good solution.

We need some departure from convexity, but not too much; some gains from specialization, but not gains without limit. And this seems to be what we see. The benefits to specialization run out because every specialist has limited capacity. If Picasso was the greatest artist of the twentieth century, why were not all paintings Picassos? Partly because of convexity of preferences: even if we think that Picasso's paintings are the best, we might like to see a mixture of Picassos and Braques. But also because Picasso could not have painted all the paintings in the world, even if he had painted all day and all night; and if he had, many of his works would not have been very good. So there is also employment for slightly less talented painters, like Braque; and even employment for the much less talented people who hang their works on park railings.

And gains from specialization also run out because too extensive specialization is boring. Technical economies of scale are almost always to be found; ultimately, they are almost always offset by human diseconomies of scale. That balance of small-scale nonconvexity and large-scale convexity is what we need.[13]

The Existence of General Equilibrium

Arrow and Debreu established precisely the way in which individual decision making by households and competitive firms might produce consistent outcomes. The conjecture of the "invisible hand" became an exact mathematical result.

Arrow and Debreu worked with a specific, simplified model of the economy in which both the sets of "things that I like" and "things that can be made" are convex. All markets are perfectly competitive, and the households and firms that trade in them are materialistic and self-regarding. Their preferences and choices are independent of those of other households and firms. Each household decides what to consume independently of the choices of others. And not only does each firm make its decisions about what to produce independently of others, its technology and methods of production are not affected by what other firms do. It is not possible, for example, that your purchases might influence mine. Or that pollution from one factory might affect the output of other firms or the welfare of households.

The Arrow-Debreu theorem shows that, if these conditions hold, there is a set of prices such that aggregate supplies will equal aggregate demands for every commodity in the economy. There will be no surpluses, and no shortages. You don't need a coordinator to achieve a coordinated outcome. The manufacture of a car requires the contributions of thousands of resources and thousands of people. But it isn't necessary for anyone to oversee the whole of that process. It is sufficient that people make decisions on the basis of the prices they see and the knowledge of their own preferences and production possibilities.

Each individual household wants food, housing, clothing, transport. But in a perfectly competitive market, no overall coordination is required to ensure that the way in which households, in aggregate, split their budgets among food, housing, clothing, and transport matches the quantities in which producers make food, housing, clothing, transport. Here too it is enough that people make decisions on the basis of their own limited knowledge.

If we don't find these things amazing, it is because we are so accustomed to the idea that market economies do mostly achieve coordination. But recall how difficult it proved to achieve the same results in a planned economy that sought coordinated outcomes through central oversight.

The abstract nature of the model must give many readers pause. This arcane mathematics seems far removed from the basic questions that motivate the study of economics. Why is Heidi rich? Why is Sicelo poor? The assumptions of the theory are obviously unrealistic. Our preferences are influenced by those of other people, different production processes interfere with each other, economies of scale are widespread. But this is not criticism enough. Because economic systems are complex, *any* model we specify involves extensive simplifying assumptions.

A model like that of Arrow-Debreu demonstrates the possibility of spontaneous order in economic systems. It does not necessarily follow that there will *be* spontaneous order. Nor does it follow that if there is coordination, or spontaneous order, the Arrow-Debreu model explains it. But some approximation to spontaneous order does seem to be a feature of real market economies, and the Arrow-Debreu model offers one coherent explanation of how such spontaneous order might come about. In the next chapter, I review a further claim for the Arrow-Debreu model of perfectly competitive equilibrium—the claim that the outcome is not only coordinated, but also efficient.

{16}
Efficiency

The History of Light

It is dark for half our lives. For most of history, artificial lighting has been too costly for widespread application in either our work or our social lives. Cro-Magnon man could not have painted in the caves of Lascaux without artificial lighting, so lamps have a long history. But the candle was the only revolutionary improvement in lighting technology before the end of the eighteenth century.

Energy technology changed fundamentally in the nineteenth century. Gas and electricity were produced centrally and distributed locally. Good-quality domestic lighting became affordable. When Thomas Edison demonstrated electric lighting at Menlo Park in 1880, huge crowds gathered to see. In the twentieth century the cost of light has fallen much more rapidly than the cost of energy. Without these improvements in the efficiency of lighting technology, we would not be able to live the lives we now do: there would not be enough energy. But what exactly do we mean by efficiency improvements? And how do we measure them?

For physicists, the amount of light (which they measure in lumens) produced per unit of energy consumed would seem a natural way to measure efficiency. And many improvements in lighting technology focused on this factor—essentially the ratio of light to heat. Light was once an incidental by-product of combustion—the flicker of a flame. Modern low-energy fittings provide light and almost no heat.

Table 16.1

● ●

Lighting Efficiency

Year	Method	Fuel	Physical efficiency (lumens/ watt)	Economic efficiency*
500,000 B.C.	Fire	Wood	0.002	70
30,000 B.C.	Lamp	Animal fat	0.015	15
1800 B.C.	Lamp	Vegetable oil	0.06	4
A.D. 1800	Candle	Tallow	0.01	0.7
1870	Lamp	Gas	0.25	0.03
1890	Lamp	Electricity	2.6	0.08
1990	Lamp	Electricity	14.2	0.00006
2000	Lamp †	Electricity	70	0.00001

* Hours of work needed to keep a hundred-watt bulb on for an hour.

† Low energy.

SOURCE: Derived from Nordhaus (1997)

Much of the gain in efficiency has come from better ways of distributing energy. Petroleum exploration and development has enabled us to substitute mineral oil for whale blubber (which was once an important source of light). We deliver gas along pipes and illuminate houses with electricity: gas, oil, or coal is burned in a central power station and sent along wires to our houses. Energy losses in electricity generation and transmission are more than offset by the greater efficiency with which households can use electrical energy.

We use more of some resources to use less of others. And this extends beyond improvements in energy efficiency. Lamps had a better light to heat ratio than open fires, and candles a better light to heat ratio than lamps. But this gain in physical efficiency had a cost. More effort was needed to find these more efficient fuels and to process them.

We can write down a list of the resources we use today to produce light. And lists of the resources we would have used a century or a millennium ago. All these lists are different—in length, in the items they contain. To compare their efficiency, we need to make precise the instinct that today's list, even if it is not shorter, represents fewer resources. The obvious means is to translate all items into a single unit, such as the hours of work needed to produce them. Table 16.1 shows the result of this calculation. A modern hundred-watt bulb produces about fourteen hundred lumens. Cro-Magnons would have had to work for twelve hours gathering fuel to sustain that level of lighting for ten minutes. It is easy to see why Braque produced many more paintings than the cave people of Lascaux.

Comparing Vectors

A vector is simply a mathematician's term for a list of numbers. If every number in one list is larger than every number in another list, the corresponding vector is larger. If some numbers are larger in one list and some larger in the other, we need to make judgments. Only a weighting scheme can allow us to rank the two vectors.

We face this problem every time we choose between alternative purchases. Consumer tests help us approach this problem in a systematic way. So when *Consumer Reports* looked at mid-size refrigerators, they rated the appliances as follows:

So which is best? The answer is not obvious. If you care about energy use, you should look at Kenmore and Maytag; for tempera-

Table 16.2

Refrigerator Features

Manufacturer	Energy use	Temperature stability	Noise	Ease of use
Kenmore	Fair	Excellent	Excellent	Very good
KitchenAid	Poor	Excellent	Very good	Very good
Maytag	Fair	Very good	Excellent	Excellent
GE	Poor	Very good	Very good	Excellent

SOURCE: Consumer Reports

ture stability, Kenmore and KitchenAid. The quietest refrigerators are Kenmore and Maytag; but if you want an appliance that is particularly easy to use, Maytag and GE are the favored choices.

But we can simplify the choice. Assuming that the prices are similar, and the *Consumer Reports* ratings are right, no one should buy the KitchenAid or the GE refrigerators. Everything the KitchenAid does, the Kenmore does as well or better; everything the GE appliance can do, the Maytag does as well or better. In these comparisons, one vector dominates the other. So your choice reduces to the Kenmore or the Maytag. That decision depends whether you care more about ease of use or temperature stability.

I can't advise you on that, but readers expect that *Consumer Reports* will. And *Consumer Reports* judges temperature stability to be more important than ease of use. By making this judgment, they rank all the appliances. They conclude that the Kenmore is the best. Indeed, under their weighting system, the KitchenAid—which is unambiguously inferior to the Kenmore and should not feature among anyone's choices—is rated above the Maytag, which is better than the Kenmore for people who care about ease of use. Once you introduce weights, you can not only choose the best, you rank all the alternatives.

The weights reflect the opinions of people at *Consumer Reports* about what we should value in a refrigerator. No doubt they are well-informed and objective. Still, you may attach more importance to ease of use than does *Consumer Reports* in finding a refrigerator. Each of us has our own personal weighting system to apply to the characteristics vectors. That is why we don't all buy the same refrigerator, even the one *Consumer Reports* recommends, and why even *Consumer Reports* is hesitant about identifying one as the best buy. But not everything is commensurable.

An Evening in Küssnacht

HEIDI: You insist on looking at everything in financial terms, Hermann. Can't you understand that some things are more important than money? Health, the environment, life itself. How can you put a price on a person, or a species?

HERMANN: Of course there are more important things than money. Life, children, relationships. And in Switzerland most people have as many material goods as anyone could reasonably want. That's precisely why we can be concerned about the environment—and why it's important that we protect it.

HEIDI: So why do you reduce everything to money?

HERMANN: When I "reduce things to money," I'm not saying that money is the goal. I'm simply using money as a means of comparison. Remember when we bought our holiday place in Umbria? We calculated what it would cost us and what we would save on hotel costs.

HEIDI: Well, you did, Hermann.

HERMANN: That's true. But we went over the sums together. That doesn't mean we go on holiday to save money. Money is just a measuring rod for costs and benefits.

HEIDI: But you can't apply that kind of calculus to the environment, or to human life.

HERMANN: Why not? Take your recycling scheme. It conserves some resources, it uses others. How can you balance one against the other except in financial terms?

HEIDI: You're missing the point. The environment is too important to be reduced to financial terms.

HERMANN: But you don't really believe that. We both hate the way electricity pylons sprout from the woods on the slopes above the lake. But even in Switzerland, it's too expensive to lay all cables underground. Life always involves choices—allocating scarce resources between competing ends. And no society is so well-endowed that it can avoid choices.

HEIDI: But you can't make all choices in this way. Some things are more important than money. How can you value a human life?

HERMANN: But we trade off money against safety every day. The cheapest way of saving lives is to invest in road improvements. Remember that bend on the road to Davos where we nearly had an accident? Five people have died there in the last ten years. They're building a tunnel to reduce the bend and the gradient. And you know you could have a safer car than the Micra, if you spent more.

HEIDI: You're incorrigible, Hermann. Only an economist could think in that way.

HERMANN: But economists must, and so should policy makers. When your friend Mieke from Novartis came round to dinner, she explained how we kill more people by delaying new drugs than we save by testing them exhaustively. And her partner Fritz works for the Swiss nuclear safety inspectorate. There have been no accidents in Switzerland, not even a Three Mile Island, far less a Chernobyl. And that's a good thing, of course. But he argued that what we spend on precautions and security is excessive. We might do more for health and longevity if we spent more on gym equipment and propaganda against eating and drinking too much.

HEIDI: Go and work out on the exercise machine while I see to supper.

Commensurability
● ●

The discussion between Heidi and Hermann raises two distinct issues. Can different objectives be treated as commensurable? And if they are commensurable, what are the terms—money, cost, fuel efficiency, or some other yardstick altogether—in which commensurability is to be measured? These issues are often muddled, because people who want to make sweeping claims for commensurability typically use money as their metric, and those who wish to deny commensurability often choose to attack the use of money as measuring rod.[1]

For some economists, all goals are commensurable. The judge and leading law and economics scholar Richard Posner takes a far more extreme position than Hermann. Posner asserts that efficiency is perhaps the most common meaning of justice—"when people describe as 'unjust' convicting a person without a trial, taking property without just compensation . . . they can be interpreted as meaning nothing more pretentious than that the conduct in question wastes resources." Even the sympathetic Todd Buchholz describes this as a "dim observation by a brilliant man" and notes that it was watered down by the third edition of Posner's treatise.[2] This illustrates the problems of defining property rights in too general a way (see chapter 6).

The right to be free of racial discrimination or sexual harassment is not a property right. Those who benefit from such a right do not have the option to sell it or transfer it; someone who proposed to give up the right not to be harassed or discriminated against, in return for a sum of money, would have misunderstood what was intended. Conversely, the right is not to be harassed or discriminated against, not an entitlement to receive large sums of money if one does suffer harassment or discrimination. "Rights as trumps," in Ronald Dworkin's striking phrase,[3] and the essence of a trump card is that it is not commensurable.

Some values in society are not commensurable in financial terms and may not be commensurable at all. The value pluralism of Isaiah Berlin[4] asserts that conceptions of what is good in society almost invariably include incompatible goals. This is not relativism: Berlin does not believe that all conceptions of the good are equally valid. But his position provides the middle ground that both Heidi and Hermann are right to seek. It is not irrational to refuse to measure human life in terms of forgone video recorders.[5] Thus refusal may lead to apparently inconsistent choices—as when we spend more to rescue someone in distress at sea than on life-saving road improvements. This is disturbing, but not necessarily irrational, in any ordinary sense of the word.

At Heidi's end of the spectrum, claims of incommensurability are often made by people who wish to deny that choices in the allocation of scarce resources between competing ends have to be made, or who wish simply to assert the primacy of their own values—what is important to you is never commensurable with what is important to me. The more assertions of incommensurability are made, the more arguments—like that between Hermann and Heidi—are necessarily inconclusive. This leads to the incoherent discourse that follows from the assertion of a multiplicity of rights. The conflicting assertions of "right to life" and "right to choose" find no common ground, and the proponents of these conflicting rights can, and do, conduct their debate only by shouting at each other or even killing each other.

If rights are trumps, only a few suits can be trumps. This makes it important to resist the designation of a wide range of desirable outcomes—paternity leave or disabled access—as "rights," which therefore have to be implemented regardless of cost. Choices in the allocation of scarce resources between competing ends have to be made. Recycling glass and paper are not worthwhile objectives in themselves, and it is reasonable to ask proponents to justify them in terms of specific costs and benefits. Environmentalists are particularly prone to sweeping claims of incommensurability. There may be environmental goals that are, in Berlin's terms, incommensurable with materialist goals; but that does not imply that environmental policies should not be assessed in consequentialist terms. Those who claim that biodiversity should be maintained regardless of cost cannot simultaneously justify biodiversity by reference to its economic benefits.

The Terms of Commensurability

Measures of efficiency require the comparison of vectors of inputs and outputs. A larger output vector from the same input is more efficient. A smaller input vector for the same output is also more efficient. This is how we could conclude that the Kenmore was a better refrigerator than the KitchenAid, the Maytag better than the GE. But it did not enable us to compare the Kenmore and the Maytag. Or even to say that a modern low-energy lightbulb is more efficient than the lanterns the Cro-Magnons used.

Consumer Reports resolved the comparison between refrigerators by weighting the characteristics of the appliances. The weights were based on the value they thought buyers would attach to these different features. In a perfectly competitive market, the price of the goods and the features of goods will correspond to the value buyers attach to them. This is the basis for using market prices to achieve commensurability, and using GDP to make comparisons of vectors of outputs between countries and over time.

The obvious problem is that the value people attach to a good or a service is the result not just of how much they want that good or service, but also how money they have. Mr. Saito did not put the extraordinary value of $82.5 million on *Portrait of Dr. Gachet* because he was uniquely devoted to great art, but because he was extraordinarily rich. The legitimacy of market values as weights depends on the legitimacy of the income distribution that gives rise to it.

Another way of approaching this issue tackles the problem directly. The purpose of an economic system is not to produce physical output, but to enhance the welfare of the households that live in it. Surely we should judge the efficiency of an economy by its contribution to the welfare of its citizens?

But how would we measure their welfare? The British utilitarians of the nineteenth century were inspired by Jeremy Bentham—whose stuffed body can still be seen in a glass case at University College, London—or Bentham's successors, such as John Stuart Mill and the mathematical economist F. Y. Edgeworth, who measured the welfare of society by aggregating the welfare—the utility—of its individual members and who looked forward to a felicific calculus that would measure progress toward their objective, the greatest happiness of the greatest number, in an objective manner.

The felicific calculus was designed to solve the knotty problem of commensurability—how to weight my utility against yours, how to decide whether greater aggregate happiness had been achieved. Sadly, progress toward the felicific calculus remains elusive, and utilitarianism fell out of fashion amongst philosophers many years ago.

Pareto Efficiency
• •

Vilfredo Pareto, Walras's successor at Lausanne, believed, like the utilitarians, that the welfare of society could be defined in terms of the individual utilities of individual citizens or households. He was content simply to list the utilities they achieved as a vector. So instead of a vector that described picture quality, sound quality, etc., a vector would list the welfare of the Smiths, the welfare of the Joneses, and so on for all the households in the economy.

It is sometimes possible to make comparisons of refrigerators without attaching any weights to the components of the vector. The Kenmore was better than the KitchenAid, because it made less noise and had better energy consumption, and other features were equally good. In a precisely analogous way, we would have a better policy, or a better allocation of resources, if we could make the Smiths or the Joneses better off without making anyone else worse off. This is described as a Pareto improvement.

In other cases, no such comparison of vectors is possible. Whether the Kenmore was better or worse than the Maytag was a matter of judgment and opinion. The Kenmore had a more stable temperature, but the Maytag was easier to use. Similarly, if the Joneses are to be better off and the Smiths worse off, an evaluation requires a weighting of the welfare of the Joneses and the Smiths. You have to judge whether the gain to the Joneses exceeds the loss to the Smiths. Ideally, you need the felicific calculus. If you use money to make the comparison, then you employ an implicit felicific calculus, which attaches a weighting to the welfare of the households concerned based on the amount of money they have.

Pareto's claim is that it is often—not always, but often—possible to avoid these judgments. And Pareto developed a further twist to this argument. If no Pareto improvement is possible—if it is not possible to make the Joneses better off without making the Smiths worse off, or vice versa, then the outcome is described as Pareto efficient.[6] An allocation of scarce resources between competing ends is Pareto efficient if it is impossible to make one household better off without making another household worse off.

It is hard not to be in favor of Pareto improvement. A Pareto improvement is the politician's dream—a policy from which there are only winners. If you could make someone better off without making anyone else worse off, wouldn't you do it? And yet you may already have a sense that Pareto is about to lead you somewhere you may not wish to go. A state of affairs might be Pareto efficient, and yet deplorable. A sadist is torturing his victims. But this outcome could still be Pareto efficient— we can only stop the torture by making the sadist worse off.

The Fundamental Theorems of Welfare Economics
● ●

Any exchange that benefits both parties and has no adverse effect on anyone else is a Pareto improvement. So an economic system can be efficient only if every possible mutually beneficial trade has occurred. This seems to link Pareto efficiency with free, competitive markets. Allowing the market economy to function freely will have the result that people will trade with each other until Pareto efficiency is achieved. For many supporters of the market economy, the argument is as simple as that. I've heard it often from practitioners of DIY economics.

It isn't as simple as that. Voluntary trade between two individuals benefits both. But it will only be a Pareto improvement if it has no adverse consequences for other people. If my purchase, or your production, affects others, it will not lead to a Pareto improvement. And it will often affect others because others want to buy the same goods as I do, or your output raises the costs of a third party.

Further—and the problem turns out to be fundamental—there is an issue of incentive compatibility. A trade that benefits the parties involved will have consequences for others if it affects the terms on which other people can trade. And this is often true. When a plane is about to depart with an empty seat, it would be a Pareto improvement if the seat was filled by a passenger willing to pay anything at all. But the airline won't do this, because if seats were regularly available for next to nothing whenever one was empty, this would affect the behavior of full-fare-paying passengers. Airlines have the sophisticated yield management systems of chapter 12 to handle precisely this problem. Their aim is not to fill the plane, but to strike a balance between filling seats and obtaining good prices for seats. If they could read minds and gauge exactly how much each passenger would be willing to pay, they could engage in perfect price discrimination[7] and achieve Pareto efficiency. But of course they can't.

So free trade leads to Pareto efficiency only in perfectly competitive markets because only perfectly competitive markets are free of these incentive compatibility problems. Market economies that are competitive but not perfectly competitive offer many opportunities for Pareto improvements. Chapters 18 through 24 will explore many instances.

But for the perfectly competitive markets described in the Arrow-Debreu framework[8] we have the fundamental theorems of welfare economics:

· Every competitive equilibrium is Pareto efficient.

· Any allocation of scarce resources among competing ends that is Pareto efficient can be achieved by a competitive equilibrium.

Don't worry: the book gets easier from here. But there is no escaping the fundamental theorems of welfare economics if we are to examine the claim that competitive markets necessarily lead to efficient outcomes. These claims are made not just by theoretical economists but by practical politicians. Ronald Reagan was not much interested in algebraic topology; but the intellectual influences on him, when finally disentangled, can be traced back to those fixed-point theorems.

part IV

THE TRUTH ABOUT MARKETS

● ● ● ● ● ● ● ● ● ● ● ● ● ● ● ● ●

{17}

Neoclassical Economics and After

Smith and Hayek

Some economists regard the Arrow-Debreu results and the fundamental theorems of welfare economics as the modern expression of Smith's invisible hand.[1] But Smith would be surprised at what is attributed to him today. Politicians and businesspeople vie in admiration for what they believe to be his doctrines. Yergin and Stanislaw's description of the revival of market economics makes frequent reference to Smith and sums up his "argument for self-interest": "The pursuit of individual interest cumulatively adds up to the overall betterment of society."[2]

This reverence for Smith even extends to hymns:

> Adam, Adam, Adam Smith
> Listen what I charge you with
> Didn't you say
> In the class one day
> That selfishness was bound to pay?
> Of all doctrines that was the Pith
> Wasn't it, wasn't it, wasn't it, Smith?
>
> —*Stephen Leacock*[3]

Was this really the Pith of Smith's doctrines? The widely quoted passage is: "By directing that industry in such a manner as its produce may be of the greatest value, he intends only his own gain, and he is in this, as in many other cases, led by an invisible hand to promote an end which was not part of his intention."

Yet on careful reading Smith does not say that selfish behavior is praiseworthy, is bound to pay, or necessarily promotes the best interests of society. When we join the shortest queue at the supermarket, we intend only our own gain and promote an end that is not part of our intention. It does not follow that our behavior is governed by self-regarding materialism, or that such behavior leads, cumulatively or otherwise, to the overall betterment of society.

The passage containing the invisible hand metaphor is not about general equilibrium theory: its purpose is to explain why merchants would continue to buy British products even if tariffs were removed. The metaphor itself originates in Shakespeare's Scottish play, *Macbeth*, and seems to have intrigued Smith. In his other major work, *The Theory of Moral Sentiments*, in which what Smith calls "sympathy" plays a central role, Smith wrote, "They [the rich] are led by an invisible hand to make the same distribution of the necessities of life, which would have been made, had the earth been divided into equal portions amongst all its inhabitants."[4]

While it is unlikely that Smith held the views popularly attributed to him, speculation as to what exactly he did think is not helpful in arriving at the truth about markets. Our purpose now is to explain economic systems that Adam Smith could not conceivably have imagined.

And that is why *The Wealth of Nations* holds only the limited interest for us today that the works of Newton have for a modern physicist or engineer.[5] Smith's important insights—such as the division of labor and the loose but prescient notion that coordination might be achieved through spontaneous order—have been absorbed and developed in the corpus of current knowledge.

Friedrich von Hayek[n] was largely neglected in modern economic thought until he was an unexpected recipient of the Nobel Prize in 1974. In the last years of his life, he was lionized by business and political leaders. It is hard to imagine many of them had read his works. Hayek's most cited work in this context is the extravagantly titled *The Road to Serfdom*, a denunciation of planning and social welfare systems.

Hayek's style is at once Delphic and dogmatic. In Hayek's mind his opponents are usually not just wrong, but mentally and morally defective. But Hayek articulated more clearly than any other twentieth-century economist the concept of spontaneous order.

And—along with a fellow Austrian, Ludwig von Mises—Hayek was one of the first to see that the information problems of planned economies were intractable. For many inside and outside the Soviet Union, central planning could be made to work with sufficiently powerful computers. Hayek understood this would never be so. Problems of incentive compatibility, and the absence of the collective knowledge created by the trials and errors of disciplined pluralism, would inevitably lead to failure.

Hayek, von Mises, and some other Central European economists of the early to mid twentieth century are sometimes described as "the Austrian school."[6] Hayek was actually an isolated figure, and the Nazi destruction of the intellectual life of Central Europe prevented the development of any continuing tradition. More recently, the conservative baton has transferred to Chicago.

The Chicago School

Almost from its foundation by John D. Rockefeller, the University of Chicago was a center of conservative economic thought.[7] Gary Becker[n] encapsulates that philosophy: "The combined assumptions of maximizing behavior, market equilibrium, and stable preferences, used relentlessly and unflinchingly, form the heart of the economic approach."[8]

As well as Becker and Friedman, Chicago figures such as George Stigler[n] and Richard Posner have played an active part in policy debates. Chicago is held responsible for various neoliberal experiments in South America and New Zealand.[9]

The centerpiece of Chicago economics is the insistence on rationality captured in Becker's statement. Becker's own most celebrated work is an economic analysis of family behavior[10] and his Nobel citation congratulates him for "having extended the domain of microeconomic analysis to a wide range of human behavior."[11] Becker sees few—perhaps no—limits to this extension. In his Nobel lecture he writes, "In the early stages of my work on crime, I was puzzled by why theft is socially harmful, since it appears merely to redistribute resources, usually from richer to poorer individuals. I resolved the puzzle by pointing out that criminals spend on weapons and on the value of their time in planning and carrying out their crimes and that such spending is socially unproductive."[12] The *Journal of Political Economy*, published from Chicago, has included articles on the economics of suicide and of language—and an exasperated response on the economics of brushing teeth.[13] But no parody is required.

Chicago was also the base for attacks on the postwar Keynesian orthodoxy of monetary and fiscal policy. Milton Friedman's counterrevolution emphasized the role of central banks controlling the supply of money relative to the importance of government adjusting levels of taxation and public expenditure.

Another Chicago economist, Robert Lucas,[n] applied "the combined assumptions of maximizing behavior, market equilibrium, and stable preferences" to macroeconomic issues "relentlessly and unflinchingly." Most theories of boom and bust—the business cycle—base their explanation on mistakes by firms or households, or on market imperfections. Perhaps there are speculative bubbles, or excess inventories; perhaps prices and wages fail to respond to supply and demand. But Chicago is unwilling to believe that markets make mistakes or fail to succeed in balancing supply and demand. Real business-cycle theory dismisses market imperfections and assumes "rational expectations"—consumers and businesses behave as if they had access to all available knowledge and infinite calculating power. Real business-cycle theory takes the assumptions of rationality in business decisions to the same extremes as Becker's description of family life.[14]

The Chicago School also recognizes the merits of the market system as a pluralist process of experiment and discovery. Some of the most compelling formulations of the arguments of chapters 9 and 10 have been presented by Chicago economists such as F. H. Knight and more recently by Almar Alchian.[15]

But the much stronger claim of the Chicago School is that competitive markets have efficiency properties unattainable under any other form of economic organization. Indeed this is now the belief of many mainstream economists. The best-selling economics textbook by Gregory Mankiw—a mainstream economist, but currently President Bush's principal economic adviser—sets out the claims clearly:

These observations lead to two insights about market outcomes:

· free markets allocate the supply of goods to the buyers who value them most highly, as measured by their willingness to pay.

· free markets allocate the demand for goods to the sellers who can produce them at least cost.

Can the social planner raise total economic well-being by increasing or decreasing the quantity of the good? The answer is no, as stated in this third insight about market outcomes.

· free markets produce the quantity of goods that maximizes the consumer and producer surplus.[16]

. . .

The equilibrium outcome is an efficient allocation of resources. The job of the benevolent social planner is, therefore, very easy: he can leave the market outcome just as he finds it. This policy of leaving well enough alone goes by the French expression *laissez-faire,* which literally translated means "allow them to do."

The benevolent social planner doesn't need to alter the market outcome because the invisible hand has already guided buyers and sellers to an allocation of the economy's resources that maximizes total surplus. This conclusion explains why economists often advocate free markets as the best way to organize economic activity.[17]

The argument Mankiw develops to support this position is, appropriately for an elementary text, informal. The most rigorous basis for such assertion is provided by a combination of the rationality postulates of Becker, the Arrow-Debreu framework of general equilibrium, the fundamental theorems of welfare economics, and a dose of individualistic political philosophy. It is time to place this last piece of the jigsaw.

Nozick and Rawls

John Rawls's *Theory of Justice,* published in 1972, and Robert Nozick's *Anarchy State and Utopia,* which appeared in 1974, are among the most influential works of modern political theory. Neither of these Harvard philosophers were proselytizing figures in the manner of the Chicago economists. Indeed the gulf between the dialogue of political philosophers and practicing politicians has perhaps never been wider than today. But both Rawls and Nozick were influential among economists, Rawls for those whose political leanings were to the left and Nozick for those who inclined right. Their frame of reasoning and the fundamental theorems of welfare economics have a natural affinity.

For Nozick, it is illegitimate to use the coercive power of the state to make some better off at the expense of others: his concept of justice requires the protection of property rights legitimately acquired or legitimately transferred. Nozick's government must achieve Pareto efficiency, but may not choose between alternative allocations that are Pareto efficient. The first of the fundamental theorems of welfare economics—every competitive equilibrium is Pareto efficient—could have been written for Nozick. The economic policy suggested is the creation of a framework that will permit competitive equilibrium to be achieved. No more, no less.

Rawls invites us to stand behind a "veil of ignorance" and order states of the world without knowing our role in them. The world economic system encompasses the different economic lives of Heidi and Ivan, Ravi and Sicelo, but we are not aware which of these people we ourselves will be. Rawls invokes what he calls the *maximin principle*—since we fear we may be Sicelo, we favor policies that will make Sicelo as well-off as possible. The Rawlsian approach not only justifies substantial redistribution, but requires it.

If the first fundamental theorem of welfare economics was written for Nozick, the second was written for Rawls. We stand behind the veil of ignorance, in search of a just mechanism for allocating scarce resources between competing ends. We are bound to choose a Pareto efficient outcome. The choice between Pareto efficient outcomes will be determined by the maximin principle. The second fundamental theorem of welfare economics—any Pareto efficient outcome can be achieved by an appropriate allocation of resources—tells us that all we need do is get the initial distribution right. Competitive equilibrium will take care of the rest. A free market economy, with income redistribution, meets the requirements of Rawls's *Theory of Justice*. Fukuyama, searching for the end of history, meets Rawls emerging from behind the veil of ignorance. We find them both in the United States at the turn of the millennium.

Nozick and the first fundamental theorem argue for the justice and efficiency of the American business model. A competitive market equilibrium is just simply by virtue of being a competitive market equilibrium. And Rawls and the second fundamental theorem argue for a more moderate version of political economy—redistributive market liberalism—to which I will return in chapter 28. With appropriate redistribution, a competitive market system will bring about a just and efficient outcome. Rawlsian justice need involve no discussion of how the economy operates, so long as we are satisfied that it is perfectly competitive. If society will only wind up the mechanism, the market will direct us toward the desired result.

The Halfway Mark

The fundamental theorems of welfare economics rest on the assumptions of the Arrow-Debreu model, and if that model were a complete description of how markets work, this book would end here. In chapter 7, I explained the mechanisms of production and exchange—gains from trade through specialization and competitive and comparative advantage—which have made modern economic systems so much more productive than subsistence economies. In chapters 8 and 9, I described the incentive compatibility problem and explained why central planning systems had struggled while market economies had, at least sometimes, evolved solutions. In chapters 9 and 10, I explained how central planning—"the single voice"—had stifled innovation and illustrated the mechanisms of disciplined pluralism that made market economies so innovative. These mechanisms have driven the coevolution of institutions and technology, which, in chapters 5 and 6, characterized the emergence of rich states.

The coordination problem remained. How does a decentralized market economy succeed in organizing the division of labor, specialization, and competitive advantage? Why does uncoordinated individual behavior not end in chaos? Chapter 11 considered that question, possibly revealing glimpses of the answer, but ending inconclusively. In

Part III, I described the best articulated response—the theory of perfectly competitive markets.

Chapter12 described the general functioning of competitive markets, and chapters 13 and 14 the workings of the markets for two peculiar, but central commodities in the market economy—the markets for risk and capital. In chapter 15, I explained the theory of general equilibrium, how it all fits together, and in chapter 16 how general equilibrium theory laid the foundations for the claim that the outcome of competitive markets is not only coordinated, but efficient.

The Arrow-Debreu results are the culmination of a long tradition in economics that emphasizes supply and demand, perfectly competitive markets, and the search for market equilibrium, conducted by independent, self-regarding agents.

Economic research since Arrow and Debreu has drawn game theory, transactions costs, and most recently behavioral economics into the mainstream of economic theory. In the Arrow-Debreu framework, interactions are anonymous and every market has many buyers and sellers. In game theory, the players are few and not anonymous. In the Arrow-Debreu framework, institutions do not exist or are dealt with in a reductionist way. Institutional, or transactions costs, economics recognizes that economic lives are lived in and through economic institutions. Behavioral economics contemplates alternative assumptions about motives and the nature of economic behavior. I will introduce game theory and institutional economics in the present chapter and take up behavioral economics in the chapter that follows.

Economic Theory After Arrow and Debreu
• •

In 1944, John von Neumann and Oskar Morgenstern published *The Theory of Games and Economic Behavior*. This approach was, after an interval, to revolutionize economic theory. The analysis of competitive markets supposes anonymous interactions among many buyers and many sellers. The fragmentation and impersonality of these markets leads to incentive compatibility—there is no need to consider the behavior and responses of other market participants. If Part III of the book was mostly concerned with these anonymous interactions, Part IV describes how the working of markets differs when these interactions are not anonymous. Game theory established mathematical tools for discussing strategic interrelationships in small groups and is essential for this analysis.[18]

Game theory has a popular appeal that fixed-point theorems will never achieve. This is partly the product of larger-than-life examples. The Prisoner's Dilemma, the most preposterous but the best known of all contributions to game theory, will appear in chapter 21. Game theory's characters are also larger-than-life. Von Neumann, born in Hungary, was one of the geniuses of his age.[19] At eighteen he was studying for three different degrees in different subjects at different universities in different countries. After making fundamental contributions to mathematics and quantum physics, he turned his attention briefly to economics, which he found "a million miles away from an advanced science."[20] Von Neumann became head of the U.S. Atomic Energy Commission—and the inspiration for Dr. Strangelove—before dying at the age of fifty-three.

John Nash was author of the principal solution concept in game theory—the Nash equilibrium—but his productive career was ended by schizophrenia. His health partially restored, he was awarded the Nobel Prize in 1994.[21] Nash was played by Russell Crowe in an Oscar-winning film of his life, *A Beautiful Mind.*

Institutional (or transactions cost) economics regards as its founder Ronald Coase,[n] a British economist who spent most of his career at the University of Chicago. His claim to fame rests mainly on two articles, published almost twenty-five years apart. The first was concerned with the theory of the firm. In the perfectly competitive world of Part III, firms played little or no role. There are many similar producers of every commodity. In Parts II and IV of this book, there are frequent references to individual firms; in Part III, almost none.

Since common sense suggests that the firm is an important institution in the modern economy, this is a loud and clear warning of the limitations of the Arrow-Debreu framework. Coase's thesis was that the boundaries of firms—islands of organization in a sea of markets[22]—were determined by the balance between the costs of alternative systems. Transactions costs in markets must be set against the problems of incentive compatibility with organizations. Is it cheaper to hire someone and tell them what to do or to negotiate contracts with potential suppliers? This make-or-buy decision is a central issue for every business.

Only in the 1970s was this approach developed much. The economic historian Douglass North[n] described how the evolution of economic institutions, particularly property rights, had provided the basis of historical development of the market economy.[23] Oliver Williamson argued that contracts between firms, and the internal structures of businesses themselves, were also determined by the costs of alternative institutional arrangements.[24] Twenty years later these ideas had developed into a comprehensive economic approach to the structure of economic organizations.[25]

Economics Evolving

Game theory and transactions costs economics allowed economists to address issues excluded from the Arrow-Debreu framework. The generation of economists who followed gave particular attention to issues of risk and information. They asked "How can coordination still be achieved if information is imperfect?" and "Why do risk markets not function as the Arrow-Debreu model requires?"

Joe Stiglitz was a leading figure in that generation, and certainly the most prolific. His work, and that of others, showed that dealing with risk and information required a much more complex truth about how markets work. In the 1990 Wicksell lectures, Stiglitz set out his revisionist stall: "For the past half century a simple paradigm has dominated the economics profession. . . . The most precise statement of that paradigm is provided by the model of Arrow and Debreu. It postulates large numbers of profit (or value) maximizing firms interacting with rational utility-maximizing consumers. . . . I want to argue in these lectures that the competitive paradigm not only did not provide much guidance on the vital question of the choice of economic systems, but what 'advice' it did provide was often misguided. The conceptions of the market that underlay that analysis mischaracterized it: the standard analyses underestimated the strength—and weaknesses—of market economies."[26]

In 1995, Stiglitz joined the President's Council of Economic Advisers and in 1997 was appointed chief economist at the World Bank. Installed at the heart of the Washington consensus, Stiglitz did not change his views—nor refrain from expressing them. He found a sympathetic listener in the World Bank's president, James Wolfensohn, who had sought to broaden the institution's remit.

But Stiglitz's outspoken views went too far for Wall Street. And more particularly, for a U.S. Treasury basking in the warm glow of American triumphalism. It became clear that Wolfensohn's continued support for Stiglitz might be at the cost of his own job, and in 1999 Stiglitz returned to research and teaching at Stanford University. In 2001, Stiglitz, along with George Akerlof and Michael Spence, was awarded the Nobel Prize for work on markets and imperfect information. That award was a formal recognition of how far modern economics had moved from the simplified theoretical framework of Arrow-Debreu and the simplified policy prescriptions of the Chicago School. Stiglitz became an increasingly public and controversial figure. I return to this controversy in chapter 28.

In the remaining chapters of this part of the book, I review successively various assumptions explicit or implicit in the Arrow-Debreu framework:

- What happens if individuals are not self-regarding utility maximizers? (chapter 18)

- What happens if information about complex products is imperfect? (chapter 19)

- What happens if our attitudes to risk are inconsistent and irrational? (chapter 20)

- How do market economies achieve cooperative, rather than self-regarding, behavior in households, teams, and businesses? (chapter 21)

- What brings about the coordination demanded by technological interdependencies, such as networks and standards? (chapter 22)

- How do market economies produce new knowledge? (chapter 23)

To list these questions seems to present a fundamental critique of the Arrow-Debreu model. The issues they raise—imperfect information, problems of technical coordination, the production of knowledge—are often described by economists as "market failures."[27] They would indeed represent failures of the market system if the Arrow-Debreu model were intended to explain the daily workings of markets—to tell us what is happening at the San Remo flower market, in the electricity trading system, or in an airline reservation network.

But that was never the purpose. The Arrow-Debreu model is a framework for understanding more clearly the nature of competitive markets, not a description of a complex modern economy. In succeeding chapters, I will describe some of the many social, political, and economic institutions that have developed to handle the problems listed above. These institutions demonstrate the success, not the failure, of the market system. The limited truth about markets that emerges from the perfectly competitive model provides a base for further exploration. That is the task of the next chapter of this book.

{18}

Rationality and Adaptation

People

Economic lives are lived by people. People like Heidi. Heidi's work is not necessary to support her family. She sometimes wonders if her family derives any financial benefit, after she has spent money on child care, domestic help, driving to school, and TV dinners. But Heidi loves teaching, loves children, and knows that she would be bored if she spent every day at home.

Pedro's economic life as an illegal immigrant is the life of rational economic man. He hates his job, although he has sacrificed almost every other part of himself to it. His behavior is mercenary. His principal aspiration is to earn enough money to stop being a rational economic man and again become a normal human being. Raoul is tempted to follow Pedro, but values his family more than his material standard of living—or theirs.

Ivan is thrilled with his work. It is, by Russian standards, secure and well paid. For the first time in his life, his working environment is competently organized. He would happily do his job for less money. Olga's salary is ludicrous. She earns more from occasional pieces of translation than a month of teaching and scholarship. But it is the latter that gives her satisfaction, and Ivan earns enough to provide what they regard as an excellent standard of living.

A few minutes spent talking to Ravi shows that what he values most is his status as an official in a prestigious state institution.

Sicelo's brother, Patrick, who works in a mine, conforms to the require-ments of rational economic man—except that he maximizes his income not for himself but for his family. Despite conversations with his brother, Sicelo himself finds it difficult to visualize what life would be like outside the village in which he has spent all his life. In any event, the family situation makes it impossible for him to take employment in the mines or in Durban.

These people are not freaks, or saints. They are often selfish. They are like you and me, and like you and me, they find it impossi-ble to separate their economic lives from other aspects of their lives. Pedro and Patrick have achieved that separation. They are both unhappy. Their lives are riven by the conflict between social and eco-nomic values which arise when societies with very different stan-dards of living are close together—as in Mexico's proximity to the United States, or the dual economy of South Africa.

Economists and Rationality

The Chicagoan emphasis on rationality is taken to extreme lengths.[1] But it is almost a badge of honor among mainstream econ-omists to seek explanations in rational or self-regarding behavior. Often, this is achieved by stretching the meaning of rationality. The approach is caricatured by Paul Samuelson.[2] "When the governess of infants caught in a burning building reenters it unobserved on a hopeless mission of rescue, casuists may argue 'she did it only to get the good feeling of doing it. Because otherwise she wouldn't have done it.'" As Samuelson observes, this "explanation" is "not even wrong."

Rationality is generally used by economists in one or the other of two senses. Rationality as consistency, and rationality as self-regarding materialism.[3] Neither of these corresponds to the ordinary meaning of the word *rational*. I may be consistent in offending my friends or eating more than is good for me, but few people would describe such behav-ior as rational. Nor is rational behavior necessarily materialistic and self-interested. We might not share Ravi's concern with his status at work or follow Patrick in sending all our earnings back to our families, but these are not irrational things to do.

Most often, economists interpret rationality as self-regarding mate-

Box 18.1

● ●

HAPPINESS AND WELFARE

We don't learn much about happiness by being told that what we do must make us happy, otherwise we wouldn't have done it. Research in at least three areas is increasing our real understanding of what makes people happy.

Statistical analysis relates descriptions of happiness (or other measures of satisfaction with life) to characteristics either of the society in which individuals live, or to characteristics of the individuals themselves. As I explained in chapter 4, people in richer countries tend to say that they are happier, but the tendency is not strong. And as societies become richer, the proportion of people who say they are happy does not rise much. Strong evidence suggests that within a country, well-off people report themselves as happier than poor people. But other variables—such as marital and employment status—are also of great importance.[*]

Neurophysiological research has begun to identify activities within the brain that are associated with what people describe as happy experiences. The role of the chemical serotonin is central. A drug like Ecstasy produces an immediate rush of serotonin, while the effect of antidepressants such as Prozac is to influence the uptake of serotonin by neurotransmitters. These relationships between behavior and serotonin uptake are found in animals as well as humans.[†]

Experience sampling asks people to describe how they are feeling at instances of time over a longer interval. Generally the highest scores are recorded when people are successfully performing absorbing and challenging tasks. Work is usually more rewarding than passive leisure activities, such as watching television. These flow experiences seem to cause states of happiness independent of the intrinsic value of the activity—thus the curious mixture of pleasure and pain involved in mountaineering and other arduous sports.[‡]

The idea that we maximize welfare by acting in accordance with fixed and predetermined preferences should be seen as an

analytic device, not a realistic description of behavior. And policies to promote happiness would not focus exclusively on GDP.

*   *Easterlin (1974); Frank (1985); van de Stadt, Kapetyn, and van de*
      Geer (1985); Lane (1991); Clark and Oswald (2002).

†   *Davidson (2000), Breiter (2001), Greenfield (2001).*

‡   *Csikszentmihalyi (1992), Loewenstein (1999).*

• •

rialism. I am writing this after putting down an excellent book by
William Easterly, a World Bank economist. Easterly is a careful and sensitive observer of the economic problems of poor countries, and chapter
24 is indebted to him. Yet Easterly begins by asking, "What is the basic
principle of economics? As a wise elder once told me, 'People do what
they get paid to do; what they don't get paid to do, they don't do.'"[4]

It is inconceivable that Easterly really believes this. The case studies
that illustrate his book immediately contradict it. An Indian widow sacrifices her own health to secure an education for her children; Sudanese
youths starve because their country is riven by a dispute over Islamic
law; an Egyptian farmer sells a clover field to take a second wife.

Economists insist on rationality because they do not like the
alternatives.[5] Self-regarding materialism is a better predictor of
behavior than altruism;[6] and Easterly's cynicism is the result of
depressing experiences working with government officials in poor
states. But the extremes of universal self-interestedness and universal altruism are not the only assumptions about behavior that might
be made. We know from our everyday lives—including our economic
lives—that reality is somewhere in between.

But such a reality is necessarily complex. There are few ways to be
rational, but many ways in which it is possible to be irrational. Self-
regarding materialism is predictable; the actions of those who balance
multiple objectives are more difficult to analyze. And this is why economists adopt a concept of rationality that reduces to self-interest. It
seems to offer an anchor in an ocean of otherwise unpredictable
human behavior. The assumption of rationality gives economics a
rigor that distinguishes it from other social sciences.

A further attraction of rationality for many economists is that conclusions can be drawn from wholly a priori reasoning. No empirical investigation is required. A joke about economists runs, "If you ask an economist to study the behavior of horses, s/he would sit at a desk and ask, 'What would I do if I were a horse?'" The analysis of economic behavior requires us to look at actual choices of firms and households, not simply to impose assumptions on their behavior. It is time to study horses.

Adaptation
● ●

Behavior is a product of the environment in which people find themselves. What Easterly really means is that people respond to what he calls incentives.[7] Easterly provides an engaged, and engaging, description of a Lahore wedding, which vividly illustrates the paradoxes of Pakistan: creativity, intelligence, and beauty, side by side with corruption, authoritarianism, and poverty. Why are Pakistani scientists able to make atomic bombs but unable to organize a vaccination program? Why are educated Pakistanis more productive in Silicon Valley than in Lahore? Why are World Bank bureaucrats more honest than Pakistani ones?

"People do what they get paid to do" is part of the answer, but a facile response. If human nature is everywhere self-interested, why is the Pakistani public service corrupt but the World Bank is not? Would James Wolfensohn, president of the World Bank, be corrupt if he were a Pakistani civil servant? You are fired if you are a corrupt World Bank official, but not if you are a corrupt Pakistani civil servant. But this is a manifestation of the problem, not its explanation.

That explanation is found in path dependency and adaptation. Both corrupt and honest behavior are self-reinforcing. A member of an organization with a reputation for its integrity will wish to expose dishonesty. A member of a corrupt organization will find it difficult to be honest. You cannot manage on your salary; you are not expected to.

The same people might be corrupt in a corrupt environment and honest in an honest one. But this is only part of the explanation: they are not the same people. We seek environments appropriate for us. A Pakistani nuclear scientist will get a better job in Pakistan than in the United States; for a Pakistani doctor or software engineer, the reverse is true. And that is why Pakistan can manufacture nuclear weapons but cannot organize a vaccination program.

Pakistani economists who are committed to economic development in poor countries will prefer to work in the World Bank than in the Pakistani civil service, which is why the World Bank employs many able Pakistanis. What would Mr. Wolfensohn do in Pakistan? The question is absurd. Mr. Wolfensohn is adapted by personality, training, and experience to the job of being a senior banker in the United States. He is not and could never have been a Pakistani civil servant.

All these aspects of economic behavior are adaptive. Adaptation means that the traits of behavior we observe are those that are most likely to be replicated in the environment in which we find them. Adaptive behavior is very different in the monastery and on the trading floor. It is the behavior that fits its environment. And in turn both the monastery and the trading floor are adapted to their purposes, though some might query their purposes. Evolution favors what is good at replicating itself, rather than what is good. This fundamental distinction is essential to understanding any evolving system.

Workers of the World, Unite!

That distinction between adaptive behavior and optimal behavior was precisely the problem Jack Welch faced at General Electric. Organizations develop processes and routines and establish values of their own. And it is important that they should do so: this is how the experience and capabilities of the organization are passed to new members.

But these values and processes may become ends in themselves rather than means to the organization's goals. The organization comes to measure the achievement of its members by their contribution to the internal cohesion of the organization rather than their contribution to its purposes. This is the nature of helpfulness, of superficial congeniality.

The same phenomenon was found in Mao's China, in Britain's electricity industry, in the later phases of Henry Ford's control of the Ford Motor Company. My own experience of Oxford University was an illuminating and instructive example.[8] The values prized within all these organizations were internally generated. Workers were praised for their diligence in regurgitating the contents of Mao's *Little Red Book*. Civil servants were promoted for the consensual skills that ensured that they spoke to ministers and the public "with a single voice." Managers were hired or fired for their devotion to Henry Ford's ideas. The rituals of Oxford University's committees, like those of the Chinese mandarinate or Ottoman empire, were pursued for their own sake, even by people who perfectly understood their futility.

In all these systems, organizational characteristics are self-reinforcing. In an organization that values helpfulness, people will tend to be promoted if they are helpful. And so they learn to be helpful and imitate the behavior of the helpful. Moreover, those whose natural instincts are helpful will be attracted by the prospect of working in such an environment, while others with different approaches and characters will go elsewhere. Helpfulness becomes ever more entrenched as a predominant value.

The common feature of these environments is that behavior that is adaptive within the organization is dysfunctional for it. Never mind that Chinese industrial production is falling, that the AGR program is billions over budget and years behind schedule, that General Motors is overtaking Ford, and that Oxford University is losing its status as an international university. It is not permissible even to say these things. This is the inability to face reality that Welch identified in GE's superficial congeniality.

Ultimately, if these structures last long enough, they resemble the organizations described in Kafka's *The Trial*. No one is in charge, and everyone is part of a system that they know is ineffective but are powerless to change.

The mechanics of these adaptive, dysfunctional relationships have never been better described than by Vaclav Havel, the playwright who became president of the post-Soviet Czech Republic. Havel writes of the greengrocer who displays the slogan "Workers of the World, Unite!"[9] As Havel points out, it is unlikely that the sign is displayed because the shopkeeper feels an irresistible impulse to acquaint the public with his ideals. Instead, "the greengrocer declares his loyalty ... by accepting the prescribed ritual, by accepting appearances as reality, by accepting the given rules of the game. In doing so, however, he has himself become a player in the game, thus making it possible for the game to go on, for it to exist in the first place." The phenomenon of self-regarding, self-perpetuating selection mechanisms is common in the public sector, but can equally be found in private sector businesses. The Western equivalent of the sign demanding that workers of the word unite is found in the meaningless sloganizing and mission statements of large corporations. These manifestations are sometimes the product of totalitarian corporate dictatorships, sometimes, as in Havel's example, the product of a self-policing culture in which no one dares to laugh. IBM's market dominance allowed it to maintain internal cultures that were not consistent with the external objectives of the organization.

For a time, but not forever. Reality must be faced if there is an external layer of selection that reviews output rather than procedure. In GE, a new management culture applied different performance criteria to business units. Ford was ultimately obliged to react to competitive pressures. Organizations that face no competition or have no mechanisms for responding to it may continue in such behavior for extended periods. The Chinese and Ottoman bureaucracies survived for centuries.

Mechanisms of Adaptation
● ●

So adaptive behavior is not necessarily efficient, or optimal, in any ordinary sense. In English, we use the word *good* in both senses, and when we describe "a good concentration camp guard," the ambiguity is obvious.[10] Similarly, a good decision or a good policy may be defined not as one that leads to good outcomes, but one that meets the perceived need of the organization for consensus among varying interests.

What is adaptive may not be efficient; confusion between adaptation and efficiency is one source of resistance to the use of evolutionary models in social sciences. It was a century before the mathematics of Darwin's ideas were properly understood. In the meantime, confusion generated by the phrase "survival of the fittest" led to an erroneous belief that evolution was a process of continuous improvement, carried moral authority, and justified assertions of racial superiority and eugenic policies.[11] The opprobrium that followed attached even to the much more careful theory of sociobiology, developed in the 1970s by scientists such as E. O. Wilson.[12]

We do not want to believe that the development of human institutions and thought is random. And it is not. While the Darwinian evolution of species is driven by chance—genetic mutations emerge accidentally—the evolution of social, political, and cultural institutions is the result of many different selection mechanisms. These include learning, imitation, and reward.

Learning enables evolution to proceed much more rapidly. Genetic selection would—eventually—breed children who did not play in busy streets, but learning and imitation produce the same results more quickly. And a genetic predisposition to listen to parental advice is adaptive. Reward is an economic selection mechanism with no simple biological analogue. Companies whose competitive advantages match their market—whose characteristics are adaptive—grow in absolute and relative size. In this way, the competitive market economy selects for the distinctive capabilities of firms.

Chicago, Salem, and Wall Street
• •

In 1953, Milton Friedman published a collection, *Essays in Positive Economics*. The arguments Friedman presented there not only defined the approach of the Chicago School but influenced the development of economics much more widely.

Friedman claimed that rationality was not an assumption about motivation, but a prediction about behavior.[13] The relationship between assumptions and predictions, a central issue for Friedman, is discussed more extensively in chapter 28. The distinction was central to his views on the nature of maximizing behavior. Even if individuals were not self-interested, self-interested behavior would drive out altruism. Firms might not seek to maximize profits, but the only firms to survive in competitive markets would be those that did maximize profits. Self-regarding, materialistic behavior would be the norm because no other behavior could persist in a market economy. This claim unites Friedman and anticapitalist protesters. And yet both are wrong. This type of argument does not show that behavior will be rational. It shows that it will be adaptive. And rational and adaptive behavior may, but need not, be the same.

In December 1998, Henry Blodget, a journalist who had found a job as an analyst at a small merchant bank, announced that a share in Amazon.com, the online book retailer, was worth at least $400. The price was then around $250. Jonathan Cohen, an analyst at the respected Merrill Lynch, countered with the suggestion (subsequently shown to be correct) that $50 was a more realistic valuation. But within a month, Amazon shares had soared beyond $400. And Blodget soared with it: he succeeded to Cohen's job at Merrill Lynch. Blodget went on to promote a wide range of Internet stocks for his new employer, most of which turned out to be worthless.

Whether Blodget believed these extravagant valuations, or whether he issued them to advance his career and bonus prospects, may never be resolved. In 2002, New York State attorney general Eliot Spitzer revealed internal memos written by Blodget that displayed less enthusiasm than his public pronouncements. In one, he described a stock Merrill was recommending as a "piece of shit."[14] But enthusiasm by Internet analysts for Internet stocks, whatever its basis, was certainly adaptive. The person who occupied Blodget's post in 1999 was bound to be wildly optimistic about the prospects for Internet stocks. No one else could have continued to hold that position, as Cohen's experience showed. Whether the individual concerned was cynical or genuine in his beliefs is relevant to how angry we should feel and how legal action should be determined. But we do not need to know the answer to that question to explain what happened.

In Blodget we recognize a familiar historical figure. In Arthur Miller's play *The Crucible,* the part of Henry Blodget is played by the Reverend Hale: "On being called here to ascertain witchcraft he felt the pride of the specialist whose unique knowledge has at last been publicly called for."[15] Both Hale and Blodget eventually understood they had helped unleash madness beyond anyone's control. The behavior of market participants in 1999–2000 was adaptive but irrational, just as it was adaptive but irrational to believe that Salem, Massachusetts, was besieged by witches in 1692.

Adaptive behavior, by definition, is self-sustaining and self-reinforcing. Honesty is adaptive in the World Bank. Superficial congeniality was adaptive in the heyday of strategic planning at General Electric. Corruption is adaptive in the Pakistani civil service. Bullishness is adaptive at Merrill Lynch.

Pursued by a Bear
● ●

An economist specializing in game theory is in the wilderness with a friend when they see a bear approaching. The theorist pulls out his laptop computer and starts to compute an optimal strategy. His colleague cries out in alarm, "Run, there is no time to waste." The economist smiles complacently. "Don't worry," he says, "the bear has to work it out too."

The joke is not particularly funny, but it contains an important truth.[16] When economists adopted game theory, they assumed rational—self-regarding, materialist—behavior. In a Nash equilibrium, each player adopts the best strategy given the strategies of all other players. Biologists also adopted game theory, but did not—could not—assume their subjects had access to laptops. They developed the concept of an evolutionary stable strategy.[17] What behavior by bears would allow them to survive and thrive, even in the face of incursion by other bears with different behavior? That sounds like the same question, but it is not. It exemplifies the difference between adaptive and rational behavior. The adaptive bear catches the rational economist. This distinction will, in chapter 21, explain why adaptive cooperators do better than rational, self-regarding maximizers.

I described in the last chapter how neoclassical economics was enhanced both by game theory and by transactions costs economics. But neoclassical rationality assumptions were imposed on both. The transactions costs solution to the wilderness dilemma is that the economist should optimize within constraints. He should do just the amount of calculation needed to find the best strategy in the light of his knowledge that every second devoted to calculation increases the chances of being caught by the bear.[18] Borrowing Herbert Simon's term (but for a very different concept), Oliver Williamson calls this optimization under constraints-bounded rationality.[19]

In this vein, transactions costs economics often degenerates into a Panglossian view of the world: institutions that exist must be the solution to some constrained-optimization problem. Economists even have a word—*recoverability*—for deducing the maximization problem to which observed behavior is the answer.

But this version of bounded rationality confronts a fundamental problem. How could the economist know when to stop calculating when he cannot know the benefits of further calculation? If we knew enough to be boundedly rational, we would know enough to be completely rational. The best answer is an evolutionary one, but such an answer leads us to adaptive, instinctive responses—such as those of the bear. And that is our behavior too. When a bear approaches—we turn and run.

Behavioral Economics

But this response is wrong. The instinct to flee from danger is powerful, and adaptive. It is wise to turn and run when faced with fire, flood, muggers, and dangerous machinery. But not when you encounter a bear. (This is probably not what you expected to learn when you bought this book, but may be the most valuable information in it.) It is in the nature of adaptive responses that they work for us in general but may be inappropriate in particular cases. Many boundedly rational decisions are mistaken, some seriously so.

You have a ticket for a play that has cost $50. On arriving at the theater, you find that you have lost the ticket. Would you buy a new ticket?

You have decided to see a play for which tickets cost $50 and on your way to the theater lose a $50 note. Do you still buy a ticket to the play?

This is one of a set of pairs of questions posed in the 1970s by two Israeli psychologists, Dan Kahneman[n] and Amos Tversky, who created the subject now called behavioral economics. Kahneman and Tversky found that practically all their subjects would still go to the play if they had lost $50, but less than half would still go if they had lost the $50 ticket.

Kahneman and Tversky did not simply challenge the standard economic assumption of rationality, but began to identify patterns of "irrationality." The ticket problem illustrates "framing." The choice we face is the same in both cases—to pay $50 to see the play, or to go home and watch television. But the way in which problems are described influences our answer.[20]

These explorations beyond rationality begin to describe how we really think. We apply conventions and rules of thumb that generally serve us well. Some are probably genetic, some the product of learning, imitation, and reward. Some are universal, some culturally specific. We occasionally apply these rules in situations where they do not work for us—many so-called irrationalities are of this kind. People we deal with may attempt to exploit these irrationalities—some ways in which they do will emerge in the next two chapters.

We behave adaptively in our economic lives, and the institutions in which we act these lives are themselves adaptive. The remaining chapters of this part of the book illustrate various areas in which adaptive individual behavior, and adaptive institutions, have co-evolved. In the next chapter, I consider how households and firms have developed mechanisms to deal with the problems of imperfect information.

{19}

Information

Perfectly competitive markets have many potential buyers and sellers of each commodity, such as apples. All apples are the same. Or perhaps all Granny Smith apples are the same. Or perhaps we can easily tell the quality of each Granny Smith apple and locate many producers of each grade. Even apples are not easy. Goods and services sold in modern market economies are often much more complex. What happens when we are not quite sure what it is we are buying?

The Wallet Auction

I have just pulled my wallet from my pocket. It is on the desk in front of me. How much will you offer for the money in it?[1] If you have read so far, you can probably guess something about my habits. But you do not really know how much I spend, or how often I visit the bank, or whether I prefer to pay with cash or a plastic card. You might speculate that $100 is in my wallet.

But you would not be wise to offer that much. Your potential profit is the difference between what is in the wallet and what you pay. If you succeeded with a $60 bid, and your assessment that $100 is in my wallet is right, you would gain consumer surplus of $40. But this won't happen. If there is more than $60 in my wallet, I will reject your proposal. If there is less than $60, I will sell it to you, but you will be worse off. The transaction doesn't make sense. The only offers I will accept are offers you should not make.

The problem is that I know what I am selling and you don't know exactly what you are buying. There is an information asymmetry between buyer and seller. And this is true of almost every transaction in a modern economy. The auto manufacturer knows more about the car than the purchaser. The clothes retailer is better informed about current fashions and the quality of materials. The supermarket knows the provenance and age of its lettuces and knows that you don't. The wallet example is striking because there is no motive for exchange except differences in information. There are no gains from trade through specialization or differences in capability.

Even when there are net gains from trade, transactions are clouded by differences in information. In the used-car market, well-informed sellers face ignorant buyers. Suppose—as in a famous model of Akerlof[n] (1970)—there are two kinds of autos, reliable ones and lemons. The seller knows which is which but it is difficult for the buyer to tell. The price of used autos will be discounted to reflect the incidence of lemons in the population. It will be an average of the values of good autos and of lemons.

But that average is a good price for the owner of a lemon, and a disappointing price for the vendor of a reliable auto. So owners of lemons will want to sell, and owners of reliable autos won't. As buyers discover this, that knowledge will push down the price of secondhand autos. But the problem is cumulative. The lower the price of used autos, the more reluctant will be owners of reliable cars to sell, and the more justifiably suspicious buyers will be. So secondhand car prices will be low, secondhand autos will be of poor quality, and many secondhand autos will be bad buys even at these low prices. This is exactly what many people experience.

If information is imperfect, some people will regret their purchases. But a less obvious problem is even more serious for the efficiency of competitive markets. Bad trades do happen, but many good trades don't. I need to sell my excellent and reliable car, but you will not pay what it is worth because you cannot be sufficiently confident of its quality. So the market will not be Pareto efficient. Allocations that would make both parties better off may not be achieved in competitive markets.

Sellers of cars try to overcome the lemons problem. They do not want you to think they are selling because the price is more than the car is worth. The small ads placed by private buyers often say, "Genuine reason for sale." "One owner" suggests a tolerant driver or a serviceable car. The social context—the buyer's knowledge of the situation, or the seller—makes the transaction possible. The most important mechanism for developing that context is reputation.

Reputation

If you want an accountant, you might go to Pricewaterhouse Coopers; for a lawyer, to Cravath, Swaine & Moore; for management advice, to McKinsey & Co. Most professional service firms still use the names of the distinguished, but deceased, individuals who set up these practices, often more than a century ago. Coca-Cola is a name invented by James Pemberton, but the modern company is relentless in maintaining its trademark. All these businesses know these names are valuable assets. Throughout the flurry of corporate restructuring and reengineering, they cling to them; that is why we have to swallow the mouthful of PricewaterhouseCoopers.

Reputation is the principal means through which a market economy deals with consumer ignorance. When we are ill, we suffer not just pain but asymmetric information. Our confidence in the physician deals with the asymmetric information, and we hope that his prescriptions deal with the pain.

Typically, this transaction has several different layers of reputation. We visit a physician, relying on the reputation of doctors in general, and on the particular reputation of Dr. Smith. If Dr. Smith is away, we may consult another member of his practice. The person we consult enjoys some reputation simply through being a medical doctor. We expect that Dr. Smith would not jeopardize his or her own reputation by associating with incompetent colleagues. We may also need to rely on the reputations of specialists whom Dr. Smith recommends, the reputations of hospitals, or the reputations of particular drugs.

Individuals and firms with established reputations—like Dr. Smith and McKinsey—have incentives to maintain them. And every day, we rely on the reputations of physicians and accountants, supermarkets and newspapers, car manufacturers and banks. We rely on them because we do not wish to train for years to diagnose our own illnesses or understand the tax code. We do not want to visit factories to see that our food is prepared in clean conditions, or to go to Iraq to see the state of affairs for ourselves. We cannot ourselves judge the reliability of the cars we buy or the solvency of the banks to which we trust our money.

It is simply wrong to think that a market economy does or could rely on the diligence of individual consumers to deal with these problems. Life is too short, and there are more interesting ways to spend it than studying the balance sheets of banks. We can never have enough information to assess the competence of our doctor, because if we did, we would not need to consult a doctor. Of course, individual experiences are the stuff of which the reputations of firms and practitioners are made. But these individual and commercial experiences take on life, and significance, only when they become part of shared social knowledge.

Reputation works best when reputations are contagious. Respected businesspeople deal with other respected businesspeople, and their continued reputation depends on behaving in this way. This is the most important mechanism for enforcing trust in business dealings. But it often breaks down. The rapid collapse of Andersen after its role in the Enron scandal was exposed illustrates how contagion can support reputation—or destroy it. Physicians, believing it important to maintain public confidence in their profession, have been notoriously slow to act against incompetent colleagues.

Advertising
● ●

My uncle was a Scottish pharmacist of scrupulous integrity. When asked by a customer to recommend a brand of expensive skin cream, he struggled between his conscience and his desire to make a sale. "Madam," he said, "the advertisements speak very well of it."

Advertising is "cheap talk."[2] We expect advertisers to say that their products are good and do not feel wiser when they do say this. To such an extent that they have mostly stopped. Copywriters have steadily drained all information from their work. Coca-Cola advertising a century ago told you that the beverage was healthful, refreshing, the preferred drink of ladies, available at any drugstore. Today, the same company tells you only that "Coke is it." In many advertisements you cannot tell what is being advertised if you do not already know.

Not only businesses advertise. We dress to impress potential employers or potential partners. Commercial advertising—for clothing, cars, or perfumes—sells goods that we in turn use to advertise ourselves. Many other species spend far more of their resources on advertisement than human beings. They devote effort to grooming, as we do, and like us, they expend resources to show off beautiful bodies. The colors and petals of birds and flowers are impressive, but nature has many more extraordinary examples of advertisement. Male grouse engage in competitive displays (leks) of their charms to females, who note the best and return to mate with the winners.[3] Bowerbirds construct arbors many times their own size to impress and attract potential partners. Human beings sometimes behave in similar ways.

In the 1970s, economists, puzzled to explain the increasing prevalence of costly but contentless advertisement in the market economy, and biologists, puzzled to explain the ubiquity of costly but pointless display in nature, came up independently with similar answers.[4] Today a general theory of advertisement is common to economics and biology.

The information that these displays contain, and effectively the only information that they contain, is the information that the advertiser is able and willing to invest resources in impressing potential partners—mates or customers. But this is important information for these potential partners because it tells them that the advertiser is well-endowed and willing to invest resources in a relationship. This is equally true of the relationship between the bowerbird and his mate and the Coca-Cola company and its customers.

The paradox—which is illustrated by extreme examples from nature such as the bowerbird and the peacock's tail—is that wasteful communication is necessary to demonstrate its truth. Cheap talk is worthless precisely because it is cheap, which is why girls were traditionally taught to value an engagement ring above a man's promise that he would still love you in the morning.

Costly and wasteful advertisement demonstrates that the advertiser is also investing in the quality of the product and a continued relationship with customers, because otherwise the costly and wasteful advertisement would serve no purpose. And—as with peacocks and bowerbirds—advertisers are thrown into the competitive presentation of ever more extensive displays.

Brown Coal

Businesses also have to trade with imperfect information. Many senior executives of energy companies made the trip in a small plane from Melbourne to the Latrobe Valley. Their destination became evident well before they saw the airport. A cloud of steam hangs over the area. The Latrobe Valley contains one of the largest deposits of brown coal in the world, and its economy is entirely devoted to burning that coal. Huge mechanical diggers shovel this plentiful but poor-quality fuel into power stations. Much of the electricity for southeast Australia is generated there.

The cash-strapped government of Victoria decided to sell the three power stations in the Latrobe Valley—Hazelwood, Loy Yang, and Yallourn. They invited sealed bids in an auction. Three foreign companies were successful. Or so they thought. The auction raised far more than had been expected, and the sale of electricity assets allowed the government to retire most of the state debt.[5] Today, however, the winners of the auction are nursing their wounds and seeking exits from what has proved an expensive venture for all of them. These companies discovered, at great cost, the "winner's curse."

The effects of liberalizing the Australian energy market were unpredictable. The government's consultants painted a rosy picture of high prices and rising demand. But that was no more credible than the patter of a used-car salesman, and the serious contenders commissioned their own studies. Estimates of the future price of electricity from the Latrobe Valley spanned a wide range. But the successful bidders expected prices at the top end of the range and pitched their bids accordingly. *That was why they were the successful bidders.*[6]

If prices had simply been in the middle of the range of estimates of informed buyers, the firms that won the auction would still have lost money handsomely. Even the average expectation of the bidders was likely to be optimistic: after all, the bidders had chosen to take part in the auction. Other firms had taken a look at the project and, more pessimistic, had decided not to become involved.

The winner's curse was discovered when the U.S. government

auctioned offshore oil blocks.[7] Oil companies learned that their winning bids were for areas where their geologists had made more bullish assessments than similar geologists, with similar training, working for competitors. The blocks companies got were the ones where their advisers had screwed up.

Deciding which firm should operate Loy Yang power station or drill for oil in the Gulf of Mexico seems very like the problem of deciding who should have the *Portrait of Dr. Gachet*. In all cases, the issue is the allocation of a scarce resource between competing ends. But there is a key difference between a "private value" auction—for *Dr. Gachet*—and a "common value" auction—for Loy Yang. In the private value auction of *Dr. Gachet,* everyone has the same (accurate) information about the appearance and provenance of the painting. If different people make different bids, it is because they have different preferences or because some are richer than others. These different bids are the result of different private values.

In the common value auction of Loy Yang, all the bidders had similar financial resources. There were no differences in preferences: no subjective or aesthetic issues were involved. Bids differed only because different firms made different (and mostly inaccurate) assessments of the value of what it was that they were buying.[8] There were no differences in private values, only differences in estimates of the common value.

The three examples of this chapter so far—the wallet auction, the used-car market, the sale of Loy Yang power station—are all examples of how market institutions that work in a straightforward way when all parties have identical, and comprehensive, information can operate in an entirely different manner when the information is imperfect. Oil companies have learned about the winner's curse. They no longer bid what they think a block is worth.

Large companies understand that auctions are complex and employ mathematical economists to devise their strategies. So governments hired their own mathematical economists to outsmart the bidders, as in the auctions of 3G mobile phone licenses in Europe in 2000.

The German government's mobile phone auction occurred at more or less the top of the technology boom in 2000. Collectively, the five companies that received licenses to operate third-generation mobile services in Germany paid 36 billion euros ($42 billion). In the cold light of day, the businesses concerned wondered what they had done: profits from providing these services will never likely approach 36 billion euros. Given the costs of rolling out networks, it is not certain that the licenses are worth anything at all. In July 2002, one of the "successful" bidders in the auction abandoned its license and wrote off its expenditure.[9]

The auction was carefully designed to avoid the winner's curse by ensuring that all bidders were well-informed about the actions of the others. But if information is imperfect, adaptive behavior can give rise to irrational outcomes. As it did with Henry Blodget's recommendations for Merrill Lynch.

Many layers of adaptive behavior contributed to this overall auction irrationality. Telecom stocks were owned by people who held exaggerated beliefs about their value. They had suffered a winner's curse in outbidding more rational investors. Senior executives of telecom companies were unreasonably optimistic about business prospects; like Henry Blodget, they would not have been in these positions otherwise. The advisers to the process hoped to be appointed as advisers in the successive auctions they knew were planned in other European countries. Given the fundamental irrationality of stock prices, many other kinds of irrational behavior were adaptive. No company could have maintained its stock market value if it failed to obtain a license.

Like Henry Blodget and Merrill Lynch, the executives of the companies that bought German phone licenses made bad decisions, in the sense that they were extremely costly to the people on whose behalf they acted or claimed to act. The decisions may have been self-interested: the individuals concerned would have found it difficult to hold their jobs if they had made different decisions (but also found it difficult to hold on to their jobs given the decisions they did make).[10]

Moving Office
● ●

Advertising and reputation are mechanisms that market economies have evolved to deal with the problems of imperfect information. They are signals that traders use to communicate. Sometimes the signals are prices themselves.

In England, the usual method of renting office space is to take a lease for a fixed period of up to twenty-five years. An occupier may move before that period ends. But the person moving out must find another tenant and remains liable for the rent originally agreed. The new rent is a matter for negotiation and will be paid by the new occupier to the original tenant.

A few years ago, my business planned to move to larger premises. The property market in central London at that time was depressed and so was the estate agent we consulted. He recommended that we should ask for a rent of £27 per square foot but was not optimistic about the prospects of an early letting. He was right. After two months, few people had inspected the property and there were no offers.

I went to see the agent and told him that we were unhappy. We were professional economists, and supply and demand were second nature to us. If no one wanted to rent our property at £27 per square foot, we should try something lower. How about £22 per square foot? The agent advised against, but we insisted. He remarketed the property at £22 per square foot. The agent was again right. A month later, almost no one had come to inspect the property and no offers had been made. He suggested we put the matter back in his practical and experienced hands. We reluctantly agreed. The asking price reverted to £27 per square foot. The following week, the agent rang me in an elated tone. A potential tenant was willing to pay £27 per square foot. There were snags: we would have to allow the new tenant six months rent-free occupation and make a contribution to his fitting-out expenses. We quickly agreed.

I debated this experience with my colleagues. It seemed to defy the laws of supply and demand. But there was an entirely sensible explanation. Properties are complicated, and idiosyncratic. It is difficult to tell what a property is like from a description. All buildings are different. It is easy to waste time visiting properties that are obviously unsuitable the moment you step in the door. The price in the particulars isn't just there to equate supply and demand. It also gives information.

When our agent advertised the property at £27 per square foot, he said to potential tenants, "This is similar to other properties for which I and my competitors ask a rent of £27 per square foot." And when we insisted on a rent of £22 per square foot, we gave confusing signals to prospective tenants and their agents. We were saying, "although this looks like a £27 per square foot property, it is a £22 per square foot property." Those who heard that statement did not necessarily think, "This is a bargain." They might equally have thought, "There is something wrong with this property, which I will discover when I spend substantial amounts of money having a surveyor inspect the building and a solicitor read the lease."

And the very economic theory we used to insist on the primacy of supply and demand suggests potential tenants were right to be suspicious. When you search for a property, you will be lucky to find one that has similar characteristics to other properties but is cheaper; you are more likely to find one that is fully priced but ideally suited to your requirements. A good agent should be trying to achieve a full price for the seller. The efficient market hypothesis should apply to the property market, and in an efficient market few bargains are to be had.

The practical wisdom of the estate agent incorporated considerable knowledge about his market. He would not have stayed in business otherwise. This does not mean he was able to explain why his market worked as it did, and he could not. But estate agents are adaptive people, and he was.

Prices of complex products convey information about products, and one of the functions of agents is to certify that information. When supply exceeds demand, as was true in that central London office market in the early 1990s, prices are not immediately cut to match demand and supply, because this would generate confusing signals. The market adjusts, somewhat imperfectly, through side payments—rent-free periods and fitting-out expenses. The stickiness of prices creates periods of surplus and shortage.

Unemployment
● ●

In a perfectly competitive market, wages and salaries should fall to equate supply and demand in each individual labor market. I have occasionally asked managers in large companies how they would react if a prospective employee offered to work for 10% less than the person who was doing the job at the moment. If the caller got an interview, it would only be because of the eccentricity of the approach. We transmitted confusing signals to the market when we cut the price of our office space to £22 per square foot, and a worker who offers to undercut existing employees gives confusing signals to the market. The natural interpretation of the offer is "I am desperate, there is something wrong with me." The firm that accepts the offer is saying, "We are more concerned with our costs than with the caliber of our staff."

In a market in which quality is important but hard to judge price competition is rarely effective or intense. And in the labor market, quality is important to both parties. The employer is concerned about the abilities and commitment of his staff; the worker wants a pleasant environment and congenial and capable colleagues.

Concepts of the "going rate" are important to the decisions of employers and employees. And since prices have an informational function as well as a market-clearing function, there are good reasons for this. But a consequence is that in the labor market, as in the property market, prices will adjust only slowly to changing economic conditions. So there is unemployment in slumps, and labor shortages in booms.[11]

And so the Arrow-Debreu model can be no more than a partial explanation of how market economies solve coordination problems. In that world, price equates supply and demand, and shortages or surpluses never occur because movements in prices eliminate them. But concepts of fair prices are not evidence of socialism, or relics of St. Thomas Aquinas.[12] They are a necessary part of our economic lives. The "going rate" is an essential tool for conveying information for the functioning of market economy. Price instability is often economically damaging, and people who disregard the going rate, as I tried to do, may impede the operation of markets rather than lubricate them.

Imperfect Information Changes Everything

In perfectly competitive markets, products are homogeneous. But markets with imperfect information exist because products are differentiated. In perfectly competitive markets, exchange is anonymous. But in markets with imperfect information, the identity of the trader is a key element of the exchange. In perfectly competitive markets, price equates supply and demand. But in markets with imperfect information, price is a means for sellers to communicate with buyers, and because price serves this function, it may fail to equate supply and demand. In perfectly competitive markets, all exchanges are efficient and only efficient exchanges occur. But in markets with imperfect information, exchanges occur that buyers regret, and trades that would benefit both buyers and sellers may not happen.

And yet market economies have been resilient, even ingenious, in developing mechanisms for dealing with problems of imperfect information. To recognize the ubiquity of imperfect information is not to mount a critique of market economies, but rather a critique of the adequacy of the perfectly competitive model as a description of how market economies work. The truth about markets is much more complex.

{20}············

Risk in Reality

Calculated, self-interested behavior in perfectly competitive markets leads to the efficient market hypothesis and forms the basis of the modern financial theory of chapter 13. That theory, at once sophisticated and practical, provides a set of tools that should enable us to manage and reduce risks in our private and business lives.

Yet reality is more complex.[1] The two preceding chapters have explained how perfectly competitive markets may operate very differently when behavior is adaptive, rather than rational, and when there are asymmetries of information. Markets in risk are particularly subject to imperfect information and vulnerable to "irrational" behavior. In fact most trading in risk markets comes from one or both of these sources; and the same combination of factors ensures that many necessary risk markets never come into being.

Our attitudes to uncertainty are born of a mixture of hopes and fears, grounded in instincts and social conditioning. Our reactions to risk are often intuitive. Some neurophysiologists argue we have a language instinct: small children manage the complex task of learning language quickly and easily.[2] The opposite seems true of probability theory: sophisticated adults find its simple mathematics hard. The most powerful argument for rationality in risk markets is that it is easy to devise strategies that make money from those who do not act rationally. That is precisely what happens.

Maurice Allais[n] is one of the few continental European economists to have won a Nobel Prize. His seminal attack on the economic theory of risk was published under the title *Critique des postulates de l'école améri-caine.*[3] Kahneman and Tversky, the pioneers of behavioral economics, pursued Allais's approach of observing subjects' choices between risky alternatives in laboratory situations.[4] All three discovered it was easy to persuade their subjects to make inconsistent choices.

And their inconsistencies were not random. The subjects were more concerned to avoid small losses than to secure gains of similar amounts. They were ready to accept low probabilities of big losses but unwilling to accept high probabilities of small losses. They liked high probabilities of small gains but took less interest in lower probabilities of big gains. Above all, they were unreasonably confident about their own judg-ments. You may recognize the feeling.[5]

Further evidence of inconsistency in behavior toward risk comes from "market anomalies"—securities market behavior that violates the efficient market hypothesis. For example, U.S. share prices tend to go up in January and down on Monday.[6] No insider knowledge is required to establish that Monday follows Sunday and January fol-lows December. These market anomalies cast doubt on the claim that the price of risky assets incorporates all publicly available informa-tion. Stocks fell by over 20% on October 19, 1987. On July 15, 2002, they dropped by 5% in the morning and rose 5% in the afternoon. These movements could not possibly be explained by new informa-tion about company prospects.

The most important market anomaly is that the "equity premium"—the historic difference between the return on stocks and shares and the return on risk-free assets—seems much too high. As financial economists have debated the "equity premium paradox," esti-mates of the size of the premium have fallen.[7] Even so, an average return of 4% to 5% over safe assets seems far more than is needed to compen-sate for extra risks. If equity returns were indeed so high, shares would almost certainly outperform bonds over all but the shortest periods of time. (This is, of course, what people selling shares advertise.)

Why do people play Powerball when only about half the takings are returned to players? The lottery offers a nicely judged combination of a small number of large prizes, together with a large number of small prizes. The jackpot provides the prospect that attracts attention; the proliferation of $100 prizes amplifies the punter's confusion about risk.[8]

Are Markets Efficient?
• •

If the efficient market hypothesis is not necessarily true, that casts doubt on market efficiency in a wider sense. In 1999–2000, securities markets around the world were disrupted by noise traders—people who buy and sell stocks without knowledge or concern for fundamental values. Insurance markets did not minimize the unavoidable costs of an accident such as Hurricane Hugo. The resulting losses were focused on individuals who had no idea of the magnitude or nature of the risks they had taken.

Procter and Gamble is one of the world's greatest marketing companies; its ability to market soaps, detergents, and cosmetics is unrivaled. The capacity of the company to forecast interest rates or to value complex derivative securities is not as great, however. When Bankers Trust salespeople put together a trading program in 1993 that appeared to offer the company lower interest rates in return for complex but unlikely risks, its treasury department welcomed the opportunity to display to senior management the profits that their skills—mostly in talking to Bankers Trust salespeople—could generate. Unfortunately the risks they had assumed materialized, and to retrieve their losses, the P&G people raised their bets. The results were predictable: P&G is unwilling to quantify its exact losses, but the settlement reached with Bankers Trust for $30 million covered only a small fraction of them. P&G was fortunate: it was a sufficiently well-resourced corporation to ride out these losses. Shareholders of the Gibson greeting card business, and residents of Orange County, were not so lucky.

Bankers Trust had established a wallet auction, and those who bought the contents of the wallet were simply[9] naive. The nature of the transaction revealed by the reported components of Kevin Hudson, the man who sold the deal on learning that P&G would go ahead with the planned transaction. "This is a wet dream . . . This is a new customer. That's the key. A customer that has never done structured leveraged proprietary trades before . . . I am wallowing in a little glory right now. Yeah. In fact, I don't even have the desire to call my other clients and beat them up this afternoon." Hudson's boss, Jack Lavin, was cruder still: "I think my dick just fell off."

Transactions at Long-Term Capital Management were much more

sophisticated. Most investment funds simply buy portfolios of stocks and bonds. A hedge fund such as LTCM trades derivatives and arbitrages between similar securities in different markets. LTCM's partners included Robert Merton[n] and Myron Scholes,[n] who won the Nobel Prize in 1997 for their contributions to financial economics. Merton and Scholes operated with experienced Wall Street traders.

Sophisticated investors can use derivative markets to insure their portfolios. By buying a put option at 10% below the current market price, you limit your maximum loss to 10%—the cost of the option is your insurance premium. After the Asian crisis and Russia's debt default in 1998, investors were particularly nervous. Long-Term Capital Management[10] sold insurance against large price changes—in either direction. In market jargon, they traded swaps and equity volatility.

The $4 billion of assets that LTCM managed may seem a lot of money, but not in the context of all the share and bond markets of the world. With this capital base, LTCM held derivative contracts worth around $125 billion. The value of the underlying securities on which these derivative contracts were based was much larger.

LTCM did not have enough capital to provide the insurance that markets sought. Its actions could transfer risks but not eliminate them—the risk of a general stock market collapse can only be shuffled round the market in a game of pass the parcel.[11] LTCM was betting that the price of the insurance the fund was selling would fall sufficiently quickly that it could buy it back at a profit. The price didn't, the fund couldn't, and LTCM was pushed to the edge of bankruptcy. LTCM's positions were so large that the Federal Reserve Board, concerned by the consequences of a collapse, orchestrated a rescue.

The underwriters of the losses of Hurricane Hugo were ignorant fools who did not know the risks they took. Participants in LTCM—the managers and investors—were clever fools whose sophistication had blinded them to the risks they took. In both cases recirculation and repackaging of risks turned a limited problem into a systemic one. A single failure jeopardized the entire Lloyd's insurance market (in one case) and the American securities market (in the other). Far from spreading risks and reducing their costs, markets in risk concentrated them and made them threatening, even fatal, to the solvency of participants.

Asymmetric Information and Adverse Selection
● ●

The risk that Seabiscuit will not come in first in the 1940 Santa Anita handicap. The risk that the Federal Reserve will unexpectedly lower interest rates. The risk that a hurricane will hit the South Carolina coast. These risks are the currency of specialist risk markets in modern market economies.

They are not, however, the principal risks that people face in everyday life. These are the risks of divorce and the breakdown of relationships, the loss of job and a career, chronic illness. You cannot insure against unwanted pregnancy or single parenthood. There is a limited market for insurance against redundancy and unemployment. The premiums are high and coverage is limited to the payment of outstanding loans.

Yet people who cannot buy protection against these threatening events do have insurance against comparatively trivial risks. Insurance against a broken windscreen, insurance against bags going missing when they are on holiday, insurance against a video recorder being stolen, or a washing machine breaking down. We can and do insure things that don't matter much, but can't and don't insure things that do.

Why is it not possible to insure against divorce? Statistics on marriage and divorce are readily available to enable an insurer to set a fair premium. But few recently married couples would buy divorce insurance. Most newlyweds think that their relationship is less likely to break down than the gloomy statistics suggest. Otherwise they would not have married in the first place. The insurance company, which looks only at statistics, takes a different view, and the premium seems high.

Soon, however, information asymmetry is reversed. Perhaps the relationship develops well, perhaps it does not. Happily married couples will not be interested in divorce insurance. Those whose marriages are rocky will. Couples visiting their insurance broker will be as representative of the whole population as couples visiting the marriage guidance counselor. This is the problem of adverse selection: the people who want the policy are bad risks. A "fair" premium based on the average incidence of divorce would be unprofitable for the insurance company.

Asymmetric information issues pervade risk markets. The insurer would sensibly raise the premium to match the characteristics of those who want policies. But this makes divorce insurance attractive only to those whose marriages are truly on the rocks. The cautious insurer must raise the premium still further. A divorce insurance market would be like the market for lemons. As in the wallet auction, there is no price at which a seller would wish to sell at which a buyer would wish to buy. So no market can exist, and there are no markets in divorce insurance.

Divorce is extreme: the gap in knowledge between the potential insurer and the insured is insurmountable. To offer marriage and divorce insurance, an insurance company would have to make an intolerable intrusion into personal affairs. For similar reasons, there is no effective insurance against unemployment or redundancy. The prospective insured is better informed about the risk than the insurer.

Markets for medical and life insurance work better. Individuals do not know much about their susceptibility to disease or their life expectancy. Inexpensive and noninvasive tests of height, weight, and blood pressure can give the insurer equivalent knowledge about the prospective policyholder's health.

Even so, adverse selection is a problem. Medical insurance is cheaper when bought by an employer for a group of workers. This is not primarily because of the employer's greater bargaining power. The insurer insists that the employer provide cover for all employees and so reduces or eliminates the adverse-selection issue. Private individuals seeking medical insurance are more than averagely likely to be sick, or to be hypochondriacs.

Markets for life and medical insurance are possible because medical knowledge is still rudimentary. But we can already identify some biological and environmental factors that cause disease and mortality—genetic defects cause Huntington's disease, smoking predisposes to lung cancer.

This is the tip of a large iceberg. The problem it raises for insurance markets cannot be solved by limiting the use of genetic information by insurers. That would only aggravate the issue of adverse selection. The only solution to the potential information asymmetry is to stop such information being collected at all—which would be impossible even if it were desirable. In fifty years, private medical and life insurance may be as difficult to obtain as divorce and unemployment insurance today, and for the same reasons.

Moral Hazard
• •

Most risks in our environment depend on the actions we take. If we have financial protection against risk, we will expose ourselves to more risks. This is the problem of moral hazard.[12] People do not allow their houses to burn down because they have fire insurance. Young women do not set out to become pregnant because there are social benefits for single mothers. But their behavior is adaptive. Social habits and economic institutions evolve together. With no fire insurance, there would be fewer chip pans and open fires. When single mothers were harshly treated, there were fewer of them.[13] As always with adaptation, cause and effect work in both directions.

The patchy evidence we have suggests that the risk of violent or accidental death in England has remained more or less constant since the thirteenth century. "The ax of the drinking companion and the neighbor's open well were regulated, to be replaced by unruly horses and unbridged streams; when these were brought under control it was the turn of unfenced industrial machinery and unsignaled locomotives; today we battle with the drinking driver" (Hair [1971], p. 24).

Given the changes in the economic and natural environment, and in legislation and regulation over the period, this constancy is extraordinary. The metaphor of the risk thermostat is powerful. We have a certain tolerance for risk and adjust our behavior to the risks in the environment. We walk more gingerly on a mountain path than a pavement. Fewer children are killed in road accidents today than eighty years ago. Roads have become more dangerous, but precautions by children and their parents have more than offset the dangers of heavy traffic.[14]

Moral hazard makes it dangerous to insure risks that are under the control of the insured. In 1982, Congress deregulated savings and loans associations.[15] But it maintained a system of insurance for their depositors. The combination proved irresistible to fools and crooks.[16] The government met losses that ultimately ran to the tens of billions of dollars while the savings and loans, and their executives, kept the gains. When those you insure can influence the risks you cover, you must supervise them.

Social Insurance of Personal Risks
• •

When people can opt out, adverse selection is a problem. If you can't easily watch what they're doing, moral hazard is a problem. The combination of adverse selection and moral hazard means that risks are best managed by groups that have other common bonds: typically families, communities, workplaces, and nations. The management of everyday risk is best and principally undertaken through social institutions. Purely economic agencies such as insurance companies and securities markets play only a minor role.

Risk sharing in social groups is effective because of the many different advantages to participation in these groups, and also because solidarity and sense of obligation come into play. The traditional marriage vow—for richer, for poorer, for better, for worse—could hardly be more explicit in identifying risk sharing as characteristic of the relationship. Only in the twentieth century did marriage become a put option, in which either party could exit the contract at a prearranged price.

But social risk sharing extends beyond family groupings. The notion that uncertainties of illness and accident should be shared in communities goes back millennia. And today it finds more formal reflection in the support of public hospitals through community philanthropy.

But medical insurance is now more often associated with a different community—the corporation. Unemployment insurance, too, shifted from communities to employers. Employers are far less vulnerable to moral hazard than either private insurers or the state, and the issue of adverse selection does not arise. An employee of a bank or a large diversified corporation could assume that, absent misconduct, there would always be a job, and so the risk of changes in technology, or a fall in demand, fell largely on the employer. The employee paid a price: pay scales related to seniority, and pensions that deferred remuneration, emphasized the long-term nature of the contract. In the last two decades of the century, many companies in the United

States and elsewhere broke these implicit contracts, and even in Japan these structures came under pressure as outsiders preached the need for "structural reform" with increasing stridency.[17] The benefit was an immediate gain in earnings per share; the cost was a reduction in the security of employment and loss of credibility in long-term commitments by employers. It is frequently said that employers "cannot afford" these commitments in the face of international competition. It is hard to interpret that statement in an environment in which reported profits grew faster than GDP.

The term *social insurance* originated in Germany in the late nineteenth century,[18] as government came to take over the insurance functions of voluntary organizations such as mutual societies and trade unions and to extend more generally the kinds of benefit they had provided to employees. This organized mutual sharing of risks is today part of the economic structure of most West European states. Government is well-placed to reduce adverse selection, because it can compel participation, but is less effective at reducing moral hazard than the social pressures of a local community. Formal social insurance schemes address the moral hazard problem by limiting the generosity of the benefits they provide, the time period for which the benefits are paid, and attaching conditions—such as tests of genuineness of the search for work—to their benefits.

Business Risk

Some economic risks are inescapable. The risk that crops will fail. Uncertainty about the growth in demand for mobile phones. Other risks are the product of the market economy itself. Intrinsic uncertainty about the size of the harvest is compounded by market volatility. No one knows how quickly the demand for mobile phones will grow, but the individual firm, and its employees and shareholders, confront the additional uncertainty of which firm will do well in the marketplace.

Business risks bring problems of asymmetric information and moral hazard. Investors should always have the tale of the wallet auction in their mind. Why are people who know more about this venture and have more influence over its outcome than I do offering a share of its potential profits to me? Why should I buy when they want to sell?[19] Many people would be better off today if they had asked that question during the stock market bubble.

The good reason for relinquishing a share of a potentially profitable investment is that the risk is too large for one individual or institution. Antonio could handle the loss of one ship, but not of three. Marine insurance would have enabled him to diversify the risk of storm at sea, but the risks associated with his own business judgment remained. Christopher Columbus could not finance a venture to find a shorter route to the spice islands of the Indies, but Queen Isabella of Castile, substantially richer, could. Sicelo's economic life is precarious because one crop failure can exhaust his assets and reserves.

Yet a business partner in Antonio's venture would sensibly be nervous of information asymmetry and moral hazard. Even if Antonio is completely honest and truthfully reveals all he knows, he may be more inclined to offer participations when he is nervous about the prospects for his trade than when he is optimistic.[20] And Antonio will certainly take more risks if he does not bear the whole consequences of failure. This is not entirely a bad thing. Optimism and risk sharing enable many more new businesses to be started and contribute to the pluralism of a market economy.

Information asymmetries extend more widely. Those who invest with Antonio will not be a random sample of the population. Investors will be those who know Antonio or believe they do. Investors, like those telecom shareholders, will be those who are more than averagely optimistic about the prospects for Antonio's trade. In all investment booms—from the tulip mania to the dot-com mania—money is raised cheaply from people who expect high returns but do not in the end receive them. Investment banks have become skilled in managing the issue process so as best to appeal to "irrationalities" in the minds of potential investors—the attraction of "prospects," their aversion to even small losses.

In chapter 14, I described how the stock market had developed, not as a primary means of raising capital for new businesses, but as a market for the sale and resale of secondary participations. An extraordinary aspect of the bubble was that the capital needs of the businesses that made IPOs were in most cases extremely small—in contrast to most previous speculative bubbles, in which large amounts had been raised for real investment in railroads, electricity cables, and construction. The IPOs were to generate liquidity, of a sort, in the imagined wealth of the promoters of fanciful schemes, and to enable banks and advisers to extract fees for their services. The actual investment that took place, mostly in telecommunications infrastructure, was largely debt financed.

Webvan was one of the more serious dot-com businesses. It allowed customers to order groceries on the Internet for home delivery. Its IPO in November 1999 valued the company, that had begun operations in San Francisco only in June, at around $8 billion. Of this, $375 million was new money raised from investors: or, to put it another way, $7.5 billion was the purported value of the stakes of the founders and the early stage investors. Fees and commissions payable to advisers were around $50 million. Webvan recruited George Sheehan, chief executive of the consulting firm Accenture, to be its chief executive. The company closed in July 2001. In common with many dot-com companies, payments to advisers and founders probably exceeded its revenue from customers.

Stock markets are not, and have never really been, important sources of capital for industry. They do allow the risks of business to be spread and diversified. But the volatility of stock markets creates its own, larger risks. And most traders are speculative: someone who believes or has been told that Cisco is a better bet than IBM deals with someone who has concluded that IBM is a better bet than Cisco.

Is Speculation Useful?

In *The Methodology of Positive Economics*, Friedman presents the example of speculative trading to illustrate the thesis that rationality is imposed by competitive market processes. He claims that market speculation is necessarily stabilizing. Speculators make money only if they buy cheap and sell dear; only speculators who make money will stay in the market for long. So prices will fluctuate less in a market with active speculation than without.[21]

Yet speculation in the stock market bubble was obviously destabilizing, driving prices to fantastic levels from which they subsequently collapsed. If all traders were perfectly rational (consistent, self-interested, profit-maximizing, well-informed), there would be no room for speculation, profitable or unprofitable. To give Friedman's argument a chance of being true, there needs to be a little bit of irrationality—noise trading—but not too much. Noise traders lose money to clever speculators. But if noise traders predominate, then speculators who base their trading on fundamental values risk oblivion as noise traders sell paper to each other at ever higher prices. And this is what happened in 1999. In the previous year, LTCM simply did not have enough money to support its—correct—judgment of market irrationality.

Odds on the different horses in a race, or the prices in the Iowa electronic market, reflect an average of assessments of their prospects. Similarly, the price of a share reflects the average of investors' views of the value of the company. This information may be helpful in guiding decisions about where new capital should be invested. But not very helpful. Banks considering lending, and firms contemplating borrowing or reinvestment, are both likely to be better informed than the stock market about business prospects. The informational function of the market is provided at large cost, and portfolio trading is—necessarily—on average unprofitable for the individuals who undertake it.

The paradox of the debacle at Lloyd's after Hurricane Hugo was that what had once been primarily an insurance market had become primarily a securities market. The participants were not deriving gains from trade by passing risks to those who could manage them most cheaply. They were exchanging risks on the basis of different beliefs about the true nature of the risks. The outcome was that the risks landed with those who did not know what they were doing and could not afford to bear them.

An omnipotent observer, who could penetrate all information asymmetries, might establish the true value of investments. There is no reason at all to think that this price is the one at which such investments actually sell in the marketplace. Most transactions in securities markets are not about sharing or spreading risks. They are like transactions in the betting shop. The people who engage in them believe they are deploying their superior knowledge. But this can never be true of more than a small minority of players.

The Truth About Markets for Risk
• •

Most financial market analysis is still based on the efficient market hypothesis, and you will probably lose more money by defying it than believing it. But temper that belief with skepticism. Rational individuals were overwhelmed by noise traders in 1999-2000. Rational behavior in financial markets is not necessarily adaptive—it wasn't for LTCM.

And what of Webvan? "When the allocation of capital is the by-product of the activities of a casino, the job is likely to be ill done," Keynes wrote in the aftermath of the bubble of 1929, but his words are equally relevant to the bubble of 2000.

The outcomes of LTCM, Bankers Trust, and Hurricane Hugo were perhaps adaptive, in the sense that people who mismanaged risk lost their jobs, their wealth, or went out of business (although not for long: John Meriwether, the creator of LTCM, was back in business fifteen months later soliciting money for his Relative Value Opportunity Fund).[22] But the outcomes were not efficient in either the technical or the ordinary sense of market efficiency.

The concept of an efficient market in risk, which manages for us the risks inherent in modern economic life, is attractive. Aesthetically attractive, because the theory of such markets is intellectually challenging yet soluble; practically attractive, because economic security is one of the principal concerns of every household.

Most of what happens in risk markets—betting, insurance, and securities markets—is not efficient in this sense. It is designed to exploit the "irrationalities" of our everyday behavior toward risk—practical rules that are adaptive in everyday life, but are not adaptive when we consult our financial adviser or our bookmaker.[23] At the same time, the risks that really concern us—the risks associated with our jobs, our relationships, our health—are not dealt with by risk markets. For these risks, we rely on the help of our friends, our social institutions, and the state.

{21}

Cooperation

The Stag Hunt

"If a deer was to be taken, everyone saw that, in order to succeed, he must abide faithfully by his post; but if a hare happened to come within the reach of any one of them, it is not to be doubted that he pursued it without scruple, and, having seized his prey, cared very little, if by so doing he caused his companions to miss theirs" (Rousseau [1791], 111).

Rousseau recognized that self-interested individuals would not necessarily cooperate even though such cooperation would make everyone better off. There is an economic need for social institutions to enforce cooperative behavior. Rousseau developed Hobbes's metaphor of the social contract—it makes sense for us all to agree to give coercive power to the state. But government is an adaptive institution: societies with the power to enforce cooperation will catch more deer than societies without. We do not necessarily need a state to solve the problem of the stag hunt. Market economies also rely on teams—groups that work together regularly. Reciprocity within groups encourages cooperation. We cooperate because we expect similar favors in future.

But modern economies require, and obtain, more cooperation than can be explained either by coercion or by reciprocity. We help other people even when we do not expect that they will have an opportunity to help us in future. If a stranger asks the way, we usually tell them. And we expect that different strangers will do the same for us. We display generalized as well as particular reciprocity. This behavior is not rational, if rationality means self-regarding materialism. But it is adaptive—societies in which people help strangers are not only nicer but more prosperous.

To the Lighthouse

The Eddystone Reef lies fifteen miles south of Plymouth at the entrance to the English Channel. A granite mass, its summit is only three feet above the water at high tide. Hundreds of ships are known to have been wrecked on it. Many that simply never returned to port probably foundered there. Other ships were driven onto the English or French coasts by captains too anxious to avoid the Eddystone.

The solution has been known for thousands of years—the lighthouse at Alexandria was one of the Seven Wonders of the Ancient World.[1] A distinctive light on a reef enables sailors to steer clear of it. Implementation is more difficult: lighting desolate rocks is not easy. The first Eddystone light was not built until 1698, and it lasted only five years before the lighthouse and its builder were swept away in a storm. No trace of either was ever found.

These technical difficulties emphasize the economic problem: Who will pay for a lighthouse?[2] The current Eddystone lighthouse— the fourth—cost £59,000 when it was built in 1882, equivalent to £2 million ($3.34 million) at current prices. This cost is small relative to potential losses of lives, ships, and cargoes. But it is a substantial sum for any individual shipowner. The benefits of the Eddystone lighthouse are widely distributed, and their incidence is difficult to identify or predict. The Eddystone light is a public good, and public goods will not be produced by self-regarding individuals in competitive markets.

The builder of the first Eddystone light was not self-regarding. Mr. Winstanley, who perished in the subsequent storm, was an eccentric but public-spirited gentleman who also constructed Winstanley's Waterworks to amuse visitors to London. He undertook the lighthouse project after two of his ships had been wrecked on the Eddystone Reef.[3]

If the Eddystone light did not exist, a major oil company might build it. Exxon, BP, and Shell each have large traffic in the English Channel, and the consequences for them of a major accident would be serious. But Exxon might reasonably ask why they should do it rather than BP and vice versa. That suggests a role for associations of like-minded people. Clubs work best when the number of beneficiaries is not large or diverse and they have a community of interest. But when there are many disparate members, the temptation is to free ride. No one feels his individual contribution is essential to the project's viability. Social pressure to participate is less intense.

If voluntary cooperation does not work or not work well enough, government can impose it. Public goods may be financed from general taxation. Or the right to impose charges may be transferred to the agency that provides the service. Lighthouses are financed today by levies on port users.

The Market in Public Goods

Social institutions, mainly government, provide a range of public goods—the police, street cleaning, national defense, a framework of rules and laws, and mechanisms for enforcing the state's laws and the private contracts of its citizens. As with lighthouses, what is provided for one is provided for all. And you cannot exclude anyone who refuses to contribute. Once built, the lighthouse shines equally brightly for all seafarers.

For a broader category of goods, it is possible but undesirable to exclude those who refuse to contribute. Perhaps it is more costly to set up mechanisms of exclusion than to allow universal access—broadcasting, public parks. Perhaps exclusion is undesirable because I benefit from provision to you—education, refuse collection. Perhaps exclusion would violate norms about the kind of society we want—medical treatment, rural transport.

These goods must be provided in productive economies, and also paid for. That requires a mechanism for deciding the level of provision and the distribution of the costs. There is variety in preferences for public goods, just as there is variety in preferences for private goods. Some people want more defense expenditure, some less. Views differ about the ways in which defense forces should be used. But no economic system can accommodate this variety of views. Whatever is provided is provided for all. There is only one army. The street is equally clean, or equally dirty, for everyone who uses it.

Incentive compatibility—how to obtain the information needed to calculate the costs and benefits of projects—is a fundamental problem for the provision of public goods.[4] Democratic governments—and undemocratic but benign governments—decide what to fund, and what not to fund, by reference to the demands of citizens. But their demands may be influenced not just by calculations of overall costs and benefits, but also by the costs and benefits to the individuals concerned.

Most interest groups—from environmentalists to abortion rights campaigners—believe, rightly or wrongly, that what they want is in the public interest. But other lobbyists simply use political processes to seek economic benefit for themselves. Naturally, people who are doing the latter say they are doing the former.

The most vociferous advocates of the construction of lighthouses hope to obtain contracts for the construction of lighthouses. Most Scottish lighthouses were built by the austere Stevenson family,[5] better known through Robert Louis Stevenson, who did not build lighthouses and instead created the romantic adventures of *Kidnapped* and *Treasure Island*. The Stevensons built lighthouses because they believed in the value of lighthouses. And they believed in the value of lighthouses because they built lighthouses. Adaptation means that characteristics match the environment.

So the level of provision of public goods is rarely decided dispassionately. Well-off people might naturally want higher levels of provision of public goods than poorer people. They can afford more parks, just as they can afford more champagne. But their votes are usually cast for lower taxes and lower levels of public provision. They assess, generally correctly, that their share of the cost will be greater than their share of the benefits. The exceptions are services, like protection of property by the police, whose benefit goes disproportionately to the better off.

When self-interested lobbying becomes dominant, voting is based on economic interest. Coalitions are formed in which I will support benefits to you if you will support benefits for me. Measures are adopted that give largesse to small groups—farmers or defense manufacturers—

for whom it is worthwhile to invest in lobbying, at the expense of small costs to a wide public. This view of politics as a marketplace is the theory of public choice, pioneered by James Buchanan[n].[6]

Public choice theory gives some insight into modern American politics. A key function of the congressman is to secure benefits for his constituents and those who have contributed to his campaign. Public choice is also relevant to kleptocracies such as the Democratic Republic of Congo, whose government is simply a vehicle for the economic interests of those who control it.

The European states in which the market economy developed fit neither of these models. Louis XIV, who built Versailles and allegedly proclaimed, *"L'état c'est moi,"* was both self-regarding and materialistic, but he was still far from an economist's model of rationality. Louis, his courtiers, and the peasants who paid for it all were acting out traditional roles in an adaptive manner. Their world cannot be explained in individualistic terms.

The French court's failure to respond sufficiently to a changing environment led Louis XVI to the guillotine in 1793. In Europe, government as social contract—a disinterested agency meeting its citizens' needs—was superimposed on structures of traditional authority. And in the United States, the founding fathers had the opportunity to create a constitution for a new nation.

For Madison and the authors of the Federalist Papers, America was primarily a republic rather than a democracy.[7] By this they meant that the citizenry would delegate the task of government to trusted men of ability. The best expression of the sentiment is found in the letter that the English Member of Parliament, Edmund Burke, wrote to his Bristol electors: "your representative owes you, not his industry only, but his judgment; and he betrays you if he sacrifices it to your opinion." John F. Kennedy's reassertion of the position differs only marginally in a substance if more considerably in eloquence "the voters selected us because they had confidence in our judgment and our ability to exercise judgment from a position where we could determine what were their own best interests, as part of the nation's interest."[8]

Disinterested government is a key element in the coevolution of social and economic institutions. European governments today often fall below the standards of disinterested government, but everyone uses that language. Even the most brazen of lobbyists claim that the public will benefit from the policies they seek. Once again altruism and self-interest both provide inadequate accounts of adaptive political and economic behavior.

Teams

We are usually more productive when we work in cooperative teams. Many species—most primates, many birds, ants—live and work in groups. But humans are among the most social of species. This sociability is fundamental to our economic organization.

Teamwork serves two purposes. Through teamwork, we can make use of the division of labor and exploit gains from specialization and differences in capabilities. An orchestra needs a violinist, a flutist, a conductor. An orchestra of thirty people sounds a lot better than thirty one-man bands and can play a much wider range of music, because the gains from specialization are large.

These benefits of specialization and capabilities were the subject of Part II of this book. They can be derived from anonymous interactions in the perfectly competitive markets of Part III. It is enough that there be a violinist and a flutist. They don't have to know each other, like each other, talk to each other. With modern technology, you could even record their separate contributions and piece them together.

But the best orchestras, like the best teams in all areas of life, are more than the sum of their parts. When you buy a budget disc, you may find it was recorded by an orchestra you have not—quite—heard of: a group of competent studio musicians who met that morning to play that score. The best recordings are made by standing orchestras: groups of people who work together frequently, develop each other's strengths, and compensate for each other's weaknesses.

Rousseau's hunt would also have gained by the huntsmen's working together, by sharing information and pooling risks. Public goods require cooperative behavior. Yet, as Rousseau explained, teams of hunters composed of self-regarding materialists would encounter problems. Everyone would do better if huntsmen focused exclusively on catching deer. But each individual member will be tempted into diversions to catch hares. If everyone does this, the hunt will catch no deer.

Today, Rousseau's problem is generally framed as the Prisoner's Dilemma. The story of the Prisoner's Dilemma has always seemed to me unnecessarily complex to illustrate its point, but since it is one of the finest of little stories, I reproduce it here. Two prisoners are arrested and put in separate cells. The sheriff admits he has no real evidence but presents the following alternatives. If one confesses, he or she will go free, and the other can expect a ten-year gaol sentence. If both confess, each will be convicted, but can expect a lighter sentence—seven years perhaps. If neither confesses, the likely outcome is a one-year sentence for each on a trumped-up charge.[9]

Prisoner 1 is uncertain what his partner in crime will do. He notes that, if she confesses, he will get seven years by confessing and ten by remaining silent. He also sees that if she does not confess, he will go free if he confesses and serve a year in gaol by remaining silent. Whatever his conjecture about her actions, he does better to confess. So he confesses. The same analysis applies to her, and she confesses. Both go to gaol for seven years.

People often miss the force of the Prisoner's Dilemma when it is first explained to them. They think that self-regarding people will want to cooperate when they see the benefits of cooperation: the Prisoner's Dilemma arises only because the prisoners do not understand the consequences of their actions. But the paradox is much deeper. The self-interested benefits of cooperation are not enough to persuade self-interested people to achieve them. Even after the Prisoner's Dilemma has been explained, and both parties understand that they will go to gaol for seven years as a result, the self-regarding action is to confess. Indeed there is some evidence that people who understand the problem posed by the Prisoner's Dilemma are *more* likely to confess than people who don't.[10]

The Prisoner's Dilemma explains why lighthouses will not be built. Replace "don't confess" by "contribute" and "confess" by "don't contribute": the inevitable outcome is that no one contributes. Replace "don't confess" by "watch for deer" and "confess" by "pursue hares": Rousseau's hunt will catch no deer. Replace "don't confess" by "cooperate fully" and "confess" by "hold back": people in organizations will never work effectively together, and joint ventures will never work. These outcomes sometimes happen. There are teams that catch no deer because their members are chasing hares, organizations whose goals are defeated because mutual suspicion is the dominant internal value.[11]

Managing the Prisoner's Dilemma
● ●

But there are also many lighthouses, successful teams, and productive organizations. Adaptive societies protect themselves from
the Prisoner's Dilemma in many ways. Two obvious mechanisms are
to change the game or to repeat it. The easiest way to change the
game is to employ an enforcer to punish anyone who confesses. If
the punishment is worse than a year's gaol, the best course of action
changes immediately: both players should keep quiet. The punishment need never be applied: the prospect of it has the desired effect.

There are many candidates for the role of enforcer. In primitive
societies, the leader of the tribe, a religious deity, or the combined
authority of both might assume the role of enforcer. Today we use the
civil and criminal law. Albert Tucker, who invented the story of the
Prisoner's Dilemma, probably used that example precisely because
criminals cannot invoke the courts to enforce nefarious agreements.
But criminals often have their own enforcers. We talk of "honor
among thieves": those outside the law create their own social institutions to handle the Prisoner's Dilemma.

But there is also honor among the honest. The social and economic lives of hunters were linked. Shirking in the forest implied
penalties around the campfire. Yet community enforcement has its
own Prisoner's Dilemma. It is in the best interests of the group for
everyone to penalize shirkers, but not necessarily in my individual
interest. We must not only penalize shirkers, but people who fail to
penalize shirkers. There is a common economic interest in the enforcement of social norms. Contagious reputation—which is valuable in
dealing with information asymmetry—also helps secure cooperation.

The best strategy for a Prisoner's Dilemma changes if the game is
repeated. The American political scientist Robert Axelrod organized
tournaments between strategies for repeated Prisoner's Dilemma.[12]
One simple strategy—tit for tat—proved successful. Tit for tat begins
with cooperation, but defects—once—every time the other player defects. Tit for tat exemplifies common features of good strategies for
Prisoner's Dilemmas. It is nice—it trusts people until proved wrong.
It is responsive—it doesn't ignore what others do. But it is forgiving—
it allows occasional mistakes.

We know that already. Tit for tat is part of our instincts and our learned behavior. The attack on Afghanistan was an inevitable response to the destruction of the World Trade Center. Even if an analysis had shown that to respond would increase, rather than reduce, the likelihood of a further terrorist attack, "do nothing" was not a course of action available to the U.S. president. Tit for tat, like fleeing from danger, is an adaptive response. Behavior, attitudes, and beliefs have developed in ways that are not necessarily self-interested but are to our economic benefit.

Cooperation Is Adaptive

That issue has wide ramifications. In the fifty years or so since the Prisoner's Dilemma problem was first formulated, economists have struggled to explain why there is so much more cooperative behavior in the world than the pursuit of self-interest would imply. There is a serious literature on why we tip waiters and taxi drivers in places we will never visit again.[13] But we just do. We conform to a social norm. That norm is part learned, part instinctive, and part enforced by the expectations of others. Only those economists who insist that human behavior is always self-regarding, whatever the evidence to the contrary, see any issue to be resolved.

For most people, and organizations, tit for tat is an instinctive response. Western societies encourage such behavior. We teach children to stand up for themselves, but we also teach them not to bear grudges. Our inclination is often to administer several tits for a tat, but this feeling tends to pass: we tell ourselves that it is not worth it. We are still not making a rational calculation. We just find the emotional price of continued animosity too high.

In chapter 19, I described how biologists and economists, working simultaneously on advertisement in nature and advertisement on billboards, had found common answers. This is also true of altruism and cooperation. Despite the image of "nature red in tooth and claw," much altruistic behavior exists in nature. Not only does the cooperative activity of ants go far beyond anything found in human societies, but birds and animals cry out to warn others of impending danger even at the cost of increasing their own exposure to that danger. And biologists do not consider rational explanations. Like bears, ants and birds have not calculated solutions to games involving reiterated Prisoner's Dilemmas. Their behavior is adaptive, not rational.[14]

These biological models show that self-interest is not the necessary outcome of competitive evolution, a view as inaccurately attributed to Charles Darwin as its economic equivalent is to Adam Smith. Because the level of natural selection is the gene, maternal—and paternal—investment in nurturing offspring is adaptive, even if it is not rational. We live in families because we have strong instincts to do so, and evolution explains why we have such instincts. This is a much more persuasive and more satisfying account of family life than the account of marriage as economic institution proposed by Gary Becker (chapter 17).

But we make sacrifices for people outside our immediate family group. When large gains are to be made from cooperative behavior, an instinct to form and enforce cooperative groups is advantageous, not just for the group, but for each individual member. It is also advantageous—in cold-blooded evolutionary terms—to be naturally cooperative, to sweat, blush, and avoid the eyes of our colleagues when we make promises we do not intend to keep. These characteristics make it possible for colleagues to trust us.

These arguments are subtle. When biologists understood that evolution did not necessarily imply self-regarding behavior, some developed theories of group selection. Natural selection would favor traits that benefited the group even if they disadvantaged the individual. But these biological arguments are mistaken.[15] In the evolution of species, the fitness of an individual has a much larger influence on reproduction than the fitness of the group to which the individual belongs. This sets a limit to cooperation in the natural environment.

But competition in business and economics mostly does take place at the level of the group. The prosperity of Heidi and Hermann, and of Sven and Ingrid, owes more to the groups to which they belong than to their own personal characteristics. An individual who can tell lies with a straight face can do well in economic life. But only so long as such people are a minority. When there are gains from teamwork, groups of self-regarding materialist individuals will not prosper. Cooperative value systems are key to the development of successful businesses. We cooperate "irrationally" because cooperation is an adaptive instinct and an acquired value.

Fire and Blood

• •

When fire breaks out in country districts, neighbors rally round to help, as they have done since humans first learned to control fire. As urban communities grew, this worked less well. A more transient population meant less solidarity, and the density of buildings made fire more dangerous.

The more complex street plans of towns also required more professional firefighters. Early fire brigades were established by insurance companies, which would arrive to minimize the damage to their policyholder's property. In the nineteenth century, the fire brigade developed into a universal service provided by local government and financed from taxes. The benefits of lighthouse provision are particularly difficult to attribute to the individuals who receive them. How can anyone know which particular ships would have come to grief on the Eddystone if the light had not been there?

But fire prevention is a private good. Most of the benefits of the fire service accrue to the people whose fires are extinguished, and businesses that are victims of major fires meet part of the costs of the fire brigades. But fire prevention is also a public good, like the lighthouse. You hope that the fire in your neighbor's house will be promptly extinguished. Even if he is overdue with his insurance premium.

But the fire service is a public good in a wider sense as well. If a pipe bursts, we turn with trepidation to yellow pages, uncertain about who will arrive, or when. If we suspect fire, we dial the emergency services, with reasonable confidence of prompt intervention from disciplined, trained officers. The organization of the fire service is an expression of social solidarity in misfortune—the same solidarity behind shared responsibility for medical or financial misfortune. Firefighting is urgent and requires constant improvization. We expect firefighters to slide down greasy poles, not wait while they negotiate fees. Firefighters need to be trusted, and to have their instructions obeyed. The effectiveness of a fire service depends on public attitudes toward it.

The only rich country in which the collection of blood is a commercial activity is the United States. There, blood donation is a means for poor people and students to enhance their incomes. In Europe, blood is obtained more or less entirely from volunteer donors, and appeals to social solidarity usually produce sufficient supplies. In 1970, a survey by the sociologist Richard Titmuss claimed that the European system produced higher quality blood more cheaply.[16] Poor people were more likely to supply infected or contaminated blood. And the commercial transaction created information asymmetry: the prospective donor might conceal his or her medical history.

Although the United States was the first rich state to experience a widespread HIV problem, the spread of disease by contaminated blood was quickly halted as competitive blood collection agencies began to test and treat their supplies. In centralized France, the blood-collecting agency and the civil servants and ministers responsible concealed mounting evidence of problems. Drawing attention to the dangers of HIV was not "helpful." Many French recipients of blood, particularly hemophiliacs, contracted AIDS as a result.[17]

The provision of public goods benefits from both solidarity and competition, and these are not always easy to reconcile. It is not beyond imagination to contemplate a world of competitive firefighting services, in which some companies win the respect of the public while others, which do not, receive fewer calls and encounter less willingness to make way for their vehicles. But no market economy organizes its fire services that way. Competitive markets for blood supply do exist, and the results are not clearly worse, or clearly better, than state-organized voluntary supplies. The complex truth about markets implies complex policy choices.

There are many public and semipublic goods in modern economies, such as blood, fire services, lighthouses. For all of them, the social context of the transaction is vital: it determines the quality of output, the quantity of output, and may influence whether they are provided at all. But economic systems don't just depend on cooperation in the provision of public goods. They need mechanisms that restrain individualistic behavior. The development of long-term relationships and the linking of social relationships with commercial ones sustains teamwork. Our predisposition is not simply to be self-regarding materialists. It is to be nice, to retaliate when we are let down, but not to bear grudges for too long. There are good adaptive reasons for this behavior. We are more prosperous as a result, both individually and collectively.

{22}

Coordination

Coordination without a coordinator is the extraordinary genius of market economies. The Arrow-Debreu model offered a possible account of how prices achieve coordinated assignment, products, and exchange even when decisions about all these things were decentralized. But the assumptions of the model exclude many difficult issues of coordination. This chapter is concerned with three different groups of coordination problems—those that arise from compatibility standards, networks, and pollution. Each of these involves an externality, which is a technological relationship between the production or consumption of one firm, or household, and the production or consumption of another firm or household. If there are externalities, there may be no perfectly competitive equilibrium and the fundamental theorems of welfare economics do not hold.

Standards

In France, Germany, and the United States, vehicles are driven on the right-hand side of the road. In Britain, Japan, and Australia, they are driven on the left. It does not matter which side of the road people use, so long as it is the same one. And once a decision has been made, large investment in that standard follows—the arrangement of the steering and pedals of cars, the positioning of street furniture, the design of intersections. Driving on one side of the road, or the other, is an unusually clear example of a coordination problem. The two options are—initially—equally good, and no intellectual or ideological commitments or commercial interests support one view or the other.[1]

Standardization began in the period of industrialization between 1750 and 1850. There is probably no strong reason why the United States, and France, chose the right, and Britain the left, but they did. Path dependency then took over. Countries made choices dictated by their colonial masters, or by larger countries in close proximity. It is now unlikely that any major country will switch—the last to change was Sweden, which moved from left to right during one extraordinary night in 1967. The QWERTY keyboard layout is another example of a path dependent solution to a coordination problem. Standards, like keyboard layouts, are everywhere. Currency is a standard. So is language. We need to use the same money, the same words, as the people around us.

Television sets need to be compatible with television broadcasts. The FCC-prescribed NSTC is used in the United States, but most of the rest of the world uses the German PAL system. The wheels of railway wagons have to be the same distance apart as the rails. And both are separated by 4′8½″ more or less everywhere. Traders want the credit card network with the most members, and cardholders want cards with the most traders. So Visa has become dominant.

Standards often emerge through competition. Early railways were built to different gauges. But there is an instability in standard setting: once a standard, not necessarily the best, gains a decisive lead, everyone else has an incentive to follow. Installed base, not technical quality, is what matters: there is no intrinsic superiority in having rails 4′8½″ apart. English is the dominant world language because it is spoken by the largest number of educated people, not because Shakespeare was a greater writer than Goethe, or because English is easy to learn.

Some standards are imposed. The Académie Française has for centuries defined what is French, and governments regulate television broadcasts. The advantages of compatibility allow bad standards—such as QWERTY—to survive. But you cannot introduce a new bad standard, and very bad standards are displaced: early word processing systems disappeared because new ones were so much superior that it was worth investing time and money to upgrade.

Many standards are constructed by industry agreements. DVD

player protocols were determined by a group of hardware and software producers. It is rare for standards to be set and controlled by private companies. Still, we see a major exception to this rule almost every day. The logo of the Microsoft Corporation appears on almost all our computer screens.

It is difficult to maintain private ownership of a standard, because the attempt to maintain control limits the rate of adoption. And being first to secure widespread adoption is key in standards battles. Sony's first videocassette recorders were designed for broadcasters and other professionals. Sony believed that its reputation and market position among experts would give the company a powerful springboard for the consumer market. Sony also believed that success in this strategy would enable it to impose its own proprietary technology, Betamax, and dominate the entire market.[2]

Sony was wrong on both counts. JVC, a subsidiary of the huge Matsushita Corporation, developed a different system, VHS, which was licensed freely. Soon, many more VHS machines than Betamax recorders were in homes. Moreover, Sony, and most other firms in the industry, misjudged how people would use their recorders. They thought they would buy camcorders to make home movies. But consumers did not use video recorders to show pictures of weddings and family holidays, or for time-shifting, but to play prerecorded movies. And for this Sony's Betamax was inferior. Since more people had VHS recorders, many more tapes were available in VHS. And so still more new purchasers preferred VHS to Betamax.

Ultimately, Sony abandoned Betamax. Apple also failed with their proprietary operating system: the price of exclusivity was low market share. Indeed the only historical example of a private standard comparable to Microsoft's is the dominance of nineteenth-century rail braking systems by Westinghouse. The company tried to reproduce its success by imposing a proprietary standard for railroad signaling, and failed.[3]

Sometimes standards simply fail to emerge. If your car needs a replacement wiper blade, you find that what you need is specific not only to the manufacturer but to model and year. The governments of most countries of the world agreed, through the International Telecommunications Union, to a common standard for mobile phones (GSM). GSM phones can be used almost worldwide—except in the United States, whose systems are not fully compatible with each other, far less with GSM. As a result, mobile phone use developed more rapidly in Europe than in the USA.

Nothing in the organization of a market economy guarantees good, or any, solution to standards issues. But these markets usually work. Often through regulation or government-sponsored agreement; sometimes through spontaneous order emerging in the marketplace; occasionally through the success of the products of one firm.

Networks

A few years ago it was still possible to holiday in the troubled but beautiful province of Kashmir. I flew to Delhi, caught a smaller plane to Srinagar, and traveled on by jeep and boat. As a porter carried my bags up a dusty track to my destination, I encountered a friend from London. What a small world, we said.

But there was really no coincidence. If I had arrived at some random point on earth, and had met an acquaintance, that would have been extraordinary. There are 6 billion people in the world, and no one can know more than a tiny fraction of them. But my arrival in Kashmir was not at all random. Travel agents in London deal with a small number of representatives in India, who deal with a few providers in Kashmir. If my friend and I had expressed similar requests, it was not surprising we should end up at the same place. We were in closely connected networks.

Network externalities is a new buzzword in business economics. Connectedness is vital, and it is best to be connected to the largest network.[4] Telephones are the archetype network externality. There is no point in being the only person with a telephone, and the more people who have them, the more valuable my phone becomes. Such network externalities seem to give huge advantages to early, large players.

But then these markets can go wrong. Either we have competing networks, and I only have access to a few of those to whom I would like to be connected; or one company, with the largest network, establishes an unassailable monopoly. The world has around 2 billion telephones, and the company with the highest proportion of this population signed up will attract most new subscribers.

This analysis has one problem. It is not how the telephone industry is organized. The world telephone system consists of many operators, large and small. Most provide service in a particular geographical area and connect each other's calls through negotiated access agreements. The same phenomenon of interacting local networks is found in other network industries, such as the banking system, gas and electricity distribution, and airlines. The many operators, large and small, organize interchange and access. These arrangements are not universal but nevertheless general enough to allow a network to function.

And the phenomenon I discovered in Kashmir explains why. In a famous sociological experiment, participants were instructed to contact a named but unknown recipient by identifying someone they knew who would be "closer" to that person. The experiment tested, and largely confirmed, the hypothesis of "six degrees of separation"— a small number of links is enough to connect anyone to anyone else.[5]

Our "small world" experiences show that overlapping clusters produce a high degree of connectedness from a modest number of direct links. Social organization solves the apparent technical and economic problem. The widespread evolution of networks in market economies is another instance of the power of spontaneous order in social and economic organization.

This spontaneous interconnectedness between competing providers is true of the most famous new network of all—the Internet. The Internet is a universal network that evolved with little regulation and outside the control of any single organization. CERN, a European physics research institute that developed the key protocols for the World Wide Web, chose to put these protocols in the public domain. Almost everyone required local telephone companies for Internet access, but regulation stopped telcos from using that power to establish a monopoly of Internet connections. Despite the wild optimism of investors, companies such as AOL, Netscape, Microsoft, and Yahoo! all failed to establish network monopolies. The potential problems of capturing network externalities effectively in a market economy don't seem to be serious in practice.

Pollution
● ●

Many externalities in modern economies arise from pollution— pollution of air, land, and water. Indeed the term *pollution* is now widely used to cover many types of externality. Noisy lawn mowers are said to emit noise pollution, offensively sited billboards represent visual pollution. But not all externalities are bad. My beautiful garden is an asset to you as well as me. Pollution can be handled by rules, by agreement between the parties, or by the creation of artificial markets in externalities. Rules against pollution are familiar enough. No litter, no busking, no horns to be sounded after eleven-thirty.

Rules against externalities work well when the objective is clear and enforcement straightforward. But this is rarely the case. No air pollution is a desirable goal, but it would mean shutting down all transport, all electricity generation, and most industrial processes. What we want is a little air pollution but not too much. So we come up with formulas like "best available technology not entailing excessive cost,"[6] which is a statement of the problem not an answer.

"The pollutor pays"[7] sounds like a simple and attractive rule, but it quickly unravels. It seems appropriate that people should pay for the pollution they cause, but the attempt to handle environmental problems through legal processes has not worked well. The problem is by now familiar: the definition of rights and rules is not obvious, but the result of a social decision. An electricity generator is not negligent in emitting carbons and sulfur dioxide until we formulate a specific rule that says he is.

Attempts to define the rules retrospectively create worse problems. How long and indirect can the chain of consequences be? Were the emissions caused by the electricity generating company, or by whoever sold the polluting fuel or financed the power station or used the electricity—or by all of these people? The pursuit of the latter route through the "Superfund" has simply ensured that funds intended to benefit victims of pollution have ended up in the hands of lawyers and has increased business uncertainty by holding individuals and companies liable for events long in the past for which they justifiably feel no responsibility.[8]

In any event, pollution is in the eye of the pollutee. You may be offended by my dress, my taste in music, or by what I read, but it would be preposterous to suggest I should compensate you for these things. Yet we do have rules against indecent exposure and display, against holding noisy parties late into the night, and against the circulation of violent and pornographic material. To make the principle of "the polluter pays" work, you have to define the default position: exactly what a world without pollution would be like.

These default positions are the product of social norms, and they change over time. It was once acceptable to deposit excrement in the street, and until recently, quite normal to allow industrial waste to accumulate in the environs of a plant. In a few decades Heidi and Hermann may find electricity pylons across tracts of beautiful countryside equally extraordinary.

Externalities may be dealt with by bargaining between the parties.[9] This works best where the externalities are big but the numbers affected small, as when I own land near your proposed factory extension or you are playing your radio too loudly. Such bargaining usually takes place "under the shadow of the law"[10] and the default position matters here also. I will bargain more confidently if I have a right, rather than a desire, to object to your factory extension or a notice says NO RADIOS TO BE PLAYED.

Markets in externalities are new. They work best for an externality like sulfur or carbon dioxide emissions with many sources. Tradable permits allow those who can reduce emissions relatively cheaply to benefit by selling rights to those for whom the costs are greater. The advantages of the competitive market—incentive compatibility and low information requirements—allow reductions in pollution to be achieved at lower cost.

Market economies solve coordination problems through a combination of spontaneous order and social institutions. Nothing guarantees that solutions will be reached or that those that are reached are efficient. But coevolution has usually produced answers.

{23}

The Knowledge Economy

Big Knowledge

It is a cliché that we live today in a knowledge economy.[1] At first sight, markets do not seem a good mechanism for producing and transmitting knowledge. Once created, knowledge can be transferred relatively cheaply to other people at little cost. If the people who create new knowledge can't protect it, they can't sell it. And if they can protect it, they will restrict its distribution. Either way, the market economy won't produce and disseminate the knowledge it needs.

Yet this doesn't really seem to happen. A remarkable feature of modern market economies is the speed with which they do create knowledge—important and unimportant. We complain about information overload, not underload. So how is new knowledge created? And how is it paid for?

Albert Einstein, a clerk in the Patent Office at Zürich, devised the general theory of relativity in his spare time. This led to the university appointment that had previously eluded him, and thereafter Einstein worked in universities. Einstein was honored wherever he went. But he never became a rich man. Not rich even by the standards of a competent investment banker. Nor did he enjoy the perquisites—the personal staff, the waiting jet—that ease the life of the modern chief executive.[2]

Charles Babbage built the first "analytical engine," or mechanical calculator, in the nineteenth century. But Babbage's machine was designed to do arithmetic. What turned a calculator into a computer was the insight that a machine that can make long strings of calculations can do almost anything—write letters, check spelling, remember addresses, and turn on the central heating. This was first realized by Alan Turing, at the time a fellow of King's, the Cambridge University college that was also home to John Maynard Keynes. At the outbreak of the World War II, Turing became a code-breaker at Bletchley Park, northwest of London. The group Turing joined, which represented the cream of British academic life, built the first operational computer.[3] Turing spent eight years working for the British government. He returned to King's College and then took a Royal Society professorship at Manchester University.[4] Prosecuted for homosexual activities, he committed suicide.

Jim Watson, while a postdoctoral research student at Cambridge, discovered, with his collaborator Francis Crick, the helical structure of DNA. The two were jointly awarded the Nobel Prize (its overall value is around $1 million) for their efforts. The ebullient Watson became one of America's leading scientists and went on to spearhead the process of sequencing the gene in the 1990s, while Crick established a more modest academic career in the United States. Neither derived any substantial financial reward (judged by the standards, for example, of a senior executive in a biotechnology company or a leading analyst of biotechnology stocks).

Relativity, computing, and DNA are probably the most important contributions to twentieth-century knowledge, and also discoveries of great commercial importance. The economic implications of computing are all around us. Relativity not only led to nuclear power but, by redefining modern physics, influenced devices from spaceships to computers. And genetics and biotechnology will transform medicine and nutrition in the next few decades.

Relativity, computing, and the double helix are ideas: antibiotics, television, and improved seed varieties are products. Slovenly practices in Alexander Fleming's laboratory led to the discovery that certain molds would kill bacteria. Although practical significance of this discovery seems obvious, it was over a decade before research by Howard Florey and Ernst Chain, sponsored by the Rockefeller Foundation, produced a drug fit for patients.[5] Antibiotics virtually eliminated infectious disease as a cause of death in otherwise healthy adults in rich countries and formed the foundation of the modern pharmaceutical industry.

Sometimes all the bits of science and engineering needed for a new product come together. Chance puts them together first, and often several people do so simultaneously. So it was with television, and Philo T. Farnsworth put them together first in the United States. Or so the courts decided when they upheld his patents. Farnsworth spent years in litigation with the Radio Corporation of America (whose chief executive notoriously said, "We don't pay royalties, we receive them"). Farnsworth ultimately won credit for the invention but little financial return: he was almost ruined by legal costs and sold out to RCA for a modest sum.[6]

The most important economic event in Palanpur in the last fifty years was the "green revolution"—the introduction of semidwarf wheat. These new varieties were bred in Mexico in laboratories funded (again) by the Rockefeller Foundation.[7]

The most important twentieth-century innovation from a private sector company is the transistor, discovered by William Shockley at Bell Laboratories in 1947. Silicon Valley is founded not on silicon, but on transistors. Yet this is a peculiar story. Bell Labs had a stunning record of technological innovation; but its owners, American Telephone and Telegraph, had agreed to an antitrust settlement a decade earlier that prevented them deriving any competitive advantage from discoveries at Bell Labs. Development of the transistor proved rewarding for Sony, and for Shockley and the company he established—Fairchild Semiconductor—but not for AT&T.[8] AT&T was broken up in a further antitrust settlement in 1982, and later the company spun off Bell Labs into an independent company, Lucent Technologies,[9] which has struggled to achieve commercial success.

Who Paid for Big Knowledge?

My sample of major twentieth-century innovations is small, and controversial. But, computing, DNA, antibiotics, television, and green revolution crops are undoubtedly innovations that helped transform our economic lives. How did they come about? Financial incentives played only a small part, and the financial rewards for the discoverers were not great. Einstein wanted to get a better job. For the others, the principal motives appear to be the excitement of the process of discovery, and the social rewards offered to the renowned scientist.

The system matters more than the heroic individual. Einstein, Turing, and Watson were geniuses. Philo Farnsworth, no genius, was an energetic entrepreneur. But relativity, computers, DNA, and television were all discoveries about to happen. If these particular individuals had not made them, others would have. Neither commercial sponsorship nor the prospect of large financial rewards played any major role.

Yet the role of government in promoting innovation is also unimpressive. The Soviet state actively promoted scientific research, but the results were poor. Russia and the USSR won eleven science Nobel Prizes in the twentieth century, compared with thirteen each for Switzerland and the Netherlands, which between them have 10% of Russia's population. Although Soviet medicine achieved high standards, no important new drugs were discovered. The evolution of electronics and computers—even for military purposes—lagged so far behind the West's that export bans on computers were used as a weapon in the Cold War.

The most extreme blight on Soviet science was Lysenkoism. Lysenko, an undistinguished biologist, gained the ear of Stalin because his theory—that evolution had no genetic basis and that any desired development was possible in an appropriate environment—fitted the modernist rationalism of socialist philosophy. The application of Lysenko's principles contributed to the Soviet famines of the 1930s, and in a horrific application of the principle of the single voice, his opponents were hounded, imprisoned, and shot.[10]

Only Einstein was employed by a government institution at the time of his discovery, but the Swiss government employed him as a clerk in the Patent Office, not to work out relativity. Private charitable foundations have been a major source of funding for innovations. The record of the Rockefeller Foundation alone—in both penicillin and the green revolution—is remarkable. With the contributions to knowledge—good and bad—from the University of Chicago, the economic effects of Rockefeller's philanthropy may outrank his creation of Standard Oil.

Philanthropy is the vehicle of pluralism in support of research. Three of the six innovations described above—antibiotics, computing, and DNA—occurred in Britain. Chauvinism in selection perhaps, but any pride I feel as a British observer relates to the past, not the present. The institutions in which the research occurred—St. Mary's

Hospital, where Fleming worked, and Oxford and Cambridge Universities—were not government agencies when that relevant work took place, but depend on state funding now. The growth of government finance and control of universities in Europe has been directly paralleled by their decline as centers of research. Europe accounted for 75% of Nobel Prizes in science before 1939; the United States has taken over 75% of Nobel Prizes in science since 1969.[11] The principal source of new big knowledge is now the pluralist higher education system of the United States.[12]

Small Knowledge

Not all knowledge achieves the exquisite abstraction of the theory of relativity, the concept of a computer, or the nature of life. Some is the product of diligent record keeping: information like the latest trades on the stock market, the telephone numbers of plumbers and car hire agencies, the route of Highway 1, and the arrangement of Manhattan streets. Such knowledge is produced and disseminated through the products designed around them: financial information systems, telephone directories, road maps, and street atlases.

In the 1929 stock market crash, share price data was distributed on "the tape." Clerks on the exchange floor would type in data, and a machine would print it out across the country. The speed of flow of information was limited by this primitive technology, and when prices plummeted on large trading volumes, the tape ran increasingly late. It was a frightening experience for speculators gathered round machines in brokers' offices. They might already have gone bust ten minutes ago.

News agencies—such as Reuters and Associated Press—reported events "down the wire" in a similar way. But these products could be delivered far more efficiently with modern electronics. Financial information could be made immediately available to screens on traders' desks. This transformed securities markets and it transformed Reuters, where imaginative managers were quick to see the potential of this new activity. The Reuters financial information service soon dwarfed the original news gathering business. The initial public offering of Reuters shares made the company more valuable than the newspapers that had owned it.[13]

But today Reuters has competitors, like Bloomberg. Both services provide continuously updated information about securities prices, bond yields, and exchange rates. They attempt to make their services attractive by adding gossip, sports information, and interviews with market celebrities—the talking heads. Although the core information provided is the same, such differentiation enables competitive providers to enter the market profitably.

Telephone companies produced lists of telephone numbers as a service to their customers. But AT&T realized that many of these customers wanted to call not Jane Doe, but a plumber or a physician or a car hire company. So they established new listings—the yellow pages—in which numbers were arranged not alphabetically by the names of the businesses, but by their commercial activities. Moreover, the telephone company could profit not only from the extra telephone use that this created, but by persuading businesses to pay to have their numbers displayed more prominently.

The yellow pages activities were spun off when AT&T was broken up. Yellow Pages became a business in its own right, and it attracted competitors, who would encourage people to use their directories by providing more convenient listings. Other firms developed annotated lists of telephone customers to sell to those irritating telemarketeers. New technologies offered opportunities for CD-ROM and Internet-based directories and alternative number information services. Today a whole range of competitive businesses are engaged in the differentiated supply of the most boring information of all—lists of telephone numbers.

The first maps were products of art and scholarship. The world grew (more of it was known) and shrank (access to it was easier). Map production became a business, and mapmakers competed in the clarity and accuracy of their mapping. A mapmaker's reputation was crucial: you would not know a map was defective until you had bought it, used it, and got lost.

Government entered the map business because the movement of large armies demanded accurate logistics and the assignment of land and mineral rights required the precise demarcation of territory. In the late twentieth century, a Global Positioning System, which enabled locations to be precisely pinpointed by satellite, was developed by the Department of Defense for the same reasons.

The basic information was—and is—produced by government as a public service. But, as with telephone listings, consumers need to use such information in many different ways. Large-scale maps are indispensable to hikers. Motorists need road atlases. We need street maps for the towns in which we live. And firms compete with each other to produce the most useful hiking maps, the clearest road atlases, the most legible street atlases. In all these ways, small knowledge is differentiated to support commercial production and dissemination.

In March 2001, the Automobile Association, which sells maps to British motorists, paid £20 million ($33.4 million) to settle a legal dispute with the Ordnance Survey, which is the government agency charged with maintaining accurate records of the terrain and what is built on it. The AA is not allowed to copy other maps. But the law does not protect the knowledge that the M1 freeway runs from London to Leeds. There is a large gray area in between, and the AA seemed to have moved too far across. "We spent a day together looking at various different sheets containing lots of different examples. There are some publishers who put deliberate mistakes in their maps," said a spokesman for the Ordnance Survey.[14]

Precious Knowledge
● ●

The AA had fallen foul of intellectual property legislation—it had infringed the Ordnance Survey's copyright. Such rules have a long history. Patents allowed people who invented new gadgets or processes—such as John Kay's flying shuttle and spinning frame—to enjoy exclusive rights to build and use them for a limited period.

Copyright allowed writers and engravers to prevent other people from copying their works without permission. This protection continued until the death of the author, and beyond. And trademarks provide an easy means by which the Coca-Cola company or Wal-Mart can stop other people from calling their products Coca-Cola or their shops Wal-Mart.

The legal structure today is far more complex. The direction of Fifth Avenue is not copyright information, but a drawing of the Manhattan streets is. The idea of relativity is not protected, nor is Einstein's explanation of it, but you cannot reproduce the article in which it was published without permission. Turing did not patent the idea of a computer, but with a good modern lawyer he might have been able to; the courts now recognize patents for business methods, so one-click ordering is exclusive to Amazon. Ricardo's concept of economic rent is now called Economic Value Added, a consulting firm's registered trademark.[15] Today there is a confused structure in which the degree of legal protection for new knowledge bears no relation at all to its originality or value.

The patents on John Kay's spinning frame were appropriated by an entrepreneur, Richard Arkwright, who became one of the richest men in England. Arkwright's approach of using intellectual property rights to establish monopolies in related businesses has become a central strategy in many industries. The most important piece of precious knowledge today is not relativity or the structure of human life: it is the software codes for Windows.

Copyright law allows Microsoft exclusivity in software codes of MS-DOS but denies Apple exclusivity in the concept of the graphical user interface: this gave the Seattle company sole rights to Windows. Intellectual property law creates this monopoly, but following court decisions in 2001 and 2002, antitrust law controls it only weakly.[16] This interaction between intellectual property rules and antitrust rules has made Microsoft one of the world's most valuable companies and Bill Gates one of the world's richest men.

Often, it is a matter of chance whether new knowledge is protected by intellectual property laws and becomes precious, or not. Over the last thirty years, great progress has been made in treating stomach ulcers, which created perpetual discomfort, and sometimes the necessity of invasive surgery, for people with stressful careers.

These conditions can now be successfully treated with drugs that control the level of stomach acidity. Two consecutive categories of drugs—the H2 receptor antagonists, Tagamet and Zantac, and the proton pump inhibitors, Losec and Zoton—have been among the most profitable drugs in the history of the pharmaceutical industry. A blockbuster drug typically relieves, but does not cure, common chronic illnesses such as depression or hypertension.

But these drugs are not the only way to treat stomach acidity. Two Australian physicians, Robin Warren and Barry Marshall, discovered that many ulcers were caused by a bacterium, *Helicobacter pylori*, which could be eliminated by an intensive program of widely available antibiotics. Chemical substances are patentable. Treatment protocols are not. Warren and Marshall's rewards for their discovery have been limited to academic kudos and the gratitude of patients.[17]

The Disney corporation is primarily a vehicle for the exploitation of the intellectual property created by its founder, Walt. No one argues that *Steamboat Willie* is the most important contribution to the canon of the English language or Mickey Mouse its most finely drawn character, but no literary products have proved more profitable. Disney copyrights and trademarks give the corporation a monopoly right to make films and merchandizing materials that exploit Disney characters, and the exclusive right to develop theme parks that feature them.

The Disney corporation is vigorous in its use of corporate lobbying to defend and extend these rights. It was one of the principal supporters of the TIPS agreement, which linked participation in the World Trade Organization to acceptance of intellectual property rules and so made ready access to Western markets by poor countries contingent on recognition of publishers' copyrights and pharmaceutical patents. Disney was also a major lobbyist for the 1998 Sonny Bono Copyright Act, which extended the copyright of corporations from seventy-five to ninety-five years from first publication. This kept Mickey Mouse under Disney control until 2023 (or such later date as Congress, which has already extended the length of copyright fourteen times, may determine).

The market economy's production of knowledge is not efficient. There are many slightly differentiated products of marginal value—in maps, in software, in pharmacology. Intellectual property law today is a morass that sometimes fosters innovation but often stifles it. Contributions to fundamental knowledge—such as those of Einstein, Turing, and Crick and Watson—are of incalculably large economic and commercial significance, but there is no mechanism, and could probably be no mechanism, for connecting value to reward.[18] Nor would it necessarily lead to a faster advance of knowledge if there were. The market has not solved the problem of generating new ideas in an orderly or efficient manner, but the social institutions of which the market economy is part have solved that problem. Along with the disciplined pluralism of today's rich states has come a pace of innovation that is both extraordinary and unstoppable.[19]

{part V}

HOW IT ALL WORKS OUT

{24} ••••••••••••••••••••••••••

Poor States Stay Poor

The Tryst with Destiny
••••••••••••••••••••••••••••••••••••••

"Long years ago, we made a tryst with destiny." On August 14, 1947, Jawaharlal Nehru accepted Indian independence from Louis Mountbatten, the country's last viceroy.[1] The birth of modern India was accompanied by high hopes and immense goodwill. These hopes and goodwill were largely the creation of Mahatma Gandhi, the remarkable leader of Indian nationalism. Gandhi had believed that only the integrity of his movement would ensure the success of its campaign and a basis for subsequent good government. As a result Nehru and his colleagues and officials were men of exceptional caliber. The architect of economic planning in India was P. C. Mahalanobis, a polymath of formidable intellect and analytic capability.[2] If planning would ever transform a poor state into a rich one, it would be in India.

The same optimism that supported India provoked new interest in development economics. The hope was that other newly independent poor countries could quickly raise their living standards. Walt Rostow described the history of economic development in terms of stages of economic growth—takeoff from an industrial society, drive to maturity once takeoff had been achieved.[3] Could similar takeoffs be achieved in poor countries?

Development economics might have taken chapter 5—how rich states became rich—as its starting point. It did not. Little attention was paid to economic history. And perhaps for good reasons. All innovations and scientific knowledge since the industrial revolution were available immediately to poor countries in the modern world. Their growth path could be accelerated through contact with already developed economies.

Technology rather than institutions was to be imported. The political framework of modern development would be very different. Government had played a limited role in the evolution of rich states and processes of central coordination almost no role at all. Productivity growth was assumed to have occurred in spite of the uncoordinated development of the market, not because of it. And the chaotic progress of uncoordinated development had led to hardship and to gross inequalities of income and wealth. Planning in countries such as postwar India could therefore not only accelerate growth but achieve fairness in its distribution. And many people thought this had happened in the Soviet Union. Not until the 1980s did the magnitude of Russian economic failure become widely apparent.[4]

So development economics looked to economic theory rather than to economic history. The modern theory of economic growth was based on a framework devised by Bob Solow[n] to describe the relationship between savings, investment, and output growth.[5] Since technology was universal, the level of output was determined by the stock of capital and so by the level of savings, the rate of growth by the rate of advance of technology. Poor countries might be trapped by low savings into low output levels, but if they could escape that trap through foreign aid and forced domestic savings, their growth potential was equal to that of productive economies.

Arthur Lewis[n]—the only black economist to win a Nobel Prize[6]—described the economies of poor countries in terms of two sectors. An industrialized sector, an enclave with the economic laws and rules of rich states, might coexist with a traditional society. An industrial sector of sufficient size would continuously attract labor and eventually take over the whole economy. Lewis's approach reemphasized a role for external help and internal coordination in achieving critical mass in the modern economy.[7]

A generation of development economists and policy makers in poor countries and international agencies believed that central direction and rapid capital accumulation could not only help unproductive economies achieve takeoff, but achieve a far more rapid take-off than had been achieved in already rich states. Virtually all poor countries followed India in introducing planning systems and state ownership. International agencies, such as the World Bank, would fill the funding gap—the transition to a higher level of savings.

It was not to be. India had sophisticated planning and substantial aid.[8] From 1950 to 1990, Indian GDP per head grew by an average of 2% per year, and the gap between India and rich states widened. Yet many poor states did worse. India was a beneficiary of those green revolution crops, which contributed far more to rural living standards than Delhi planners. Latin American economic growth was lower than that of India, and most countries in sub-Saharan Africa are today poorer than at independence. Only in Asia have once poor countries narrowed the gap in productivity and living standards. Productive economies have continued to grow richer, and their growth has been stable. In rich states, productivity rarely falls: even New Zealand has seen its economy grow slightly in absolute terms since 1984.[9]

Shoes
• •

What went wrong? The growth models above contain no institutions—firms, industries, or governments. If you have capital, labor, and technology, output follows. But imagine introducing in Sicelo's village the capital, technology, and methods of organization that are used on Sven's farm in Sweden. They wouldn't work (literally). The difference in capital per head is only a small part of the story. Without changes in the organization of landholding, without a reorganization of social relationships, without an educational revolution, and without the infrastructure—from roads to repairmen—needed for different methods of production, imported capital could never be usefully employed.

Although this hypothetical experiment is absurd, it is not so far from what has happened with large-scale projects in poor states. Output is a function not just of capital and labor but of institutions, in industrial sectors as in the traditional economy.

In one widely cited early work of development economics, P. N. Rosenstein-Rodan[10] illustrated the need for a "big push"—an organized, coordinated approach to takeoff—with the example of a shoe factory. If a poor country began industrialization by establishing a shoe factory, where would it find demand for its products? Its workers would not want to spend all their incomes on shoes. Lewis's industrial sector would need to develop many activities at once. Development required the simultaneous establishment of a shoe factory, a clothing factory, a bicycle factory. Shoe workers could use their income to buy clothes and bicycles, and bicycle workers would buy shoes. A planning agency could coordinate this simultaneous development.

Fifty years later, anticapitalist journalist and author Naomi Klein visited a shoe factory in the Philippines.[11] She did not find it a pleasant experience, and no sensitive person from a rich state would. Most employees of the factory were young women, daughters of peasant families. They worked long hours under tight discipline for low wages, living in small dormitories shared by four or six people. They had been lured by bright lights, depressed by lack of opportunities in their remote villages, encouraged to send money back to support their families.

These workers did not buy all the shoes they made. They did not buy any of them. Rosenstein-Rodan's problem had been solved by exporting the factory's entire output. The shoes were branded by Nike and bought for kids in rich states at a price that represented a month's wages for a Filipino assembly worker.

In Tanzania, the World Bank financed the Morogoro shoe factory. It was built with modern equipment and shoemaking technology to satisfy all Tanzania's demand for shoes and have capacity for exports to Europe.[12] The Morogoro shoe factory was not a success. Its equipment regularly failed because of lack of maintenance and shortages of spare parts. Workers and managers stole from the plant. The Morogoro plant was designed like a modern Western shoe factory, with aluminium walls and no ventilation system, inappropriate for the Tanzanian climate. The Morogoro shoe factory never operated at more than 5% of capacity and never exported a single shoe. It closed in 1990.

Naomi Klein did not need to go to the Philippines to see the unpleasantness of early-stage industrialization. She could have read accounts of conditions in English factories during the industrial revolution, or Korean economic development in the 1950s. What she saw in the Philippines was Rostow's "takeoff" as it had been in England and Korea. It would be wonderful—and very profitable—if the technology, capital, and equipment used productively in rich states could be transferred to poor countries that have not simultaneously evolved a matching set of social, cultural, and political institutions. The Morogoro shoe factory is a memorial to how difficult that is.

Morogoro is a sad case. As is Tanzania itself. Julius Nyerere stands out among the corrupt and vainglorious politicians of modern Africa for his decency and integrity. A socialist who believed in planned development, he devoted himself to the welfare of his people in twenty-one years as president. The state he ruled united Tanganyika—a beautiful area of East Africa, transferred from German to British control over World War I—and the spice island of Zanzibar.

Tanzania received extensive aid, as public agencies and private donors supported a hopeful development in a depressing environment. Western advisers filled the hotels of Dar es Salaam—Nyerere could never have found people of the quality who had managed India's central planning from the country's internal resources.[13] Yet Tanzanian GDP per head is lower today than when Nyerere became president. After his retirement, Nyerere faded from view, conceding, with the honesty and modesty that had characterized his life, that he and his policies had failed.[14]

India's development is also littered with failed projects. The high hopes of Indian planners were frustrated by endemic corruption at lower levels of politics and bureaucracy. Corruption spread upward as the Gandhi dynasty extended its power. But India's saving grace was commitment to democracy. As the failures of Indian economic planning became evident in the 1980s, the battery of state controls was progressively dismantled.[15]

India remains desperately poor. Technology has improved life expectancy and reduced infant mortality[16] as much as it has contributed to economic development. So population growth has meant that growth has not varied living standards by much. As with China, the poor economic performance of the mother country contrasts with the achievements of people of Indian origin outside India.[17] Institutions matter, and output is not simply a product of capital, labor, and technology.

Government as Theft
•••••••••••••••••••••••••••••••••••••••

In Menton, the terrace where I write overlooks Cap Martin, a beautiful wooded peninsula. The family of the late president Mobutu of Zaire still owns four villas in its most exclusive quarter. The part of central Africa bounded by the Congo River is rich in mineral resources—copper, cobalt, zinc, tin, nickel, uranium, and diamonds. But these riches have harmed the country, not helped it. The Congo has been a magnet for thieves—the curse of Kurtz.[18] The area was first looted by King Leopold II of Belgium, who also spent his profits on the Côte d'Azur.[19] One of the Mobutu villas is on an avenue named after Leopold's wife.[20]

The Congo then became a regular Belgian colony. While Britain and France sought an orderly process of decolonization, the Belgians just packed up and (mostly) went home. The state quickly collapsed into four zones. Most mineral resources were in the province of Katanga, ostensibly ruled by Moise Tshombe, a Western puppet. Patrice Lumumba, the first prime minister, was murdered, with the connivance of Western security agencies. Dag Hammarskjöld, the Swedish secretary-general of the United Nations, died in a mysterious plane crash on a peacekeeping mission.[21]

Joseph Mobutu, army commander, proclaimed himself head of state in 1965 and maintained that claim until his death thirty-two years later. He established and kept control through terrorism and bribery. His principal associates were known as *grosses légumes* (fat vegetables). In the 1970s, Western banks lent heavily to the ostensible government of Zaire, Mobutu's name for his country (and its currency, of steadily declining value). There was aggressive competition to give Mobutu money. Walter Wriston (the Citibank CEO who was later to write *The Twilight of Sovereignty*) memorably remarked that "the country does not go bankrupt,"[22] and Citibank was a large lender. Zaire ran up debts it could never repay while its leaders became immensely rich. As private lenders withdrew, the World Bank filled the gap.[23] Much of the borrowed money never reached Zaire but was channeled directly into foreign bank accounts by Mobutu and the *grosses légumes*.

Before Mobutu's death in 1997, copper and cobalt production had collapsed. Even the power lines and equipment had been stolen. In the words of the American ambassador, "Mobutu has not only killed the golden goose, he's eaten the carcass and made fat from the feathers."[24] The diamond trade was mostly under the control of bandits. Mobutu himself, surrounded by his presidential guard, occupied a boat on the Congo River, the only place where he could feel safe.

The history of Western involvement in the Congo has been entirely disgraceful. Western countries destabilized its politics, supported terrorizing governments and armed oppositions, and gave criminals the trappings of statesmen. The motives were cynical, but the policies futile. The Congo is in anarchy, mineral production has collapsed, and large amounts of money have been handed to thieves by international agencies and commercial banks. It is hardly credible that the World Bank continued to lend to the Mobutu regime for over twenty years.

The Congo's external debt today is around $15 billion. This is a purely notional figure because it can never be repaid. Its existence is an obstacle to economic development, but such economic development is not likely. The process described in Lewis's two-sector model has operated in reverse. Depreciation of capital in the modern sector has led to relapse to a traditional economy based on subsistence agriculture.

The Congo has been extreme, but the general experience of sub-Saharan Africa since 1960 makes grim reading. Natural resource endowments may actually damage economic development because these resources distort the structure of economic institutions.[25] Nigeria—rich in oil—has been ruled by a succession of dictators whose grand larcenies have institutionalized corruption throughout Nigerian life.[26]

In the nineteenth century, economic institutions in Australia and the western United States were distorted by gold discoveries. The oil wealth of Saudi Arabia makes balanced economic development impossible.[27] Some rich states—Norway and Iceland—have managed bountiful resource endowments well. Others—such as Switzerland and Japan—may have benefited from their absence.

Tom Friedman, the herald of globalization, notes a still greater paradox. If you are really looking for societies characterized by unrestrained greed and weak government, sub-Saharan Africa is the place to find them. "Come to Africa—it's a freshman Republican's paradise. Yes, sir, nobody in Liberia pays taxes. There's no gun control in Angola. There's no welfare as we know it in Burundi, and no big government to interfere in the market in Rwanda. But a lot of their people sure wish there were."[28]

The "governments" of these countries are corrupt businesses, more akin to the Mafia than to public services. "Failed states" describe situations—as in Afghanistan or Somalia—where no group of warlords is sufficiently dominant to be described as government, in contrast to the monopoly of oppression in Saddam's Iraq, Mobutu's Zaire, and Mugabe's Zimbabwe. Rich states function through a variety of established social conventions and political institutions, which were not successfully transplanted to Africa during short periods of colonial occupation.[29]

Dependencia

Colonial regimes in countries of settlement put in place the building blocks of successful market economies. This did not happen in countries that experienced only colonial occupation. Perhaps this occupation not only failed to promote economic development, but actually hindered it.

For more than one Latin American theorist of the process of growth: "The now developed countries were never underdeveloped, though they may have been undeveloped."[30] The implication is that undevelopment is a state of nature, but underdevelopment an imposed status. The poverty of poor countries (victims of the international economic system) is the corollary of the prosperity of rich countries—*dependencia*. To escape from this servitude, their growth path must be fundamentally different from the history of today's rich states. Although the model is very different from Solow's growth theories, that implication is the same.

Such arguments have obvious attractions for economists and politicians in poor states. They also appeal to people in rich states who feel guilty about their own prosperity. We tell children not to leave food while others starve. The children point out that the food they leave is not available to the starving—a response that gets to the heart of the matter. There is no fixed pool of food, and neither by clearing my plate nor eating less do I make food available to people thousands of miles away.

The most coherent models of victimhood were developed by the

Economic Commission for Latin America (ECLA), established in 1947. The commission's articulate spokesman was the Argentine Raoul Prebisch. Hans Singer developed a similar argument in England at about the same time, and their description of dependency has become known as the Prebisch-Singer thesis.[31]

The central claim is that industrializing Europe imposed on "peripheral economies"—like Argentina and New Zealand—an obligation to specialize in primary goods—agricultural products and natural resources. Since technological advance was in and around manufacturing production, this led to a widening gap in incomes between the center and the periphery. Peripheral economies could only achieve growth by withdrawing from the international trading system and developing their own manufacturing sectors. The policies that follow are not very different from those that were pursued without success in India, and they were equally unsuccessful in Latin America.

There are elements of truth in dependency theory. Resource-rich economies may find themselves at a disadvantage—the curse of Kurtz.[32] The headquarters of a corporation creates spillovers—management training, research and development facilities, needs for supporting services—that are not needed for branch offices. And many countries have protected their fledgling industrial sectors from competition in the early stages of economic development. The most striking exception, Britain, was also the first developing nation.

But there has been rapid technological advance in agriculture, in oil production, and in mining, just as in manufacturing. And some peripheral economies—such as Australia's—have prospered. The different economic experiences of Australia and Argentina do not originate in differences in relationships between these peripheral economies and the center but in the economic, social, and political institutions of the peripheral economies themselves.

Dependency theory is a poor explanation of Latin America's disappointing economic performance. And has faded from view. The Brazilian economist Fernando Cardoso was an associate of Prebisch's and a leading proponent of the dependency thesis.[33] When he became finance minister in 1993 and president the following year, he followed policies of an impeccably conventional nature. Cardoso suffered the humiliation of being forced to announce a currency devaluation from a public lavatory to which mobbing crowds had forced his retreat. But his tenure of office can be rated a moderate success.

Poor but Happy
● ●

India's planners, Nyerere's advisers, and the Economic Commission for Latin America wanted poor states to be like rich states. Nyerere may have had different objectives, although it was never clear what they were. Mobutu, with no concern for his people, sought—and achieved—the trappings of extreme wealth for himself. The common assumption is that the values of the modern economic system are universal.

Yet some communities, with little or no exposure to that modern economic system, are happy. Visitors to Ladakh, an inaccessible province in the Himalayan foothills, repeatedly observe the cheerful demeanor of its people.[34] Only in the 1930s did the West discover that the central plains of New Guinea were densely populated by tribes that had developed their own agriculture, politics, and culture in an environment cut off from external influences for thousands of years.[35] The lives of these people seemed full and satisfying.

But their autonomy was destroyed forever by the arrival of visitors in airplanes and helicopters carrying transistor radios. Once material goods become available, people want them, and some will make great sacrifices of personal well-being to obtain them. Perhaps for themselves, perhaps for the benefit of families—that is why the Mexican Pedro is in Los Angeles and Sicelo's brother, Patrick, works in the South African gold fields.[36]

The relationship between expectations and achievement is central to happiness, and that is why the juxtaposition of different economic lives in South Africa and on the Mexican border creates such social tensions and personal distress. Anthropologist Colin Turnbull contrasted the well-adjusted forest people, the Itun, with the Ik hill tribe:[37] the Ik, facing environmental deterioration and a reduced standard of living, had retreated into a selfish materialism that might disturb even Gary Becker.

Individuals may be attracted to industrial jobs and unfamiliar places by illusions about other lifestyles, and misjudgments about their own prospects. And perhaps economic development requires that people make such mistakes—or are forced into a modern sector because they have no choice. The first farmers may have had lower standards of living than nomads.[38] Working conditions in Britain's industrial revolution were horrific, and some people argue that standards of living declined.[39] The growth of agriculture and the industrialization of Britain ultimately raised material standards of living for everyone, and by large amounts, but these effects were not immediate.

It is easy to romanticize life in what we consider primitive societies. Agriculture in peasant communities is rarely the healthy outdoor life enjoyed by Sven: it normally involves long days of backbreaking toil. The myth of Shangri-la is an enduring image in Western thought, and few descriptions survive critical scrutiny. But it remains true that our economic lives are not our only lives, and happiness comes from the range of our experiences, not the quantity of material goods found in our homes.

Eastern Europe

The gap between expectation and achievement was wide in Eastern Europe, and these countries achieve particularly low scores for self-reported happiness.[40] The collapse of Soviet influence in Eastern Europe in the late 1980s, followed by the disintegration of the Soviet Union itself, created many and varied new states. The architecture of the capital cities of Slovenia, Hungary, and the Czech Republic demonstrates the strength of their European heritage. Tiny Baltic countries like Estonia and Latvia look naturally to Scandinavia, failed states like Romania and Moldova sit on the edge of Europe, and Tajikistan and Uzbekistan enjoy an uneasy relationship with other Asian Islamic republics.

Experience since the communist collapse has varied widely. The most successful economies were always geographically and culturally close to established rich states of Western Europe. If the Czech Republic had been independent after World War II, it would probably today be a rich European state. Poland, whose modern territory includes much of German Prussia, Hungary, for long joined in empire with Austria, and Slovenia are today the most promising Eastern European economies.

Russia itself is the largest new state. Experience here is not encouraging. Mikhail Gorbachev's attempts to reform the Soviet system failed: it proved impossible to introduce economic pluralism without undermining political centralism. And all structures of economic and political authority depended on that centralization.

The combination of pluralism in economic matters with centralism in political affairs has been more successfully achieved in China. China inherited from Mao a dysfunctional economic system. And perhaps this was almost an advantage. The economy of the Soviet Union did, after a fashion, work. In China, change could only be for the better; in Russia, change need not have been for the better and was not. From 1990 to 2000, Chinese economic growth averaged 10% per year, while Russia's GDP fell by half.

The assets of the Soviet state were rapidly transferred to the private sector. Too rapidly. Much former state property fell into the hands of criminals. Anatoly Chubais, leader of the Russian economic reform process, reportedly said, "They are stealing absolutely everything and it is impossible to stop them. But let them steal and take their property. They will then become owners and decent administrators of this property."

But they did not. The new Russian oligarchs were more concerned to transform the assets they controlled into negotiable currency than to develop them. Having secured economic power, they used it to extend their political influence. The lack of legitimacy of the new distribution of income and wealth, and the corruption of Russian politics, aggravated inherent political and economic instability. The experience of Argentina should have acted as a warning. The mechanisms and consequences of Russia's allocation of state assets mirrored Argentina's allocation of empty land, and the adverse results may be as enduring.

Foreign investors had initially seen Russia as an opportunity for the profitable transfer of capital and technology. But these hopes were shaken by large-scale defaults on Russian debt, increasing disillusionment over Russian willingness to protect the interests of investors in Russian businesses, and the steady decline of the Russian economy. The fall in of output in Russia's "capitalist" phase is without precedent among large countries in peacetime. Once again, the application of capital and technology failed in the absence of an appropriate economic, political, and social infrastructure.

{25} ····························

Who Gets What?

People
··

Heidi ($3,000) is a schoolteacher in Switzerland. Sven ($2,000) is a farmworker in Sweden. Ivan ($900), a telecommunications engineer in Moscow. And Ravi ($300) is an accountant with the State Bank of India. The figures in parentheses are their monthly earnings. Although a dollar buys more in India than in Switzerland—purchasing power parities differ from official exchange rates—their earnings correctly rank their material standards of living. Heidi is best off, followed by Sven, Ivan, and Ravi. Why?

There are productivity theories and bargaining theories of income distribution. In productivity theories, earnings reflect the value of an individual's contribution. If people don't earn very much, that is because what they do or make isn't worth very much. In bargaining theories, earnings reflect the distribution of power in society. If people don't earn very much, that is because they do not have control over political institutions and the means of production.

Productivity theories appeal to the rich. Their good fortune is the result of their own abilities. If they take out a lot, it is because they have put more in. Bargaining theories appeal to the poor. They can blame their status on the unfair organization of society. If they receive only little, it is because others have taken out more.

Productivity theories appeal to the political right. Inequality is the inevitable, even fair, result of differences in abilities. People dissatisfied with their economic lives should put in more personal effort. Bargaining theories appeal to the political left. Inequality is the result of social and political injustice. People dissatisfied with their economic lives should seek political power through collective action.

The right won the Cold War and the left lost, so productivity theories have the upper hand today. The profits of Goldman Sachs and Coca-Cola are the fruits of victory. The rewards of investment bankers and CEOs may seem outlandish to you and me, but the market tells us they are worth it. After declining for decades, income inequality within rich states has again increased in the last twenty years (see Box 4.1).

But can these theories explain the different economic lives of Heidi and Ivan, Ravi and Sven? Whose output is more valuable, Heidi's or Ravi's? I don't know how to answer that question and am certain that the people who hired Heidi and Ravi, or sign their paychecks, have not thought about it. But it is even less plausible that Heidi earns so much because she is a tough negotiator, or that Swiss teachers are a uniquely influential political group. Most people do not know their personal productivity, nor are they often able to bargain over wages. Productivity theories and bargaining theories are both inadequate descriptions of how rewards are determined in market economies. But a synthesis helps toward the answer.

The Product of Teams
● ●

Rousseau's hunters did better by cooperating to catch a deer than by individually chasing hares. But when he or she did kill a deer, who got what? Each member must receive at least as much meat as he or she could get catching hares, otherwise the team would fade into the forest. But even after each has had that much, there is venison to spare. This surplus is the economic rent attributable to the team: by analogy with the rents to Saudi oil described in chapter 12, it is the difference between the revenues of the hunt and the minimum needed to keep them together.

How is that meat to be distributed? The simplest solution would be for the hunt to divide the catch equally among the members. But one team member might be better than others at catching hares. She might suggest that only the surplus, the economic rent, be divided equally, and if she would otherwise leave the team, it might be best for all to agree. Or a member might be a particularly skillful hunter. If he has the opportunity to defect to another team, the hunt would be wise to offer him a larger share. It would be Pareto efficient, and members might agree that it was fair. These factors reinforce each other.

Even if team members have similar skills and alternative opportunities, they may have different roles. The conductor isn't necessarily the most talented member of the orchestra or the most important, but simply the person who fulfills the coordinating function. Great conductors can, and do, impose their style—as can bad conductors—but the quality of the sound depends principally on the score and the musicians. Even if all hunters are equally skillful, a team may need a leader, just as an orchestra needs a conductor. As with which side of the road we drive on, it is often more important that there be a decision than what the decision is. Should we hunt north or south tomorrow?

Leadership roles are universal in human society. The leader may be the best hunter, but this is not a necessary, or even a sensible, way to choose. Weber[1] explained how leadership roles may be filled by tradition—the incumbent king, or CEO, breeds or chooses a successor. This is how Louis XVI succeeded Louis XV on the throne of France and Jeff Immelt succeeded Jack Welch in the top spot at General Electric.[2] The leader may achieve that position by personal charisma or be chosen by a rational process, such as democratic election or selection by a search committee of the board. All these mechanisms—dynasty, anointment, meritocratic search, election, and charisma—are found in economic life.

Leaders almost always seek a larger share and are usually in a position to get it. The maximum the leader can extract, if membership is voluntary, is the whole of the economic rent: otherwise members defect in pursuit of hares. But if team members cannot opt out, the leader may try to eat the whole animal. Citizens of countries cannot easily opt out, and the shareholders of companies can opt out only by finding someone to take their place. The last kings of France tried to eat more and more of the animal, as did Mobutu, and as do some chief executives.[3] The only limit to this rapacity is that the leadership is overthrown, as happened to Louis XVI and some executives.

The allocation of rewards by teams reflects a complex balance of factors. How much do members contribute to the work of the team? What alternatives are available to them? Political factors, and norms and traditions, matter too. Both productivity and bargaining play a role in arriving at the final outcome.

Economic Rents

The surplus from teamwork—the difference between the value of the deer caught by the team and the hares that could be captured by its members working individually—is the economic rent created by the team. The concept of economic rent was introduced in Box 12.1, as the difference between the cost and selling price of Saudi oil, or the operating costs and yield of fertile land. The "margin of cultivation" describes the marginal oil, or marginal land, for which (unlike Saudi oil or fertile land) receipts only just cover costs. But the concept of economic rent is quite general. It is the difference between the value of a resource or collection of resources and the value that these resources could generate in other uses.

The economic rent created by the Coca-Cola corporation is the difference between the revenues of the company and the revenues that would be derived if the company was broken up and its capital, its plants, and its workers were employed elsewhere. A rough-and-ready measure is the difference between Coca-Cola's profits and what you would earn by putting its capital in the bank. Madonna's economic rent is the difference between the profits from her stage appearances and sales of albums and what she would earn in her next best job. I will not speculate on what that job might be. The economic rent created by Harvard Business School is the difference between the value created by that institution and the value that would be created if its faculty and students were dispersed elsewhere. The concept is clear enough, but measurement is impossible.

Ricardo's framework is equally applicable to soft drinks, pop stars, and universities. The least successful firm in the soft drink business will earn just enough to satisfy its shareholders and employees. It is at the industrial "margin of cultivation." Coca-Cola has a competitive advantage over that firm and earns economic rent equal to its competitive advantage.

In Madonna's world, there are many wannabee stars. Most never get a recording contract—they are, in Ricardo's language, outside the margin of cultivation. Her economic rent is the difference between her earnings and those of someone who is just talented enough to attract the attention of an agent or record company. This is probably no more than the person concerned could earn in an everyday job, as a hairdresser or shop assistant.

The possibility of large Madonna-type rents illuminates another aspect of the life of hungry painters at the Colombe d'Or. Popular music, and painting, are activities in which the distribution of rewards is particularly uneven. The rewards to those who are outstandingly talented are outlandishly high.[4] Eventually, Braque no longer needed to exchange his paintings for food and sold them at high prices. The prospect of the high returns earned by top sportsmen, pop stars, actors, and lawyers prompts many to enter these activities, few of whom succeed. The small possibility of Madonna-like success ensures a crowd of hopefuls at studio doors. It makes sense—and is often necessary—for them to share some of their potential rewards with sponsors.[5]

Patrons of young artists hope that a few successes will compensate for the many pictures that will never have any real commercial value. The painter values the certain return now. His attitude to risk has a convexity property: he prefers the average of the rewards of stardom and the likelihood of penury to taking a chance on one or the other. No doubt most of the pictures Paul Roux accepted in lieu of payment for board and lodging turned out to be worthless. The collection at the Colombe d'Or demonstrates that despite these mistakes he still benefited himself as much as he benefited the artistic community he supported.

Madonna earns rent as an individual, and Coca-Cola earns rent as a corporation. At Harvard, we see both. The faculty earn individual rents, like Madonna, from their star talents. The institution—like Coca-Cola—creates its own economic rent. It adds value through teamwork—the division of labor allows professors to teach their speciality rather than the whole of management, and the reputation of the institution makes the whole more valuable than the sum of the parts.

Bargaining to a Perfectly
Competitive Equilibrium
● ●

But all economic rents result from scarce factors. Coca-Cola has a distinctive brand. Madonna has a unique talent. HBS has a distinguished faculty and an enviable reputation. A perfectly competitive market has many buyers and sellers, and none is large enough, or distinctive enough, to have significant influence over price. No scarce factors: no distinctive brands, unique talents, distinguished faculty, or enviable reputations. Few economic rents exist in a perfectly competitive market.

In a perfectly competitive market Coca-Cola cannot earn economic rents because it must compete not only with other manufacturers of colas, but with other producers of Coca-Cola. In a perfectly competitive market Madonna cannot command high fees because clones can provide identical services. In a perfectly competitive market Harvard must compete with other institutions indistinguishable from it. In a perfectly competitive market all university professors are the same. In a perfectly competitive market there will be no surplus from the successful stag hunt: competing teams of hunters will crowd the forest until only sufficient deer can be caught to make deer hunting on a par with chasing hares. The margin of cultivation is always at the front door.

Game theory's framework of individuals bargaining over rents offers a quite different account of spontaneous order. Imagine a large group of people trying to decide on an allocation of scarce resources between competing ends. They have different skills and capabilities, which could be put to many different uses. No one will agree to a proposed allocation unless he or she benefits. There must be gains from trade.

Individuals must gain from trade. But so must states. And groups of individuals—such as firms—are free to form groups and trade among themselves and with other groups. No group should agree to a proposed allocation if they could do better by opting out and forming a mini-economy of their own.

A group that could do better by staying out of a planned allocation is called a blocking coalition. Given enough individuals and firms of each kind—given enough pluralism in the economy—one and only one allocation cannot be blocked. It is exactly the allocation that would emerge from the Arrow-Debreu model of competitive equilibrium.[6] Bargaining theory and the Arrow-Debreu model give identical results. There are no economic rents, nothing left to bargain over. If there are no scarce factors in an economy, bargaining and productivity theories converge. This is an intriguing result, but it probably does not reveal much of the truth about markets. In modern economies, many factors are scarce and there are many sources of rents. The acquisition and defense of rents, and bargaining and dispute over their distribution, are the main influences on income distribution.

Rent Seeking

Economic rents are returns to scarcities—the exceptional talents of individuals, the distinctive capabilities of corporations. But not all individuals have scarce talents, not all corporations have distinctive capabilities. If scarcity does not naturally exist, perhaps it can be invented, and rents garnered anyway. The grant of monopolies has been a source of patronage and revenue for governments for thousands of years and continues today in poor countries and corrupt states.[7] In postcommunist Russia, the Orthodox Church won an alcohol monopoly. Tax-free status entered the Russian language as *ofshorraya zona*.

The costs of monopoly to the public are usually greater than profits of monopolists. Monopoly closes down disciplined pluralism and stifles innovation in products and technology. The monopoly often goes to the best lobbyist, not the best competitor. So gains from trade due to specialization and differences in capabilities are likely to be lost.

Under disinterested government, it is difficult to earn rents by buying monopolies or tax concessions. Rent seeking is most common in rich states in areas of genuine public interest in restricting entry— such as protection from untrained doctors, unsafe aircraft, and dishonest financial advisers. But all entry restrictions, whatever their rationale, can create rents, and those who have entered lobby for tightening entry restrictions still further. Friedman, following Gellhorn, provides an extended list of the skills needed—such as knowledge of barber history and barber law—to be allowed to cut hair in some American states.[8] When supervising bodies are more vigorous in monitoring the standards of prospective entrants than of established practitioners, that is a warning that regulation is directed more toward increasing rents than maintaining standards.

Many economic resources are scarce, and mechanisms are needed to regulate access. Mineral resources are limited, and broadcast spectrum is scarce. Unless we allow indiscriminate development, construction sites will be limited and permission to develop them valuable. These restrictions often create large rents, and firms will spend correspondingly large sums to get them. A government that creates or assigns these resources can impose heavy taxes, or large up-front fees, for their use—as with specific taxes on oil and mineral deposits, or the allocation of spectrum for mobile phone companies. These fees and taxes yield revenue and discourage rent seeking.

Rent seeking impedes the functioning of a market economy—the pursuit of gains from trade through specialization and differences in capabilities. It limits innovation though disciplined pluralism. It corrodes the integrity of politics. These adverse political and economic effects often reinforce each other.

Rents and Competitive Advantages

Firms derive rents from their competitive advantages. Coca-Cola earns rents because it is well inside "the margin of cultivation"—its returns are much better than those of an ordinary soft-drinks business. The competitive advantage is not the secret recipe for the fizzy water. In 1985 the company replaced the classic formula with a flavor that users preferred in blind tasting. The result was disastrous. Consumers identify with the brand for other reasons. Coke is indeed it.

Chapter 7 described other corporate competitive advantages, past and current. The brands and reputation of Marlboro and McDonald's. The structure of relationships established by Toyota. The depth of management capabilities at General Electric. Microsoft's ownership of the Windows interface. The quality of production-line engineering achieved by BMW and Mercedes and the associated brands.

Shareholders take the lion's share of business rents. Firms with competitive advantages earn returns in excess of the cost of capital, and the market capitalization of these companies is much greater than the value of the plant, machinery, and inventories that they use in the business.[9] But successful companies share rents with workers and customers. This enhances the rent itself. Companies with competitive advantages are good companies to do business with, good companies to work for.

Managers of the largest corporations had felt insulated from the stock market. In 1980, General Motors dismissed contemptuously an inquiry from its largest shareholder, the Californian public employees retirement plan, about its succession planning. In the 1980s, corporations were urged to direct economic rents exclusively to shareholders. The threat of hostile takeover focused managers on the pursuit of "shareholder value." Imaginative financiers put together packages that made it possible to attack even the largest of companies. Michael Milken, who put together some extraordinary deals for shady figures in the United States, was jailed, and the firm for which he worked, Drexel Burnham Lambert, went into liquidation.[10] But the effect of his activities led to a continuing emphasis on shareholder value even if Milken himself was out of business.

As this trend developed, executives in large corporations no longer compared themselves with those who had risen to the top of other professions or large organizations—top lawyers or doctors, civil servants, managers of nationalized industries. The comparison was with dealmakers and financiers, and they revised both the amounts they were paid and the ways in which they were paid it. While their salaries rose, the real growth in pay came from bonuses and stock options (call options on the company's shares). This gave a strong incentive to ensure that share prices continued to rise, and some professional managers became extremely rich men. Steve Ross of Time Warner and Michael Eisner of Disney each received over a billion dollars for their services.[11]

Companies could satisfy the stock market and add value to executive share options only by reporting earnings growth faster than the growth of their business—increasing the rents from scarcity and competitive advantage. But how was this to be achieved in markets that were becoming more competitive, not less, as a result of globalization? Analysts and commentators struggled during the bubble to find answers to this question.

The talking heads suggested rents might come from consolidation in firms with stronger competitive advantages. The analogy of

Microsoft was widely used, but chapter 22 showed how unusual in business is the control of a proprietary standard by a single firm. The history of past technological revolutions, such as railways, electricity, and automobiles, is that most benefits go, through competition, to consumers.

The Very Rich

Forbes magazine produces an annual list of the richest Americans.[12] Three names are always close to the top: Bill Gates, Warren Buffett, and Robson Walton. Bill Gates is too well-known to need description. Robson Walton is the son of Sam Walton, founder of Wal-Mart. The company, still based in Bentonville, Arkansas, where Sam grew up, is the world's largest retailer and, with over a million workers, the world's largest private sector employer.

Warren Buffett is the most successful investor in history. Buffett and his partner, Charlie Munger, control the investment company Berkshire Hathaway. Berkshire Hathaway owns a number of businesses—such as America's largest reinsurer, Geico—and has major stakes in other companies, including Coca-Cola. This portfolio, which today is worth around $40 billion, has grown from negligible beginnings through Buffett's continued success in choosing investments.[13]

Buffett still lives in the bungalow in Omaha, Nebraska, he bought in 1957. He has never been a Wall Street figure—although he was for a time chairman of Salomon Brothers, after illegal activities by the bank's traders jeopardized the value of his investment. His favorite drink is Cherry Coke (he switched from Pepsi and became Coca-Cola's principal shareholder). The annual meetings of Berkshire Hathaway, at which Buffett delivers a lengthy and engaging homily, attract huge audiences to Omaha: many small shareholders have become rich by following Buffett.[14] Buffett, now seventy-three, harbors no dynastic ambitions. On his death, the Buffett Foundation will become the world's largest charity.

Both Buffett and Walton are modern American heroes and with reason. Sam Walton's habits were even more modest than Buffett's, and he drove a utility pickup until his death.[15] Both became extraordinarily rich through their own remarkable abilities, and conducted uncomplicated lives and businesses with transparency and integrity.

The economic rents of Wal-Mart come from its competitive advantage over other general retailers. Sears Roebuck was for decades the largest chain store. Kmart, Wal-Mart's closest rival, went into chapter 11 protection in 2001. Walton was quick to see the potential of out-of-town shopping and positioned Wal-Mart stores outside small towns across America. Wal-Mart also pioneered the effective use of information technology to match stock to consumer needs. The sheer scale of the Wal-Mart business means that a margin of 2% on its sales yields $7 billion of profit, and the Walton family, as legatees of Sam, enjoy a substantial share.

Microsoft, although ubiquitous, is a much smaller company: Wal-Mart employs twenty times as many people and its sales are ten times greater. Gates is as rich as Walton because Microsoft, unlike Wal-Mart, enjoys a near monopoly, while Wal-Mart is in a competitive market. Microsoft's rents are much larger relative to its sales.

One of the richest men outside the United States—perhaps the richest—is the sultan of Brunei, a tiny state on the western coast of Borneo, whose offshore oil reserves produce around 70 million barrels of oil per year—more, per head of population, than Saudi Arabia. The sultan's brother, Prince Jefri, became internationally famous for extravagance. The royal family is reported to own 350 Rolls-Royce cars. In London, Jefri allegedly kept forty prostitutes on standby at the Dorchester Hotel and was for many years the principal customer of Asprey's, the most expensive shop in the city and perhaps the world until he finally bought the store itself. The effect of Jefri's expenditure and incompetence were to reduce the family fortune from $110 billion to a more manageable $40 billion.[16]

The riches of Walton, Gates, and the sultan are all based on economic rents—derived from, respectively, the competitive advantage of Wal-Mart, the dominance of Windows, and the oil reserves of Brunei. The individuals concerned are entitled to a large share of these rents—the sultan, through tradition and heredity; Gates, through his role in the foundation of the company; Robson Walton, through a combination of the two.

It is clear who pays what the sultan, Gates, and Walton spend.

The users of Brunei's oil, the customers of Wal-Mart and Microsoft. Motorists, Wal-Mart shoppers, and Windows users pay willingly. Even if they resent the wealth of these men, they value the product: there are mutual gains from trade. But who contributed to the resources of the Buffett Foundation?

Buffett's investment strategy has always been based on identifying sustainable economic rents. "As a child the clanging of the trolley car would put a thought in Warren's mind. All of that traffic with no place to go but right by the Russells's house, he would say—if only there were a way to make some money off it."[17] Buffett's investment coups—in American Express, the *Washington Post*, Gannett, Gillette, and Coca-Cola—are all in businesses with strong competitive advantages, yielding sustainable economic rents.

Buffett simply understood the truth about markets better than the talking heads of Bloomberg television. Yet the rents created by Wal-Mart, Microsoft, and Brunei oil did not exist before Walton opened his stores, Gates founded Microsoft, and the sultan invited oil companies to drill. American Express, the *Washington Post*, and Coca-Cola would all have been powerful rent-generating businesses if they had never heard of Warren Buffett. Buffett's gains were made at the expense of less successful investors—advisers and their clients with less understanding of the truth about markets. Buffett's contempt for Wall Street is legendary. In December 1986 he wrote, under the heading "How to Tame the Casino Society" that "if a graduating MBA asks me how to get rich in a hurry, I hold my nose with one hand and point to Wall Street with the other."[18]

Who Gets What?

Productivity and bargaining theories of income distribution are synthesized in the theory of economic rent. Many rents are the product of scarce talents in individuals or competitive advantages in firms; some reflect arbitrage gains of securities houses or the rent-seeking activities of successful lobbyists. The creation of rents is the result of a combination of productivity and bargaining.

Where rents are the product of the scarce talents of individuals—Madonna—then it is obvious who benefits from the rents. But most rents in modern economies are the product of teams or can only be effectively exploited through teams. The distribution of rents within teams is the result of a combination of individual productivity and internal bargaining.

The most important influence on our incomes is the teams we belong to. Many teams and kinds of team are relevant to world income distribution. These teams include the residents of the canton of Zürich, the Organization of Petroleum Exporting Countries, the shareholders and employees of Wal-Mart stores, the family of the late Sam Walton, the citizens of Brunei and its ruling family, the executive directors of the Disney corporation.

Some teams are highly exclusive. If you were not born a Walton or in the household of the sultan of Brunei, marriage to an existing member is the only way to join the team. Wal-Mart, on the other hand, recruits employees and shareholders actively. If you want to join, it will very likely have you. The canton of Zürich is less exclusive than the Waltons but more so than Wal-Mart. It will admit you if you are a citizen of another Swiss canton or, selectively and reluctantly, if you were born elsewhere. The more exclusive the club the more valuable is membership.

Heidi and Sven have high material standards of living because they are members of many different teams, and the organization of these teams has evolved over centuries in a highly sophisticated manner. Not only to exploit fully the division of labor to the greatest possible extent, but also to manage information, pool risks, achieve cooperation and coordination, generate knowledge, and to do so within an extensive and elaborately developed set of conventions and rules. Sicelo is a member of almost no economic teams, barely deriving benefit even from the division of labor. Ravi and Ivan are members of fewer teams, and some of these are ineffective—because of poor internal organization or because they are not directed to relevant social and economic objectives.

{26}
Places

Küssnacht

Heidi benefits from a division of labor that Adam Smith could never have imagined as he wandered round the pin factory. Smith had been paid by students to whom he delivered lectures and acted as private tutor to the Duke of Buccleuch. But the modern division of labor in education would have astonished him. Heidi takes her own children to a caregiver while she teaches larger groups of other people's children. This division of labor makes mass education possible. Sicelo's children can learn only the little their mother knows.

Heidi sees two hundred children each week and is paid by the canton of Zürich. She teaches: Gary Becker would say she develops their human capital. That will yield direct benefits for them—they earn more because they are better educated. And it will benefit their future employers—banks, manufacturing businesses, the canton itself. Their education and skills will enhance the social, political, and economic infrastructure that makes life pleasant, and possible, for Heidi—safe streets, stable institutions.

Heidi is contributing to innumerable products, and large numbers of people help to make Heidi's economic life possible. Her car alone required thousands of workers. Heidi does not know who they are, and no one need know who they are. This is the power of spontaneous order. The pin factory would have been unaware of all those who contributed to its much simpler product. But Nissan probably can identify most of those who made Heidi's Micra. The modern division of labor makes complex products possible, but it also reduces the anonymity of exchange of the perfectly competitive market.

Heidi benefits from this detailed division of labor, in which differing capabilities and specialization are exploited fully. Sicelo is part of a small, largely isolated community, producing mostly for its own use. This is the most important reason why Heidi is so rich and Sicelo so poor.

Heidi also shares various economic rents. Her Swiss nationality is important. The division of labor from which she benefits so much is supported by an elaborate and extensive economic infrastructure. Heidi benefits every day from the competitive advantages of national and international brands and the skills and reputation of local traders. She enjoys the advantages of cooperative structures that operate at every level of Swiss society, and from the coordination that gives her access to the world's most efficient rail system, an electricity grid, a network of cash machines: a comprehensive list of elements of this Swiss economic infrastructure would occupy the remaining pages of this book. Her economic life is conditioned by the elaborate structure of rules and conventions, mostly tacit, that govern Swiss society and create large and enduring rents.

Heidi also benefits from rents created by Swiss corporations. They are derived from competitive advantages of international businesses like Nestlé and Novartis, from the worldwide reputation of Swiss banks for prudence and discretion, and the specialist skills of those small chemical and engineering businesses scattered along the lakeshores and in the lower valleys. Their exports are the dynamic of the Swiss economy.

Heidi and Hermann benefit directly from these rents through their modest portfolio of shares. Hermann also shares some of the rents of his Swiss bank. The bank prefers to employ Swiss nationals, and as a result Hermann earns a comfortable living without the pressures of the financial services industry in Manhattan or London. Because of the competitive achievements of the business for which he works, Hermann is probably paid more than someone of his abilities, education, and experience would secure anywhere else in the world. This is not to downplay his skills and achievements. Hermann is good at his job, and his organization is successful because all are good at their jobs. The team is more than the sum of its parts, and the team rewards are distributed among the parts.

But the pool of talent on which internationally successful Swiss businesses can draw is limited. Although large enough to support these businesses, their very success has created pressures. The division of labor itself limits the resources available to the international sectors of the Swiss economy. Not everyone can work in a bank, or an engineering firm: these businesses, and the people who work in them, require architects and accountants, shop workers and car mechanics, town planners and schoolteachers. Their earnings are set by reference to the earnings of people who work in the internationally competitive sector of the economy. That is both fair and necessary if there are to be car mechanics as well as engineering workers. This is why Heidi is one of the best-paid schoolteachers in the world.

Ravi has friends in Mumbai who are as well qualified to teach as Heidi and earn a fraction of her salary. But Ravi's friends do not speak German and would mostly prefer to live in their familiar environment. Swiss schools prefer staff knowledgeable about Swiss culture and society. And it is unlikely that an Indian teacher would be allowed to work in Switzerland. Puerto Rican nurses relieve nursing shortages in the United States and keep down the pay of American nurses, while creating scarcities in Puerto Rico and raising wages there. But nursing skills are unusually transferable. Barriers to mobility protect the economic rents of Swiss nationals and limit the potential for equalization of earnings internationally.

Heidi's material standard of living is the product of three interrelated groups of factors. She benefits from an extensive and well-coordinated division of labor, domestically and internationally. She is part of a complex set of social, political, and economic institutions that have evolved to manage the problems of information, risk-sharing, cooperation, and coordination in rich states. And directly and indirectly she shares in numerous economic rents from Swiss institutions and Swiss corporations.

Kivik

Sven and Ingrid have their feet up in front of the television in their Kivik home. Sven and Ingrid are agricultural workers, like most of the population of the world, today and throughout history. But few have imagined farming as it is for Sven and Ingrid.

Most agricultural workers engage in arduous physical labor. The energy expended on a Swedish farm comes almost entirely from machinery. Most agricultural workers worry about weather and diseases. So do Sven and Ingrid; but their finances are largely insulated from the productivity of their crops and they are able to control animal and pest diseases.

Although well educated—both have a spattering of foreign languages—Sven and Ingrid are no intellectuals. They do not read much, their recreations are sports and television. They enjoy almost everything that romantics have admired in rural life—a job outdoors, contact with nature, freedom and flexibility to manage their day without close supervision—with few of its disadvantages. They have a regular salary, extensive social benefits, a wide range of opportunities and new experiences; they do not work particularly hard.

Sven and Ingrid are well-off for much the same reasons that Heidi and Hermann are well-off. They benefit from the same finely demarcated and well-organized division of labor as Heidi and Hermann. The social and economic infrastructures of Switzerland and Sweden have many differences, but both are sophisticated, developed market economies And the rents that Switzerland earns from Novartis and Nestlé, from speciality chemicals and engineering, Sweden obtains—not quite—from Abba and Volvo, and from other branches of precision engineering.

Yet Sven's economic position is more vulnerable than Heidi's. It is not economic to grow wheat in Sweden on a large scale. The profitability of the farm depends on the Swedish government and the Common Agricultural Policy. This farm support is under pressure.[1]

And while some others could do Heidi's job, many millions, with modest training, could do Sven's. In some rich countries, work like Sven's is undertaken by migrant workers at low wages. Many potential migrants are in the candidate states of the European Union. The union that represents Sven understands well that the willingness of other Swedes to share rents with Sven may be eroding and that the Swedish and West European clubs to which he belongs may become less exclusive.

Moscow
• •

Ivan and Olga are discussing, as they often do, the extraordinary political events through which they have both lived. The initial excitement of perestroika in the 1980s, when change became possible. The collapse of the Soviet Union and Soviet system, which followed. The mixture of corruption and chaos, opportunity and innovation, that they see around them today, at once exhilarating in its potential and depressing in its outcomes.

Why did the planning systems of the Soviet Union fail so comprehensively? Disciplined pluralism proved far more innovative than central direction. The considerable talents of Russian scientists and engineers—like Ivan—achieved little. They were most effective in developing the country's military capabilities. Defense objectives were relatively clear, with few limits on the resources devoted to them. This was the basis of the Soviet Union's one great achievement—the defeat of Nazi Germany. The development of military technologies was impressive, though not comparable to that of the United States. Russia put the first man in space.

But in other spheres the record was poor. Standards of Russian medicine were often high, but advances in medical protocols and in pharmacology were imitative. And Soviet consumer goods were laughably bad. When Heinz drove his Trabant across the border in October 1989, the failure of communism was most clearly demonstrated in the shop windows of the Kurfürstendamm.

The inefficient, chaotic processes of competitive markets manufactured cars in the quality of Mercedes and the quantities of Volkswagen, while the East produced Trabants. The disorganized experimentation of the American computer industry created the personal computer—a competitive weapon so fearsome that the U.S. defense establishment tried to stop the Russians from getting hold of it. The task forces of the USSR, like the task forces of IBM, produced nothing.[2]

But Soviet planning was not just insufficiently innovative. It was also inefficient. It managed the division of labor and the associated problems of information and coordination far worse than market economies. The Soviet regime had opted out of the international division of labor, but the resources and size of the Soviet economic bloc could have yielded large gains from specialization and differences in capabilities.

But incentive compatibility prevented effective exploitation. Central authorities lacked the information needed to develop the distinctive capabilities of their citizens and businesses. And citizens and businesses themselves lacked incentives to exploit and extend these capabilities. The mechanics of coordination were less effective under central direction then in the spontaneous order of market economies.

No economy has ever been so vulnerable to rent-seeking as the collapsed Soviet Union. Russia is rich in natural resources. Its centralized economy had established many monopolies of production, communication, and transportation. Western firms, anxious to do the business that had been opened to them, required political and economic connections. Never have so many rents been on offer in such a short space of time. The beneficiaries of the process were the politically well connected, managers of established Russian businesses, and criminal gangs. Public choice—the self-amplifying cycle of political corruption and economic rent-seeking described by Buchanan's model (p. 294)—found its fullest expression. As oligarchs bought politicians, they could demand further favors.[3]

Few rents in Russia are derived from scarce talents or the competitive advantages of firms. Talents are plentiful; organizations that can exploit them effectively are scarce. Some Russian firms have competitive advantages—relative to each other—but none have competitive advantages in the global market. International businesses bring their own competitive advantages to Russia, but rents from their Russian operations are future hopes not present realities.

Ivan and Olga do not share the rents of Russia's rent-seeking society. By working for an American company, Ivan experiences American business as it really is, not the caricature of it that has been imposed on the former state sector. AT&T is a successful worldwide business with competitive advantages, but is not profitable in Russia. It pays Ivan more than it need but far less than it would pay a similarly qualified worker in the United States. That is the price Ivan pays for living in an ineffectively coordinated environment that has developed few of the social, political, and economic conventions and institutions that underpin a market economy.

Mumbai

●●●

Ravi is, as often, discussing politics with his friends. They focus on the frustrations of young, well-educated Indians over the inability of their country to realize its potential.

British influence on the structure of Indian institutions remains both wide-ranging and superficial. Ravi's accountancy qualification is modeled on its British equivalent. The atmosphere of the bank in which he works would be familiar to someone who had worked in an American bank thirty years ago. The framework for the endless debates of Ravi and his friends is still provided by the mild and benign socialism that captured the intellectual life of Britain for a large part of the twentieth century (its government for a much shorter time, but one that covered the period of Indian independence).

And yet so much about their economic lives and social environment is Indian. For example, the open good humor that has led so many visitors to India to fall in love with the country. The debates of Ravi and his friends are intense but also full of laughter, which is one reason they are so frequent. They will go on arguing late into the night. It has never occurred to them that these debates may be part of the problem rather than part of the solution.

India is spontaneous, but while Switzerland and Sweden display spontaneous order—everyone falls into allotted roles with a minimum of conscious direction—India seems to exemplify spontaneous disorder. The theorems of Arrow and Debreu, the mathematics of complexity, show how disorganized systems might yield ordered outcomes, but they do not demonstrate that they will. And in India disorder seems to remain.

The best reason for believing that economic systems will drift toward order is that selection functions through disciplined pluralism. India has elements of pluralism—its mixture of civilizations is one of its joys—but its pluralism is often undisciplined. And in many respects Indian society is not pluralist at all.

In a village like Palanpur, the economic roles of individuals are largely determined by caste, religion, and gender. This traditional organization establishes division of labor—that is its economic function. But it does so in a way that does not allow differences in capabilities to emerge, far less be exploited, and it cannot easily handle change.

Ravi could not hold the job he does had he not been born into a well-off—by Indian standards—middle-class household in Mumbai. Only exceptional talents and good fortune would permit Indians from humble backgrounds to achieve as much. Nandini will bring up their sons to similar aspirations; only gradually is it understood that daughters might fulfill these roles.

The State Bank of India is not a pluralist institution in origin or intention. Its objective—often pursued with skill and integrity—is to promote the economic development of the country as seen through the eyes of the Indian government, and the directors and managers of the State Bank.

Today, India has an increasingly competitive banking system. Not very competitive—it is in the nature of bankers, from Walter Wriston down, to hold conventional views and to follow the instincts of the herd. The bubble touched even the Bombay Stock Exchange. Still, some of Ravi's circle are successful entrepreneurs. Two of his friends are employed in high-tech businesses in California.

Supporting institutions for the market economy can be found in embryonic form in Mumbai. Traders have competitive advantages, brands, and reputations. India is full of nepotistic networks of cooperation, many of them devoted to rent-seeking, many still engaged in petty deceit and corruption. Ravi and his friends are honest but take pride in knowing the ropes and, occasionally, pulling them to get things done. Increasingly, they understand that the successful coordination of economic systems is not the result of either government direction or personal contact, but systems of organization.

KwaZulu Natal

All this is very distant from Sicelo's life in KwaZulu Natal. Sicelo ekes out a living from subsistence agriculture, as his parents and grandparents did before him, and as he expects his children to do. For Sicelo, the division of labor does not extend much beyond some villagers focusing on crops and others on animals: most, including Sicelo, do both.

Sicelo is in distant contact with that international economy through his brother Patrick. There are large rents from gold mines. Mostly they went to those who discovered and developed the mines.

These enterprises did not see any economic or political need to share these rents and did not do so. Even from a narrowly self-interested perspective, this may not have been a wise decision. Yet the experiences of the Congo, Nigeria, and Saudi Arabia demonstrate that rich resources are a mixed blessing for a poor country.

The institutions of a modern market economy, imported to South Africa by Dutch and British settlers, were set beside a traditional economy based on subsistence agriculture. The settlers attempted to preserve the two systems separately, to draw on the subsistence sector for unskilled labor, and yet to protect the living standards of low-skilled white workers. This impossible balancing act ultimately led to apartheid—morally repulsive, and in the end politically and economically unsustainable.

But none of this affects or affected Sicelo much. Even now, he derives no benefit from the economic rents that come from South Africa's resources; in any event, these rents are not so large that a fair share would make much difference. Sicelo is marginal to the international economy, and the international economy is marginal to him. Sicelo derives little benefit either from rents or the international division of labor, and his standard of living is based on simple agriculture on unpromising land. In common with much of the population of sub-Saharan Africa, he has one of the lowest material standards of living in the world. There is occasional joy in Sicelo's world—wedding feasts are extended celebrations for the whole village—but life is hard.

{27}

The American Business Model

Enlightenment and Modernity

Adam Smith, Adam Ferguson, and the eighteenth-century scholars of the Enlightenment were concerned not just to describe the emergence of spontaneous order in social and economic affairs, but to prescribe for a better society. *The Wealth of Nations* was published in 1776, just after Massachusetts colonists had thrown tea into Boston Harbor. The architects of the American and French republics hoped to design ideal social and political institutions on scientific lines. That rationalist vision has dominated social sciences ever since.

The Enlightenment was to become modernity, and to influence not just economics, politics, and sociology, but all areas of cultural and intellectual life. The rise and fall of modernity—the attempt to reassess knowledge from first principles on a rationalist basis—is most clearly exemplified in architecture. From the 1920s, modernist architects—freed by technology from the constraints of conventional building design—set their classical traditions aside. This enabled them to rethink the relationship of buildings to function. In Le Corbusier's famous phrase, "a house is a machine for living in." In this spirit, he designed the first tower blocks in Marseille in 1952. Modernist architecture swept across the world.

This was all a terrible mistake. The architectural commentator

Charles Jencks famously announced that the modernist era ended on July 15, 1972, when the Pruitt-Igoe housing project in St. Louis was demolished.[1] The project, constructed less than twenty years earlier, had won many architectural awards as a pointer to modernist urban living. But a house was not a machine for living in. The scheme failed to meet the social needs of its residents and fell victim to crime and vandalism. Its emphasis on functionality proved, in the end, not to be functional.[2] Postmodern architecture is eclectic, draws on many historical traditions, and offers multiple interpretations of function and appearance. In the last century, art, literature, music, theater, and cinema all experienced analogous transitions from modernity to postmodernism.

It is strange that economics and business should be the last bastions of modernity.[3] A book has an author, a building an architect, a constitution has its framers. We can try to divine the intentions of these creators and believe that knowledge of such intentions might help us to understand their books, their buildings, their constitutions. That is why we study authors as well as texts and resist the postmodernist claim that there is only the text. An economic system has no architect. There is nothing but the text to study.

The contrast between the eclecticism of the postmodern and the functionalist design of social engineers has been described by Jean-François Lyotard as the contrast between "little stories" and "grand narratives."[4] The most extensive "grand narrative" was Marxism, which purported to offer a unified explanation of human history and a prescriptive view of a just structure of society, linked by an assertion of historical inevitability.

The American Business Model
● ●

And so at the start of the twenty-first century, the American business model (ABM) plays the role in political economy that socialism enjoyed for so long. All political positions, even hostile ones, are defined by their relationship to it. Globalization and privatization have displaced capital and class as the terms of discourse. The label *market forces* immediately evokes hostile or supportive reactions. The term *Washington consensus* is for some a statement of inescapable realities of economic life; it is demonized in many poor states as an attack on democracy and living standards. The right has determined the terms of political debate.

The philosophy of the ABM, as articulated by Milton Friedman, is of government as referee. "It is important to distinguish the day-to-day activities of people from the general customary and legal framework within which these take place. The day-to-day activities are like the actions of the participants in a game when they are playing it; the framework, like the rules of the game they play.... These then are the basic roles of government in a free society: to provide a means whereby we can modify the rules, to mediate differences among us on the meaning of the rules, and to enforce compliance with the rules on the part of those few who would otherwise not play the game" (Friedman [1962], 25). [5]

The claims of the American business model are of four kinds:

- **self-interest rules**—self-regarding materialism governs our economic lives.

- **market fundamentalism**—markets should operate freely, and attempts to regulate them by social or political action are almost always undesirable.

- **the minimal state**—the economic role of government should not extend much beyond the enforcement of contracts and private property rights. Government should not itself provide goods and services, or own productive assets.

- **low taxation**—while taxation is necessary to finance these basic functions of the minimal state, tax rates should be as low as possible and the tax system should not seek to bring about redistribution of income and wealth.

Among those sympathetic to the ABM, there are two views of how market fundamentalism is to be reconciled with the minimal state. Some proponents believe an antitrust policy is needed to preserve competitive markets. For others, even that degree of government intervention is inappropriate.[6]

The ABM, Economic Theory, and Economic Efficiency
●●●●●●●●●●●●●●●●●●●●●●●●●●●●●●●●●●●●●●●

The ABM case is often founded on arguments of general principle. This is not a book about moral philosophy, or the ethics of markets. But moral issues are fundamental for many people. Some supporters of the ABM see government action in economic matters as an attack on liberty, an improper use of the coercive power of the state. Freedom of contract requires a minimal state; market fundamentalism and low taxation are immediate corollaries.

Although people who believe this mostly also believe that the ABM is economically efficient, presumably they would still favor it if it were not. If it could be shown that some regulation of markets would make everyone, or very many, people better off, they would still judge it wrong for government to implement it. Others find the premise of self-interested motivation morally repugnant. Even if it is true, it ought not to be true, and social institutions should restrain greed rather than accommodate it. The accountability of democracy is preferable to the anonymity of markets. If market fundamentalism, the minimal state, and low taxation are necessary for economic efficiency, material sacrifices must be made to secure a just society. But people who hold this view tend also to believe that such sacrifices would not be large. This clash of moral values cannot be resolved by economics; perhaps it cannot be resolved at all. The issue for this book is narrower: it is the relationship between political structures and economic outcomes. The claim that the ABM is the only route to material prosperity has given it its political power and intellectual influence.

In chapters 16 and 17, I described how the Arrow-Debreu model and the fundamental theorems of welfare economics could be combined with the political philosophies of Nozick and Rawls to provide a theory of political economy. This is the intellectual foundation of the ABM. Adding Nozick's conservative political philosophy to the mix yields its final proposition—low and nonprogressive taxation.

A Rawlsian approach leads to redistributive market liberalism.[7] This version of political economy broadly accepts the first three elements of the ABM—self-interest, market fundamentalism, and the minimal state—but rejects the fourth, the impermissibility of redistribution. It is both proper and necessary for government to use taxes and benefits to secure a just distribution of income. Free markets are combined with high levels of state provision of social benefits and public services. Redistributive market liberals, less skeptical of the value of state intervention than supporters of the ABM, generally support a vigorous competition policy.

Is Greed Good?

The largest difficulty the ABM encounters in attracting support stems from its unattractive account of our behavior and our characters. Some practitioners revel in this unflattering self-description. Al Dunlap, author of *Mean Business,* writes, "If you want a friend, get a dog. I'm not taking any chances, I've got two." John Gutfreund, chairman of Salomon Brothers, one of the most aggressive investment banks of the 1980s, said successful traders must wake up each morning "ready to bite the ass off a bear."[8]

Lester Thurow, economist and former dean of MIT's Sloan School of Management, offers intellectual support for this materialist perspective "Wealth has always been important in the personal pecking order, but it has become, increasingly, the only dimension by which personal worth is measured. It is the only game to play if you want to prove your mettle. It is the big leagues. If you do not play there, by definition you are second rate."[9]

In the most extreme versions of the American business model, it is a mistake to deplore materialism and regard selfishness as a vice. Greed is good: nice guys finish last. The rambling but strident philosophy of Ayn Rand, Alan Greenspan's former mentor, proclaims the virtues of selfishness under the title *objectivism.*[10] The logical conclusion of extreme individualism is that concern for others is an emotion that can properly be called on only to the extent that we feel it spontaneously. Private charity is the only proper mechanism of redistribution, and any further claim by the community would infringe on our autonomy.

In an alternative view, ethical issues that puzzled great thinkers from Aristotle to the present disappear in a haze of confusion and goodwill. Modern advocates of "corporate social responsibility" and well-meaning businesspeople claim that if only self-interest is interpreted sufficiently widely, there can be no conflict between self-interest and the public good.[11] As when Charles Wilson asserted that "what was good for our country was good for General Motors, and vice versa."[12] History interpreted his remark as malign, but it was simply naive.

A more plausible argument is that there is simply a dichotomy between economic life and public morality. The values appropriate to business are just different from those appropriate to our private lives. As Goethe observed at the beginning of the industrial revolution, "Everything which is properly business we must keep carefully separate from life."[13] Goethe's position mirrors Milton Friedman's: "The social responsibility of business is to maximize its profits."[14]

This position is acceptable to many businesspeople because it puts few restrictions on their behavior. The corollary is the general contempt among intellectuals for business and those who engage in it. A wasp has been named after Gutfreund, *Eruga gutfreundis:* "She stings and paralyzes the insect, and then lays her egg on its back. The hatched larva feeds off its host's blood for about six months before devouring the money spider."[15] The dichotomy between economic values and ordinary values achieves sophisticated expression from philosophers like Michael Walzer, who identifies "spheres of justice,"[16] criteria for distinguishing the proper boundaries of the market.

Greed as Motive

But the primary objection to the description of human behavior in the ABM is not that it is immoral, but that it is incorrect. Greed is a human characteristic, but not, for most people, a dominant one. The minority for whom it is an overriding motive are not people we admire. Nor do we think of them as successful: they do not "leave their footsteps in the sand of time." When we read that Hetty Green, possibly the richest woman in history, dressed in secondhand clothes to secure admission to a charity hospital for her injured son,[17] we feel sadness and even sympathy that she made such a mess of things. Our sense of what constitutes a good life is similar to that which Aristotle described two millennia ago. Most of us still find Thurow's assertion that those who do not achieve great wealth are "by definition, second-rate" bizarre.

Politics is attractive to people obsessed by financial reward—such as Mobutu, although even Mobutu was more interested in money as a means to power rather than an end in itself.[18] Productive economies have adopted systematic, and usually successful, policies to exclude such people from public life. Those who enter politics in Europe or the United States today may have other personality disorders, but not that one.

And modern business is not appealing to the truly greedy. Building successful businesses requires considerable abilities and hard work. Successful businesspeople—from Andrew Carnegie, in the nineteenth century, the ruthless steel tycoon who wrote that "a man who dies rich dies disgraced," to Bill Gates in the twentieth century—regard building a successful business as a primary, not an intermediate, goal. That is what they tell us and we should not disbelieve them.[19] When Carnegie or Gates declared their intention to crush competitors, they were not trying to persuade us to like or admire them.

Even in financial services, self-interest is not an overriding motivation. Donald Trump is perhaps the most aggressive and high-living American trader of the last two decades. Yet Trump's autobiography begins with "I don't do it for the money." He goes on, "I've got enough, much more money than I'll ever need. I do it to do it. Deals are my art form."[20]

What of Warren Buffett? His motives are complex. Buffett's biographer reports, "It's not that I want money," Warren replied. "It's the fun of making money and watching it grow."[21] Which is, presumably, why Buffett still lives in that Omaha bungalow and enjoys nothing more than a Nebraskan steak washed down with Cherry Coke.

The aspiration of the bond traders at Salomon Brothers described by Michael Lewis was to be regarded by their peers as a Big Swinging Dick. He reports that "what really stung the trader . . . was not their absolute level of pay but their pay in relation to the other bond traders."[22]

This is not to deny that self-interested materialism is an important feature of economic life. Economic systems based on appeals to work for the common good will fail. But self-interest is necessarily hedged by the complex institutions of modern economic, social, and political life—formal regulation and implicit rules, mechanisms of reputation and coordination, instincts and structures of cooperation, feelings of solidarity. Without that, the answer to Arrow and Hahn's question—"What will an economy motivated by individual greed . . . look like?"—is indeed the commonsense one they cite: there will be chaos. Modern societies did not develop ethical norms that limit and deplore self-regarding materialism out of perverse desire to restrain entrepreneurial spirits.

Economic motivations are complex, multifaceted, and not necessarily consistent. The study of human behavior is empirical. It cannot rely solely on introspection and a priori assumptions. Still less should it rely on introspection and a priori assumptions that do not correspond to experience. The best starting point is to expect that behavior will be adaptive—that people will behave in the way they are normally expected to in the circumstances in which they find themselves. This expectation will sometimes be false. Economies would not develop otherwise.

Property Rights

The ABM emphasizes the central importance of property as an institution, so central that its defense is the principal function of the state. The Arrow-Debreu framework generally takes a distribution of property rights as its starting point. This assumes that the nature of property rights is obvious. But property rights are socially constructed. Property rights can be defined in many ways and allocated among individuals, households, and firms in many ways.

Milton Friedman, unlike many of his less sophisticated followers, understands this: "What constitutes property and what rights the ownership of property confers are complex social creations rather than self-evident propositions." But, he goes on, "in many cases, the existence of a well specified and generally accepted definition of property is far more important than just what the definition is."[23]

But Friedman produces no evidence for this conjecture, and experience of economic history and geography demonstrates the opposite. The development of agriculture, of employment, and of limited liability companies is an evolution from one group of definitions of property rights to another. The legitimacy of property rights determined the different economic experiences of Argentina and Australia. We continue to argue over the scope of intellectual property and the nature of media regulation in a pluralist society. It is not easy to see how the current coevolution of technology and institutions in the Internet and genome will play itself out. But no one could think that the outcome of these debates doesn't matter.

"Let them steal," said Anatoly Chubais, mirroring Friedman.[24] Russia's economic disaster is an enduring reproach to those who claim that the only requirement of a market economy is a system of private property rights. The quality of economic institutions—which it is too simple to characterize as property rights—is the most important difference between rich and poor states.

The possibility of many different property rights regimes, with differing effects on economic efficiency, is a fundamental challenge to the efficiency claims of the Arrow-Debreu model. The fundamental theorems of welfare economies can be true only with respect to a particular structure of property rights. And it is then no longer possible to claim that any particular competitive equilibrium is Pareto efficient. A different property rights regime could—and probably would—make everyone better off.

The Truth About Markets
. . . .

Misunderstandings about motivation and simplification of property rights are not the only problems. Markets function effectively only if they are embedded in social institutions that are poorly—if at all—accounted for within the ABM.

(1) (chapter 19) Information in complex modern economies is necessarily incomplete and imperfect. Competitive markets fail when there are major differences of information between buyers and sellers. Transactions usually take place within a social context. We prefer to deal with people we know. Or we rely on trusted suppliers, or trusted brands. This social context develops, and is necessary, to deal with these differences (asymmetries) of information.

(2) (chapter 20) Markets for risk do not work as described in the efficient market model of chapter 13. Most of the important risks we face are not handled through the market, but in households,

among communities, and by government. Securities markets are better described as arenas for sophisticated professional gambling than as institutions that minimize the costs of risk bearing and allocate capital efficiently among different lines of business.

(3) (chapter 21) Most economic activity cannot be organized by negotiations between large numbers of potential buyers and potential sellers in impersonal markets. We need to work in organizations and in teams, and to cooperate in small groups. Self-interested individuals would often fail to cooperate with each other, even when it was in their mutual best interests. Corporate cultures, ethical values, and the blending of working and social lives are all necessary for effective cooperation.

(4) (chapter 22) It is often true that coordination is more effectively achieved through mechanisms of spontaneous order than central direction. But spontaneous order does not emerge immediately and infallibly. Many coordination mechanisms are the product of government interventions, social institutions, and agreements among firms.

(5) (chapter 23) Knowledge and information are key products in complex modern economies. They cannot be produced in competitive markets in which there are many buyers and sellers of each commodity. Nonmaterialist motivations—the thrill of discovery and the satisfactions of philanthropy—have been more important stimuli to innovation than profit seeking.

That ABM is deficient for its naive approach to issues of human motivation, its simplistic analysis of structures of property rights, its inability to maintain efficiency in the face of imperfect information, its misleading account of markets in risk, its glossing over of problems of cooperation and coordination, and its failure to describe the generation of the new knowledge on which its very success depends.

The Distribution of Income and Wealth

There is a final problem for the ABM—the legitimacy of the distribution of income and wealth that results from it. The fourth premise of the ABM denies that this distribution is a proper concern of government in a market economy. If differences in income and wealth are the result of differences in productivity, and these are in turn the consequence of differences in effort, talent, and skill, redistribution of income and wealth is potentially inefficient. If rewards to differences in efforts, talents, and skills are suppressed, then talents and skills will not be fully exploited. This is not a conclusive argument against redistribution, but redistribution may involve a high price in economic efficiency.

Yet, as chapter 25 demonstrated, it is hard to believe that differences in income and wealth are completely, or even mainly, explained by differences in effort, talent, and skills. Why does Heidi earn so much more than Ravi, Sven more than Ivan? Why is Sicelo so poor? Bill Gates made an important contribution to the personal computer industry, but his wealth would allow him an annuity of $3 billion per year for the rest of his life. Are his effort, talent, and skills really so exceptional? Do they justify an income many thousands of times greater than that of—say—Alan Turing? Would Gates have put in much less effort if the prospective reward had been, say, only $1 billion per year?

If GDP would fall by $3 billion if Gates stayed at home, then we are all better off by paying him $3 billion to come to work. But it is not likely that this is true. We certainly don't know that it's true. And even if it were true, we might still be able to cut a deal, in which he agreed to come to work for only $1 billion per year. Most of Gates's reward is economic rent. I suspect he likes his job more than people who struggle to work each morning to earn much smaller sums.

And what of the people on the trading floor of securities houses? They are valuable to their employers, which is why they receive multimillion-dollar bonuses. But trading profits are mostly arbitrage gains, whose impact on GDP is small. GDP might be higher if securities markets were less active and less liquid. Corporate executives are paid a lot not because of their productivity, which is impossible to measure, but because of their bargaining power. They take a slice of the rents they control.

The complexity of the way in which market rewards are determined makes it impossible to argue such rewards are necessarily just or efficient. Thoughtful conservatives like Friedman and Nozick do not make that claim: they assert instead that interference with the process that gives rise to them would be unjust, because it would involve illegitimate state coercion.[25]

Some people might agree with this argument. But many would not. And that disagreement is itself a problem. If the distribution of income and wealth in the market economy does not meet widely shared notions of legitimacy, that distribution will be expensively disputed. The direct and indirect costs of litigation and crime may be a serious burden on the market economy. In Argentina, and modern Russia, problems of legitimacy have led to structures of politics that have blocked effective economic development.

The American Business Model and the American Economy

If the American business model is not a plausible description of how market economies function, why is the American economy so successful? The answer should by now be obvious: the ABM does not describe the American economy. We do not look to Norway or Switzerland for societies populated by the exclusively self-interested; but nor do we look to the United States. We point instead to countries such as Nigeria or Haiti, in which there is an insufficient basis of trust for market institutions to develop. Or to Colin Turnbull's description of the Ik hill people, whose social institutions had been shattered by adversity, and for whom callous materialism had led to a spiral of economic decline.[26]

The ability to form supportive groups that enhanced the lives of individuals and households but did not involve the processes of government has always been a distinguishing feature of American society. Tocqueville once more: "The most democratic society on earth is found to be the one where men in our day have most perfected the art of pursuing the object of their common desires in common and have applied this new science to the most effect."[27] The market economies of rich states depend on such institutions. The most important today is the corporation. Corporate man, the epitome of the American submergence of the individual in the company, was once the butt of jokes. But corporate men, and corporate women, are the social individuals who make the economic lives of Americans rich and fulfilling.

{28}

The Future of Economics

Most people who are not economists think that economics is about forecasting. If you tell the person next to you at a dinner party that you are an economist, you do not rise in their esteem. They expect that you will be opinionated, boring, and wrong. They will ask you what is going to happen to interest rates, or whether there will be a recession or a recovery, without any real interest in the answer. If you say, as I do, that you are not that kind of economist they will express polite surprise that there is any other sort of economist, and turn to talk to the person on the other side.

The talking heads who make these forecasts on Bloomberg television and CNBC are the best-paid economists. But they are not taken seriously by other economists, or indeed by anyone but themselves, and not always by themselves: they are popular entertainers, whose professional status lies somewhere between astrologers and the weather forecasters.

The contents of this book are a more accurate reflection of the activities and conclusions of mainstream professional economists. The material here reflects a bias toward microeconomics—the study of individual households, firms, and markets—rather than macroeconomics—the study of broad economic aggregates, GDP, inflation, and growth. But this reflects the balance of economic research as a whole, and the areas in which new knowledge has recently been obtained. Of the fifty or so Nobel Prize winners in economics since the inception of the award in

1969, only around half a dozen have been given for work in macroeconomics. (See Appendix.)

Since Samuelson defined the course of modern economics in 1947, the dominant paradigm has been generally called neoclassical economics. Neoclassical economics is founded on twin assumptions: that human behavior is best described by rational-choice models and that economic activity tends toward equilibrium. The analysis in this book is, broadly, in this tradition. And for many economists, these principles define economics. Thus, for Chicago's Gary Becker[n], "the combined assumptions of maximizing behavior, market equilibrium, and stable preferences, used relentlessly and unflinchingly, form the heart of the economic approach" (p. 234).

The term *neoclassical economics* evokes intense hostility—most of all, from other social scientists. And this is not surprising. Economists are imperialist and arrogant.[1] They have sought to displace psychology by emphasizing rationality and maximization, and to invade sociology, anthropology, political theory, and law with economic explanations of behavior. The Chicago School's analyses of marriage, crime and punishment, and law and economics provide good, if extreme, examples. Economists are often found in the role of intellectual supporters of conservative political positions. And—perhaps this leads to the most intense and widespread resentment—economists have claimed for their analysis a scientific status that they deny to other approaches to the analysis of human behavior—and with it an authority to pronounce on current events—yet neither that authority, nor that status, seems borne out in their ability to explain or predict evolving economic events.

Economics as Science

In chapter 17, I described the transition in economics that occurred in the middle of the twentieth century. The literary discourse and institutional commitment exemplified by elegant style and involvement in affairs was displaced by mathematical argument and statistical analysis: Keynes gave way to Samuelson. The declared objective was to build economics on the model of natural science. Samuelson's purpose was to establish "operationally meaningful theorems"—

propositions about the world that could, at least in principle, be tested in the manner of an experiment in a scientific laboratory. Milton Friedman's 1953 essay "The Methodology of Positive Economics" was, among professional economists, probably his most influential contribution.[2] The philosopher Daniel Hausman has caustically commented that it is probably the only essay on methodology that most economists have ever read.[3] For a long time, it was certainly the only essay on methodology that I had ever read.

Friedman argued that the realism of the assumptions of a theory was irrelevant to the validity of the theory. This view is often called the F-twist by economists. An economic model should be judged by its predictions, and an established theory could be displaced only by one that made at least equally good predictions. It is easy to see why this argument was popular. The criticism that economies are often out of equilibrium and choices frequently irrational is dismissed as irrelevant. The only valid criticism of the neoclassical paradigm is an alternative view of the world that offers at least equally definitive statements about behavior.

But there are many ways to be irrational, and an infinity of disequilibrium positions. So Friedman was setting a challenge that was never likely to be met and has not been met. The only contender as an alternative universal theory was the Marxist explanation of economic behavior in terms of class and power relations. As Marxism failed, and the United States came to dominate the economic world, neoclassical economics achieved almost total dominance.

But economists today occupy a methodological time warp. They adhere to a primitive form of positivism, an interpretation of the nature of scientific knowledge that strutted its brief hour upon the stage as the paradigm of neoclassical economics was framed, but is an interpretation heard no more, or at least hardly at all, among philosophers of science today.

It was always widely recognized that Friedman's assertions were, at least, exaggerated.[4] A model or theory is, by its very nature, a simplification or abstraction from the world, and it is therefore correct to point out that the realism of assumptions is never a decisive test of a model or theory. But it does not follow that the realism of assumptions is not a relevant test at all. We dismiss a variety of crackpot theories of everything on the basis that their assumptions do not relate to our perception of reality, and if we could not do this, there would be no possibility of scientific progress. Moreover, as the philosopher of science Nagel[5] explained in a critique of Friedman's argument, assumptions may be unrealistic in different ways: simplification should not be conflated with falsehood.

But there are larger problems with Friedman's emphasis on prediction and Samuelson's quest for operatively meaningful theorems. Verification and falsification of economic theory are difficult to achieve. If only economics could experience such decisive tests, as Galileo's demonstration that different objects dropped from Pisa's leaning tower reached the ground at the same time, or the experiment which exploited an eclipse of the sun to confirm Einstein's theory of special relativity.

Yet nothing like this happens, or can happen, in economics. We see complex events unfolding in the economic world, but it is always difficult to assess exactly what economic theory has been supported, and which refuted. Philosophers now know this as the Duhem-Quine problem or the underdetermination thesis. These insights, which were most extensively developed by Quine in the 1950s and 1960s, came just too late to feed into the mainstream of neoclassical economic thought.[6]

To turn a theory into a specific prediction about a complex world, it is usually necessary to make a variety of additional assumptions (auxiliary hypotheses). But if the prediction proves false, does the fault lie with the theory or the additional assumptions? Since we rarely know, it is difficult to establish a definitive test of the truth of any theory.

The most decisive experiment in social sciences was the division of Germany, described in chapter 3. But even in that case, defenders of Marxism or of economic planning seek refuge in auxiliary hypotheses— what was implemented was not true socialism, the planning systems were not appropriately designed—to immunize their theories from the superficially overwhelming evidence of their failure.

The underdetermination problem is pervasive in economics. Students of economics 101 are quickly introduced to the phrase *ceteris paribus*—the range of auxiliary hypotheses that would need to be maintained for a prediction to hold. A common joke is that an economist is someone who can explain tomorrow why what he forecast yesterday did not happen today. Underdetermination has rarely been better expressed.

So fifty years after Friedman's "Methodology of Positive Economics," it is still hard to give a definitive description of the truth about markets, to point to a list of verified hypotheses and contrast it with a list of falsified ones. When George Stigler writes, "Let me predict the outcome of the systematic and comprehensive testing of behavior in situations where self-interest and ethical values with wide verbal allegiance are in conflict. Much of the time, most of the time in fact, the self-interest theory will win,"[7] Amartya Sen responds acerbically, "the evidence for this belief presented by Stigler seems, however, to be largely confined to predictions made by Stigler himself. . . . The fact is there have been very few empirical testings of this kind . . . while assertions of conviction are plentiful, factual findings are rare."[8]

Indeed, it is difficult to think of any issue on which a position once held by a substantial, respected group of economists has been vacated as a result of empirical refutation. Perhaps the Phillips curve—an empirical correlation between unemployment and inflation that broke down after the oil shock of the 1970s—falls into this category. But then I turned again to Mankiw's elementary textbook, and discovered an entire chapter devoted to the Phillips curve: and that George Akerlof, receiving the Nobel Prize in 2001, described the Phillips curve as "probably the single most important macroeconomic relationship."[9]

No modern chemistry textbook describes the phlogiston theory. No physics laureate commends the theory that the sun rotates the earth. The progress of economics is more accurately described by changing fads and fashions, in which Keynesianism gives way to monetarism, enthusiasm for rational expectations waxes and wanes, game theory attracts attention, disappoints, and is then seized on with renewed enthusiasm.

But normal science is by no means free of this phenomenon. Thomas Kuhn famously described the progress of science in terms of paradigm shifts. There are phases of accumulation of knowledge within a particular frame of reference until the utility of that frame of reference is exhausted, and the subject acquires renewed vigor from a new paradigm. Economics lies somewhere between the progressive development of knowledge familiar in natural sciences and the evanescent schools of thought of literary criticism.

Could Economics Be True?

● ●

Modern philosophers of science are skeptical of the claim that scientific knowledge resides in claims to some essential truth, statements that describe the world as it really is. But it is a lot easier to see how physicists might make such claims than economists. It is hard to believe, for example, that anyone could suppose that Becker's theory of marriage might explain marriage in the same way, for example, that Maxwell's equations explain wave motion. Yet it is difficult to see another interpretation of Becker's account of the purposes of his work. "The economic approach to the family interprets marriage, divorce, fertility and relations among family members through the lens of utility-maximising behavior. . . . The rational choice model provides the most promising basis presently available for a unified approach to the analysis of the social world by scholars from the social sciences."[10] This theory of the family is not offered as an alternative perspective on the economic dimension of social relationships that might supplement more conventional accounts, but as a better approach that supersedes them.

Faced with such a claim, most people who are not economists will immediately dismiss the assertion as ridiculous, and they will be right. In the Nobel Prize lecture from which that quotation is drawn, Becker claims support for his theory from the empirical observation— surprising, he suggests—that rich people are less likely to divorce than poor. But even supposing the facts were correct, economic theories cannot be tested in this way. In England from the time of Henry VIII to the mid–nineteenth century, divorce was possible only by securing the passage of a special act of Parliament, and the few divorcées were extremely affluent. In polygamous societies, rich men have many wives. Any prediction about the divorce rate is wholly contingent on auxiliary hypotheses about the actual divorce law that is in force and the culture of society. Becker's theory cannot be falsified, or verified, in the manner he supposes.

It seems absurd for debate to be polarized between the assertion that models based on rational choice and equilibrium are uniquely and completely descriptive of human behavior and the contrary claim that such models have no explanatory value at all. But this is essentially the choice that Friedman's approach imposes, and many economists impose this choice on themselves and their critics. And their insistence that economic theory is true, in the same sense that these economists suppose physics to be true, leaves no room for middle ground. The commonsense position of believing that models based on equilibrium and rational choice might be relevant in some situations but not others is not available. The laws of thermodynamics are either false or always true; and if economic theory is to rival physics, valid economic models must have similarly universal application.

The stridency of this approach, and the dogmatism and imperialism that follow from it, repels most people who have not completed a graduate course in economics (and, indeed, it repels many people who begin an undergraduate course in economics). Many professional economists display an ideological fervor of the kind maintained by those who believe themselves in possession of fundamental truths to which others are blind. The hectoring but misplaced self-confidence that follows leads those dinner party companions to seek more congenial conversation.

Until I began writing this book, I had not realized the extent to which economists had cut themselves off from the ordinary discourse of intellectual life. This isolation is not only from developments that are obviously of central relevance to the work economists do, such as the mathematics of nonlinear, nonmaximizing, dynamic systems and the development of evolutionary psychology; but equally from broad currents of contemporary thought, such as postmodernism or the modern philosophy of science that has succeeded the former "received view."[11]

In his 2001 presidential address to the American Economic Association, Robert Hall took as his subject the stock market bubble that had collapsed so dramatically the year before.[12] Hall asserted that the bubble was consistent with rational behavior. He made this claim by extending the concept of rationality to cover behavior that is consistent with some coherent (though false) set of beliefs. In Hall's Ely lecture, we hear the voice of a profession communicating only with itself. How can it be possible to take the most extraordinary set of events in recent economic history and find so little of interest to say about it?

Knowledge in Economics
● ●

It is not difficult to put together an account that makes better sense of good economics (including that of Samuelson and Friedman) than the methodological positivism which they espouse. Such an account displays the opportunities both for a more eclectic development of the subject and for a more constructive relationship with those who develop other, and different, forms of knowledge.

The Arrow-Debreu general equilibrium model (chapter 15), Akerlof's lemons model (chapter 19), or the Prisoner's Dilemma (chapter 21) are powerful and influential economic models that have had a major influence on the development of economics. One common feature of all these models is that no one seriously suggests that they are true. I once used the Akerlof model of the used-car market in a lecture. When I finished my talk and invited questions, a representative of the trade association for automobile dealers, the Retail Motor Federation, rose to explain that the model was invalid since used-car dealers were people of the highest integrity.

Even if what he said was correct, he had missed the point. The Akerlof model is not about the car market, just as the Prisoner's Dilemma is not about the U.S. penal system. The illustrations are metaphors, vivid ways of describing the properties of mathematical models—the story of the Prisoner's Dilemma was reportedly invented by Tucker when he was asked to give an account of his work to a nonspecialist audience.

The power of these models is not that they mirror nature, but that they illuminate it. The implications of both the lemons model and the Prisoner's Dilemma are unexpected, and forceful. Both have generated a large literature—in the case of the Prisoner's Dilemma, it runs to thousands of articles and several books—that develop applications and extensions of the basic idea. People—economists or not—who have understood these models regularly find new applications in their everyday experience.

The Arrow-Debreu model is different. We can ask whether the model is correct—did those Nobel laureates get the mathematics right? (they did)—but not whether the model is true. A Samuelsonian might argue that it generates "operationally meaningful theorems," but it is difficult to understand what would be entailed, even in principle, in a test of the proposition that equilibrium exists. The theorem offers a possible element of an answer to the difficult issue of how complex economic systems create spontaneous order. But its main value is in the identification of auxiliary hypotheses—the types of assumptions that would be required if common claims about the nature and efficiency of economic systems were to be valid. By focusing attention on these issues—how market economies overcome, or fail to overcome, potential obstacles to equilibrium or efficiency—it has provided a framework for applied research. This is a more limited achievement than that expected by those who thought that such an approach could provide analyses of social affairs comparable in scope and power to the laws of thermodynamics, but that was always a forlorn hope.

And so the test of an economic model is not its truth or falsehood, but its utility. A good model in economics produces what Peter Jay has described as an OIC (oh, I see)[13] moment, as once puzzling features of the empirical world fall into place. The Prisoner's Dilemma is useful in precisely this way. The paradox is startling, but is encountered in a wide range of problems and situations. The model can be developed and extended to illuminate new problems and situations. These criteria of usefulness are necessarily subjective. And the selection of appropriate models for particular problems requires skill and judgment and may be the subject of reasoned and reasonable disagreement. This is not science as positivists might once have described it, but it is not far from the reality of what most scientists do.

Through Thomas Kuhn, we have understood that alternative ways of looking at the natural world may simply be incommensurable alternatives, and this seems obviously and inevitably true of the social world. Richard Rorty denies that the achievements of physics are possible because physics describes the world as it, in some sense, really is—the mirror of nature: instead, physics draws its strength from the practical utility of its techniques. There are echoes of Friedman in this conclusion, but it implies a radically different and more circumscribed role for the status of economic reasoning.[14]

Economic Models

The growth of large-scale computing power led the postwar search for economic truth in another direction: an attempt to build large models comprehensively descriptive of economic systems. These exercises have largely been abandoned: they did not produce accurate predictions or many other insights.[15] The task of large-scale modeling has more recently been taken up by business consultants, who offer quantitative descriptions of firms and markets, estimates of the profitability of nuclear power stations, and the value of mobile phone licenses. They believe that by incorporating more and more features of the world in their models, they improve the quality of their description. The power of spreadsheets today runs far ahead of the quality of the data or the capacity of those people who build these models to understand the worlds they describe.[16]

The error of principle—the reason these models will never be useful—was exposed three centuries ago in Suarez Miranda's story of the cartographers who set out to produce the most accurate possible map: They "set up a Map of the Empire which had the size of the empire itself and coincided with it point by point. Succeeding generations understood that this Widespread Map was Useless and not without impiety they abandoned it to the inclemencies of the sun and the winters." The search for realism destroyed the purpose of the map: a map can be useful precisely because it simplifies and omits.[17] But how to simplify, what to omit? Economic models are maps for the market economy. A map can be false but never true just as Arrow and Debreu's mathematical proof might have contained errors. We seek the simplest map adapted to our purpose, and that is why we need hiking guides as well as road maps, and street atlases. The "little stories," or economic models, of this book are to be judged in the same way.[18]

I once debated the relationship among social sciences with some anthropologists. We adjourned to a pub, and someone bought a round of drinks; the discussion naturally turned to the reasons why. For the economists, the explanation was obvious: the practice of buying rounds minimized transactions costs, reducing the number of exchanges between the patrons and the bar staff. The anthropologists saw it as an example of ritual gift exchange and described the many tribes that had developed similar customs. I proposed a test between the competing hypotheses: Did you feel cheated or victorious if you bought more rounds than had been bought for you? Unfortunately the economists and the anthropologists gave different answers to that question.

I now realize that the attempt to test competing explanations was mistaken, drawing on the inappropriate analogy of those extraordinary moments experienced by Galileo or in the validation of relativity. It would never be possible to establish the truth of one explanation of such social behavior at the expense of the other. Both the transactions cost theory and the taxonomy of gift exchange contributed to a partial understanding of why people adopt these social conventions: neither could provide the whole story.

Social behavior needs to be understood in many dimensions, and at many levels. The anthropologist Clifford Geertz, following Gilbert Ryle, has written of "thick description."[19] A wink is a contraction of the eye muscles but also a social signal. When the doorbell rings an electrical connection is completed that triggers a hammer in a metal box. A stranger seeks to gain admittance. A policeman arrives to tell parents of an accident to their child. All these can be accurate but incomplete accounts of the same phenomenon. Thick description embraces them all.

The child prodigy Jedediah Buxton, taken to see *Richard III*, observed (correctly) that it contained 12,445 words.[20] As a postmodernist would recognize, he saw the same play as his parents, and yet a different one. Becker's description of family life as a means of deriving economies of scale is one account; the evolutionary biologist sees the family as a means of facilitating parental investment in offspring has a different perspective; and poets who describe the family in terms of mutual love provide a further strand of explanation. There is no incompatibility and no need to choose among these elements of thick description. The economic imperialism that seeks to "explain" all behavior by reference to rational choice is misconceived, as is a purely anthropological account that denies or disregards the economic functions of social practices.

The Politics of Economics

Economics and economists reached a peak of popularity in prestige in the 1960s. This was the heyday of planning in governments and business, to which economists were thought to contribute. The rapid growth experienced in almost all rich states since the end of World War II seemed to vindicate Keynesian principles of demand management.

The most widely read economist of the time was John Kenneth Galbraith, whose literary gifts matched those of Keynes. Galbraith, a liberal who was appointed ambassador to India by John Kennedy, poked gentle fun at corporate America in such works as *The New Industrial State* and *The Affluent Society,* and also wrote the best account of 1920s speculative bubble in *The Great Crash.* Galbraith was never in the mainstream of professional industrial economists, but among those who held similar political positions.

The relationship between economics and businesspeople has always been complex. In the 1960s, almost every large corporation had a chief economist with a professional staff, but their job would be forecasting macroeconomic events and industry trends. Their advice would rarely be sought on microeconomic issues such as pricing, industry evolution, or market positioning. With most economists liberal by persuasion, the few who were interested in the behavior of those who wished to apply their analysis—such as Mike Scherer, whose textbook conveyed an encyclopedic knowledge of American business to a generation of students—would do so on behalf of the Department of Justice in enforcing the antitrust law.[21]

The gap was filled by business strategists. The principal economist to have succeeded as business guru—Michael Porter—disguised his training and the origins of his analysis.[22] The micreconomic theory in this book—particularly that of chapters 19 to 23—has much to contribute to an understanding of modern corporations and the environment in which they operate; but economists have made little attempt to sell their wares.

So the public role of the economist, then and now, mostly concerns government and dealing with government. This was—is—odd. Economists may design and describe markets, but are rarely hired by those who made decisions in markets. In those antitrust issues, economists would increasingly describe behavior in terms that were not recognized by those whose behavior was described.

This golden age of the professional economist came to an abrupt end. Formal planning systems went into decline, and accelerating inflation from the 1960s, exacerbated by the 1973 oil shock, meant that confidence in macroeconomic policies declined. As economies went wrong, politicians would increasingly make jokes at the expense of economists. But economists, sensitive to market trends, reinvented themselves, as cheerleaders for conservative, market-oriented policies, and a new simple theory—monetarism—supposedly took the place of the Keynesian economics which had supposedly been discredited.

Milton Friedman became the professional economist best known to a wider public. Friedman and other Chicago economists, including Gary Becker, contributed columns to popular newspapers and magazines and helped establish a conservative image of the profession. This was reinforced when economists such as Jeffrey Sachs played a role in devising reforms in Latin America and post-Soviet Eastern Europe. These economists found support from a business community ready to promote their views (to influence public policy, not business policy) and organizations such as the American Enterprise Institute, the Cato Institute, and the Hoover Institute helped give them a popular platform.

The arguments put forward by Greg Mankiw that I quote on page 201 are more intellectual than those Ronald Reagan, Margaret Thatcher, or either George Bush would espouse, but these politicians draw comfort from the perception that solid academic arguments can be found in support of their positions. And they influence a generation of students. As Mankiw himself observes, quoting Paul Samuelson, the most successful of all writers of economics textbooks: "I don't care who writes a nation's laws, or crafts its advanced treaties, if I can write its economics textbooks."[23] (This is before Mankiw took a position in the Bush administration.)

Current Policy Controversies

But a majority of working economists—including the leaders of the neoclassical tradition, such as Kenneth Arrow and Paul Samuelson—were, like most social scientists, predominantly liberal. Many economists found a means of reconciling their neoclassical economics with liberal sentiments in redistributive market liberalism, a doctrine described in a previous chapter and, as I noted there, popular with economists but with few other people. The focus of resulting tensions was the World Bank and the IMF. These international agencies, which employ many capable economists, were charged with implementing conservative policies in poor countries. Implementation of these measures was almost always controversial.

Under James Wolfensohn, with Stiglitz as chief economist, the World Bank established an intermediate position, emphasizing poverty reduction as a goal in contrast to the IMF's emphasis on macroeconomic stability. The tension burst into the open, however, after Stiglitz was forced out of the World Bank by the U.S. Treasury and, encouraged by his receipt of the Nobel Prize, published a blistering attack on the IMF under the title *Globalization and Its Discontents.*

Stiglitz's attack was too personalized, however, and a counterblast by Ken Rogoff, chief economist at the IMF, reduced what should have been a debate about the relationship between economic knowledge and economic policy to a spat between individuals and institutions. The central message—that economics provides at best little support for conventional political wisdom about market efficiency and the simplifications of the American business model—was lost. Stiglitz was cheered by antiglobalization protesters with little appreciation of what the argument was really about.

The stock market bubble confronted economists with different challenges. The public debate was dominated by pundits: George Gilder of *Forbes ASAP,* Kevin Kelly of *Wired* and *New Rules for the New Economy,* James Glassman and Kevin Hassett of *Dow 36,000.* These people were not credentialed economists, but they announced the irrelevance of traditional principles of business economics and market valuation in the face of new technology and a changed political environment. Few serious economists made public pronouncements on the bubble, perhaps wisely. Bob Shiller, whose observations in 1996 had given rise to Alan Greenspan's famous remarks about "irrational exuberance," was savaged by commentator George Will,[24] for whom the continued rise of the stock market demonstrated the error of Shiller's claim that valuations were unsustainable.

Shiller was, of course, right, and the book in which he defined his views, published just as the bubble burst in the early months of 2000, became a *New York Times* best-seller. But the "new economy" stories did not die. Stock values, even if well below their historical highs, remained extraordinary by historic standards. Faith in future productivity gains was used to explain how tax cuts would reduce, not increase, the widening fiscal deficit. America's massive trade deficit and rapidly growing external liabilities—to most external observers, a demonstration that the country was living beyond its means—were proclaimed by politicians as an illustration of the enthusiasm of the rest of the world for investment in an American economic miracle.

One domestic critic came to the fore. Paul Krugman is a mainstream economist whose seminal work in trade theory was not far below the level that, had he not become such a controversialist, might have won him a Nobel Prize. In the 1990s, he discovered a taste, and a capacity, for popular writing and became a regular contributor to newspapers and magazines. In 2000 he began a twice weekly op-ed column in the *New York Times* and, in using this platform to become America's most widely read economist, reestablished a liberal public profile for economists. Krugman rapidly became not just a critic of the economic policies of the Bush administration, but of its wider record, and in 2002 *Washington Magazine* called him the most influential political columnist in America.[25]

The Students Are Revolting

Anyone who has taught economics in the last two decades will have recognized that many students are unhappy with what they are taught. They are drawn to social sciences by their interest in people and affairs; but a large number, perhaps most, do not find this interest satisfied by rational-choice theories and mathematical models. Particularly women: while other social sciences—anthropology, law, psychology, and sociology—now generally have a majority of female students, men predominate in economics. At the top twenty U.S. institutions, three men graduate with a Ph.D. in economics for each woman.[26] Few senior economists are female: no woman has yet received the Nobel Prize in economics, and I counted only a handful of female economists in the bibliography to this book.

Some students do find the dominant rational-choice paradigm, its universalism and its rigorous but not too difficult mathematics appealing, and it is, of course, predominantly from this group that the next generation of teachers is drawn. There is nothing unusual about this—this professional development is the means by which Kuhn's scientific paradigms are perpetuated. What is unusual is the dissatisfaction engendered in those who are lost along the way.

An explosion of such dissatisfaction occurred—in Paris, of course—

in 2000 when a group of students signed a petition critical of the material they were taught, engagingly and pointedly describing the state of the subject as autistic. The petition attracted the attention of the French education minister, Jack Lang. He commissioned a report by a senior French economist, which was somewhat supportive of the students' search for a broader curriculum. Olivier Blanchard, perhaps the leading French economist in the United States, joined Bob Solow to rebuke the protesters in *Le Monde*. The movement continues, with a Web site and a newsletter, although an increasing proportion of its content is now devoted to repetitive tirades against neoclassical economics.[27]

If the French students reacted through voice, the more disturbing reaction is through exit. The proportion of students reading economics peaked in the 1980s. Since then, it has been in steady decline. The fall in the numbers taking economics in high school is particularly marked. Students hoped for material that would help explain the complex nature of social life or enable them to make money in business or the stock markets. They were disappointed.

The Future of Economics

But I find economics enjoyable and exhilarating. And precisely because economic concepts not only illuminate the complex nature of social life, and help make money in business and on the stock market. I hope that the reader who has reached this far will have shared some of that enjoyment and exhilaration. No other subject can yield so many of those "oh, I see" moments, when everyday events are illuminated by the single penetrating insight that an economic theory or economic model can deliver.

These moments of revelation are very different from the profound dullness of Hall's Ely lecture, or the essential silliness of Becker's analysis of marriage and crime. Many economists are today inching ever more slowly toward the end of a cul-de-sac, and others have simply taken a wrong turn: but it would be a serious mistake to reject the corpus of neoclassical economics because some of it is not interesting, because some of its practitioners devise applications as misconceived as they are ingenious, or because the supposed findings of neoclassical economics, like the writings of Adam Smith, have been adopted by conservative politicians who understand little of their substance. Neoclassical economics is not a true account of the world, a mirror of nature—the scientific pretensions of many economists are overblown—but once that concept is put aside its models have many instructive applications, and I have sought to demonstrate some of these in this book.

With the end of grand narratives, or universal theories, and the abandonment of claims to find principles of comparable generality to the laws of thermodynamics, should come a recognition that a useful economics is necessarily and appropriately eclectic. Behavioral economics, which relies on observing what people do rather than imposing assumptions about behavior on them, has much to contribute. Many of the developments in adjoining sciences—the applied mathematics of complexity, synchronicity, the insights of evolutionary biology—will change the way we think about economic issues. Rational choice modeling will continue to have a major role, but the attempt to squeeze all economic behavior, far less all human behavior, into this single framework is bound to fail. Friedman's methodological approach, which seems to deny the freedom to pick and choose when neoclassical models are appropriate and when not, invites comprehensive rejection, and that is indeed how many have reacted. Economics is necessarily and appropriately an eclectic subject. Keynes commented:

> The study of economics does not seem to require any specialized gifts of an unusually high order. Is it not ... a very easy subject compared with the higher branches of philosophy or pure science? An easy subject, at which very few excel! The paradox finds its explanation, perhaps, in that the master-economist must possess a rare *combination* of gifts. He must be mathematician, historian, statesman, philosopher—in some degree. He must understand symbols and speak in words. He must contemplate the particular in terms of the general, and touch abstract and concrete in the same flight of thought. He must study the present in the light of the past for the purposes of the future. No part of man's nature or his institutions must lie entirely outside his regard. He must be purposeful and disinterested in a simultaneous mood; as aloof and incorruptible as an artist, yet sometimes as near the earth as a politician.[28]

{29}

The Future of Capitalism

The assumptions of the ABM are false, but that does not imply their opposites are true. Some people think economic behavior is mostly altruistic, political mechanisms of allocation are always preferable to the anarchy of the market, government should control and preferably own all productive assets, and highly progressive taxation should be imposed to bring about an egalitarian distribution of income and wealth. But not many people think so, and I doubt if many of them will have read this far.

The economic world is complex. Self-interest is an important motivation, but not an exclusive motivation. Our other concerns influence work and business lives as well as personal lives. We need the approbation of our friends, the trust of our colleagues, the satisfaction of performing activities that are worthwhile in themselves and give others pleasure. These motives are not materialistic, but that does not mean they are not economic. They are an essential part of the mechanisms through which successful business operates. Without them business and economic systems would be impoverished—in material as well as other terms.

Markets work, but not always and not perfectly. Pluralist market structures promote innovation, and competitive markets meet many consumer needs, but there is no general reason to believe that market outcomes are efficient. Social and economic institutions manage the transmission of information in market economies. These institutions depend on culture and values, laws and history. In the perfectly competitive model, and the simplicities of the ABM, it is obvious what the rules of a market economy should be and easy to enforce them. The description of products and the definition of their properties is also obvious and easy.

But market economies have been successful relative to other societies precisely because the rules that govern them are not obvious to frame and easy to implement, and rich states have evolved complex governance structures embedded in other modern social and political institutions. That allows the development of sophisticated products that consumers are confident to buy and use without needing to understand them. Market economies handle well coordination problems associated with logistics—coordination between manufacturers and component suppliers, reliable deliveries, overall balances between supply and demand. They do less well when even temporary imbalances are intolerable—as in electricity supply, when the lights go out. Mercury Energy did restore supplies to Auckland, but seven weeks is a long time.

But markets do not necessarily succeed at all, or succeed in producing good outcomes, when other forms of coordination are required, as for networks and standards. And markets for risk and capital, dominated by speculative traders, are prone to bubbles and overshooting. These fluctuations in securities markets destabilize markets for goods and services and divert resources from productive activities to the pursuit of small arbitrage gains.

The very concept of a market for labor is offensive to many people, and with cause: workers are citizens as well as suppliers of labor, and enjoy rights that are not held by apples, pears, software—or corporations. Laws that prohibit slavery and regulate the organized sex industry are hardly controversial. They restrict freedom of contract on the grounds that even voluntary transactions may degrade society and deprive individuals of dignity. The issue is not whether the labor "market" should be subject to social and legal regulation, but the nature and extent of such regulation. That is a matter for moral judgment, social values, and empirical evidence.

Many services cannot be provided in competitive markets. Public goods like lighthouses, environmental protection, police and defense, and the framework of rules within which the modern market economy operates. There are natural monopolies, in water and electricity distribution, road and rail networks, air traffic control. Other services—such as education and health—could be provided by competitive markets but are generally not. It is desirable to find pluralist structures for these industries, but acceptable market solutions will not spontaneously emerge.

Economists have, as I described in chapter 28, claimed a scientific status and a prescriptive role that is not capable of being supported by our existing knowledge of economic systems. Keynes once hoped that economies might become like dentistry: a technical subject that attracted no ideological involvement. This chapter is written in the spirit of economics as dentistry.

Motives and Incentives
• •

With the rise of the modern corporate economy in the twentieth century—the emergence of corporations such as ICI, General Motors, and General Electric—came the rise of the professional manager. These individuals saw themselves and were seen by others as comparable in status to leaders of other professions—top solicitors, accountants or surgeons, judges and senior civil servants. They were paid accordingly. Performance bonuses were unknown, as insulting and inappropriate as a bonus to a distinguished judge or a tip to a helpful accountant.

This ethos began to break down in the 1980s. The rise of the ABM allowed the claim that greed was good. The continual rise in the stock market generated very large earnings in the financial services sector, and managers who engaged with financial institutions naturally compared their own salaries with Wall Street bonuses.

Top American executives took larger and larger sums of money out of the corporate till. So long as share prices were rising, few objections were raised. It became normal for American chief executives to receive tens, even hundreds, of millions of dollars in bonuses and share options. Only as the stock market crashed in the new century did the extent to which senior managers at companies like Enron and WorldCom had run them for their own enrichment and aggrandizement become widely apparent. And the failure of these businesses took with it an army of advisers—such as the accounting firm Andersen—for whom it had been adaptive to collude.

Within the ABM framework, preventing political or corporate corruption is a matter of institutional design. The public-choice model of politics assumes that public officials will be self-regarding and structures its minimal state around that assumption. The principal-agent model of the corporation attempts to align the incentives of managers with those of shareholders.

But the difference between corrupt and honest public administration, between corrupt and honest business, is not the result of differences in rules. Laws against corruption are often more draconian in corrupt states than in disinterested ones; extensive rules are more often the symptom of a problem than its solution. The attempt to structure elaborate incentive schemes to align the interests of managers and shareholders did not eliminate fraud: it provoked it.

Incentive compatibility and adaptive behavior explain why this is so. The integrity of an institution is not the product of its governance structure, but of the values of those who work within it. Many different value systems will be supported by adaptive, self-reinforcing behavior. If institutions are designed on the assumption that individuals are self-interested, self-interested behavior will be adaptive within them. If the premise is that people are not to be trusted, that expectation will be fulfilled.

The purely instrumental motivations of the ABM are ultimately self-defeating. It is not true that profit is the purpose of a market economy, and the production of goods and services is a means to it: the purpose is the production of goods and services, profit the means. The happiest people are not those who single-mindedly pursue happiness; the most profitable companies are not the most profit oriented.[1] Successful individuals, and successful companies, adapt their behavior and their capabilities to the environment that they face. The consequences of adaptation resemble the *outcome* of maximization, but are not the *product* of maximization. The motion of the planets follows a system of differential equations despite the inability of the planets to compute the solutions. The song and flight of birds displays a beauty and efficiency of design that was not part of the intention of the birds, or of any other agency. We do better to flee the bear than to calculate an optimal strategy, and to follow the advice of park rangers is better still. Sometimes we understand best when we do not try too hard to understand.

Self-interested behavior by managers of large companies is corrosive of the integrity of companies, just as self-interested behavior by government officials is corrosive of the integrity of government. The central premise of the ABM—that economic life is or could be successfully organized around the instrumental behavior of self-regarding materialists, constrained only by externally imposed rules—is mistaken. And the mistake threatens both the viability and legitimacy of market systems. In both politics and business, the rise of the ABM created the very problem of controlling self-interest it purported to solve.

So the distribution of income and wealth and the process by which that distribution is established must, like the structure of market institutions itself, enjoy legitimacy if the market economy is to survive and evolve. Many failures of the market economy follow from this failure of legitimacy. Russia, obviously; also Argentina and New Zealand.

Government in the Embedded Market

The embedded market describes the successful market systems of Western Europe—and the reality of the United States. The embedded market does not function within a minimal state. Productive economies have the largest, most powerful, and most influential governments the world has ever seen. Throughout most of history—and in poor countries today—government rarely impinged on the everyday lives of ordinary people, like Sicelo or the villagers of Palanpur.

In rich states, we are always conscious of the influence of government. We pay its taxes on every transaction we make, and most of us also receive social benefits. Regulation governs everything we do, from the way we drive to the butter we spread on our bread. We look to government to provide a wide range of goods and services, from education to rubbish collection. The market economy relies on intermediate institutions greater than individuals, smaller than governments. The most important of these are corporations. But there are many others.

For conservatives, the economic role of government is confined to defining and enforcing private property rights and the integrity of the market—codifying and applying the rules. For liberals, the economic role of government is to determine through democratic process how society wishes scarce resources to be allocated between competing ends, and to direct the activities of businesses and households to bring that allocation about. Neither of these models describes the function of government accurately. The complex institutions of the market economy developed largely without central direction and constantly evolve. Government is an agent in that evolution, not a bystander; but government cannot control the process and should not seek to. Because markets are embedded in social institutions, it is not only, or mainly, by voting that we influence the development of the market economy. Economic policy is not a list of things the government should do. We make economic policy as consumers, employers, entrepreneurs, and shareholders. We influence economic policy when we conform to, or resist, the norms and values of the market economy. Economic policy is as much about social attitudes and customary behavior as about law and regulation.

Keynes' vision of economics as dentistry implies that its practitioners be seen as technicians with specific skills, not coventurers on an ideological crusade. My purpose is to exemplify rather than to offer wide-ranging prescription. Indeed a principal objective is to demonstrate that, with the failure of grand narrative, there are no wide-ranging prescriptions. There are some general principles—the recurrent difficulties of incentive compatibility, and the overriding necessity for disciplined pluralism. But the premise is that economic understanding, like plumbing and dentistry, is a piecemeal process of acquired knowledge, driven by little stories.

Perfect Competition or Disciplined Pluralism? (Chapters 12–16)

Market economies did not succeed because businesspeople were cleverer than politicians. They succeeded because disciplined pluralism is more innovative and more responsive to customer needs than centralized decision making.

Most rich states have policies to maintain competition. But competition policies are often predicated on the assumption that the world should be aligned with the perfectly competitive market model of Part II. If the world does not conform to the model, the fault lies with the model, not the world. Part III demonstrated why market economies are not perfectly competitive and could not be efficient if they were.

Disciplined pluralism implies that rivals pursue differentiated strategies and the more successful of them earn rents. Competition policy should not seek to eliminate these rents: if it tries, it will diminish pluralism. The purposes of competition policy are to promote pluralism and make discipline effective.

Forces that work for pluralism today can work against them tomorrow. It seems paradoxical that the very success of Standard Oil, or Microsoft, forces us to act against these companies to maintain both discipline and pluralism. But that is how it must be. The case for the market economy is not that the democratic decisions of the market are better than the democratic decisions of the electorate—"Microsoft has a monopoly because we want it to have one." The pluralist processes of competition within the market economy reveal information and promote innovation more effectively than any centralized organization, public or private. The battle to maintain pluralism never ends.

General Equilibrium and DIY Economics (Chapter 15)

Every government is confronted by rent-seeking lobbyists. Farmers ask for agricultural support, manufacturing industries seek protection from international competition, workers in declining industries seek subsidies for their products. DIY economics flourishes here. At first sight, every economic activity promotes jobs and either adds to exports or substitutes for imports: every subsidy increases competitiveness. And, as I explained in chapter 15, the people who present these arguments know, from their own experience, the truth of what they say: they often genuinely believe their self-interested arguments promote a wider good.

But the lobbyists do not know, from their own experience, the general equilibrium context—the adding up of constraints for the economy as a whole—within which they operate. Their misleading partial perspective often leads them to argue for policies that are not in their own interests, far less those of the public at large.

The case against price controls, tariffs, subsidies, and tax breaks is not that the market always gets it right. The direct consequences of these policies are always to benefit the rent-seeking group, and although others usually bear substantial costs, it is often hard to identify who they are. There should be a strong presumption against arguments that are based on generalized economic benefit—growth, employment, efficiency, "competitiveness"—from measures that are specific to an industry. There is generally no way of demonstrating the claimed benefits, other than through DIY economics; and only by establishing a general principle is it possible to deflect the queue of lobbyists who today stretch round Capitol Hill.

Rationality and Adaptation (Chapter 18)

We behave adaptively in our economic lives. Adaptive behavior will reproduce itself in the environment in which it is found. We cooperate much more than rational self-interested individuals would because it is adaptive for us to do so (chapter 21). But it is also adaptive for us to follow the rules of dysfunctional cultures whose outcomes do not benefit us or the organizations themselves.

Adaptive behavior is determined by social and business values we impose on each other—the phenomenon of contagious reputation (chapter 19) is a good example—and the prevailing values of a market economy are key to its success. This is an important part of the explanation of why Norway and Switzerland are rich states and Kenya and Indonesia are not.

The maxim that greed is good has set back the cause of economic development in the East, undermined the legitimacy and performance of the market economies of the West. There is no substantive difference between the pyramid schemes that crippled the Albanian economy in the mid-1990s and the stock market bubble of 1999–2000. We shall only gradually learn how much the competitive advantages of businesses in rich states have been eroded in the pursuit of unsustainable reported growth in earnings: banks that have lost the loyalty of their employees; pharmaceutical companies whose pipelines are increasingly empty; media companies that have alienated their creative talent; insurance companies that no longer have the confidence of their customers.

The selection mechanisms of competitive markets deal, not necessarily quickly, with inappropriate but internally adaptive cultures in business organizations. Because adaptive behaviors are self-reinforcing, these cultures are difficult to alter, as chief executives seeking to impose change on their organizations complain. The extreme case is the government minister who, powerless to change personnel, has no influence on the organization of which he or she is nominally the head. For many effective businesses, this is a good thing: chief executives come and go, taking their absurd visions and missions and legions of strategy consultants with them.

Adaptive bureaucracies impose an appearance of rationality on decision making. The British program of advanced gas-cooled reactors was carefully analyzed; but the numbers these analyzes contained were nonsense and, except in a formal sense, irrelevant to the decisions that were made. Dot-com valuations of 1999, and mobile phone bids of 2000, were justified by elaborate spreadsheets. These exercises gave the appearance of rationality to adaptive processes, but often made decisions worse by concealing the reality of decision making and blurring responsibility for it.

Because behavior is adaptive, not rational, we support social institutions that interfere with our freedom of choice. Odysseus tied himself to the mast to resist siren voices. That is why there are subsidies to pensions and compulsory contributions; taxes on things we know we ought to avoid, such as alcohol, tobacco, and gambling; subsidies to things we think we should have, such as libraries, concerts, and adult education.

Social norms and legislation define the nature of adaptive behavior in economic life; we favor norms and legislation that change economic behavior, including our own. Odysseus would not have been impressed by the argument that the behavior he fears, being irrational, will not happen. And nor are we.

Information (Chapter 19)

Asymmetric information is endemic in modern market economies. It is easy to conclude that the remedy for asymmetric information is to tell consumers more, either by regulation or by recognizing disclosure of risks as a legal defense.

Yet, as these examples illustrate, such measures are almost useless. The normal market mechanism for dealing with asymmetric information is reputation. When we place a deposit with a bank or visit a doctor, we rely on the reputation of the bank and the doctor to assure the security of our deposit and the wisdom of the advice.

No regulation can ensure that banks will not go broke or that doctors will make correct diagnoses. And regulation directed to information disclosure—rules that compel banks to display their balance sheets or require doctors to fully explain risks and prognoses—do not work well either. The bank's balance sheet is out-of-date, incomprehensible, and anyway conveys little relevant information. We don't want to hear long extracts from medical textbooks when we visit our doctor. We want to trust their professional competence.

Self-regulation has one advantage over statutory regulation. Self-regulating entities—companies, groups of professionals—have the information to do it, and a government agency does not. And one disadvantage. Self-regulating entities do not have much incentive to take regulation seriously, and government does. Yet again, the problems of information and incentives interact. Regulation can get the best of both worlds by giving insiders incentive to undertake policing that only they have the information to perform. Self-regulation is stimulated by external supervision.

Risk in Reality (Chapter 20)

Market economies manage uncertainty expensively but badly. Private markets fail to provide effective protection against the principal risks of life—accidents, redundancy and unemployment, and relationship breakdown. Moral hazard and adverse selection are widespread. We are bad at assessing risks and calculating probabilities. The major risks of life cannot be handled by markets.[2] The policy choices we have are between letting risks lie where they fall or trying to manage them through social institutions.

If risks lie where they fall, costs to unlucky victims may be very high. If there is no social provision for misfortune, the only recourse for victims is to blame misfortune on someone else. The possibility of such recourse may bear little relationship to the reasonableness of the claim, and none to the severity of the misfortune. Legal processes are costly to all parties and often ineffectual in compensating real distress. It is profoundly shocking that almost none of the billions of dollars spent pursuing and settling asbestos claims relieves the suffering of mesothelioma victims.[3] At the same time, the risk of being sued has become an additional hazard of modern life. Hence playgrounds made so risk-free, or at least so liability-free, that any normal child would be too bored to use one.[4]

When private markets and the tort system fail, and they mostly do fail, the major risks of daily life are better managed by social insurance. Social insurance differs from private insurance in that payments are not actuarially matched to expected costs.

Social insurance expresses social solidarity. Membership cannot be optional, because that leads to free riding, moral hazard, and adverse selection. But solidaristic institutions need not, and should not, only be agencies of the state. Large companies are the most efficient providers of unemployment and work accident insurance for their employees. Companies and fellow workers can distinguish the malingering from the unfortunate, with a flexibility that no rule-bound bureaucracy can achieve. Yet the expectation that an ordinarily competent employee of a major private company or public authority could expect job security—at a price, in all but exceptional circumstances—has been shattered as companies have asserted they cannot afford to provide jobs for life anymore. In the market revolution this discovery was quickly followed by the discovery that the state could not afford to bear such costs either.

The risks of economic fluctuations, of illness, accident, unemployment, broken homes and marriages, are inescapable. Society has no choice but to afford them. But its institutions can increase or reduce their costs: partially collectivizing them reduces the cost by spreading them, but invites moral hazard. Sharing risks within communities achieves the best balance among these conflicting forces.

Coordination (Chapter 22)

Standards and networks in a market economy require coordination. Government can impose coordination. Coordination can be established by private agreement among firms. Or it can emerge from the spontaneous operation of market forces. These mechanisms are not incompatible, or mutually exclusive. Standards are often the product of a combination of these forces. Governments have imposed broadcasting standards and required interconnection to telecom networks; agreements between hardware producers established standards for compact and video discs; banks and airlines created networks to provide compatible payment systems and interlining facilities; VHS, Windows, and Visa became dominant in market-based competition.

In the United States, the competing networks of bank cash machines (ATMs) usually charge for using the machines of another network. In France, an agreement brokered by the Banque de France ensures that all cards can be used in all machines. The American structure puts pressure on providers to be cost-efficient and makes it competitively attractive to install machines—the largest provider is now the software company EDS. Customers like universal acceptance and free use; and they also like low bank charges. It is not obvious which system seems better.

The personal computer industry evolved as it has today, with industry standards based on Intel processors and Microsoft operating systems, as a result of a market process: standardization emerged from an apparent chaos of competing systems as a consequence of consumer choices. It is unlikely that any regulatory structure could have worked as well.

In the mobile phone industry, however, the absence of a single standard in the United States meant that development and use of cell phones lagged well behind that of Europe, in which a common standard was agreed and imposed by regulatory fiat. The result was not only that use of mobile telephony grew faster in Europe, but that European firms such as Nokia and Ericsson became world market leaders in the provision of hardware for the industry.

Rules and Property Rights (Chapter 6)

The term *property rights* invites us to believe that it is easy to define what they are and to require observance of them. But the rules of a market economy are extensive, and largely implicit. They are determined and enforced more by social convention than legal process. Government is only one agent in the simultaneous evolution of technology, market institutions, and the social and political context.

Once, consumers relied mainly on the retailer's reputation when they bought goods and services. The growth of product branding and national advertising meant that they could rely on the quality of packaged goods made in large manufacturing plants. The rise of chain stores restored power to the retailer. But consumers now relied on the retailer's brand and the scientific skills of its head office rather than their personal knowledge of individual shopkeepers.

These developments were driven by changing technology and the increasing complexity of products. These factors in turn determined the success and failure in the marketplace of different businesses. The support of evolving law protected trademarks and prohibited misleading advertising. Other innovations in the rules of a market economy, such as the development of limited liability, required more deliberate legal and regulatory structures.

New policies are required to establish a legal framework for new activities—such as with the Internet and the genome—and to modify old rules to meet modern technologies. Good rules cannot be made by general principle: solutions are usually specific to technology and a market. The legal framework of both the genome and the Internet has mistakenly been allowed to depend on judicial interpretation of legislation directed to quite different purposes. Government must often be proactive rulemaker, not referee.

The ABM emphasizes freedom of contract, and responsiveness in contract design has been a strength of the market economy. The flexibility of the common law systems of the English-speaking world has been a source of competitive advantage for financial services and for the legal business itself. But genuine freedom of contract is prohibitively expensive. We don't negotiate contract terms when we buy most goods and services because we would never get out of the shop, or on the train.

Market fundamentalists might ask why we need a company law. After all, shareholders and managers are free to make any agreements with each other they like. This is not a realistic proposal because negotiation is costly and litigation over the interpretation of idiosyncratic contracts overwhelmingly costly.[5] That is why there are so many standard forms and procedures even in common law countries and why we need systems of registration for corporations and securities.

Pay, Taxes, and Benefits (Chapter 25)
● ●

What people earn is the most important factor in their economic lives. Even the smallest business needs a pay policy. Government is the largest employer in all productive economies, and the dominant employer in many sectors, from education to waste collection. So government pay policy for its own employees has an economy-wide impact. The sharing of income within households and families is the most important mechanism of redistribution. Charity and philanthropy also play a role, but that role is today much smaller than that of formal tax and benefit systems. Social policies not only reallocate income among households, but within families and across lifetimes.

If either productivity theories or bargaining theories were true to the exclusion of the other, policy for income distribution would be relatively easy. Productivity theory allows little scope to influence the distribution of income. Productivity is fixed by technology and the market; any interference with the implied distribution involves losses greater than the amounts redistributed. Bargaining theories imply that earnings are politically determined, both within organizations and in the nation as a whole. There is more or less unlimited scope to implement a democratic conception of fairness in rewards.

But both theories have elements of truth without being the complete truth. And anyone who has ever had to determine pay in the real world recognizes the conflicting pressures of politics and the market, of efficiency and fairness. The very fact that pay needs to be determined demonstrates that the market does not tell the whole story: if it did, you would not need to have a remuneration committee or tell a human resources director to fix a pay scale. But justice in the distribution of income must be tempered by realism.

Almost all rich states have set a minimum wage. A legal minimum forces a change in the distribution of rents within organizations. It raises the costs of activities—such as cleaning, supermarket checkouts, services, and fast food—that use casual, unskilled labor. This will increase their price and reduce demand for them. The balance between more pay and fewer jobs is an empirical question, and the consequences cannot be estimated without detailed quantitative research. But social norms about wages are a flexible and responsive mechanism that no statutory regime can ever replicate.[6]

The Future of Poor States
● ●

The disparities of income and wealth in the world today are an affront to any reflective person. Money and economic growth do not necessarily buy happiness, but money and economic growth could certainly buy more happiness for Sicelo and his family.

But we who live in rich states are not rich because those who live in poor states are poor. It is simply not true that the market economy and the world trading system are structured in ways in which the rich gain at the expense of the poor. If the nineteen rich states of chapter 4 traded only with each other and had no economic dealings with the rest of the world, their standard of living would not fall by much. Most of their trade is already among themselves.[7] The most important consequence would be a rise in energy costs. Rich states are rich because of high productivity, which results from their effective exploitation of the division of labor and their own modern technology, skills, and capabilities.

In such a divided world, the standard of living of poor countries would also fall, perhaps by relatively more. The small number of poor countries that are resource rich—such as the Congo and Saudi Arabia—would lose. But, as described in chapter 24, these resources so distort the structure of their economies that the long-run benefit is uncertain. More serious would be the loss of equipment—from oil production facilities to telecommunications switching equipment—that could not be manufactured at all without access to Western technology.

Nor are poor countries poor because of a "funding gap" that it is within the capacity of rich states to bridge. The effectiveness of aid given in the past, not particularly generously, is low. It is easy to make an emotional case for debt relief, but the issues are complicated. Campaigners invite us to imagine that the inhabitants of poor countries spend much of their day working to pay off the debts that we imposed on them. The reality is that most of the money lent to highly indebted governments has gone and can never be recovered. The practical consequence of indebtedness is that it limits the capacity to borrow more. Since much of what was previously borrowed was stolen or wasted, this may be a good rather than a bad outcome.[8]

The difference between rich and poor states is the result of differences in the quality of their economic institutions. After four disappointing decades, development agencies have recognized this and used their authority to demand reforms. But the prescriptions have often been facile. What was offered to Russia was not American institutions, but the nostrums of the American business model. The institutions of the market—secure property rights, minimal government economic intervention, light regulation—were supposed to be simple and universal. If these prescriptions were implemented, growth would follow.

But the truth about markets is far more complex. Rich states are the product of—literally—centuries of coevolution of civil society, politics, and economic institutions. A coevolution that we only partially understand and cannot transplant. In the only successful examples of transplantation—the Western offshoots—entire populations, and their institutions, were settled in almost empty countries. The appeal of the American business model today, as of Marxism yesterday, is the suggestion that the history of economic institutions, the structure of current society, and the path of future development have a simple economic explanation and an inevitable outcome. This is as misleading a view of political economy as the Marxist one.

There is no grand narrative, only little stories. But the need for grand narrative is so firmly ingrained in human thinking that the fruitless search for it will never end. This book is dedicated to those for whom a partial understanding of complex reality is better than the reassurance of false universal explanations.

{appendix} •
Nobel Prizes in Economics

The Nobel Prize in economics was established in 1968 by the Bank of Sweden. Like the other Nobel Prizes (for physics, chemistry, medicine, literature, and peace) it is awarded by the Swedish Academy of Sciences on the recommendation of a specialist subcommittee after wide consultation.

The Nobel Prize in economics has always been controversial. Many people (including many economists) feel that economics is not, or not often, characterized by definitive and seminal advances in knowledge of the kind recognized by the science prizes. Even if that is true, the Nobel Prize list is a good indication of what a well-informed group judge to be the most important developments in modern economics and the most important contributors to these developments.

I suspect that the entire group of laureates would have made only a handful of appearances on Bloomberg television in total. There are few prizes in macroeconomics—Milton Friedman (1976), James Tobin (1981), Robert Lucas (1995), and arguably Franco Modigliani (1985) and Robert Mundell (1999). Macroeconomics—the study of inflation, interest rates, and aggregate employment—is a much less important part of academic work in economics than most people might suppose. But there have also just been fewer good new ideas in macroeconomic theory in the last fifty years than in other branches of economics.

About two-thirds of Nobel prizes in economics have gone to the United States, and this despite an attempt by the organizers to lean over backward to favor non-Americans: it is hard to argue that the average achievement of the non-Americans is as high. But the proportion of awards in economics going to the United States is no higher than in sciences. Several awards—Engle (2003), Granger (2003), Heckman (2000), McFadden (2000), Haavelmo (1989), Klein (1980), and arguably Frisch (1969) and Tinbergen (1969)—have been made in econometrics. Econometrics is not, as many people believe, the application of mathematics to economics. Most economic theory is now developed mathematically—indeed there is an inappropriate premium for expressing ideas in this way, and the mathematics used is often trivial. Econometrics is the application of statistical techniques to economic data sets. The development of these methods has partly compensated for the inability of economists to engage in controlled experiments, and the sophistication of statistical technique in econometrics now runs far ahead of its development in other subjects—such as medical statistics—where similar problems arise. The state and contribution of econometrics requires another book, however, and I am not the person to write it.

The majority of prizes have been given for microeconomic theory—the functioning of individual markets for goods and services, the concerns of this book. Most agree that macroeconomics will develop from a microeconomic base, although that has now been said for many years without major practical consequence.

Economic Science: Laureates and Prizes

Name	Country	Year	Subject
George A. Akerlof	USA	2001	Asymmetric information
Maurice Allais	France	1988	The theory of markets and efficient utilization of resources
Kenneth J. Arrow	USA	1972	General equilibrium theory

Name	Country	Year	Subject
Gary S. Becker	USA	1992	"For having extended the domain of microeconomic analysis to a wide range of human behavior and interaction, including nonmarket behavior."
James M. Buchanan Jr.	USA	1986	Public choice
Ronald H. Coase	UK	1991	Theory of the firm, property rights, and transactions costs
Gerard Debreu	USA	1983	General equilibrium
Robert F. Engle	USA	2003	Time series analysis
Robert W. Fogel	USA	1993	Quantitative economic history
Milton Friedman	USA	1976	Macroeconomics
Ragnar Frisch	Norway	1969	Economic dynamics
CWJ Granger	UK	2003	Time series analysis
Trygve Haavelmo	Norway	1989	Econometrics
John C. Harsanyi	USA	1994	Game theory
Friedrich von Hayek	Austria/UK	1974	Economic systems
James J. Heckman	USA	2000	Econometrics
John R. Hicks	UK	1972	General equilibrium theory
Daniel Kahneman	USA	2002	Behavioral economics
Leonid Vitaliyevich Kantorovich	USSR	1975	Optimization modeling
Lawrence R. Klein	USA	1980	Econometrics
Tjalling C. Koopmans	USA	1975	Optimization modeling
Simon Kuznets	USA	1971	Empirical studies of economic growth
Wassily Leontief	USA	1973	Input-output analysis

Name	Country	Year	Subject
Arthur Lewis	UK	1979	Development economics
Robert E. Lucas Jr.	USA	1995	Real business cycle theory
Harry M. Markowitz	USA	1990	Finance theory
Daniel L. McFadden	USA	2000	Econometrics
James E. Meade	UK	1977	Trade theory
Robert C. Merton	USA	1997	Finance theory
Merton H. Miller	USA	1990	Finance theory
James A. Mirrlees	UK	1996	Asymmetric information
Franco Modigliani	USA	1985	Macroeconomics and finance theory
Robert A. Mundell	Canada	1999	Exchange rates and currency areas
Gunnar Myrdal	Sweden	1974	Economic systems
John F. Nash Jr.	USA	1994	Game theory
Douglass C. North	USA	1993	Application of economic theory to economic history
Bertil Ohlin	Sweden	1977	Trade theory
Paul A. Samuelson	USA	1970	"For the scientific work through which he has developed static and dynamic economic theory and actively contributed to raising the level of analysis in economic science."
Myron S. Scholes	USA	1997	Finance theory
Theodore W. Schultz	USA	1979	Development economics
Reinhard Selten	Germany	1994	Game theory
Amartya Sen	India	1998	Welfare economics
William F. Sharpe	USA	1990	Finance theory

Name	Country	Year	Subject
Herbert A. Simon	USA	1978	Decision making
Vernon Smith	USA	2003	Behavioral economics
Robert M. Solow	USA	1987	Theory of economic growth
A. Michael Spence	USA	2001	Asymmetric information
George J. Stigler	USA	1982	Industrial structures, functioning of markets, and causes and effects of public regulation
Joseph E. Stiglitz	USA	2001	Asymmetric information
Richard Stone	UK	1984	National income accounting
Jan Tinbergen	Netherlands	1969	Economic dynamics
James Tobin	USA	1981	Finance theory and macroeconomics
William Vickrey	USA	1996	Asymmetric information

{glossary} •••••••••••••••••••••••

absolute advantage	See COMPETITIVE ADVANTAGE.
balance of payments	The difference between a country's exports and imports (its current account surplus or deficit), which is necessarily matched by a growth or decline in its net asset position in the rest of the world.
bounded rationality	Choice from within a limited set of alternatives. Used in two different senses. The first (the original, due to Herbert Simon) assumes that the impossibility of assembling sufficient information constrains, largely arbitrarily, the possibilities considered, and so people choose alternatives that are "good enough."
	The second (popularized by Oliver Williamson) supposes that rational choices are made from within a subset of all possibilities that are themselves rationally chosen, i.e., balancing the costs of obtaining information against the benefits.
	Thus one interpretation effectively abandons conventional assumptions of rationality; the other transforms it into metarationality.

call option	The right to buy a security at a fixed price (even if its market price has risen in the meantime). Thus you share the upside, but not the downside, of its movements. In return for this, you pay a premium.
comparative advantage	A country (or less commonly an individual) has a comparative advantage in the activities that it is relatively best at. See page 84. Distinguish from competitive (absolute) advantage.
competitive advantage	A firm has a competitive (absolute) advantage in activities that it performs better than other firms. Absolute (competitive) advantage governs the activities of firms, while comparative advantage governs the activities of countries and individuals. This is because firms with no competitive (absolute) advantages are pushed out of business, while countries and individuals with no competitive advantage are pushed into low-value activities in which they have comparative advantage.
competitive equilibrium	A competitive market in which supply and demand are equal.
competitive market	A market in which all buyers and sellers are sufficiently small that none has a significant effect on the price.
convexity	In a convex set, any average of two points in the set is also in the set. A convex curve has the property that any line that joins two points on it lies above the curve. The practical implication of convexity is that averages are preferred to extremes.
derivative	A security whose value is based on (derived from) the value of another security—see, for example, PUT and CALL OPTIONS.
division of labor	The breaking down of tasks into a number of specialized activities.
economic rent	The amount that a firm, individual, or other resource is paid in an activity above what is needed to attract it to that activity. It is competition between buyers when the factor is scarce that creates economic rent.

economies of scale | Falling average costs of production that are the result of higher levels of output.

efficient market hypothesis | The theory that information about the past and future prices of securities is fully incorporated in their prices. Takes a weak form (past data conveys no information), semistrong form (all publicly available information is incorporated), strong form (all information, whether public or not, is incorporated).

equity premium | The difference between returns on stocks (shares) and returns on risk-free assets.

futures contract | An agreement to buy or sell a commodity or security at a future date at a fixed price agreed now.

general (competitive) equilibrium | A position in which all competitive markets in an economic system are simultaneously in equilibrium.

gross domestic product | The total value of output (before depreciation) produced within the boundaries of a state.

gross national income | The value of output (before depreciation) produced by factors of production owned by residents of a state. National income and domestic product differ from each other by the amount of net property income from overseas.

incentive compatibility | A property of allocation mechanisms under which no agent can gain an advantage by strategic behavior.

information asymmetry | A characteristic of a market in which one side (buyer or seller) is better informed about the properties of the good or service than the other (seller or buyer).

intellectual property | Rights created by copyright, patent, or trademark legislation and associated regulations.

market anomalies | Observed deviations from the efficient market hypothesis.

mercantilism | A theory of international trade (widely held before Adam Smith and still adhered to by some devotees of DIY economics) that draws

	an analogy between the exports and imports of states and the revenues and expenses of firms.
noise trader	A buyer or seller (especially in securities markets) whose behavior does not reflect views about the fundamental value (prospective earnings, etc.) of what he or she is buying.
Pareto efficiency	The property of an allocation of resources in which no one can be made better off without making someone else worse off.
Pareto improvement	A change that makes some people better off and no one worse off.
path dependency	A dynamic process in which behavior is affected indefinitely by initial conditions.
primary market	The initial sale of a good or service (especially of a security).
productivity	Labor productivity in output per unit of labor (per head, per hour worked). Total factor productivity is output per unit of all inputs (including, in particular, capital inputs). Productivity without qualification usually (but not always) refers to labor productivity.
purchasing power parity	The rate of exchange between different currencies at which a representative bundle of goods would cost the same in each country or currency zone.
put option	The right to sell a security at a fixed price at a future date, even if its market price has subsequently fallen.
random walk theory	The theory that future security-price movements are independent of past movements.
secondary market	The resale of an item that has already been sold in a primary market (especially in securities markets).
winner's curse	A property of allocation mechanisms in which the winner overpays for the good, service, or security received. A failure of incentive compatibility.

{notes} •

Part I: THE ISSUES

Chapter 1: A Postcard from France
• •

1. Austria, Belgium, Finland, France, Germany, Greece, Ireland, Italy, Luxembourg, the Netherlands, Portugal, Spain. The three other European Union members as of January 1, 2004, Britain, Denmark, and Sweden, have opted out of the single currency.
2. GRONINGEN[W] reference.

Chapter 2: The Triumph of the Market
• •

1. Fukuyama (1989, 1992).
2. Mintzberg (1994) recounts these developments.
3. Yergin and Stanislaw (1998), 10.
4. Ibid., 398.
5. Gates (1995, 1999).
6. Lowenstein (1995).
7. Greenspan (1963) in Rand (1967).
8. There is also a statistical issue here: if the United States were divided into individual states, many would be richer than the U.S. average, and some very rich indeed.

Chapter 3: People
• •

1. A fine discussion of many of these issues is in Olson (1996) and this section draws significantly on his arguments.
2. This led to the 1997 Asian crisis; see chapters 5 and 24.

3. Hoffman (2000) estimates capital per head in 1994 at $54,000 for the United States and $13,000 for Mexico.

4. Between 1950 and 1960 the West German economy grew at over 8% a year and unemployment fell from 11% to 1%.

Chapter 4: Figures
● ●

1. Ten further countries joined the European Union in 2004. None of these would have qualified as rich countries for the purposes of Table 4.1.

2. Quah (1996).

3. Measured height and weight follow the normal distribution—a standard statistical distribution—which is often fitted to the distribution of examination marks. Hours of television watching is lognormal. The observation of these standard statistical properties in data generated by processes with random elements forms the basis of econometrics.

4. World Bank, 2001 World Development Indicators, Table 2.8.

5. Schultz (1998), Milanovic (1999), and Melchior et al. (2000) begin the process of assessing the inequality of household incomes across the world. For a survey of these issues and those of Box 4.1 see Gottschalk and Smeeding (1997).

6. How the product of a team is divided among its members is a central economic issue, to which I return in chapter 25. For the moment, however, it is enough to say that some division of the team's output happens.

7. Lanjouw & Stern (1998).

8. And even with productivity twenty times Indian levels, Swedish wheat is not really economic: without the support of the European Union's Common Agricultural Policy, it is unlikely that wheat would be grown in Kivik at all (see chapter 26).

9. The Komi republic is about a thousand miles northeast of Moscow, with good skiing around its capital, Syktyvkar. In 1994–95 oil leaks from the Kharyaga-Usinsk pipeline produced a spill three times the size of *Exxon Valdez*'s.

10. Nathan Rothschild died on July 28, 1836, probably from either staphylococcus or streptococcus septicemia, which came either from an abscess on his back or from the surgeons' knives used to treat it. This story is told in David Landes (1998), xvii–xviii.

11. Heston and Summers (1991); World Bank (1993). For Penn World Tables, see PENN^w.

12. Landes (1998) has an extended discussion of this. See also Sachs (2000). Sachs, a forceful proselytizer for the American business model, needs to reconcile the universality of his prescription with manifestly large differences in productivity and living standards. Hence the emphasis on climate. In Sachs's model poor countries are poor because they are too hot for capitalism.

13. Fukuyama (1992), 49–50.

14. Kornai (1992), 179; World Bank, 2001 World Development Indicators, Table 3.13.

15. Inglehart et al. (1998), Table V128.
16. Ibid.
17. See also Lane (1991), Oswald (1997), and the WORLD DATABASE OF HAPPINESS.ʷ
18. UNDP (2002).
19. Steckel (1995), 1914.
20. Transparency International (2001), 234.
21. World Bank, 2001 World Development Indicators, Table 2.8.
22. IMF World Economic Outlook 2000, Inflationʷ www.imf.org/external/pubs/ft/weo/2000/02/data/.
23. UNDP Human Development Index 1998. However, some poor states, e.g. Malawi and the Indian state of Kerala, have high literacy rates.
24. Inglehart et al. (1998), Table V264.
25. IMD (2002), Freedom House (2002).
26. Maddison (1993), Table A-2 of 2000 ed.
27. Freedom House (2001), 11.
28. Inglehart and Baker (2000), 19–55.
29. Inglehart et al. (1998), Table V70, Table V77.

Chapter 5: How Rich States Became Rich
●●

1. On the subject matter of this chapter, see Diamond (1997), Landes (1998), and Baumol (2002) for contrasting but integrative perspectives from science, history, and economics.
2. Stringer and Gamble (1993); Diamond (1997), 40–41, Tattersall (1995); Wells (2002).
3. Tudge (1998).
4. Flannery (1973), Smith (1995), Grigg (1992).
5. Aristotle (1984), 1258a39–1258b7.
6. See for example Dickens (1977).
7. "Among the loveliest inventions of the human mind," said Goethe (1809).
8. Weber (1930), Tawney (1926), Merton (1936), Samuelsson (1961).
9. See Fisher (1989) for an account of the European origins of U.S. economic development.
10. Smith (1976), bk. 1, chap. 8.
11. Friedman (2000).
12. Soto (2000) provides an intriguing discussion of these issues, and the discussion here reflects his approach.
13. North (1990) stresses the significance of the North West Ordinance of 1787 in establishing a secure structure of property rights in the United States. There is some force in this. English property law still rests on the fiction that land rights derive from the crown, a fiction difficult to maintain in the postrevolutionary United States, and the North West Ordinance was adopted to provide a basis for modern property law. But the attempt to substitute the federal gov-

ernment for the crown as the source of land rights largely failed in the face of a different local reality. See Soto (2000).

14. Gold was discovered in California in 1848, when San Francisco had a population of eight hundred. In 1849 alone, eighty thousand people migrated to California (the '49ers). The lag in communication with Washington and the scale of the influx relative to the existing infrastructure made government control of developments impossible. Rohrbough (1997).

15. O. Marshall (2000).

16. See, for example, Shumway (1991) and Bethell (1993).

17. There may have been worse prime ministers in rich states than Muldoon, but not many. Even after his electoral defeat, he cost the country a large part of its foreign exchange reserves by insisting on maintaining the exchange rate until he was removed from office.

18. New Zealand, 1998 Report of Mercury Energy Inquiry.

19. There is an extensive literature on the New Zealand reforms. Almost all of it is congratulatory in tone; the congratulation relates to the fact that the reforms have happened. See, for example, Evans et al. (1996), which is a careful survey of the program, but then derives lessons from the "success" of the reforms without substantive discussion of effects. Douglas et al. (2002) is similar. It is presumably self-evident that the results will be beneficial, and therefore there is no need to inquire into the consequences. This is a feature of much commentary on the American business model. Dalziel and Lattimore (1999) give factual background, and Hazledine (1998) provides an informed critical assessment of what happened in New Zealand.

20. See Kay, *Financial Times,* (August 30, 2000).

21. Pomeranz (2000) describes the issue and the range of views taken. Landes's (1998) discussion is close in spirit to the arguments here.

22. These quotations from Louise Le Comte and Evanske Huc respectively are found in Landes (1998), 342.

23. Kornicki (1998), Buzo (1999), Jeffries (2001).

24. Mitsui, Mitsubishi, Dai Ichi Kangyo, Sumitomo, and Sanwa.

25. See Economic Intelligence Unit (2002), Buzo (1999), Jeffries (2001), Amsden (1989).

26. There is extensive discussion of the Asian "miracle." The World Bank's (1993) presentation attracted responses from Krugman (1994), Young (1995), Little (1996).

27. This discussion rests heavily on Maddison (2001).

28. de Long[w].

29. Maddison (2001).

30. I shall follow a convention of ignoring short sea crossings.

31. The EU candidate states (apart from the two small islands of Malta and Cyprus) are at best poor intermediate; several are simply poor. The gap is much larger than at the accession of Greece and Portugal.

Part II: THE STRUCTURE OF ECONOMIC SYSTEMS

Chapter 6: Transactions and Rules
● ●

1. The Federal Communications Commission (FCC) is the government agency charged with regulating communications by radio, wire, television, satellite, and cable.
2. The condominium arrangement gives the owner of a unit a transferable package of rights against the condominium. In England, an apartment owner simply rents the apartment, but with a long lease—often 99 years—and the right to assign it. Australian law makes the individual the legal owner of his part of the building (strata title).
3. Nor to the common "battle of forms," in which each party sends the other its own assertion of the contract.
4. Bertram (1865), Roughley (1951), FISH[w].
5. A malt extract spread.
6. Durham (1991) includes a variety of accounts of genetic and cultural coevolutions.
7. The average length of job tenure in the United States is 6.6 years (as against 10.6 years in Europe). ILO[w].
8. The economics of enclosure has an extensive literature, recently developed by McCloskey (1989), McCloskey (1991).
9. A story told most effectively by Chandler (1963). See also Hannah (1976).
10. Sulston and Ferry (2002).
11. Wolff (1998) is an entertaining discussion of these issues.
12. Napster allowed users—estimated at 50 million—to share compressed audio files. Merriden (2001).
13. See Davies (2001) and Sulston and Terry (2002) for an account of the problem of gene sequencing.
14. The living thing was a genetically modified bacterium; the case was *Diamond v. Chakrabarty*.
15. An extensive literature uses property rights in an extremely broad sense, e.g., Demsetz (1964), Furbotn and Pejovich (1977). Barzel (1997) says that "the insurer is thus one of the owners of the building: he or she owns the fire occurrence attribute of the building." (p. 61). North (1990) defines property rights as "the rights individuals appropriate over their own labor and the goods and services which they possess." This definition—narrow by economists' standards—is still much wider than property as it would be defined by legal theorists.

Chapter 7: Production and Exchange
● ●

1. His work on the concerns of this book—Youngson (1959)—is disappointingly judicious and inconclusive.

2. Youngson (1966).
3. This derives from Robbins (1935): "Economics is a science which studies human behavior as a relationship between ends and scarce means which have alternative uses," p. 16.
4. St. Paul is now full of tourists, although the nearby Fondation Maeght is one of the world's most beautiful galleries. There are many more attractive and less visited hill villages around Nice—Peillon, for example, is magical.
5. Buchet (1993).
6. According to legend, the Manhattes tribe sold Manhattan Island to Dutch settlers for $24 in 1626. Warren Buffett, following calculations by David Dennis, has claimed that the money invested at 6% interest would today be sufficient to buy the island back. Since it is not clear that the Manhattes tribe owned it, the issue of who got the better deal will reverberate forever.
7. "One man draws out the wire, another straightens it, a third cuts it, a fourth points it, a fifth guides it at the top for receiving the head." A. Smith (1976), 14.
8. "What a blessing it was that the idea of cooperation . . . came and prevailed to take the place of this chaotic condition in which the virtuous academic Know-Nothings about business were doing what they construed to be God's service in eating each other up." John D. Rockefeller to W. O. Inglis, quoted in Chernow (1998), 4.
9. Neale and Goyder (1980) describe the evolution of U.S. antitrust law.
10. By rejecting the proposed takeover of Honeywell, another large U.S. corporation. The U.S. Department of Justice had already agreed to the merger.
11. The Atlanta pharmacist was John Pemberton, whose business was bought by Asa Griggs Chandler, who developed the business with wide distribution and aggressive advertising. Chandler ran Coke for twenty-five years before becoming mayor of Atlanta in 1916.
12. For an elaboration of the relationship between competitive advantage and firm capabilities, see Kay (1993).
13. This example was used in Ricardo's *Principles of Political Economy* (1817).
14. Own estimates from world trade statistics.
15. Own estimates from Swiss trade statistics.
16. Porter (1990) has repopularized the emphasis on industrial "cluster" noted by Alfred Marshall a century before.

Chapter 8: Assignment

1. This account of the history of the *Portrait of Dr. Gachet* is based heavily on Saltzman (1998).
2. Gachet (1994).
3. Van Gogh's brother, Theo, was an art dealer who died soon after the painter, and Theo's sister effectively commercialized van Gogh's work: *Gachet* was first sold in 1897 for 225 francs.

4. In July 2002, Rubens's *Massacre of the Innocents* was sold for £49.5 million, which then equaled $76 million.

5. The art historian Louis Anfray has alleged that the Musée d'Orsay version is a copy by another artist (Landais [1999]).

6. Editions 1999—*Le Docteur Gachet*, exhibition catalog.

7. Jennings and Sambrook (2000).

8. The distinction between exit and voice is due to Hirschman (1970).

9. Marx (1875), 12.

10. Kornai (1992), chap. 7.

11. "Any observed statistical regularity will tend to collapse once pressure is placed upon it for control purposes." Goodhart (1984), 96.

12. Buchan (1997) provides an entertaining history of the evolution of moneys. Del Mar (1895) is exhaustive.

13. Radford (1945).

14. See Magee (2003).

15. Condorcet (1785), Arrow (1950, 1951a).

16. Lynch and Kahn (2000), 21–34.

17. The California crisis might alternatively be interpreted as a manifestation of a more fundamental problem: that individuals themselves cannot be expected to have consistent preferences on social issues. Since Enron's collapse, it has become fashionable to pin the blame on that company.

18. Vickrey (1961, 1962).

19. For auction design, see Bulow and Klemperer (2002), AUCTIONS[w].

20. See the repeated attacks by one art critic on what he described as a Serota clique dominating British art administration: Sewell (1994).

Chapter 9: Central Planning
● ●

1. The two-week trip was dogged by incident and surrounded by controversy but increased Khrushchev's popularity at home and (especially) abroad. Jasny (1965), Talbott (1971).

2. Hosking (1992), 358–59.

3. The Great Leap Forward is described in scholarly detail by MacFarquhar (1993) and with literary skill by Chang (1992). See also Karnow (1973) and Teiwes (1999).

4. Josephson (1995) describes some of the many grandiose schemes planned during the history of the Soviet Union.

5. Knudsen and Ford's comments are found in Halberstam (1987) which provides an immensely readable account of the decline of Ford and the role of its proprietor in that decline. The fall of Wang is described in Kenney (1992).

6. Chen Yuen in Story (2003).

7. Caro (1974).

8. Henney (1988), 17.

9. These figures include capitalized interest up to the date of effective operation.

Source: own calculations based on data from CEGB and Nuclear Electric reports. The best account of this disaster is Burn (1978). Some more recent analysis is in Green (1995).

10. Department of Energy (1976), 15–16, quoted by Henderson (1977), 192.

11. This story is told in Hannah (1982), although since Hannah's history was authorized by the Electricity Council, some reading between the lines is required.

12. "One thing that you might think would count, but which in fact is given no attention whatever, is whether or not your advice has been any good": an anonymous civil servant, Henderson (1977). "It is much more important for a paper to be competent than for it to be right or enlightening."—Sir Samuel Brittan, (1971) p. 53.

Chapter 10: Pluralism

1. In 1981, the year Welch became CEO at General Electric, his predecessor, Reg Jones, was voted the best CEO in America by a poll of other chief executives, and by a considerable margin. Goold and Campbell (1987), 273.

2. These quotes from Havermesh (1986), 181, 202.

3. Welch (2001), 104.

4. Reported in S. M. Cohen (1982).

5. Mintzberg (1994) describes the rise and fall of strategic planning in companies in parallel with the rise and fall of planning in national economies.

6. Welch (2001), 104.

7. The last British nuclear plant, Sizewell B, was one of the few nuclear plants built to an American design after the Three Mile Island incident in 1979.

8. Welch (2001), 97.

9. Flatow (1992), chap. 11.

10. The history of Xerox Parc is told by Hiltzik (1999).

11. Xerox "was cursed by the Chester Carlson vision . . . all you have to do is give us the right technology and the world would come to us." Paul Strussman, former Xerox chief technology officer, in Hiltzik (1999).

12. The history of the development of personal computers is told by Ceruzzi (1998). There is a bookshelf of hagiography of Gates and Microsoft: see, for example, Ichbiah and Knepper (1991) and, of course, Gates's own self-congratulation in Gates (1995, 1999).

13. Leadbeater (2000).

14. Cassidy (2002) is the best account of the dot-com boom.

Chapter 11: Spontaneous Order

1. For surveys of the Scottish Enlightenment thinkers, see Berry (1997) and Broadie (1997).

2. Paley (1802), Hume (1779).

3. Ferguson (1767), 187.
4. Which became the title of a book by Richard Dawkins (1991, new ed.).
5. Dawkins (1989) proposed the idea of "memes" as a social analogue to genes. Blackmore (1999) is the most extensive development of the notion. As Dawkins says in his introduction to that book, "any theory deserves to be given its best shot." But its best shot is disappointing.
6. In the nineteenth century, the battle between Lamarckian evolution and Darwinian evolution was won by Darwin: characteristics acquired during life cannot be genetically transmitted. But, as with French, they can be transmitted in other ways.
7. Arrow and Hahn (1971), vii.
8. Kornai (1992) is a source of evidence on repeated coordination failures in planned economies.
9. In 1990, U.S. steel capacity was 60% of Soviet capacity—on calculations from OECD data.
10. Wal-Mart, founded by Sam Walton in 1962, is now the world's largest retailer.
11. Yergin and Stanislaw (1998) begin their book with an admiring description of the Izmailovo outdoor market. In the United States, however, Wal-Mart is more important.
12. Price discontinuities resulting from supply shortages routinely generate consumer protests in market economies.
13. Lynch and Kahn (2000), 21-34.
14. See, for example, Bunday (1996).
15. Heilbroner (1955), 214.
16. Weaver (1948), 536. See also Johnson (2001), 46-49.
17. Gladwell (2000) provides a popular discussion of "tipping points," the characteristics of systems with this property.
18. For an introduction to chaos theory, see Gleick (1988); for economic and other social applications, Kiel and Elliott (1996).
19. The modern emphasis on path dependency in economics originates from Arthur (1989), 116-31.
20. The QWERTY problem was described by P. A. David (1985) who shares with Arthur the credit for finding this approach. For (unpersuasive) responses from American business model (ABM) supporters, see Liebowitz and Margolis (1990).
21. For a basic introduction to the issues and personalities, see Waldrop (1994).
22. Darwin (1859).
23. Due in particular to the empirical work of Wilson (1971), who will reappear in other contexts, and the theoretical insights of Hamilton (1964).
24. For discussions of the relationships between social insects and human social processes, see Ormerod (1998) and Kirwan (1993).
25. Simon (1969).
26. Kauffman (1995, 2000).
27. Although Waldrop (1994) regards Arthur as one of the founders, other economists, such as Arrow, have played an active role in Santa Fe work.

Part III: PERFECTLY COMPETITIVE MARKETS

Chapter 12: Competitive Markets
●●

1. Expert evidence in antitrust cases is the principal source of (lucrative) consultancy work for professional economists.

2. The inclination to view resource reserves and resource availability in physical rather than economic terms is deep rooted. The Club of Rome report (Meadows et al. [1972]), which predicted that the world would by now have run out of several major resources—gold, silver, mercury, zinc—is only one example of a large literature that goes back many centuries. We are dependent on oil because (for the moment) oil is plentiful, just as we were once even more dependent on coal (which was then plentiful and, at a price, still is) and earlier still on wood (which was then plentiful). This does not mean that no resource shortages can ever arise, but it is unlikely they will arise in the way many environmentalists think.

3. About 30% of world oil production comes from the Middle East, another 20% from rich states (principally the United States, UK, Canada, and Norway).

4. R. E. Williams (1997), Suzuki (1997).

5. Brunekreeft (1997) describes the structure of the UK electricity generation system.

6. Klopfenstein (1989).

7. Levy (1989).

8. The industry was privatized in 1990. In England and Wales there were two generating companies and twelve regional distribution businesses. The nuclear power stations initially remained in public ownership; the AGRs (see chapter 9) were sold in 1996.

9. See Brunekreeft (1997).

10. The National Grid continues to operate a central control room, which assures continuity of supply while bids and offers determine the associated financial settlements. Analogous arrangements are found in all other electricity markets.

11. Prices were raised in 1974 to levels that equate to $20 per barrel (in 2002 dollars).

12. The most famous Dutch flower market, at Aalsmeer, operates quite differently, with a clock and an auction mechanism. The "Dutch auction" is different from the "English auction," used for *Dr. Gachet*.

13. The New York Stock Exchange is an auction market, in which specialists facilitate trade but do not take positions on their own account. On NASDAQ, buyers and sellers are matched electronically. The American Stock Exchange is also an auction market, but some specialists act as dealers.

14. Most individual markets have their own price reporting systems. "Real-time price feeds," i.e., up-to-date pricing information, is available from market services such as Reuters and Bloomberg. Delayed price quotes (even a fifteen- or twenty-minute delay is thought to destroy the value of information to professional traders) are readily available on the Internet for many markets.

15. The Hunts began buying silver in 1973 and aggressive accumulation in 1979. It is claimed that at the peak of the market (the price of silver rose from $2 per

ounce in 1973 to $54 in 1980) they controlled half the deliverable (i.e., not in jewelery and heirlooms) supply. In early 1980 the price collapsed. The two Hunt brothers became bankrupt and were eventually convicted of market manipulation.

16. The International Tin Council collapsed on October 24, 1985. See "ITC Pulls the Plug on Supporting the Tin Market," *Metals Week: Tin Section* 1985, 1. Rodger, "Dented Image in the Can Market," *Financial Times*, October 28, 1985, 11. Crabtree et al. (1987).

17. A forward market is a derivatives market. How these work is described in the next chapter.

18. Kanfer (1993), Carstens (2001), Gregory (1962).

19. Soros became a major philanthropist, particularly in Eastern Europe, and wrote books skeptical about the American business model (Soros [1998, 2000]).

20. Tsurumi (2001).

21. Wholesale electricity prices fell substantially in 2001.

Chapter 13: Markets in Risk

1. Bernstein (1996) is a brilliant study of the history of risk analysis and risk markets.

2. IOWA^W.

3. *Economist,* August 2, 2003, 70.

4. This sounds paradoxical. If Lochnagel wins the five-o'clock race at Ascot, isn't it obvious that those who backed Lochnagel won and others lost? In a sense, yes. And yet it might have been that the odds on Lochnagel were shorter than the horse's form deserved, so that if you had (hypothetically) made a hundred similar bets, you would have lost. When you buy a lottery ticket, you make a mistake—you almost certainly should not bet at such poor odds. But if the winning ticket is yours, chance redeems your mistake.

   When people succeed in risky situations, the outcome is a mixture of their good judgment and their good luck, and it is impossible to disentangle the elements of the two. This is of central importance to considering successful businesses and successful businesspeople. To what extent were Henry Ford, William Morris, Bill Gates people who had the good judgment to choose the right number, or the lucky people whose number came up?.

5. Kendall (1953).

6. See for example, Carhart, 1997.

7. Black and Scholes (1973).

8. Jensen (1978).

Chapter 14: Markets in Money

1. "This was a venture, sir, that Jacob serv'd for . . . was this inserted to make interest good?" *Merchant of Venice,* act 1, sc. 3, l. 85.

2. "Ancient Egypt was doubly fortunate, and doubtless owed to this its fabled wealth, in that it possessed two activities, namely pyramid building as well as the search for the precious metals, the fruits of which, since they could not serve the needs of man by being consumed, did not stale with abundance." Keynes (1936), 131.

3. See *Economist,* August 2, 2003.

4. N. Ferguson (2001).

5. Many derivative packages are of this kind.

6. Fama and French, 2001.

7. Insider trading is the use of information gained through a relationship with the firm—e.g., as director or adviser. It is now illegal in Britain, the United States, and many other countries.

8. See, for example, estimates of rates of return to higher education in Harkness and Machin (1999).

9. These "intangible assets" are the capitalized value of rents arising from competitive advantages. This is why "Tobin's q"—the ratio of the market value of a company to its tangible assets—can appropriately exceed one.

10. Putnam (2000).

11. "Americans of all ages, all conditions, all minds, constantly unite." Tocqueville (1835), 489.

Chapter 15: General Equilibrium

●●

1. Note that this is true of any coordinated system, whether the coordination is designed or not.

2. Henderson (1986).

3. As in the repeated suggestion that practical businessmen rather than economists or financiers should fix interest rates.

4. *England's Treasure by Foreign Trade* is a work of the 1620s by Thomas Mun. As is typical of DIY economics, it is hard to pin down precisely what mercantilists thought; hence Viner's description of it as "essentially a folk doctrine" (*International Encyclopedia of Social Sciences,* 1968).

5. The workers who threatened Kay actually preceded the Luddites, followers in the early nineteenth century of the (possibly mythical) Ned Ludd. A picture of Kay fleeing is found at LUDDITE[W].

6. Marshall described his methodology of economics as follows: "(1) Use mathematics as a shorthand language, rather than as an engine of inquiry. (2) Keep to them till you have done. (3) Translate into English. (4) Then illustrate by examples that are important to real life. (5) Burn the mathematics. (6) If you can't succeed in 4, burn 3. This last I did often." A. Marshall (1925), 427.

7. Keynes (1936).

8. The works described are Hicks (1939), Samuelson (1947), Arrow and Debreu (1954), Debreu (1959). Overviews are found in Koopmans (1957), and a definitive textbook is Arrow and Hahn (1971).

9. The original fixed-point theorem is due to Brouwer. The version commonly employed by economists is by Kakutani (1941), pages 451–59.

10. Although the general idea of convexity has always been known, the mathematics of convex sets was fully developed only in the twentieth century, Hardy, Littlewood, and Polya (1934), and applied to economics even later.

11. Langlois, Roggman, and Musselman (1994), 214–20; Etcoff (1994); Perrett et al. (1994).

12. This discussion concerns the stability as well as the position of equilibrium. Convexity is relevant to both.

13. Lyapunov's theorem shows how many small nonconvexities can be consistent with overall convexity if the numbers of firms, industries, etc., are sufficiently large. Aumann (1964), 39–50.

Chapter 16: Efficiency
● ●

1. Pearce (1992) attempts to resolve this muddle, but continues to assert universal commensurability. This follows almost inescapably from the rationality postulates described in chapters 17 and 18.

2. Buchholz (1999), Posner (1998).

3. Dworkin (1977), chap. 4; Waldron (1984), 153–67.

4. Berlin (2000).

5. For a summary of the standard economic approach to the value-of-life issues, see Jones-Lee (1976). For a well-balanced background to why this approach is untenable, see Douglas and Wildavsky (1982).

6. Often called a Pareto optimum.

7. Perfect—"first degree"—price discrimination tailors the price for each good sold precisely to its user so that all consumer surplus is extracted.

8. Arrow (1951b).

Part IV: THE TRUTH ABOUT MARKETS

Chapter 17: Neoclassical Economics and After
● ●

1. For example, for James Tobin[n] the invisible hand is "one of the great ideas of history and one of the most influential." Tobin (1992), 117.

2. Yergin and Stanislaw (1998), 398. More or less the same phrase is found at the beginning of the book, page 24.

3. Leacock (1936). These are not Leacock's own views.

4. Smith (1759), 184–85 For a discussion of the role of the "invisible hand" metaphor in Smith's work, see Rothschild (2001), chapter 5. The original "invisible hand" seems to be found in Shakespeare:

Come seeling night
Scarf up the tender eye of pitiful day
And with thy bloody and invisible hand
Cancel and tear to pieces that great bond
Which keeps me pale.
           —*Macbeth, act 3, sc. 2, l. 119.*

5. See the discussion of DIY economics in chapter 15.

6. Austrian economics is often today used simply as a description of right-wing and libertarian sentiment, sometimes combined with resistance to the application of mathematical technique. These features make the label attractive to many DIY economists: see, for example, the reading lists on economics offered on the Amazon.com Web site. A discussion of the various meanings of Austrian economics, with a judicious summary—"economists (and other intellectuals in Austria today) are cognizant of—and proud of—the earlier Austrian school . . . but see themselves today simply as a part of the general community of professional economists" (p. 149)—is found in Kirzner's essay in the *New Palgrave*.

7. Although Thorstein Veblen, whose trenchant criticism of the consumption of the rich is still readable today (Veblen [1899]), was a faculty member. However, Veblen's personal habits were as uncongenial as his views and he was asked to leave.

8. There is a—possibly intentional—trap in this quotation. At a quick reading, it seems to describe self-interested behavior. On a more careful reading, it does not: the behavior is not relentless and unflinching, but the economist who studies it. This difficulty in distinguishing consistent behavior from self-interested behavior recurs repeatedly: see below.

9. Although the Chicago influence in New Zealand is widely cited (Easton [1994]), the reality is less clear. "There is a view in New Zealand that the reforms were driven by Chicago. It is certainly true that Friedman's *Free to Choose* was read widely in New Zealand . . . But to the best of my knowledge none of those most closely involved in the reform process ever studied at Chicago. In fact the most common academic background . . . was probably the University of Canterbury." Brash (1996).

10. The key feature of this account is that it contains no ethics or norms, or more precisely, that what we describe as ethics or norms are adopted as the result of self-interested calculation, e.g., honesty may be the best policy, but will be abandoned if it ceases to be the best policy. Honesty is not a trait of character. "Someone is honest only if honesty, or the appearance of honesty, pays more than dishonesty." Telser (1980), 27–44. See also Becker (1968).

11. Becker (1973, 1974, 1981).

12. Becker (1993), 8.

13. Hamermersh and Soss (1974), Blinder (1974).

14. It follows that only unpredicted—and unpredictable—shocks create cyclical fluctu-

ations in economies. Moreover, the closely related "Lucas critique" excludes most empirical testing of these models, because the information generated (including the results of the test itself) should be incorporated in public knowledge.

15. Producer surplus is economic rent (see Box 12.1).
16. Mankiw (2004), 149–50.
17. Knight (1921), Alchian (1950).
18. Dixit and Nalebuff (1991) is an accessible introduction. Binmore (1994, 1998) relates game theory to some of the wider issues of this book.
19. Macrae (1992).
20. Quoted in Strathern (2001), 300.
21. Nasar (1998).
22. "I was once in the habit of telling pupils that firms might be envisaged as islands of planned coordination in a sea of markets." Richardson (1972), 883. Richardson goes on to say, "This now seems to be a highly misleading account."
23. North and Thomas (1973), North (1990).
24. O. E. Williamson (1975).
25. Milgrom and Roberts (1992).
26. Stiglitz (1994), 5. This volume is a good introduction to his approach.
27. The term *market failure* was popularized by Bator (1958). For the interpretation of market failure as violation of Arrow-Debreu assumptions, see Ledyard (1988).

Chapter 18: Rationality and Adaptation

1. See note 11, chapter 17.
2. Samuelson (1993), 143.
3. Amartya Sen[n] has done much to clarify these issues. See Sen (1987), 12–22; Sen (1988).
4. Easterley (2001), xii.
5. This argument and the answer to it is well described by Gintis (2000): "The most common informal argument is reminiscent of Louis XIV's *après moi le déluge* defense of the monarchy: drop the assumptions and we lose the ability to predict altogether. The models developed recently . . . show that we have little to fear from the flood."
6. Though cf. Stigler: "Let me predict the outcome of the systematic and comprehensive testing of behavior in situations where self-interest and ethical values with wide verbal allegiance are in conflict. Much of the time, most of the time, in fact, the self-interest will win." Stigler (1981), 176. Note that Stigler predicts the result, he does not report results, and in fact, as Sen (1987) notes, few such tests have been made. Correct predictions—demand curves slope downward—can be derived in many ways: see Becker (1962).
7. Easterly's quotation is immediately followed by another: "People respond to incentives; all the rest is commentary." Easterly (2001), xii.
8. Kay (2000), OXFORD[w].

9. Havel (1985), 29–31.
10. MacIntyre (1981), 57–59.
11. Francis Galton was not only a major figure in the development of scientific genetics but a sponsor of the eugenics movement.
12. Wilson (1975). Wilson was subject to a variety of tirades and famously had a pitcher of water poured over him at the American Association for the Advancement [*sic*] of Science.
13. "The relevant question to ask about the assumptions of a theory is not whether they are descriptively realistic, for they never are, but whether they are sufficiently good approximations for the purpose in hand. And this question can be answered only by seeing whether the theory works, which means whether it yields sufficiently accurate predictions." Friedman (1953), 15.
14. This was 24/7 Media.
15. Miller (1953).
16. In another—also instructive—version of the joke, the game theorist runs. The colleague says, "You can't run faster than the bear." The economist responds, "I only need to run faster than you." JOKES[W].
17. Maynard Smith (1982), Taylor and Joncker (1978).
18. O. E. Williamson (1985).
19. Gigerenzer et al. (1999) reports that Simon "once remarked with a mixture of humor and anger that he had considered suing authors who misuse his concept of bounded rationality to construct ever more complicated and unrealistic models of human decision making." (p. 12).
20. Kahneman and Tversky (2000).

Chapter 19: Information
● ●

1. The wallet problem is due to Stiglitz, who would occasionally attempt to auction his wallet to a class.
2. "Cheap talk" is a threat or promise that is not credible because it pays to make the promise or threat but not to carry it out.
3. Cronin (1991), pages 222–26, describes this and other similar biological phenomena.
4. For the biological explanations, see Zahavi (1975). The economics of signaling was pioneered by Spence (1973) and the specific application to advertising by Nelson (1974).
5. AUSTRALIA[W].
6. Thaler (1991) discusses this (and other economic paradoxes).
7. Capen, Clapp, and Campbell (1971).
8. Bulow and Klemperer (2002), Borgers and Dustmann (2001) KLEMPERER[W].
9. The Sonera/Telefonica consortium.
10. Since the auction, all the successful bidders have new chief executives, as has Merrill Lynch. Henry Blodget was barred for life from the securities industry as part of a plea bargain with New York Attorney General Spitzer.

11. The first extensive argument that information issues were an explanation of cyclical unemployment was given by Leijonhufvud (1968), who suggested that it was the correct interpretation of the argument of Keynes's General Theory.

12. "Matthew Parris . . . has reminded us that most people do not escape the market system . . . Parris writes of an aunt of his who believes that there is such a thing as a fair price or wage that can be determined by contemplation rather than the state of the market . . . I have made a few soundings of my own among business journalists, who might be expected to have a higher degree of sophistication." Brittan (1996), 49.

Chapter 20: Risk in Reality

1. For a review of the current status of this theory, see Starmer (2000).
2. Pinker (1994).
3. Allais (1953).
4. Kahneman and Tversky (2000) is a collection of their work.
5. Adam Smith observed that "such in reality is the absurd confidence which almost all men have in their own good fortune, that whenever there is the least probability of success, too great a share of it [investment] is apt to go to them [mining projects] of its own account." A. Smith (1976), chap. 7, pt. 1. See Shiller (2000), pages 142–46 for a demonstration that only the methods of empirical research have changed.
6. Shleifer (1999), Siegel (1998), survey market anomalies. The January effect is discussed by Siegel, page 254, the 1987 crash by Shiller (2000), pages 88–95.
7. The equity premium paradox was first described by Mehra and Prescott (1985) and elaborated by Benartzi and Thaler (1995). See Dimson et al. (2002) for evidence on it.
8. Haigh (1999) gives a thoughtful discussion of the structure of lotteries.
9. Thomson (1998) p.125. The settlement with Proctor and Gamble was only one of several pieces of litigation that engulfed Bankers Trust. In 1995, its chief executive, Charles S. Sanford, retired early, outstanding suits were settled, and the bank was subsequently absorbed into Deutsche Bank.
10. The story of LTCM is told by Lowenstein (2000).
11. This is the undiversifiable risk for which the equity risk premium is the reward.
12. Arrow[n] (1971) is a seminal discussion of moral hazard and adverse selection.
13. The proportion of single women in the U.S.[n] who are mothers doubled between 1970 and 2000.
14. Adams (1995), 12–13.
15. Barth (1991), White (1991), Calavita et al. (1997).
16. Including Charles Keating.
17. Shleifer and Summers (1988). "When asked how GE had managed to increase its earnings by 14% per year, Vice President Frank Doyle replied, 'We did a lot of violence to the expectations of the American workforce'": Hay and Moore (1998), quoted in Hutton (2002).
18. For a history of social insurance, see Dilnot, Kay, and Morris (1984), chapter 1.

19. "Part of selling bonds for Salomon was persuading yourself that a bad idea for Salomon was a good idea for a customer." M. Lewis (1989), 162.

20. And yet new issues—IPOs—are more frequent when stock markets are high. (Ritter [1991]). This is another case where adaptation provides a more compelling account of behavior than rationality—see the discussion in the previous chapter.

21. "People who argue that speculation is generally destabilizing seldom realize that this is largely equivalent to saying that speculators lose money, since speculation can be destabilizing only if speculators on the average sell when the currency is low in price and buy when it is high." Friedman (1953), 175.

22. Lowenstein (2000), 236.

23. For an introduction to these issues of behavioral finance see Shleifer (1999). For a practical guide, Belsky and Gilovich (2000), Shefrin (2000).

Chapter 21: Cooperation
● ●

1. The Pharos of Alexandria, built around 280 B.C., was a marvel for the combination of its scale of construction and the technological sophistication of its mirrors. Forster (1982), Fraser (1984).

2. Socrastus—named on the Pharos and identified as its architect by Pliny—was probably in fact the public-spirited courtier who paid for it. Fraser (1984), 19.

3. Winstanley is described by Bathurst (1999), page 59, as "an English eccentric of the finest breed."

4. Groves and Ledyard (1977, 1980).

5. Bathurst (1999).

6. Buchanan and Tulloch (1962), Downs (1957), Buchanan and Tollison (1972, 1984).

7. See the discussion in Zakaria (2003).

8. Langford (1996), Kennedy (1956).

9. The Prisoner's Dilemma was one of the problems devised in early exploration of game theory at the Rand Corporation after World War II. Supposedly devised by Merrill Glood and Melvin Dresher, the problem was posed in story form by Albert Tucker to explain his research to Stanford psychologists.

10. Marwell and Ames (1981).

11. The "folk theorem" of game theory (see, for example, Fudenberg and Tirole [1991], chapter 5), so called because its attribution is unclear, claims that all such strategies are Nash equilibrium in an indefinitely repeated game. We behave as we are expected to.

12. Axelrod (1984, 1997).

13. Basu (2000).

14. See Cronin (1991) for an explanation of these biological models. See Frank (1988) for a development of their economic analogues. Gintis (2000) describes both.

15. The classic statement of group selection arguments is Wynne-Edwards (1962), which helped provoke the decisive refutation by G. C. Williams (1966).

16. Titmuss (1970).

17. This kind of problem is associated with a single voice. It was equally "unhelpful" for British civil servants to warn of the possible dangers of "mad cow disease." Their cover-up does, however, seem to have been less egregious and, fortunately, the results less disastrous.

Chapter 22: Coordination

1. Kincaid (1986).
2. Levy (1989).
3. Prout (1922).
4. See Kelly (1998), Shapiro and Varian (1999).
5. Travers and Milgram (1969), 425–33. The small-world phenomenon is well illustrated at ORACLE OF BACON[w] and in Watts (1999).
6. This vacuous phrase has been adopted as policy by the European Union.
7. This similarly vacuous concept has been lauded by the OECD (1975).
8. According to estimates by Dixon (1996), 36% of expenditures under the Superfund to that date related to transactions costs rather than clearing up pollution.
9. Buchanan and Stubblebine (1962), Demsetz (1964).
10. Mnookin and Kornhauser (1979).

Chapter 23: The Knowledge Economy

1. See, for example, Shapiro and Varian (1998); also "new economy" writers such as Kelly (1998), Leadbeater (2000), and Coyle (2001).
2. Bodanis (2000), Clark (1979).
3. The Bletchley Park project, once highly secret, has now generated extensive literature—Hinsley and Stripp (1993), Enever (1994), Butters (2000)—and a film *(Enigma)*.
4. In the last years of his life, Turing was a pathbreaker in the understanding of the mathematics of spontaneous order in nonlinear dynamic systems of the kind described in chapter 10. His paper on the chemical basis of morphogenesis was published in 1952, shortly before his death. Hodges (1992).
5. Very little happened following Fleming's now famous discovery. The drug could only be useful if it could be absorbed and produced in large quantities, and Florey had difficulty securing even philanthropic funding for this research. Judson (1980).
6. Schwartz (2002), Fisher (1997), Godfrey and Sterling (2001).
7. Norman Borlaug, an American whose principal work was undertaken at the International Maize and Wheat Center in Mexico, received the Nobel Peace Price in 1970 for his contribution to the green revolution.
8. Freiberger and Swaine (2000), Kaplan (1999).
9. Lucent was floated off from AT&T in 1996 at $27 per share. The share price reached a high of $84 in the bubble, but in 2002 fell below $2.
10. Sheehan (1993).

11. Own calculations using data from NOBEL[W].
12. The vast majority of U.S. higher education institutions are state controlled, but the major research centers—such as Harvard, Yale, Princeton, Chicago, and Stanford—are private institutions that raise most of their own funding.
13. Read (1999).
14. *Guardian*, March 6, 2001.
15. See Stern et al. (2001), Ehrbar (1998).
16. In 2001, the government settled its action in return for minor concessions by Microsoft after higher courts had critized the conduct of presiding judge Jackson. A number of individual states continued to pursue the case, unsuccessfully.
17. Marshall (2002).
18. See David Hume Institute (1997) for a skeptical review of current intellectual property law.
19. Baumol (2002).

Part V: HOW IT ALL WORKS OUT

Chapter 24: Poor States Stay Poor
● ●

1. Collins & Lapierre (1975).
2. On Mahalanobis, see Yergin and Stanislaw (1998), chapter 3, and Chakravarty (1988).
3. Rostow (1953).
4. Kotkin (2001).
5. Harrod (1939), Domar (1957). See Solow (1970) for an exposition (Growth Theory).
6. And the only economist from a poor country. Lewis was, when he received his prize, vice-chancellor of the University of the West Indies, although his principal work was done in England. Amartya Sen is credited to India by the Nobel Prize Committee, but his career has been spent in Britain and the United States.
7. Lewis and Schultz (1953).
8. Although India and China are among the largest recipients of aid, because of their size the per capita figure is amongst the lowest. As an aid recipient, it is clearly an advantage to be a small country.
9. Maddison (2001).
10. Rosenstein-Rodan (1943); see also his 1961 article.
11. "It was in Cavite that I finally found a piece of unswooshed space, and I found it, oddly enough, in a Nike shoe factory." Klein (1999), 203.
12. The sad story of the Morogoro shoe factory is told in World Bank (1995).
13. World Bank (2002).
14. A moving obituary in the *Economist* (October 21, 1999) concluded, "He was a magnificent teacher: articulate, questioning, stimulating, caring. He should never have been given charge of an economy."
15. See for example, Desai (2001).

16. Life expectancy at birth: India has risen from thirty-two years at independence to sixty-three years today, partly driven by a fall in infant mortality from over 200 per 1,000 live births to below 70. Adlakha (1997), World Bank (2002).
17. Gidoomal (1997).
18. Kurtz is the central character of Joseph Conrad's masterpiece, *Heart of Darkness* (1902). Drawing on Conrad's own experience of Leopold's Congo, the book is still an extraordinary evocation of the corrupting effect of resource-based wealth. Francis Ford Coppola's remarkable *Apocalypse Now* is based on *Heart of Darkness*, and Michaela Wrong picked up the theme in her description of the Mobutu era, *In the Footsteps of Mr. Kurtz* (2000).
19. Hochschild (1999) is a shocking account of the Congo under Leopold's rule.
20. Danish architect Georg Hans Tesling constructed this estate.
21. This history is recounted in Wrong (2000).
22. *New York Times,* September 14, 1982.
23. There is currently extensive discussion of a formal bankruptcy regime for countries: Rogoff and Zettelmayer (2002).
24. Wrong (2000), 113–14.
25. Sachs and Warner (1995).
26. Maier (2000).
27. Saudi Arabia derives 35% of GDP and 85% of government revenue from oil.
28. Friedman (1999), 350.
29. Ayittey (1998).
30. A. G. Frank (1965).
31. Prebisch (1950), Singer (1950). Dependency theory is still at the heart of ECLA thinking—see ECLA[w], C. Kay (1989).
32. Though diamond-rich Botswana has been the most successful economy in sub-Saharan Africa.
33. Cardoso and Faletto (1979).
34. Norberg-Hodge (1991).
35. Diamond (1997), 352–53.
36. A long tradition in economics, though not a mainstream one, has seen demand as stimulated by supply. See Veblen (1899), chapter 16, or more recently Galbraith (1986): "He or she surrenders to the will of the purveyor of the beer, cigarettes, deterent, or political purpose."
37. Turnbull (1961, 1973).
38. B. D. Smith (1995), Flannery (1973).
39. Thompson (1968), Mokyr (1999), Hartley and Crafts (2000), Hartwell (1971).
40. HAPPINESS[w].

Chapter 25: Who Gets What?

• •

1. Weber (1930, 1947).
2. See Welch (2001), chapter 26, for a description of this process, in which the golf course played a large role.

3. In the last days of the 1990s boom, several CEOs extracted hundreds of millions of dollars from their failing companies. *Financial Times,* July 30–August 1, 2002.

4. Frank and Cook (1995) provide an entertaining exposition of this phenomenon—and its relationship to the division of labor.

5. Afterward, the successful will wish they had not agreed to this—this is why legal disputes between pop stars and their managers are almost routine.

6. This theory is due to Shubik (1959) and Scarf (1962).

7. The Thurn and Taxis family remains one of the richest in Europe as a result of the communications monopoly it enjoyed in the Hapsburg Empire for three centuries. THURN[W].

8. Friedman (1962), 142.

9. The ratio of the market value of companies to the value of their tangible assets rose to unprecedented levels during the bubble.

10. Bruck (1989).

11. Chrystal (1991). In December 1997, Michael Eisner of Disney exercised options worth $60 million. Conyon and Murphy (2000).

12. In 2001 the top ten in the *Forbes* list were Gates, Allen, and Ballmer of Microsoft, Buffett, Larry Ellison of Oracle, and five members of the Walton family.

13. Lowenstein (1995).

14. BUFFETT[W].

15. Ortega (1999) provides a more skeptical account.

16. In 2000, action in the English courts and by his brother, the sultan, finally brought Jefri's activities to a halt (*Newsweek,* December 10, 2000).

17. Lowenstein (1995), 4.

18. *Washington Post,* December 4, 1986.

Chapter 26: Places
● ●

1. In 2002, the European Commission proposed substantial reductions and redirection of agricultural support, but these seem likely to be defeated by opposition, particularly from France.

2. Graham (1998).

3. Freeland (2000), S. E. Cohen (2000).

Chapter 27: The American Business Model
● ●

1. For modernism and postmodernism in architecture, see Jencks (1986).

2. Jacobs (1961) developed these arguments with great literary skill; Certeau (1984) adopts a similar approach on a wider canvas.

3. Though less surprising that those involved in business and economics should not be receptive to postmodernism. Among the postmodernists, comment on busi-

ness and economic issues rarely rises above tired Marxist clichés—see, for example, the turgid works of Jameson (1992). The scientific pretensions of postmodernism were deliciously parodied by Sokal, who succeeded in publishing a crude parody in the journal *Cultural Studies*. Sokal and Bricmont (1998). None of this precludes the possibility that postmodernist truths about business and economics exist.

4. Lyotard (1992).
5. Milton Friedman's *Capitalism and Freedom* (1962) is probably the best description of the American business model within a framework of social and political philosophy. For a less restrained version, see Gilder (1984).
6. Attitudes to antitrust litigation against Microsoft are a litmus test of this latter distinction.
7. See for example Meade (1964), Turner (2002) for an exposition of redistributive market liberalism.
8. Dunlap (1996), xii.
9. Thurow (1999), 15.
10. Rand (1990a, 1990b).
11. See, for example OECD (2001), and for a critique, Henderson (2001).
12. Wilson's observation was made in testimony to the Senate Armed Services Committee on his nomination as secretary for defense in the Eisenhower administration (quoted in *New York Times*, February 24, 1953). It is often reproduced as "what's good for General Motors is good for America," a significantly different statement.
13. Goethe (quoted in Manser [1987], 45).
14. *New York Times*, September 13, 1970. See also M. Friedman (1962), chap. 8.
15. Attributed to Ian Gauld, taxonomist at the British Museum, in Vitullo-Martin and Moskin (1994).
16. Walzer (1981).
17. Crossen (2001), 213.
18. Wrong (2000), 20.
19. Gates (1995, 1999).
20. Trump (1987), 1.
21. Lowenstein (1995), 20.
22. M. Lewis (1989), 88.
23. M. Friedman (1962), 26–27.
24. Quoted in Freeland (2000), 67–68.
25. "I find it difficult to justify either accepting or rejecting [the capitalist ethic] or to justify any alternative principle. I am led to the view that it cannot in and of itself be regarded as an ethical principle; that it must be regarded as instrumental or a corollary of some other principle such as freedom." Friedman (1962), 165–66.
26. Turnbull (1973).
27. Tocqueville (1835).

Chapter 28: The Future of Economics

● ●

1. See Lazear (2000) on economic imperialism.
2. Friedman (1953).
3. Hausman (1992), 162.
4. Hands, D.W. (2001) is an excellent introduction to methodological issues in economics.
5. Nagel (1963).
6. See, primarily, Quine (1951, 1969).
7. Stigler, 1981.
8. Sen, 1987.
9. Mankiw, 2004, Akerlof, 2001.
10. Becker, 1993.
11. The term is due to Suppe (1977).
12. Hall (2001).
13. Jay (2000), xi–xii.
14. Kuhn, 1961, Rorty, 1979.
15. See OECD (1993) for a skeptical, informed review of the performance of economic forecasters..
16. See the National Audit Office (2001) for comment on the elaborate spreadsheet models built to justify public-private partnerships..
17. From "Travels of Praiseworthy Men" (1658) by J.A. Suarez Miranda in Jorge Luis Borges's "Of Exactitude in Science" in *A Universal History of Infamy* (1972).
18. For discussions of models in similar vein by major contemporary economists see Akerlof (1984), Krugman (1995).
19. Geertz, 1973, chap. 1.
20. Boyle (2000), xi
21. Scherer, 1970.
22. Porter (1980, 1985) set out the industrial organization theory of the Harvard economics department of the 1970s, almost without attribution, in terms comprehensible to business people.
23. Mankiw (2002), v.
24. See Taleb (2001) for a discussion of these issues.
25. AEA Report on the status of women in the economics profession, 2003.
26. A collection of these articles is in Krugman (2003).
27. See Fulbrook (2003) for an account of the post autistic economic movement, or POST AUTISTIC^w.
28. Quoted by Mankiw (2004), 32.

Chapter 29:The Future of Capitalism

••

1. Collins and Porras (1994).
2. Despite imaginative proposals to extend their scope, as in Shiller (2003).
3. Hensler et al. (2001).
4. "The new equipment is so boring . . . that children make up dangerous games, like crashing into the equipment with their bicycles." Howard (2001), 4.
5. This was probably decisive in ending individual underwriting by names at Lloyd's.
6. I have written books on the tax and benefit system (Dilnot, Kay, and Morris [1984]; Kay and King [1990]), and while I don't now hold all the views I did then, I still urge the reader to read (or better still buy) them.
7. See chapter 7, note 14.
8. See Easterly (2001) for a discussion of some of the issues.

{bibliography} ● ● ● ● ● ● ● ● ● ● ● ● ● ● ● ● ●

Adams, J. 1995. *Risk*. London: UCL Press.

Akerlof, G. A. 1970. "The Market for Lemons: Quality Uncertainty and the Market Mechanism." *Quarterly Journal of Economics* 84 (August): 488–500.

———. 1984. *An Economic Theorist's Book of Tales*. Cambridge: Cambridge University Press.

———. 2001. *Behavioural Macroeconomics and Macroeconomic Behaviour*. Nobel Prize Lecture, Stockholm.

Albert, M. 1990. *Capitalisme contre capitalisme*. Paris: Seuil; trans. P. Haviland, as *Capitalism vs. Capitalism*. New York: Four Walls Eight Windows, 1993.

Alchian, A. A. 1950. "Uncertainty, Evolution and Economic Theory." *Journal of Political Economy* 58: 211–21.

Allais, M. 1953. "Le comportement de l'homme rationnel devant le risque: critique des postulants et axioms de l'école américaine" *Econometrica* 21 (4) (October): 503–46.

Amsden, A. H. 1989. *Asia's Next Giant: South Korea and Late Industrialization*. New York and Oxford: Oxford University Press.

Aristotle. 1984. *Politics*. Ed. J. Barnes. Princeton: Princeton University Press.

Arrow, K. J. 1950. "A Difficulty in the Concept of Social Welfare." *Journal of Political Economy* 58: 328–46.

———. 1951a. *Social Choice and Individual Values*. New York: Wiley.

———. 1951b. *An Extension of the Basic Theorems of Classical Welfare Economics*. Berkeley: University of California.

———. 1971. *Essays in the Theory of Risk-Bearing*. Amsterdam and London: North-Holland.

Arrow, K. J., and G. Debreu. 1954. "Existence of an Equilibrium for a Competitive Economy." *Econometrica* 22 (3) (July): 265–90.

Arrow, K. J., and F. H. Hahn. 1971. *General Competitive Analysis*. San Francisco: Holden-Day.

Arthur, W. B. 1989. "Competing Technologies, Increasing Returns, and Lock-In by Historical Events." *Economic Journal* 99 (March): 116–131.

Atkinson, A. B. 1970. "On the Measurement of Inequality." *Journal of Economic Theory* 2: 244–63.

———. 1983. *The Economics of Inequality.* Oxford: Oxford University Press.

Augar, P. 2000. *The Death of Gentlemanly Capitalism: The Rise and Fall of London's Investment Banks.* Harmondsworth: Penguin Books.

Aumann, R. J. 1964. "Markets with a Continuum of Traders." *Econometrica* 32: 39–50.

Axelrod, R. 1984. *The Evolution of Cooperation.* New York: Basic Books.

———. *The Complexity of Cooperation: Agent-Based Models of Competition and Collaboration.* Princeton: Princeton University Press.

Ayittey, G. B. N. 1998. *Africa in Chaos.* New York: St. Martin's Press.

Ball, D. B. 1991. *Financial Failure and Confederate Defeat.* Urbana: University of Illinois Press.

Barth, J. R. 1991. *The Great Savings and Loan Debacle.* Washington D.C.: American Enterprise Institute Press.

Barzel, Y. 1997. *Economic Analysis of Property Rights.* 2nd ed. Cambridge: Cambridge University Press.

Bass, T. A. 1999. *The Predictors.* London: Allen Lane.

Basu, K. 2000. *Prelude to Political Economy: A Study of the Social and Political Foundations of Economics.* Oxford: Oxford University Press.

Bathurst, B. 1999. *The Lighthouse Stevensons.* New York: HarperCollins.

Bator, F. M. 1958. "The Anatomy of Market Failure." *Quarterly Journal of Economics* 72 (3) (August): 351–79.

Baumol, W. J. 2002. *The Free-Market Innovation Machine: Analyzing the Growth Miracle of Capitalism.* Princeton and Oxford: Princeton University Press.

Becker, G. S. 1962. "Irrational Behavior and Economic Theory." *Journal of Political Economy* 70: 1–13.

———. 1968. "Crime and Punishment: An Economic Approach." *Journal of Political Economy* 76 (2) (March-April): 169–217.

———. 1973. "A Theory of Marriage: Part I." *Journal of Political Economy* 81 (4) (July-August): 813–46.

———. 1974. "A Theory of Marriage: Part II." *Journal of Political Economy* 82 (2) (March-April): S11–S26.

———. 1981. *A Treatise on the Family.* Cambridge, Mass.: Harvard University Press.

———. 1993. "The Economic Way of Looking at Behavior (Nobel Lecture)." *Journal of Political Economy* 101 (3) (June): 385–409.

Belsky, G., and T. Gilovich. 2000. *Why Smart People Make Big Money Mistakes.* New York: Fireside.

Benartzi, S., and R. H. Thaler. 1995. "Myopic Loss Aversion and the Equity Premium." *Quarterly Journal of Economics,* February, 73–92.

Berlin, I. 2000. *The Power of Ideas.* Ed. H. Hardy. Princeton: Princeton University Press.

Bernstein, P. L. 1996. *Against the Gods: The Remarkable Story of Risk.* New York and Chichester: John Wiley and Sons, Inc.

Berry, C. J. 1997. *Social Theory of the Scottish Enlightenment.* Edinburgh: Edinburgh University Press.

Bertram, J. G. 1865. *Harvest of the Sea*. London: John Murray.

Bethell, L., ed. 1993. *Argentina since Independence*. Cambridge: Cambridge University Press.

Binmore, K. G. 1994. *Game Theory and the Social Contract*. Cambridge, Mass.: MIT Press.

———. 1998. *Just Playing*. London and Cambridge, Mass.: MIT Press.

Black, F., and M. Scholes. 1973. "The Pricing of Options and Corporate Liabilities." *Journal of Political Economy* 81 (May-June): 637–59.

Blackmore, S. 1999. *The Meme Machine*. Oxford: Oxford University Press.

Blinder, A. S. 1974. "The Economics of Brushing Teeth." *Journal of Political Economy* 82 (July-August): 887–91.

Bodanis, D. 2000. *E = Mc²: A Biography of the World's Most Famous Equation*. London: Macmillan.

Borgers, T., and C. Dustmann. 2001. "Strange Bids." *CEPR Discussion Paper* 3072 (November).

Borges, J. L. 1972 "Of Exactitude in Science." In his *A Universal History of Infamy*. Trans. N. T. di Giovanni. New York: Dutton.

Boyle, D. 2000. *The Tyranny of Numbers: Why Counting Can't Make Us Happy*. London: HarperCollins.

Brash, D. T. 1996. *New Zealand's Remarkable Reforms: 5th Annual Hayek Memorial Lecture*. London: Institute of Economic Affairs.

Brealey, R. A., and S. C. Myers. 1981–99. *Principles of Corporate Finance*. 6 eds, New York and London: McGraw-Hill.

Breiter, H. C. et al. 2001. "Functional Imaging of Neural Responses to Expectancy and Experience of Monetary Gains and Losses." *Neuron* 30 (May): 619–39.

Brittan, S. 1971. *Steering the Economy*. Harmondsworth, Penguin.

———. 1996. *Capitalism with a Human Face*. London: Fontana Press.

Broadie, A., ed. 1997. *The Scottish Enlightenment: An Anthology*. Edinburgh: Canongate.

Bruck, C. 1989. *The Predators' Ball: The Inside Story of Drexel Burnham and the Rise of the Junk Bond Raiders*. New York: Penguin.

Brunekreeft, G. 1997. *Coordination and Competition in the Electricity Pool of England and Wales*. Baden-Baden: Nomos-Verlag.

Buchan, J. 1997. *Frozen Desire: An Enquiry into the Meaning of Money*. London: Picador.

Buchanan, J., and G. Tulloch. 1962. *The Calculus of Consent*. Ann Arbor: University of Michigan Press.

Buchanan, J. M., and W. C. Stubblebine. 1962. "Externality." *Economica* 29: 371–84.

Buchanan, J. M., and R. D. Tollison, eds. 1972. *Theory of Public Choice: Political Applications of Economics*. Ann Arbor: University of Michigan Press.

———. 1984. *Theory of Public Choice: II*. Ann Arbor: University of Michigan Press.

Buchet, M. 1993. *La Colombe d'Or: St Paul de Vence*. Paris: Editions Assouline.

Bucholz, T. 1999. *New Ideas from Dead Economists*. New York: Plume.

Bulow, J., and P. Klemperer. 2002. "Prices and the Winner's Curse." *Rand Journal of Economics* 33 (1) (spring): 1–21.

Bunday, B. D. 1996. *An Introduction to Queuing Theory*. New York: Halsted Press.

Burgess, S., and H. Rees. 1996. "Job Tenure in Britain, 1975–1992." *Economic Journal* 106: 334–44.

Burn, D. 1978. *Nuclear Power and the Energy Crisis: Politics and the Atomic Industry.* London: Macmillan Press.

Butters, L. 2000. *Bletchley Park: Home of Station X.* Andover, Pitkin Unichrome.

Buzo, A. 1999. *The Guerrilla Dynasty: Politics and Leadership in North Korea.* Boulder, Colo.: Westview Press.

Calavita, K. H., N. Pontell, and R. H. Tillman. 1997. *Big Money Game: Fraud and Politics in the Savings and Loan Crisis.* Berkeley, Calif., and London: University of California Press.

Cannan, E. 1927. *An Economist's Protest.* London: P. S. King.

Capen, E., R. Clapp, and N. Campbell. 1971. "Competitive Bidding in High-Risk Situations." *Journal of Petroleum Technology* 23 (1): 641–53.

Cardoso, F. H., and E. Faletto. 1979. *Dependency and Development in Latin America.* Trans. M. M. Urquidi. Berkeley: University of California Press.

Carhart, M. M. 1997. "On Persistence in Mutual Fund Performance." *Journal of Finance* 52 (1) (March): 57–82.

Caro, R. 1974. *The Power Broker.* New York: Knopf.

Carstens, P. 2001. *In the Company of Diamonds: De Beers, Kleinzee, and the Control of a Town.* Athens, Ohio: Ohio University Press.

Cassidy, J. 2002. *Dot.Con: The Greatest Story Ever Sold.* New York: HarperCollins.

Castles, I. 1998. "The Mismeasurement of Nations: A Review Essay on the Human Development Report 1998." *Population and Development Review* 24 (4) (December): 831–45.

Certeau, M. de. 1984. *The Practice of Everyday Life.* Berkeley: University of California Press.

Ceruzzi, P. E. 1998. *A History of Modern Computing.* Cambridge, Mass., and London: MIT Press.

Chakravarty, S. 1988. "Mahlanobis, P. C." In J. Eatwell, M. Milgate, and P. Newman, eds., *The New Palgrave: A Dictionary of Economics.* London: Palgrave Macmillan.

Chandler, A. D., Jr. 1963. *Strategy and Structure: Chapters in the History of the Industrial Enterprise.* Cambridge, Mass.: MIT Press.

Chang, J. 1992. *Wild Swans: Three Daughters of China.* New York: Anchor Books.

Chernow, R. 1998. *Titan: The Life of John D. Rockefeller.* New York: Random House.

Chrystal, G. 1991. *In Search of Excess.* New York: Norton.

Clark A. E., and A. J. Oswald. 2002. "A Simple Statistical Method for Measuring How Life Events Affect Happiness." *Working Paper, University of Warwick.*

Clark, R. W. 1971. *Einstein: The Life and Times.* New York: World Publishing Co.

Cohen, S. F. 2000. *Failed Crusade: America and the Tragedy of Post-Communist Russia.* New York: W. W. Norton.

Cohen, S. M. 1982. "For General Electric, Planning Crowned with Success," *Planning Review,* March.

Collins, J. C., and J. I. Porras. 1994. *Built to Last: Successful Habits of Visionary Companies.* New York: HarperBusiness.

Collins, L., and D. Lapierre. 1975. *Freedom at Midnight*. London: Collins.

Condorcet, Marquis de. 1785. *Essai sur l'application de l'analyse à la probabilité des décisions rendues à la pluralité des vois*. Paris.

Conrad, J. 1902. *Heart of Darkness*. Ed. Nicolas Tredell. New York: Columbia Press, 1999.

Conyon, M. J., and K. J. Murphy. 2000. "The Prince and the Pauper." *Economic Journal* 110 (467): 640–71.

Coyle, D. 2001. *Paradoxes of Prosperity: Why the New Capitalism Benefits All*. New York and London: Texere.

Crabtree, J., G. Duffy, and J. Pearce, eds. 1987. *The Great Tin Crash*. London: Latin America Bureau.

Cronin, H. 1991. *The Ant and the Peacock*. Cambridge and New York: Press Syndicate of the University of Cambridge.

Crosland, C. A. R. 1956. *The Future of Socialism*. London: Jonathan Cape.

Crossen, C. 2001. *The Rich and How They Got That Way*. New York: Crown Business.

Csikszentmihalyi, M. 1990. *Flow: The Psychology of Happiness*. London: Rider.

Currie, W. 1994. "The Strategic Management of a Large Scale IT Project in the Financial Services Sector." *New Technology, Work and Employment* 9 (1): 19–29.

Dalziel, P., and R.. Lattimore. 1999. *The New Zealand Macroeconomy: A Briefing on the Reforms*. 3rd ed. Greenlane, New Zealand, and Oxford: Oxford University Press.

Darwin, C. R. 1859. *On the Origin of Species by Means of Natural Selection*. Ed. G. Beer. Oxford: Oxford University Press. 1996.

David, P. A. 1985. "Clio and the Economics of QWERTY." *American Economic Review* 75 (2): 332–37.

David Hume Institute. 1997. *Innovation, Incentive and Reward*. Edinburgh: Edinburgh University Press.

Davidson, R. J. 2000. "Affective Style, Psychopathology and Resilience." *American Psychologist*. November, 1196–1214.

Davies, K. 2001. *The Sequence: Inside the Race for the Human Genome*. London: Weidenfeld & Nicolson.

Dawkins, R. 1989. *The Selfish Gene*. New ed. Oxford: Oxford University Press.

———. 1991. *The Blind Watchmaker*. New ed. London: Penguin Books.

Debreu, G. 1959. *Theory of Value: An Axiomatic Analysis of Economic Equilibrium*. New Haven: Yale University Press.

Del Mar, A. 1895. *History of Monetary Systems*. London: Effingham Wilson.

Demsetz, H. 1964. "The Exchange and Enforcement of Property Rights." *Journal of Law and Economics*, October, 11–26.

———. 1967. "Towards a Theory of Property Rights." *American Economic Review* 57 (2): 347–59.

Department of Energy. 1976. *The Structure of the Electricity Supply Industry in England and Wales: Report of the Committee of Inquiry*. Cmnd. 6388. London: HMSO.

Desai, A. V. 2001. "The Economics and Politics of Transition to an Open Market Economy." *Prime Ministers Advisory Council Report, Technical Paper*, 155.

Diamond, J. M. 1997. *Guns, Germs and Steel: The Fates of Human Societies*. London: Jonathan Cape.

Dickens, A. G. 1977. *The Age of Humanism and Reformation: Europe in the Fourteenth, Fifteenth and Sixteenth Centuries.* Englewood Cliffs, N.J., and London: Prentice-Hall.

Dilnot, A. W., J. A. Kay, and C. N. Morris. 1984. *The Reform of Social Security.* Oxford: Clarendon Press.

Dimson, E., P. Marsh, and M. Staunton. 2002. *Triumph of the Optimists: 101 Years of Global Investment Returns.* Princeton: Princeton University Press.

Dixit, A. K., and B. J. Nalebuff. 1991. *Thinking Strategically.* New York: W. W. Norton and Co., Inc.

Dixon, L. S. 1996. *Fixing Superfund.* Santa Monica, Calif.: Rand Institute for Civil Justice.

Domar, E. D. 1957. *Essays in the Theory of Economic Growth.* New York: Oxford University Press.

Douglas, M., and A. Wildavsky. 1982. *Risk and Culture: An Essay on the Selection of Technical and Environmental Dangers.* Berkeley and London: University of California Press.

Douglas, R., R. Richardson, and S. Robson. 2002. *Spending Without Reform.* London: Reform.

Downs, A. 1957. *An Economic Analysis of Democracy.* New York: Harper and Row.

Dunlap, A. J., with B. Andelman. 1996. *Mean Business: How I Save Bad Companies and Make Good Companies Great.* New York: Fireside.

Durham, W. H. 1991. *Coevolution: Genes, Culture and Human Diversity.* Stanford, Calif.: Stanford University Press.

Dworkin, R. 1977. *Taking Rights Seriously.* London: Duckworth.

———. 1984. "Rights as Trumps." In J. Waldron, ed., *Theories of Rights.* Oxford: Clarendon, 153–67.

Easterlin, R. 1974. "Does Economic Growth Improve the Human Lot?" In P. A. David and W. B. Melvin, eds., *Nations and Households and Economic Growth.* Palo Alto, Calif.: Stanford University Press.

Easterly, W. 2001. *The Elusive Quest for Growth: Economist's Adventures and Misadventures in the Tropics.* Cambridge, Mass., and London: MIT Press.

Easton, B. 1994. "Economic and Other Ideas Behind the New Zealand Reforms." *Oxford Review of Economic Policy* 10 (3): 78–94.

Eatwell, J., M. Milgate, and P. Newman, P. eds. 1998. *The New Palgrave: A Dictionary of Economics.* London: Palgrave Macmillan.

Economist Intelligence Unit. 2002. *Country Profile: North Korea 2002/2003.* London: Economist Intelligence Unit.

"Editions 1999." 1999. *Un ami de Cézanne et van Gogh: le docteur Gachet.* Paris: Editions de la Réunion des Musées Nationaux.

Ehrbar, A. 1998. *EVA: The Real Key to Creating Wealth.* New York: John Wiley and Sons.

Eichengreen, B., C. Wyplosz, and J. Tobin. 1995. "Two Cases for Sand in the Wheels of International Finance." *Economic Journal* 105 (January): 162–72.

Enever, T. 1994. *Britain's Best Kept Secret: Ultra's Base at Bletchley Park.* Stroud: Alan Sutton.

Engerman, S. L., and R. Z. Zallman. 1986. *Measuring the Transaction Sector.* NBER Studies in Income and Wealth. Chicago: University of Chicago Press.

Etcoff, N. L. 1994. "Beauty and the Beholder." *Nature* 368 (March 17).

Evans, L., A. Grimes, B. Wilkinson, and D. Teece. 1996. "Economic Reform in New Zealand, 1984–95: The Pursuit of Efficiency." *Journal of Economic Literature* 34 (4) (December): 1856–902.

Fama, E. F., and K. R. French. 2001. "Disappearing Dividends." *Journal of Financial Economics* 60: 3–43.

Fearon, P., and A. Moran. 1999. *Privatising Victoria's Electricity Distribution*. Melbourne: Institute of Public Affairs.

Ferguson, A. 1767. *An Essay on the History of Civil Society*. Ed. Fania Oz-Salzberger, New York: Cambridge University Press. 1996.

Ferguson, N. 2001. *The Cash Nexus: Money and Power in the Modern World, 1700–2000*. London: Allen Lane, Penguin Press.

Firebaugh, G. 1999. "Empirics of World Income Inequality." *American Journal of Sociology* 104 (May): 1597–630.

Fisher, D. E. 1997. *Tube: The Invention of Television*. Fort Washington, Pa.: Harvest Books.

Fisher, D. H. 1989. *Albion's Seed*. New York: Oxford University Press.

Flannery, K. 1973. "The Origins of Agriculture." *Annual Reviews of Anthropology* 2: 271–310.

Flatow, I. 1992. *They All Laughed—from Lightbulbs to Lasers: The Fascinating Stories Behind the Great Inventions That Have Changed Our Lives*. New York: HarperCollins.

Forster, E. M. 1982. *Alexandria: A History and a Guide*. With an introduction by L. Durrell. New ed. London: Michael Haag.

Frank, A. G. 1969. *Latin America: Underdevelopment or Revolution: Essays on the Development of Underdevelopment and the Immediate Enemy*. New York and London: Monthly Review Press.

Frank, R. H. 1985. *Choosing the Right Pond*. New York: Oxford University Press.

———. 1988. *Passions within Reason: The Strategic Role of the Emotions*. New York: Norton.

Frank, R. H., and P. J. Cook. 1995. *The Winner-Take-All Society*. New York: Free Press.

Fraser, P. M. 1984. *Ptolemaic Alexandria*. Oxford: Clarendon Press.

Freedland, J. 1998. *Bring Home the Revolution: How Britain Can Live the American Dream*. London: Fourth Estate.

Freedom House. 2001. *Freedom in the World: The Annual Survey of Political Rights and Civil Liberties*. New York: Freedom.

———. 2002. *Freedom in the World: The Annual Survey of Political Rights and Civil Liberties*. New York: Freedom.

Freeland, C. 2000. *Sale of the Century: The Inside Story of the Second Russian Revolution*. New York: Times Books.

Freiberger, P., and M. Swaine. 2000. *Fire in the Valley: The Making of the Personal Computer*. New York: McGraw-Hill.

Friedman, M. 1953. "The Methodology of Positive Economics." In *Essays in Positive Economics*. Cambridge and Chicago: Chicago University Press and Cambridge University Press.

Friedman, M., with R. D. Friedman. 1962. *Capitalism and Freedom*. Chicago and London: University of Chicago Press.

Friedman, T. 1999. *The Lexus and the Olive Tree*. New York: Anchor Books.

Fry, M., ed. 1992. *Adam Smith's Legacy*. New York: Routledge.

Fudenberg, D., and J. Tirole. 1991. *Game Theory*. Cambridge, Mass.: MIT Press.

Fukuyama, F. 1989. "The End of History." *The National Interest,* summer, 3–18.

———. 1992. *The End of History and the Last Man*. London: Hamish Hamilton.

Fulbrook, E. ed. 2003. *The Crisis in Economics*. London: Routledge. .

Furbotn, E. G., and S. Pejovich. 1972. "Property Rights and Economic Theory: A Survey of Recent Literature." *Journal of Economic Literature*. 10 (4) (December): 1137–62.

Gachet, P., with comments by A. Mothe. 1994. *Les 70 jours de van Gogh à Auvers*. Saint-Ouen-L'Aumône: Éditions du Valhermeil.

Galbraith, J. K. 1955. *The Great Crash 1929*. Boston: Houghton Mifflin.

———. 1958. *The Affluent Society*. Boston: Houghton Mifflin.

———. 1967.*The New Industrial State*. Boston: Houghton Mifflin.

———. 1986. *The Anatomy of Power*. London: Hamish Hamilton.

Gates, B., with N. Myhrvold and P. Rinearson. 1995. *The Road Ahead*. New York: Viking.

Gates, B., with C. Hemingway. 1999. *Business @ the Speed of Thought: Using a Digital Nervous System*. New York: Warner Books.

Geertz, C. 1973. *The Interpretation of Cultures*. New York: Basic Books.

Gidoomal, R. 1997. *The UK Maharajas: Inside the South Asian Success Story*. London: Nicholas Brealey.

Gigerenzer, G., and R. Selten. eds. 2001. *Bounded Rationality: The Adaptive Toolbox*. Cambridge, Mass., and London: MIT Press.

Gigerenzer, G., et al. 1999. *Simple Heuristics That Make Us Smart*. New York: Oxford University Press.

Gilder, G. F. 1984. *The Spirit of Enterprise*. New York: Simon and Schuster.

Gintis, H. 2000. *Game Theory Evolving: A Problem-Centered Introduction to Modeling Strategic Interaction*. Princeton: Princeton University Press.

Gladwell, M. 2000. *The Tipping Point: How Little Things Can Make a Big Difference*. Boston: Little, Brown.

Gleick, J. 1988. *Chaos: Making a New Science*. New York: Penguin.

Godfrey, D. G., and C. H. Sterling. 2001. *Philo T. Farnsworth: The Father of Television*. Salt Lake City: University of Utah Press.

Goethe, J. W. von. 1809. *Elective Affinities*. Translated by and with an introduction by R. J. Hollingdale. London: Penguin, 1971.

Goodhart, C. 1984. *Monetary Theory and Practice: The UK Experience*. London: Macmillan.

Goold, M., and A. Campbell. 1987. *Strategies and Styles: The Role of the Center in Managing Diversified Corporations*. Oxford: Basil Blackwell.

Gottschalk, P., and T. M. Smeeding. 1997. "Cross-National Comparisons of Earnings and Income Inequality." *Journal of Economic Literature* 35 (June): 633–87.

Graham, L. R. 1998. *What Have We Learned about Science and Technology from the Russian Experience?* Palo Alto Calif.: Stanford University Press, 38–40.

Green, R. J. 1995. "The Cost of Nuclear Power Compared with Alternatives to the Magnox Program." *Oxford Economic Papers* 47: 513–24.

Greenfield, S. A. 2000. *The Private Life of the Brain*. London: Allen Lane, Penguin.

Greenspan, A. 1963. "The Assault on Integrity." In A. Rand. *Capitalism: The Unknown Ideal*. New York: Signet, 1967.

Gregory, T. 1962. *Ernest Oppenheimer and the Economic Development of Southern Africa*. Cape Town: Oxford University Press.

Grigg, D. 1992. *The Transformation of Agriculture in the West*. Oxford: Basil Blackwell.

Groves, T., and J. O. Ledyard. 1977. "Optimal Allocation of Public Goods: A Solution to the Free Rider Problem." *Econometrica* 45: 783–809.

———. 1980. "The Existence of Efficient and Inventive Compatible Equilibria with Public Goods. *Econometrica* 48.

Haigh, J. 1999. *Taking Chances: Winning with Probability*. Oxford: Oxford University Press.

Hair, P. E. H. 1971. "Deaths from Violence in Britain: A Tentative Survey." *Population Studies* 25 (1): 5–24.

Halberstam, D. 1987. *The Reckoning*. New York: Morrow.

———. 1992. *The Best and the Brightest*. New York: Fawcett.

Hall, R. E. 2001. "The stock market and capital accumulation." *American Economic Review* 91 (5): 1185–1202. .

Hamermesh, D. S., and N. M. Soss. 1974. "An Economic Theory of Suicide." *Journal of Political Economy* 82(1) (January-February): 83–98.

Hamilton, W. O. 1964. "The Genetical Evolution of Social Behavior." *Journal of Theoretical Biology* 7: 1–52.

Hands, D. W. 2001. *Reflection without Rules*. Cambridge: Cambridge University Press.

Hannah, L. 1976. *The Rise of the Corporate Economy*. London: Methuen.

———. 1982. *Engineers, Managers and Politicians: The First Fifteen Years of Nationalized Electricity Supply in Britain*. London: Macmillan.

Hardy, G. H., J. E. Littlewood, and G. Polya. 1934. *Inequalities*. Cambridge: Cambridge University Press.

Harkness, S., and S. Machin. 1999. *Graduate Earnings in Britain, 1974–1995*. DfEE Research Report 95. London: Department for Education and Employment.

Harrison, L. E., and S. P. Huntington, eds. 2000. *Culture Matters*. New York: Basic Books.

Harrod, R. 1939. "An Essay in Dynamic Theory." *Economic Journal* 49 (193): 14–33.

Hartley, K., and N. Crafts. 2000. "Simulating the Two Views of the British Industrial Revolution." *Journal of Economic History* 60 (3) (September): 819–41.

Hartwell, R. M. 1971. *The Industrial Revolution and Economic Growth*. London: Methuen.

Hausman, D. M. 1992. *The Inexact and Separate Science of Economics*. Cambridge: Cambridge University Press.

Havel, V. 1985. *The Power of the Powerless: Citizens against the State in Central-Eastern Europe*. London: Hutchinson.

Havermesh, R. B. 1986. *Making Strategy Work*. New York: Wiley.

Hay, K., and P. Moore. 1998. *The Caterpillar Doesn't Know: How Personal Change is Creating Organizational Change*. New York: Free Press.

Hazledine, T. 1998. *Taking New Zealand Seriously: The Economics of Decency*. Auckland, New Zealand: HarperCollins New Zealand Ltd.

Henderson, D. 1977. "Two British Errors: Their Probable Size and Some Possible Reasons." *Oxford Economic Papers* 29 (2): 159–205.

———. 1986. *Innocence and Design: The Influence of Economic Ideas on Policy.* Oxford: Blackwell.

———. 2000. "False Perspective: The UNDP View of the World." *World Economics* 1 (1) (January-March).

———. 2001. "Misguided Virtue: False Notions of Corporate Social Responsibility." *Hobart Paper* 142. London: Institute of Economic Affairs.

Henney, A. 1988. *The Economic Failure of Nuclear Power in Britain.* London: Greenpeace.

Hensler, D. S. Carrol, M. White, and J. Cross. 2001. *Asbestos Litigation.* Santa Monica Calif.: U.S. Rand Institute for Civil Justice.

Heston, A., and R. Summers. 1991. "The Penn World Table (Mark 5): An Expanded Set of International Comparisons, 1950–1988." *Quarterly Journal of Economics* 106 (2) (May): 327–68.

Hicks, J. R. 1939. *Value and Capital: An Inquiry into Some Fundamental Principles of Economic Theory.* Revised ed. Oxford: Clarendon Press. 1946.

Hiltzik, M. A. 1999. *Dealers of Lightning: Xerox Parc and the Dawn of the Computer Age.* New York: HarperBusiness.

Hinsley, F. H., and A. Stripp, eds. 1993. *Codebreakers: The Inside Story of Bletchley Park.* Oxford: Oxford University Press.

Hirsch, F. 1976. *Social Limits to Growth.* Cambridge, Mass.: Harvard University Press.

Hirschman, A. O. 1970. *Exit, Voice, and Loyalty: Responses to Decline in Firms, Organizations, and States.* Cambridge, Mass.: Harvard University Press.

Hochschild, A. 1999. *King Leopold's Ghost: A Story of Greed, Terror and Heroism in Colonial Africa.* Boston: Houghton Mifflin.

Hodges, A. 1992. *Alan Turing: The Enigma.* New York: Simon and Schuster.

Hoffman, A. 2000. "Standardized Capital Stock Estimates in Latin America: A 1950–94 Update." *Cambridge Journal of Economics* 24: 45–86.

Hosking, G. 1992. *A History of the Soviet Union.* London: Fontana.

Howard, P. K. 2001. *The Lost Art of Drawing the Line.* New York: Random House.

Hume, D. 1779. *Dialogues Concerning Natural Religion.* London.

Hutton, W. 2002. *The World We're In.* London: Little, Brown.

Ichbiah, D., and S. L. Knepper. 1991. *The Making of Microsoft: How Bill Gates and His Team Created the World's Most Successful Software Company.* Rocklin, Calif.: Prima Publications.

IMD. 2002. *The World Competitiveness Report.* Lausanne: IMD.

Inglehart, R., and W. E. Baker. 2000. "Economic Levels of 65 Societies, Superimposed on Two Dimensions of Cross-Cultural Variation." *American Sociological Review* 65 (February): 19–51.

Inglehart, R., M. Basañez, A. Moreno, and M. Moreno. 1998. *Human Values and Beliefs: A Cross-Cultural Sourcebook: Political, Religious, Sexual, and Economic Norms in 43 Societies.* Ann Arbor: University of Michigan Press.

Jacobs, J. 1961. *The Death and Life of Great American Cities.* New York: Random House.

James, K. R. 2000. "The Price of Retail Investing in the UK. *FSA Occasional Paper* 6 (February).

Jameson, F. 1992. *Postmodernism: Or the Cultural Logic of Late Capitalism*. London: Verso Books.

Jasny, N. 1965. *Khrushchev's Crop Policy*. Glasgow: George Outram and Co.

Jay, P. 2000. *Road to Riches or the Wealth of Man*. London: Weidenfeld and Nicolson.

Jeffries, I. 2001. *Economies in Transition: A Guide to China, Cuba, Mongolia, North Korea and Vietnam at the Turn of the Twenty-First Century*. New York: Routledge.

Jencks, C. 1986. *What Is Post Modernism?*. New York: St. Martin's Press.

Jennings, A., and C. Sambrook. 2000. *The Great Olympic Swindle*. New York: Simon and Schuster.

Jensen, M. 1978. "Some Anomalous Evidence Regarding Market Efficiency." *Journal of Financial Economics* 6:. 95–101.

Johnson, S. 2001. *Emergence: The Connected Lives of Ants, Brains, Cities and Software*. New York: Scribner.

Jones-Lee, M. W. 1976. *The Value of Life: An Economic Analysis*. London: Martin Robertson.

Josephson, P. R. 1995. "'Projects of the Century' in Soviet History: Large-Scale Technologies from Lenin to Gorbachev." *Technology and Culture* 36 (3): 519–59.

Judson, H. F. 1980. *The Search for Solutions*. New York: Rinehart and Winston.

Kagel, J. H., and A. E. Roth. eds. 1995. *The Handbook of Experimental Economics*. Princeton: Princeton University Press.

Kahneman, D., and A. Tversky, eds. 2000. *Choices, Values and Frames*. New York and Cambridge: Russell Sage Foundation and Cambridge University Press.

Kakutani, S. 1941. "A Generalization of Brouwer's Fixed Point Theorem." *Duke Mathematical Journal* 8: 451–9.

Kakwani, N. C. 1980. *Income Inequality and Poverty: Methods of Estimation to Policy Applications*. New York: Oxford University Press.

Kanfer, S. 1993. *The Last Empire: De Beers, Diamonds and the World*. New York: Farrar, Straus & Giroux.

Kaplan, D. A. 1999. *The Silicon Boys and Their Valley of Dreams*. New York: William Morrow and Co.

Karnow, S. 1973. *Mao and China: From Revolution to Revolution*. New York: Viking Press.

Katzenstein, P. J. 1984. *Corporatism and Change: Austria, Switzerland and Politics of Industry*. London and Ithaca: Cornell University Press.

Kauffman, S. A. 1995. *At Home in the Universe: The Search for Laws of Complexity*. New York and Oxford: Oxford University Press.

———. 2000. *Investigations*. Oxford: Oxford University Press.

Kay, C. 1989. *Latin American Theories of Development and Underdevelopment*. New York: Routledge.

Kay, J. A. 1993. *Foundations of Corporate Success: How Business Strategies Add Value*. Oxford: Oxford University Press.

———. 1996. *The Business of Economics*. Oxford: Oxford University Press.

———. 2000. "Oxford: A Lost Cause?" *Prospect*.

Kay, J. A., and M. A. King. 1990. *The British Tax System*. 5th ed. Oxford: Oxford University Press.

Kelly, K. 1998. *New Rules for the New Economy*. London: Fourth Estate.

Kendall, M. 1953. "The Analysis of Economic Time Series, Part I: Prices." *Journal of the Royal Statistical Society* 96: 11–25.

Kennedy, J. F. 1956. *Profiles in Courage*. New York: Harper Perennial, 2000.

Kenney, C. 1992., *Riding the Runaway Horse: The Rise and Fall of Wang Laboratories*. Boston: Little Brown.

Kenrick, J. 1979. "Expanding Imputed Values in the National Income and Product Accounts." *Review of Income and Wealth*, December, 349–63.

Keynes, J. M. 1936. *The General Theory of Employment, Interest and Money*. London: Macmillan.

Kiel, L. D., and E. W. Elliott. 1996. *Chaos Theory in the Social Sciences: Foundations and Applications*. Ann Arbor: Michigan University Press.

Kincaid, P. 1986. *The Rule of the Road: An International Guide to History and Practice*. Westport, Conn.: Greenwood Press.

Kirman, A. 1993. "Ants, Rationality and Recruitment." *Quarterly Journal of Economics*. 108 (February): 137–56.

Klein, N. 1999. *No Logo*. New York: Picador.

Klopfenstein, B. C. 1989. *The Diffusion of the VCR into the United States*. London and Newbury Park, Calif.: Sage Focus Editions.

Knight, F. H. 1921. *Risk, Uncertainty and Profit*. Boston and New York: Houghton Mifflin.

Koopmans, T. C. 1957. *Three Essays on the State of Economic Science*. New York: McGraw-Hill.

Kornai, J. 1992. *The Socialist System*. Oxford: Oxford University Press.

Kornicki, P., ed. 1998. *Meiji Japan: Political, Economic and Social History. 1868–1912*. London: Routledge.

Kotkin, S. 2001. *Armageddon Averted: The Soviet Collapse, 1970–2000*. Oxford: Oxford University Press.

Krugman, P. 1994. "The Myth of Asia's Miracle." *Foreign Affairs* (November-December).

———. 1995. *Development, Geography and Economic Theory*. Cambridge, Mass.: MIT Press.

———. 1996. *The Self-Organizing Economy*. Oxford and Cambridge, Mass.: Blackwell.

———. 2003. *The Great Unraveling*. New York: W. W. Norton.

Kuhn, T. 1961. *The Structure of Scientific Revolutions*. Chicago: University of Chicago Press.

Landais, B. 1999. *L'Affaire Gachet: l'audace des bandits*. Paris: Layeur.

Landes, D. S. 1998. *The Wealth and Poverty of Nations*. New York: W. W. Norton.

Lane, R. E. 1991. *The Market Experience*. Cambridge: Cambridge University Press.

Langford, P., ed. 1996. *The Writings and Speeches of Edmund Burke*. Vol. 3, *Party, Parliament and the American War*. Oxford: Clarendon Press.

Langlois, J., L. Roggman, and L. Musselman. 1994. "What Is Average and What Is Not Average about Attractive Faces?" *Psychological Science* 5: 214–20.

Lanjouw, P., and N. Stern, eds. 1998. *Economic Development in Palanpur over Five Decades*. Delhi: Oxford University Press.

Lazear, E. P. 2000. "Economic Imperialism." *Quarterly Journal of Economics*. February, 99–146.

Leacock, S. B. 1936. *Hellements of Hickonomicks in Hiccoughs of Verse Done in Our Social Planning-Mill*. New York: Dodd, Mead and Company.

Leadbeater, C. 2000. *Living on Thin Air: The New Economy*. London: Viking.

Ledyard, J. O. 1988 "Market Failure." In J. Eatwell, M. Milgate, and P. Newman, eds. *The New Palgrave: A Dictionary of Economics*. Basingstoke: Palgrave Macmillan.

Leijonhufvud, A. 1968. *On Keynesian Economics and the Economics of Keynes*. London and New York: Oxford University Press.

Levy, M. R. 1989. *The VCR Age: Home Video and Mass Communication*. Newbury Park, Calif.: Sage Publications.

Lewis, A., and T. W. Schultz. 1953. *The Economic Organization of Agriculture*. New York: McGraw-Hill.

Lewis, M. 1989. *Liar's Poker: Two Cities, True Greed*. New York: Penguin.

———. 2000. *The New New Thing*. New York: W. W. Norton.

Lewis, W. A. 1954. "Economic Development with Unlimited Supplies of Labor." *Manchester School* 22 (May): 139–91.

Liebowitz, S. J., and S. E. Margolis. 1990. "The Fable of the Keys." *Journal of Law and Economics* 33 (April): 1–25.

Little, I. 1996. *Picking Winners: The East Asian Experience*. London: Social Market Foundation.

Loewenstein, G. 1999. "Because It Is There: The Challenge of Mountaineering . . . for Utility Theory." *Kyklos* 52: 315–44.

Lowenstein, R. 1995. *Buffett: The Making of an American Capitalist*. New York: Random House.

———. 2000. *When Genius Failed: The Rise and Fall of Long-Term Capital Management*. New York: Random House.

Lynch, L., and M. Kahn. 2000. *California's Electricity Options and Challenges*. San Francisco: California Public Utilities Commission.

Lyotard, J. F. 1979. *The Postmodern Condition: A Report on Knowledge*. English translation. Manchester: Manchester University Press.

MacFarquhar, R. 1983. *The Origins of the Cultural Revolution*. Vol. 2, *The Great Leap Forward. 1958–1960*. Oxford: Oxford University Press.

MacIntyre, A. 1981. *After Virtue: A Study in Moral Theory*. Notre Dame, Ind.: University of Notre Dame Press.

Macrae, N. 1992. *Johan von Neumann*. New York: Pantheon.

Maddison, A. 1993. *Monitoring the World Economy, 1820–1992*. Paris: OECD.

———. 2001. *The World Economy: A Millennial Perspective*. Paris: OECD Development Center Studies.

Magee, C. S. P. 2003. "Third Party Candidates and the 2000 Presidential Election." *Social Science Quarterly* 84 (3) (September).

Maier, K. 2000. *This House Has Fallen: Midnight in Nigeria*. New York: Public Affairs.

Malkiel, B. G. 1996. *A Random Walk down Wall Street: Including a Lifecycle Guide to Personal Investing*. New York: W. W. Norton.

Mankiw, W. G. 2004. *Principles of Economics.* 3rd ed. Ohio: South Western Mason, 149–50.

Manser, M. H. 1987. *The Pan Chambers Book of Business Quotations.* London: Chambers.

Mardel, M. 1996. "The Triumph of the New Economy." *Business Week,* December 30, 70.

Marshall, A. 1925. *Correspondence with Professor A. L. Bowley.* London: Macmillan.

Marshall, B. ed. 2002. *Heliobacter Pioneers.* Carlton, Victoria: Blackwell Scientific.

Marshall, O. 2000. *English-Speaking Communities in Latin America.* Basingstoke: Macmillan.

Marwell, G., and R. Ames. 1981. "Economists Free Ride, Does Anyone Else?" *Journal of Public Economics* 15: 295–310.

Marx, Karl. 1875. *Capital.* Trans. D. McLellan. Oxford: Oxford University Press, 1999.

Maynard Smith, J. 1982. *Evolution and the Theory of Games.* Cambridge: Cambridge University Press.

McCloskey, D. N. 1989. *The Open Fields of England: Rent, Risk, and the Rate of Interest, 1300–1815.* Cambridge: Cambridge University Press.

——— 1991. "The Prudent Peasant: New Findings on Open Fields." *Journal of Economic History* 51 (2) (June): 343–55.

McMurrin, S. M., ed. 1981. *The Tanner Lectures on Human Values.* Salt Lake City: University of Utah Press.

Meade, J. 1964. *Efficiency, Equality and the Ownership of Property.* London: Allen and Unwin.

Meadows, D. H., D.L. Meadows, J. Randers, and W. W. Behrens III. 1972. *The Limits to Growth.* New York: Signet Books.

Mehra, R., and E. C. Prescott. 1985. "The Equity Premium: A Puzzle." *Journal of Monetary Economics* 15 (March): 145–61.

Melchior, A., K. Telle, and H. Wiig. 2000. *Globalization and Inequality: World Income Distribution and Living Standards, 1960–1998.* Norwegian Institute of International Affairs, Royal Norwegian Ministry of Foreign Affairs Studies, Foreign Policy Issues, Report 6B.

Merriden, T. 2001. *Irresistible Forces: The Business Legacy of Napster and the Growth of the Underground Internet.* Oxford: Capstone.

Merton, R. K. 1936. "Science, Technology and Society in Seventeenth-Century England." In G. Sarton, ed., *Osiris: Studies in the History and Philosophy of Science, and on the History of Learning and Culture.* Vol. 4. Bruges: St. Catherine Press.

Milanovic, B., 1999. *True World Income Distribution. 1988 and 1993: First Calculation Based on Household Surveys Alone.* World Bank, Development Research Group.

Milgrom, P., and J. Roberts. 1992. *Economics Organization and Management.* Englewood Cliffs, N.J.: Prentice-Hall.

Miller, A. 1953. *The Crucible.* New York: Viking Press.

Ministry of Finance. 2002. *Economic Survey 2001–2002.* Government of India.

Mintzberg, H. 1994. *The Rise and Fall of Strategic Planning.* New York: Free Press.

Mnookin, R., and L. Kornhauser. 1979. "Bargaining in the Shadow of the Law." *Yale Law Journal* 88: 950–97.

Mokyr, J., ed. 1999. *The British Industrial Revolution: An Economic Perspective.* Boulder, Colo., and Oxford: Westview Press.

Nagel, E. 1963. "Assumptions in Economic Theory." *American Economic Review,* 53 (May): 211-19.

Nasar, S. 1998. *A Beautiful Mind.* New York: Simon and Schuster.

National Audit Office. 2001. *Managing the Relationship to Secure a Successful Partnership in PFI Projects.* London: HMSO.

Neale, A. D., and D. G. Goyder. 1980. *The Antitrust Laws of the United States of America.* Cambridge: Cambridge University Press.

Nelson, P. 1974. "Advertising as Information." *Journal of Political Economy* 82 (4) (July-August): 729-54.

Norberg-Hodge, H. 1991. *Ancient Futures: Learning from Ladakh.* San Francisco, Calif.: Sierra Club Books.

Nordhaus, W. 1997. "Do Real-Output and Real-Wage Measures Capture Reality?: The History of Lighting Suggests Not." In T. Bresnehan and R. Gordon, eds. *The Economics of New Goods.* Chicago: University of Chicago Press.

Nordhaus, W. D., and E. C. Kokkelenberg, eds. 1999. *Natures' Numbers.* Washington, D.C.: National Academy Press.

North, D. C. 1990. *Institutions, Institutional Change and Economic Performance.* New York: Cambridge University Press.

North, D. C., and R. P. Thomas. 1973. *The Rise of the Western World: A New Economic History.* Cambridge: Cambridge University Press.

Nozick, R. 1974. *Anarchy, State and Utopia.* New York: Basic Books.

Oakeshott, M. J. 1962. *Rationalism in Politics and Other Essays.* London: Methuen.

OECD. 1975. *The Polluter Pays Principle: Definition, Analysis, Implementation.* Paris: Organization for Economic Cooperation and Development.

———. 1993. *Improvement of Economic Forecasts.* Paris: Organization for Economic Cooperation and Development.

———. 2001. *Corporate Social Responsibility: Partners for Progress.* Paris: Organization for Economic Cooperation and Development.

Olson, M. 1996. "Big Bills Left on the Sidewalk: Why Some Nations Are Rich, and Others Poor." *Journal of Economic Perspectives* 10 (3): 3-24.

Ormerod, P. 1998. *Butterfly Economics: A New General Theory of Social and Economic Behavior.* New York: Pantheon Books.

Ortega, B. 1999. *In Sam We Trust: The Untold Story of Sam Walton, and How Wal-Mart Is Devouring America.* New York: Times Business.

Oswald, A. 1997. "Happiness and Economic Performance." *Economic Journal* 107: 1815-31.

Paley, W. 1802. *Natural Theology; Or Evidences of the Existence and Attributes of the Deity, Collected from the Appearances of Nature.* London.

Pearce, D. W. 1992. "Green Economics." *Environmental Values* 1 (1): 3-13.

Perrett, D. I., K. A. May, and S. Yoshikawa. 1994. "Facial Shape and Judgements of Female Attractiveness." *Nature* 368 (March 17): 239-42.

Pinker, S. 1994. *The Language Instinct: The New Science of Language and Mind.* New York: W. Morrow and Co.

Polanyi, K. 1944. *The Great Transformation.* New York: Farrar and Rinehart, Inc.

Pomeranz, K. 2000. *The Great Divergence: China, Europe and the Making of the Modern World Economy.* Princeton, N.J. and Oxford: Princeton University Press.

Porter, M. E. 1980. *Competitive Strategy* New York: Free Press.

———. 1985. *Competitive Advantage.* New York: Free Press.

———. 1990. *The Competitive Advantage of Nations.* New York: Free Press.

Posner, R. A. 1987. "The Law and Economics Movement." *American Economic Review* 77 (2) (May): Papers and Proceedings of the Ninety-Ninth Annual Meeting of the American Economic Association, 1–13.

———. 1998. *Economic Analysis of Law.* 5th ed. New York: Aspen Law & Business.

Prebisch, R. 1950. *The Economic Development of Latin America and its Principal Problems.* New York: United Nations.

Pritchett, L. 1997. "Divergence, Big Time." *Journal of Economic Perspectives* 11 (3) (summer): 3–17.

Prout, H. G. 1921. *A Life of George Westinghouse.* New York: American Society of Mechanical Engineers.

Putnam, R. D. 2000. *Bowling Alone: The Collapse and Revival of American Community.* New York and London: Simon and Schuster.

Quah, D. 1996. "Twin Peaks: Growth and Convergence in Models of Distribution Dynamics." *Economic Journal* 106 (437) (July): 1045–55.

Quine, W. V. O. 1951. *From a Logical Point of View.* Cambridge, Mass.: Harvard University Press.

———. 1969. *Ontological Relativity and Other Essays.* New York: Columbia University Press.

Rabin, M. 1998. "Psychology and Economics." *Journal of Economic Literature,* March, 11–46.

Radford, R. A. 1945. "The Economic Organization of a POW Camp." *Economica.* November, 189–201.

Rand, A. 1967. *Capitalism: The Unknown Ideal.* New York: Signet.

———. 1990a. *Introduction to Objectivist Epistemology.* New York: Meridian Books.

———. 1990b. *The Voice of Reason: Essays in Objectivist Thought.* New York: Meridian Books.

Rawls, J. 1972. *A Theory of Justice.* Cambridge, Mass.: Belknap Press of Harvard University Press.

Read, D. 1999. *The Power of News: The History of Reuters.* Oxford: Oxford University Press.

Rhodes, M. 2000. "Past Imperfect?: The Performance of UK Equity Managed Funds." *FSA Occasional Paper Series* 9 (August).

Ricardo, D. 1817. *On the Principles of Political Economy in Taxation.* London.

Richardson, G. B. 1972. "The Organization of Industry." *Economic Journal* 82: 883–96.

Ridings, W., and S. McIver. 1997. *Rating the Presidents.* Secaucus, N.J.: Citadel Press.

Robbins, L. C. 1935. *An Essay on the Nature and Significance of Economic Science.* London: Macmillan.

Rogoff, K., and J. Zettelmayer. 2002. "Early Ideas on Sovereign Bankruptcy Reorganization: A Survey." *IMF Working Paper* 2/57.

Rohrbough, M. J. 1997. *Days of Gold: The California Gold Rush and the American Nation.* Berkeley and London: University of California Press.

Rorty, R. 1979. *Philosophy and the Mirror of Nature.* Princeton: Princeton University Press.

Rosenstein-Rodan, P. N. 1943. "Problems of Industrialization of Eastern and Southeastern Europe." *Economic Journal* 53 (June-September): 202–11.

———. 1961. "Notes on the Theory of the Big Push." In H. S. Ellis and H. C. Wallich, eds., *Economic Development for Latin America.* New York: St. Martin's Press, chapt. 7, B.1, 342–45.

Rostow, W. W. 1953. *The Process of Economic Growth.* New York: Norton.

Rothschild, E. 2001. *Economic Sentiments, Adam Smith, Condorcet and the Enlightenment.* Cambridge, Mass. and London: Harvard University Press.

Roughley, T. C. 1951. *Fish and Fisheries of Australia.* London and Sydney: Angus and Robertson.

Rousseau, J. J. 1791. *The Social Contract and Discourses.* Trans. G. D. H. Cole. London: J. M. Dent, 1913.

Sachs, J. 2000. "Notes on a New Sociology of Economic Development." In L. E. Harrison and S. P. Huntington, eds. *Culture Matters.* New York: Basic Books, 29–43.

Sachs, J., and A. Warner. 1995. "Natural Resource Abundance and Economic Growth," Discussion Paper 517a. Cambridge, Mass.: Harvard Institute for International Development.

Sala-i-Martin, X. 2002. "The 'Disturbing Rise' of Global Income Inequality." *NBER Working Paper* 8904 (April).

Saltzman, C. 1998. *Portrait of Dr. Gachet: The Story of a van Gogh Masterpiece, Modernism, Money, Collectors, Dealers, Taste, Greed and Loss.* New York: Viking.

Samuelson, P. A. 1947. *Foundations of Economic Analysis.* Cambridge, Mass.: Harvard University Press.

———. 1993. "Altruism as a Problem Involving Group Versus Individual Selection in Economics and Biology." *American Economic Review* 83 (2) (May): 143–48.

Samuelsson, K. 1961. *Religion and Economic Action.* Trans. E. G. French, ed., and introd. by D. C. Coleman. Stockholm: Svenska Bokforlaget.

Scarf, H. E. 1962. *An Analysis of Markets with a Large Number of Participants.* Philadelphia: Ivy Curtis Press.

Scherer, F. M. 1970. *Industrial Market Structure and Economic Performance.* Boston: Houghton Mifflin.

Schultz, J. P. 1998. "Inequality in the Distribution of Personal Income in the World: How It Is Changing and Why." *Journal of Population Economics* 11: 307–44.

Schumpeter, J. A. 1942. *Capitalism, Socialism and Democracy.* New York: Harper and Brothers.

Schwartz, E. I. 2002. *The Last Lone Inventor: A Tale of Genius, Deceit, and the Birth of Television.* New York: HarperCollins.

Sen, A. K. 1987. *On Ethics and Economics.* Oxford: Basil Blackwell.

———. 1988. "Rational Behavior." In J. Eatwell, M. Milgate, and P. Newman, eds. *The New Palgrave: A Dictionary of Economics.* Basingstoke: Palgrave Macmillan.

Sewell, B. 1994. *The Reviews that Caused the Rumpus.* London: Bloomsbury.

Shanks, M. 1961. *The Stagnant Society: A Warning*. Harmondsworth: Penguin.

Shapiro, C., and H.R. Varian. 1999. *Information Rules: A Strategic Guide to the Network Economy*. Cambridge, Mass.: Harvard Business Press.

Sheehan, H. 1993. *Marxism and the Philosophy of Science: A Critical History*. Atlantic Highlands, N.J.: Humanities Press International.

Shefrin, H. 2000. *Beyond Greed and Fear: Understanding Behavioral Finance and the Psychology of Investing*. Boston, Mass. and London: Harvard University Press.

Shiller, R. J. 2003. *The New Financial Order: Risk in the 21st Century*. Princeton: Princeton University Press.

———. 2000. *Irrational Exuberance*. Princeton and Chichester: Princeton University Press.

Shleifer, A. 1999. *Inefficient Markets: An Introduction to Behavioral Finance*. Oxford: Oxford University Press.

Shleifer, A., and L. Summers. 1988. "Breach of Trust in Hostile Takeovers." In A. Auerbach, ed. *Corporate Takeovers: Causes and Consequences*. London: University of Chicago Press.

Shubik, M. 1959. "Edgeworth Market Games." In A. W. Tucker and R. D. Uce, eds. *Contributions to the Theory of Games*. Vol. 4. Princeton: Princeton University Press, 207–78.

Shumway, N. 1991. *The Invention of Argentina*. Berkeley and Oxford: University of California Press.

Siegel, J. J. 1998. *Stocks for the Long Run*. New York and London: McGraw-Hill.

Simon, H. A. 1969. *The Sciences of the Artificial*. Cambridge, Mass.: MIT Press.

Singer, H. 1950. "The Distribution of Gains between Investing and Borrowing Countries." *American Economic Review* 40: 473–85.

Smith, A. 1759. *The Theory of Moral Sentiments*. Indianapolis: Liberty Press. 1976.

———. 1976. *An Enquiry into the Nature and Causes of the Wealth of Nations*. Ed. R. H. Campbell and A. S. Skinner. Oxford: Oxford University Press.

Smith, B. D. 1995. *The Emergence of Agriculture*. New York and Oxford: Scientific American Library.

Sokal, A. D., and J. Bricmont. 1998. *Fashionable Nonsense: Postmodern Intellectuals' Abuse of Science*. New York: Picador.

Solow, R. M. 1970. *Growth Theory: An Exposition*. Oxford: Oxford University Press.

Soros, G. 1998. *The Crisis of Global Capitalism: Open Society Endangered*. New York: Public Affairs.

———. 2000. *Reforming Global Capitalism*. New York: Little, Brown.

Soto, H. de. 2000. *The Mystery of Capital: Why Capitalism Triumphs in the West and Fails Everywhere Else*. New York: Basic Books.

Spence, A. M. 1973. *Market Signaling: Information Transfer and Hiring and Related Process*. Cambridge, Mass.: Harvard University Press.

Starmer, C. 2000. "Developments in Non-Expected Utility Theory." *Journal of Economic Literature* 38 (June): 332–82.

Steckel, R. H. 1995. "Stature and the Standard of Living." *Journal of Economic Literature* 33(December): 1903–40.

Stern, J. M, J. S. Shiely, and I. Ross. 2001. *The EVA Challenge: Implementing Value-Added Change in an Organization.* New York and Chichester: Wiley.

Stigler, G. J. 1981. "Economics and Ethics." In S. M. McMurrin, ed. *The Tanner Lectures on Human Values.* Vol. 2. Salt Lake City: University of Utah Press.

Stiglitz, J. E. 1994. *Whither Socialism?.* Cambridge, Mass. and London: MIT Press.

———. 2002. *Globalization and Its Discontents.* London: Penguin.

Stone, R. 1986. "Nobel Memorial Lecture 1984: The Accounts of Society." *Journal of Applied Econometrics* 1 (1) (January): 5–28.

Story, J. 2003. *China: The Race to Market.* London: FT Prentice Hall.

Strathern, P. 2001. *Dr Strangelove's Game: A Brief History of Economic Genius.* London: Hamish Hamilton.

Stringer, C., and C. Gamble. 1993. *In Search of the Neanderthals: Solving the Puzzle of Human Origins.* London: Thames & Hudson.

Sulston, J., and G. Ferry. 2002. *The Common Thread: A Story of Science, Politics, Ethics and the Human Genome.* New York: Bantam.

Suppe, F. 1974. *The Structure of Scientific Theories.* Urbana: University of Illinois Press.

Suzuki, N. 1997. *Measuring the Degree of Competition in the U.S. Milk Market.* London: National Research Institute of Agricultural Economics, MAFF.

Talbott, S. 1971. *Khrushchev Remembers.* London: André Deutsch.

Taleb, N. N. 2001. *Fooled by Randomness.* New York: Texere.

Tattersall, I. 1995. *The Last Neanderthal.* New York: Macmillan.

Tawney, R. H. 1926. *Religion and the Rise of Capitalism.* New York: Harcourt Brace (preface, 1937).

Taylor, P., and L. Joncker. 1978. "Evolutionarily Stable Strategies and Game Dynamics." *Mathematical Biosciences* 40: 145–56.

Teiwes, F. C., with W. Sun. 1999. *China's Road to Disaster: Mao, Central Politicians, and Provincial Leaders in the Unfolding of the Great Leap Forward, 1955–1959.* Armonk, New York: M. E. Sharpe.

Telser, L. G. 1980. "A Theory of Self-Enforcing Agreements." *Journal of Business* 53 (1): 27–44.

Thaler, R. H. 1991. *The Winner's Curse: Paradoxes and Anomalies of Economic Life.* New York and Toronto: Free Press and Maxwell Macmillan.

Thatcher, M. 1993. *The Downing Street Years.* London: HarperCollins.

Thompson, E. P. 1968. *The Making of the English Working Class.* Harmondsworth: Penguin.

Thomson, R. 1998. *Apocalypse Roulette.* London: Macmillan.

Thurow, L. C. 1999. *Building Wealth: The New Rules for Individuals, Companies, and Nations in a Knowledge-Based Economy.* New York: HarperBusiness.

Titmuss, R. M. 1970. *The Gift Relationship: From Human Blood to Social Policy.* London: Allen and Unwin.

Tobin, J. 1978. "A Proposal for International Monetary Reform." *Eastern Economic Journal* 4: 153–59.

———. 1992. "The Invisible Hand in Modern Microeconomics." In M. Fry, ed. *Adam Smith's Legacy.* London: Routledge.

Tocqueville, A. de. 1835. *Democracy in America.* Ed. and trans. H. C. Mansfield and D. Winthrop. Chicago: University of Chicago Press, 2000.

Transparency International. 2001. *Global Corruption Report.* Berlin: Transparency International.

Travers, J., and S. Milgram. 1969. "An Experimental Study of the Small World Problem." *Sociometry* 32 (4) (December): 425–33.

Trump, D., with T. Schwartz. 1987. *Trump: The Art of the Deal.* London: Century.

Tsurumi, M., ed. 2001. *Financial Big Bang in Asia.* Aldershot: Ashgate.

Tudge, C. 1998. *Neanderthals, Bandits and Farmers: How Agriculture Really Began.* London: Weidenfield and Nicolson.

Turnbull, C. D. 1961. *The Forest People.* London: Pimlico, new ed., 1993.

———. 1973. *The Mountain People.* London: Pimlico, new introd. 1994.

Turner, J. A. 2001. *Just Capital: The Liberal Economy.* London: Macmillan Publishing.

Ullman, J. E. 1988. *The Anatomy of Industrial Decline.* New York: Quorum.

United Nations Development Program. 2002. *Human Development Report.* New York: Oxford University Press.

van de Stadt, H., A. Kapetyn., and S. van de Geer. 1985. "The Relativity of Utility." *Review of Economics and Statistics* 67: 179–87.

Veblen, T. 1899. *The Theory of the Leisure Class: An Economic Study of Institutions.* London: Routledge/Thoemmes Press. 1994.

Vickrey, W. 1961. "Counterspeculation, Auctions and Competitive Sealed Tenders." *Journal of Finance* 16: 8–37.

———. 1962. *Auction and Bidding Games.* Philadelphia: Ivy Curtis Press.

Vitullo-Martin, J., and J. R. Moskin. eds., 1994. *The Executive's Book of Quotations.* New York and Oxford: Oxford University Press.

von Neumann, J., and O. Morgenstern. 1944. *The Theory of Games and Economic Behaviour.* Princeton: Princeton University Press.

Waldron, J., ed. 1984. *Theories of Rights.* Oxford: Oxford University Press.

Waldrop, M. M. 1994. *Complexity: The Emerging Science at the Edge of Order and Chaos.* New York: Simon and Schuster.

Walker, D., and E. E. Coleridge. 1992. *Report on an Inquiry into Lloyd's Syndicate Participations and the LMX Spiral.* London: Lloyd's of London.

Walzer, M. 1981. "Philosophy and Democracy." *Political Theory* 9 (3): 379–99.

———. 1984. *Spheres of Justice: A Defense of Pluralism and Equality.* Oxford: Robertson.

Watts, D. J. 1999. *Small Worlds: The Dynamics of Networks between Order and Randomness.* Princeton and Chichester: Princeton University Press.

Weaver, W. 1948. "Science and Complexity." *American Scientist* 36: 536–44.

Weber, M. 1930. *The Protestant Work Ethic and the Spirit of Capitalism.* London: Allen and Unwin.

———. 1947. *The Theory of Social and Economic Organization.* Trans. A. R. Henderson and T. Parsons. New York: Free Press of Glencoe.

Welch, J., with J. A. Byrne. 2001. *Jack: Straight from the Gut.* New York: Warner Books.

Weldon, F. 2001. *The Bulgari Connection.* London: Flamingo.

Wells, S. 2002. *The Journey of Man.* London: Allen Lane.

White, L. J. 1991. *The S&L Debacle: Public Policy Lessons for Bank and Thrift Regulation.* New York: Oxford University Press.

Williams, G. C. 1966. *Adaptation and Natural Selection: A Critique of Some Current Evolutionary Thought.* Princeton: Princeton University Press.

Williams, R. E. 1997. *The Political Economy of the Common Market in Milk and Dairy Products in the European Union.* Rome: Food and Agriculture Organization of the United Nations.

Williamson, O. E. 1975. *Markets and Hierarchies.* New York: Free Press.

———. 1985. *The Economic Institutions of Capitalism: Firms, Markets, Relational Contracting.* New York: Free Press.

Williamson, O. E., and S. G. Winter, eds. 1991. *The Nature of the Firm: Origins, Evolution and Development.* New York: Oxford University Press.

Wilson, E. O. 1971. *The Insect Societies.* Cambridge, Mass.: Harvard University Press.

———. 1975. *Sociobiology, the New Synthesis.* Cambridge, Mass.: Belknap Press of Harvard University Press.

WM Company. 2002. *A Comparison of Active and Passive Management of Unit Trusts.* Edinburgh: Virgin Money Personal Finance.

Wolff, M. 1998. *Burn Rate: How I Survived the Gold Rush Years on the Internet.* London: Weidenfield and Nicolson.

World Bank. 1993. *The East Asian Miracle, Economic Growth and Public Policy.* Oxford: Oxford University Press.

———. 1995. *Bureaucrats in Business: The Economics and Politics of Government Ownership.* Oxford: Oxford University Press for World Bank.

———. 1997. *Expanding the Measure of Wealth: Indicators of Environmentally Sustainable Development.* Washington, D.C.: World Bank.

———. 2001. *2001 World Development Indicators.* Washington, D.C.: World Bank.

———. 2002. *Tanzania at the Turn of the Century: World Bank Country Study.* Washington, D.C.: World Bank.

Wriston, W. B. 1992. *The Twilight of Sovereignty.* New York: Scribner.

Wrong, M. 2000. *In the Footsteps of Mr. Kurtz: Living on the Brink of Disaster in the Congo.* New York: HarperCollins Publishers.

Wynne-Edwards, V. C. 1962. *Animal Dispersion in Relation to Social Behavior.* London and Edinburgh: Oliver and Boyd.

Yergin, D. I., and J. Stanislaw. 1998. *The Commanding Heights: The Battle between Government and the Marketplace That Is Remaking the Modern World.* New York: Simon and Schuster.

Young, A. 1995. "The Tyranny of Numbers: Confronting the Statistical Realities of the East Asian Growth Experience." *Quarterly Journal of Economics* 110 (August): 641–80.

Youngson, A. J. 1959. *Possibilities of Economic Progress.* Cambridge: Cambridge University Press.

———. 1966. *The Making of Classical Edinburgh. 1750–1840.* Edinburgh: Edinburgh University Press.

Zahavi, A. 1975. "Mate Selection—a Selection for a Handicap." *Journal of Theoretical Biology* 53: 205–14.

Zakaria, F. 2003. *The Future of Freedom.* New York: W. W. Norton.

{index}

WITHDRAWN

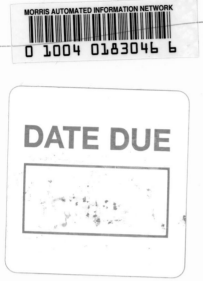